17-D 5

SOCIAL DEVELOPMENT
IN TWENTY FIRST CENTURY

Social Development
in
Twenty First Century

By
Mohammad Abbas Khan

ANMOL PUBLICATIONS PVT. LTD.
NEW DELHI - 110 002 (INDIA)

ANMOL PUBLICATIONS PVT. LTD.
4374/4B, Ansari Road, Daryaganj
New Delhi - 110 002
Ph.: 23261597, 23278000
Visit us at: www.anmolpublications.com

Social Development in Twenty-first Century

First Published, 2005

ISBN 81-261-2130-0

PRINTED IN INDIA

Published by J.L. Kumar for Anmol Publications Pvt. Ltd., New Delhi - 110 002 and Printed at Mehra Offset Press, Delhi.

Contents

Preface

Social Development is a relative term. It varies from society to society and culture to culture. In fact, every society has its own ideals and defined ways of behaviour in life and time. The communities or persons, who deviate from the set pattern, always create problems for others. Gradually, these problems take root in the social system and establish notorious institutions, which over a period of time become incurable and caste their shadows, for years to come. Thus, the questions raised and strengthened by certain elements or events are termed as social issues. The Sociologists have the crucial responsibility of seeking answers to these questions. They have to be cautious in finding ways to eradicate the hindrances and reform the elements, responsible for them and subsequently pave the way for Social Development. They are not the policemen of society and they cannot punish the guilty, they are simply supposed to suggest the formula of remedies and forward an ever-lasting solution, with a defined programme for development, with a goal to reform the society.

Social Development has taken place in our country at a fast pace and our society has beautified its face. But, in typical climate of our country, many a hurdle have also been created. Spread of education and civility have helped a new class, known as noble citizenry, come up. But, ironically, this newly emerged group has developed a sort of superiority complex towards others, which is a bad sign in itself. For a healthy Social Development, emergence of a new civilized community is required. No doubt, there are a number of books on the subject, yet , a dearth for comprehensive books always remains there. This endeavour is in order to fill this room only. Hopefully, this modest work would be welcome by all circles.

-Editor

1

Introduction

Most of the identifications of sociologists with a particular 'theory' indicates not as much their commitment to a process of formal theorizing as to their affirmation of an ideology. Most theoretic attempts towárds formalization either end up in application of theory to explain a marginal or insignificant segment of reality or to near abandonment of formal explanations in the face of social realities of macroscopic relevance. This is particularly true for functional theory in sociology, but its parallelism for other 'theories' would not entirely be unfounded. In a formal sense, functional propositions have a teleological character. All institutional interactions and linkages constituting a system must be homoestatiscally integrated. In case of a social system, as examined by philosophers of science, for instance, Ernest Naegel and Karl Hempel, these prerequisites of formalization simply do not exist. The isomorphism between organic system and social system does not exist. In the absence of homology between the two systems functionalist theorizing in sociology takes recourse to metaphors and analogies.

However, these metaphors or analogies in sociology drawn on the model of the organic systems have undergone deeper and variegated logical and intuitive transformations, based on both in-depth observation of comparative social systems and refinement of the logical structure of categories. The richness of observational experiences in cross-cultural settings has in progressive stages contributed to the conceptual refinements in functional sociology. In this process, one witnesses ascendancy of metaphoric reasoning over that of simplistic analogy. The emphasis shifts not only to systems in self-maintenance but also in self-transformation. Merton's portrayal of basic similarity between the functional and dialectical paradigms particularly takes note of this point. Others have been inclined rather to giving up the nomenclature of functional sociology by encompassing it in the very structure of sociological craftsmanship. These tendencies clearly indicate the triumph of 'metaphor' over 'analogy' in the paradigm of functional analysis. Analogous mode of theorizing does not disclaim formal theory. Its commitment to positivism or even scientism persists. Its claim to value neutrality is rather strong and it sharply distinguishes between science and ideology. All attempts towards model-building using organic assumptions about society may belong to this category of theorizing. Its catholicity in respect of system maintenance or consensus as being the primary tendency of societies is uncompromising. The place for conflict in this paradigm only exists as a deviation.

It might appear that during the fifties the functionalist orientation in the Euro-American setting began to undergo a metaphoric transformation. Merton's adumbration of a middlerange theory was its beginning, but the contributions of Talcott Parsons and N.J. Smelser in the *Economy and Society,* and those of Lewis Coser and Ralph Dahrendorf later, tend to manifest its nearmaturation. What does this metaphor of functionalism imply? The answer to this question may be briefly summed up as: (1) Assumption of a system in a process of self-maintenance within its internal-external setting through dual mechanisms, (a) that of socialization at the level of personality, and (b) of institutionalization at the level of roles or human activities. (2) Postulate of consensus in the maintenance of the system (derived from the above premises) together with possible *autonomy* of conflict in the system triggering needs for. (3) Rewor-king of consensus leading to even radical social transformations. Smelser's explanation of the industrial revolution falls within this category of functionalist metaphor. The nature of this conflict might even inhere dialectical reasoning occasionally through .the process of polarization on binary lines or as arising out of a symmetry of values or power. Most conflictual situations imply such a symmetry. But, the notion of dialectics as used here departs basically from its formulation in Marxism, where it is endowed with evolutionary historicity. The use of dialectics in functionalist metaphor, especially in the early works of Parsons and the contributions of Coser and Dahrendorf, are of structuralist variety. Parsons, in his thesis on 'evolutionary universals', does depart from this cognitive frame. But he used the term 'evolution' without being fully historical. (4) The functionalist metaphor treats change both as adaptive deviation from the dominant system pattern as well as an occasional system transformation. It thus deals both with changes in the system as well as changes of the social systems. Implicit distinction here is between what is normal and what is historical. In actual practice, however, the studies using functionalist metaphor abound to the near-paucity of social movements or revolutionary transformations. (5) The metaphor of functionalism commits itself strongly to scientific methods and empirical techniques. Indeed, its major contribution to sociology has been not only in the domain of conceptual categories but more prominently in the fabrication of tools of observation, analysis of data and construction of social reality. On this account, however, functionalist sociology has been charged with 'abstracted empiricism', scientism, fallacies of instrumentation and reification. But, most of these refer only to the abuses of certain tools of investigation rather than their logic of discovery.

We have dwelt at some length with this metaphoric shift in functionalism in sociology in order to balance the perspective in our evaluation of the Indian sociology. In most critical commentaries functionalism has been charged with being an ideology of status quoism, bourgeoisie conservatism and mindless positivism. It is also considered to be devoid of a radiological content. In his treatment of Talcott Parsons, Elvin Gouldner makes most of these points with only one exceptional departure in his perception, that is, possibilities of convergence between the Marxist and the western (an euphemism for functional) sociology. Though critical of functionalism of Talcott Parsons, Gouldner does not discard totally the metaphors of this theoretical orientation which he has used effectively in his own studies of complex organization. The idea of theoretical convergence, however, is evocative of the general crisis in sociological theorizing. This refers to a host of cognitive and historical forces generated during the past few decades in the western societies that impel most social scientists to move away from the quest for formal theory. C. Wright Mills' quest for 'sociological imagination' was a product of this crisis and the quest for a new metaphor.

One may ask: why substitute metaphor for theory? There is a basic reason. A theory in its formal sense implies a historicity and near-universal validity. It refers to a level of abstraction where the specificities of historical experiences become blurred if not evanescent. However, at this level of theorizing, the social science products, though high in explanatory power, are low in social relevance. Tautologies replace reasoning. In such a situation, even intuitive reasoning begins to take better of social science theory. The hiatus between the formal and the substantive becomes acute. The metaphoric thinking in sociology is a halfway house between abstracted and empty formalism and dense substantive empiricism in social sciences. I must, however, confess that such metaphoric tension is not only characteristic of functional sociology. One might witness similar tensions in Marxism and phenomenological sociology as well. The search for 'parameters' in place of 'variable' by Peter Worsely, and for middle range theory by Merton only refer to this dilemma of sociological theorizing. An important implication of this, however, is that functionalism as a metaphor offers possibilities of creative variations in different socio-historical contexts. This point assumes significance when we try to analyze the elements of functionalism in Indian sociology.

Social Context

Cognitive structure and methods in Indian sociology have been deeply conditioned by colonial historical experience. One does notice in this context some dissociation between the sociological works of the Indian sociologists and the foreigners, especially the colonial administrators-turned-sociologists or social anthropologists. In the works of C.H. Hutton and W Wiser, the elements of early functionalist orientation tend to be obvious, but not so is the case of pioneer sociologists, G.S. Ghurye, Radhakamal Mukherjee and D.P. Mukherji who were all engaged in monumental efforts to understand the Indian reality.

The difference of perspective here is not to much of social anthropology as against sociology. The difference is primarily between the colonial and the nationalistic perspectives. The British administrators and scholars tended to look at the Indian society from the framework of comparative functionalism and comparative history. The objective was not only to understand but also to govern. The mix of politics with social science in the works of these scholars is an affirmation of social conditioning of theory and its metaphoric existence. The recurrent themes in the early sociological and social anthropological writings of western scholars on India tend to revolve around a series of polarities, such as caste-race, primitive-civilized, peasantry-aristocracy, country-city, outcaste-Brahmin, Hindu-Muslim, etc., which posits, on the one hand, questions of cultural lag, or evolutionary back-dating, regression and, on the other, structural dissociation or autonomy for each of the polar categories. Effort seldom was to see the interconnections between these structures in a historical civilizational depth. For instance, the British administrators always portrayed village as an autonomous reality which indeed it was not. Perhaps to see the place of an Indian village in the background of its organic linkages with regions, of the towns, capital city or sacred city would have involved the dynamic unity of the economy, polity and culture of the Indian society which colonialism was systematically attempting to play down.

The shift of emphasis in the treatment of such systems as village, caste, tribe, family, kinship, etc., in heuristic isolation of the one from another by early British and other foreign social anthropologists and sociologists becomes the centre piece of Indian functional sociology which was to be continued by some Indian sociologists even after independence. The mainstream of the early Indian sociologists, however, did not succumb to such temptations. In their writings we find emphasis on history, civiliza-tional unity and continuity, identification of regions and their eco-nomic, political and cultural integration, both internal and in the context of the nation as a whole, the study of social structures, such as caste and class, agrarian strata and political economic systems in comparative historical frame of reference, and analysis of the place of the Indian tradition and forces of transformation within it, in the context of western contactsi both colonial and non-colonial. The dominant themes of these studies appear to have their anchorage in these sociologists' quest for national identity, systematic needs of development and change through reform, synthesis and innovation in the culture and social structure. The cultural and political encounter with the west and its sociological implications for our society constituted the central matrix of their consciousness and their intellectual response.

The theoretical choices in most writings of the pioneers of Indian sociology were at best eclectic, emphasis generally being on comparative historical and ideological foci. An interplay of vague theoretical responses ranging from the British evolutionism to German historicism, from American institutionalist and regional sociology to Vedantic dialectics, an Indianized form of Marxism, reflect the intellectual perspective of this age of macroscopic sociology. Though application of functionalism in the works of social anthropologists of this period could be discerned, especially in their studies of caste and tribes, it did not dominate the theoretical orientation of the Indian sociology of the forties and about. The culture of 'research methodology' which began to dominate the sociological thinking and practice in the fifties had not yet emerged in India and most sociological researches were based on individual scholar's own entrepreneurship, innovate the insights and intuitive sensitivities. The emphasis on a methodology, which forms the most significant element in the functionalist metaphor of sociology, was thus non-existent in this period of Indian sociology.

Practical Aspects

The fifties saw in India a shift from the earlier tradition of macroscopic sociology of the pioneers to what may be called, for the lack of a more expressive term, 'specific sociologies' of individual entities and sub-systems. This also coincided with the rise of a culture of research methodology, 'scientific' precision in tools of observation and reproduction of interpretive meanings from facts. It was also a move away from philosophical and historical anchorage of categories of sociology and its broader and bolder intuitive generalizations. Such efforts in sociology, which referred to matrices of civilization, cultural movements and comparative history of institutions, were now treated as of no 'scientific' consequence or even as 'unsociological'. The meaning of sociology in this phase of research does indeed seem to identify sociology with a set of categories in systematic logical interconnection, which had all the frills of a science. Emphasis on structure, role and status, power, institutions and value processes of institutionalization, differentiation and change, in categorical sense, constituted the vocabulary of this new sociology. This tendency was reinforced by rapid influx of American-British textbooks in sociology and contacts between scholars from these countries and our own scholars.

When we closely observe the process of inclusion and exclusion of categories in the sociology of the fifties in India, we witness two major consequences: one, it indeed developed a more tightly structured and logically closed system of concepts. Concepts were such that could be easily operationalized (most of them were already operationalized in the western setting), had close empirical referents, were devoid of obtuse historico-philoso-phical generalities, and intuitive value judgments. Most importantly, the feedback between categories and empirical verification became more rigorous and the basic element of the sociological craft. Secondly, the problems which now sociologists began to select for study were more specific and defined largely in microscopic setting. The selectivity of problems was determined by this internal shift of orientation in the cognitive and methodological self-image of sociology; but it was also influenced by external factors, such as governmental funding of research in specific developmental areas, setting of styles by foreign sociologists, and the continuity of past traditions in the choice of problems for research.

The most popular areas of research in sociology during the fifties were village community, tribe, caste, family and religion. In addition, many studies of planning and development constituted specialized concerns by a considerable amount of sponsored research. The studies of village community were undertaken with a variety of frames of reference, but three tendencies could be clearly discerned. These are evaluative studies trying to diagnose sociologically the interaction between village social structure and institutions and the targets of planned socio-economic development. Such studies only accidentally tried to offer generalized postulates about the nature of the village community. These studies were not designed as such for construction of social reality in the context of a 'theory'. Metaphoric associations could, nevertheless, be associated in their findings: that institutions do not inhibit development, that social structure and its hierarchy, especially economic power, does tend to channelize the benefits of development to a narrow caste-class grove, and that factors both within the village as well as without constitute the forces of social change, especially mass communication and politicization. Most studies of community development and panchayati raj in the villages come closer to confirming this. No criticism of the structure of public policy, however, was implied or attempted in these village studies.

In addition to the above, we have two types of preeminently sociological studies of village community in India during the fifties. One, which drew its inspiration from the British social anthropology, its emphasis being on the construction of the structure of village as a social entity, with all ramifications of its internal differentiation and external linkages. Emphasis here was not so much on values, traditions and ideas as on categories of status, role, power and institutions in totality, generating processes of interaction. Bailey's village studies in Orissa come closer to the explication of this orientation, but several studies could be included in this category. The second kind of village studies have their inspiration in the American social anthropology led by Robert Redfield and his associate Milton Singer. In these studies, there was a designed conceptual project that we have analyzed else-where as that of civilization and tradition. More than on social structures, focus here was directed on the structure of values, institutions and traditions. The forces of social and economic changes were in these studies seen within the framework of the integrative and conflictual mechanisms of tradition. Hence, the study of festivals, rituals and deities along with the ethnography of the village. The teams led by Singer and Marriott have generated considerable material on village reality in India.

The village studies conducted by prominent Indian sociologists during this time, such as M.N. Srinivas, S.C. Dube, A.R. Desai and others, though bearing some impress of both the above orientations, belong, to my mind, to different approaches. Among the Indian sociologists, Desai clearly followed Marxist orientation in his studies. Dube's Indian village is a sociological construction of a village in all its facets of integration and tensions, primarily undertaken from a role-status differentiation perspective. Dube also attempts to analyze the processes of change in response to both internal and external forces. Srinivas carried the sociological perspective much deeper in his studies and offered as it were a masterly synthesis of both structure and tradition as analytical categories. It is this unique effort in the village sociology of Srinivas that constitutes a distinctive contribution.

The studies of caste were an organic part of the village studies. The processes of caste differentiation, mobility and hierarchy constituted its main foci. Much data was generated on the mobility in the caste system through the processes of sanskritization, westernization and accumulation of resources and power. The phenomenon of dominance and cultural persistence in the operation of caste hierarchy was particularly investigated. In all these studies, not only the element of segregation but also unity of the worldview of pollution and purity was highlighted as the main thread that rendered caste studies symptomatic of the changes in Indian structure and tradition. The principles of commu-nity and cooperation, the symbiotic role of the *jajmani* system, and the aspiration to move up in caste hierarchy within the cultural matrix of pollution-purity were aspects which drew the attention of sociologists.

The attributes of functional analysis in Indian sociology are in popular image associated with this phase of village and caste studies. It, however, needs to be closely examined. The factors which impel sociologists to characterize these studies as functional are first, an overt systemic assumption about village and caste within the framework of principles of cooperation and compatibility. In the caste system it was assumed through the universal dominance of the pollution-purity values and in the village context the integrative relationships of caste, *jajmani* and family, kinship and social ecological distinctiveness. Thus, a consensual worldview about the social structure of the village and caste was an implicit element in most of these studies. The entire debate on whether village could be treated as a valid *sociological* reality for investigation or whether the village had a collective consciousness as a unit of social reality related to this theme. The principles of communality in rural social relationships were indeed overportrayed. Oscar Lewis, in his studies of factions in villages, drew a very benign picture of these otherwise contentious and jealous institutions. He went even so far as to suggest usage of this institution for developmental purposes.

The second aspect of these studies relates to their treatment of social change. The notion of change in most of these studies is that of systematic adaptations. The time dimension is simply diachronic. The notion of conflict exists but it is reconcilable within the overarching canopy of the structure and tradition. The historical sensitivity is missing from most paradigms of changes used by this generation of sociologists. On the issues of policy of change and its phenomenology sociologists do not raise any questions; they do not even attempt to judge it or evaluate it. They simply accept the model of change as sponsored by the state as given. The critical element in sociological thinking is thus largely mute. Thirdly, these studies are conducted with much methodological sophistication. Meticulous care is taken about the objectivity of observations, recording of data, and the use of designs of investigation. The 'scientific' sociological craft dominates in these studies, which is also an organic part of the functionalist culture in social science.

Despite all this, the affinity of these studies to functionalism is simply metaphoric. The teleological assumption about the nature of either caste or village as a system is at no stage projected, nor it is substantiated. On the contrary, the systems both of caste and village are exposed to serious doubts qua systems, their linkages outcrossing the confines of a local ecology in case of the village or lineage and kinship in case of caste. The system boundary of both these entities tends to be regional if not pan-Indian in character. At this level of exposure, homoestasis self-corrections are ineffective and nebulous. On the contrary, contradictions are generated by the forces outside the system which not only cannot be accommodated but call for restructuration of roles and values. Bailey's concept of 'bridge action', Srinivas' focus on village disputes and Orenstein's portrayal of inter-village rivalries and tensions, not only draw our attention to the conflicts in the systems of village and caste but also their pervasive dynamic significance. This dynamics is not always intra-systemic as most crucial contradictions emerge from state legislatibn, constitutional enfranchisement of people and jural reforms in social, economic and political rights. These several forces contributing to sanskriti-zation, to which Srinivas drew attention of sociologists, had them in the making in the process of census operation initiated during the British rule. The literature on the sociology of caste and village of this period does visualize the systems in states of adaptive accommodation, but it also leaves the system boundaries undefined and also the encounter that these systems have with outside systematic forces reflect often that contradiction. Such formulation of the system properties does at no account harmonize fully with a functionalist model. Its similarity with this model is only metaphoric.

The same is the case of the studies of religion. Srinivas' *Religion and Society among the Coorgs of South India* might be cited as the best sociological study of this period. It has obvious links with structural notions, especially in the analysis of rituals. But it also indicates the multiplier ideological inconsistencies in the co-existence of the Sanskritic and non-Sanskritic rituals and beliefs. Srinivas writes:

> Both the Sanskritic and non-Sanskritic modes of propitiation exist cheek by jowl as far as the bulk of Coorgs are concerned. The more enquiring of the men see the two modes of propitiation as mutually inconsistent, but such inconsistency does not seriously trouble anyone. All over India, Sanskritic and non-Sanskritic customs, often involving beliefs, regarded as mutually inconsistent, are found existing together. Usually, the non-Sanskritic custom, either drops out or is transformed to suit the Sanskritic custom, but this process takes a very long time. There is also no doubt, however, that the non-Sanskritic customs of every caste as well as those of sects and peripheral groups are continually being Sanskritized. This has been happening for over 2,000 years all over India (1952: 167).

The above passage to illustrates the fact that in Srinivas' study of the structure of rituals the emphasis on the historical process is not subdued. Within the framework of interaction over time the Sanskritic and non-Sanskritic elements in religious beliefs and rituals undergo self-transformation, which is not merely adaptive but total. To understand it, one has to not only go beyond the static or even diachronic time frame, look through the passage of history. Thus, we once again witness but also in whatever functionalist orientation that may exist in the analysis of rituals, the tendency to go beyond it, to search for transformative principles through history. Such a cognitive frame is obviously not of functionalism, even though it is replete with functionalist metaphors. Other studies of religion under the inspiration of the Redfield's model of organization of tradition conducted by several sociologists and anthropologists in India also bear affinity to a similar sense of history. This is clearly highlighted later in the works of L.P. Vidyarthi and Milton Singer, among others.

Structuralist Constructions

Indian sociology in the sixties and seventies underwent major changes both in theoretical orientations and ideologies. The debate initiated by Dumont and Pocock towards the end of fifties on the one hand, and on the other, the increase of self-consciousness among the Indian sociologists about the nature of their discipline and its objective, led to new theoretic tensions. It also contributed to the widening of the substantive base of sociology as it moved from caste and village studies to that of agrarian structure, peasantry, social movements and social history. The sociological thinking became more analytical from its highly descriptive ethnographic orientation of the past. Even in the village studies, now emphasis shifted from cataloguing of mere facts to discussions of principles and categories. In the use of categories the method of using analytical typologies becomes prominent introducing the shift from the notion of continuation to that of levels in the understanding of the dynamics of social change. There is both a substantive and meta-theoretical shift in the sociology of this period. Substantively, the unit is no longer a territory or a single entity but a system defined conceptually or even axiomatically with the help of a set of categories. This renders these studies simultaneously more theoretical as well as more comparative. The conceptualization of systems or changes therein through categories like 'tribe, caste and nation', 'caste, class and power', 'mind', 'body' and 'wealth' (Pocock, 1974), etc., which are seen to proliferate during this period, though not all equally rigorous in methodology, tend to highlight the change. This was also the period of substantive differentiation of socio-logical research interests. The questions of 'equality and inequality', 'peasantry' and social movements particularly became new interests of sociologists. The spur to studies of peasantry and agrarian structure came from the field of economics, and the historians' works generated the interest in the studies of social movement.

The exposure of sociology to economics and history, with ensuing new trends in these disciplines, introduced new theoretical and conceptual sensitivities in sociology. Marxological orientation in agrarian studies, quite popular among the dominant group of economists, and the studies of social history, the movement with subtle linkages with the Annales School of French History among the Indian historians, to my mind, also influenced the theoretical preferences of some sociologists studying peasantry and peasant movements. Historical studies in the areas of kinship and family were conducted which used historical material and geneaologies and also family cycle and its self-reproduction from one generation to another. I.P Desai's study of family cycle in a township effectively countered the theory of continuum in the family change.

During the seventies and eighties, however, the same trend in the selectivity of problems and conceptual orientations persisted. Only we now come across some systematic studies of social structures which have a clearly Marxist orientation in conceptual design. Studies also tend to have more regional and macroscopic dimension in their cognitive organization.

In totality, the contributions of sociologists during the sixties to eighties can be seen as a period of differentiation rather than consolidation of methods or paradigms. In some aspects, especially in dialectical or Marxist orientation, one might see elements of revival of the traditions of the early forties-fifties when Marxism was seriously debated among sociologists at several centres of learning. But 'revival' would not be adequate to describe the new phenomenon, since Marxism now has two additional characteristics: first, emphasis on empirical fieldwork and secondly, interpretive elasticity and cognitive differentiation. Marxism was not used now merely as critical social philosophy or as a tool for analysis of historical data, but as a project for empirical observation of facts and generation of data. Hence, many village studies, studies of agrarian systems, of townships and industrial centres and social movements were conducted using Marxological methods. During this period, one thus finds that along with the tendency of structural and comparative historical studies, which continue to dominate, the Marxological studies, particularly by a number of sociologists of the younger generation, come into being.

The three rather novel conceptual and methodological orientations of this period are: structuralist, typological and dialectical. The linkages, however, among the three orientations are so close that it would be difficult to identify any particular work of this time with anyone of these specific approaches. The structural as well as structuralist notions in the study of caste, religion, knowledge and culture interpenetrate during this period. Within the overall structuralist framework, one does come across notions of substantive relationships and their implication to the system under study. The studies are not entirely formal. In the typological studies, which use analytic type categories, we find preeminent role of observation, construction and interpretation of concrete institutions and relationships. It is for this reason that allusion to neo-Weberanism in such studies by some sociologists would have to be qualified. In essence, these studies bear closer resemblance to monographic studies of rural and caste structures during the fifties. Their sophistication in terms of analysis and use of categories is, however, so designed that the power of their generalizations tends to be wider and more logically anchored. Otherwise, the notions of system, differentiation of structures, institutions and adaptive changes are as much part of the studies using typologies as were in the former village studies. Amongst the functionalist metaphor these studies do not share the teleological assumptions but the notions of system, structure and change in these studies quite harmonize with the functionalist metaphoric contents. This would be as much true for many studies of agrarian structure, social stratification and cultural institutions as of the studies of social movements.

As we mentioned above, the study of social movements and revolution had come to be recognized as an important new element of the functional metaphor of sociology. It may be interesting to investigate as to how far the contemporary studies of social movements in India depart qualitatively in their paradigmatic content from this model. The sequence of events in the functional analysis of social movement for structural change are: initial dissatisfaction with existing condition, initial resistance and binary differentiation of interest groups, positive-negative emotional tensions and rationalizations of these interests, covert processes of handling these tensions by mobilization of resources and ideas, etc., supportive tolerance of new ideas without commitment to specific responsibilities, positive attempts to select specific new ideas and demands which will become objects of commitment, and finally suitable transformation in the structure to incorporate the new system (see, Parsons and Smelser, 1956: 249-74).This sequence inheres the life cycle of social processes which initiate fundamental changes in the social structure as well as lead to its transformation.

The pertinent question in the sociology of social movements that arises is as to whether all paradigms of movement studies inhere a model of structural transformation or revolution, and whether the outcome of all social movements are structural transformation. Obviously, the answer to both of these questions would be in the negative. It is more as a matter of emphasis and not theoretic conditioning that social movement sociology deals with structural transformations as social change. It would not be without basis to suggest, therefore, that with the coming into fashion of agrarian sociology and social movement, the functional metaphor in sociological practice has not withered away. One could even establish its persistence in many such studies. Both the notions of conflict and contradiction as we mentioned above have been incorporated in the structure of the functionalist metaphor.

The new development in the sociology of the seventies or the eighties is not so much the decline of the functionalist metaphor as such, as the rise of the systematic dialectical-materialist 'theory' for the understanding of social reality. It is still in its nascent form, and does not have, particularly in sociology, much wealth of data to fall back upon in order to test the validity and plasticity of its categories; but it has to its credit some serious efforts in all these directions. Much more basic work in India in the dialectical materialist analysis is being done by economists and a group of historians rather than sociologists. It would thus be premature to go into the question of theoretical consolidation or synthesis of the alternative metaphors of functional and dialectical materialism in Indian sociology.

However, the nature of internal differentiation within the Marxist paradigm during the past two to three decades, the debates on the notions of 'caste' and 'clan', the nature of the infrastructure versus the superstructure, the role of structural differentiation and integration or even institutionalization in the socialist revolutionary societies (which necessitate recall of functionalist metaphor as such) and their sub-systems, the existence of teleological notion of immanent historical formations within the paradigm of Marxism, etc., tend to suggest both possibilities of convergence and co-existence of the two major metaphors in the contemporary world of sociology. In India, to look for convergence as such would be premature as the bulk of work continues to have anchorage in the functionalist metaphor of sociology. In the absence of concrete and comparative studies of Indian reality by the alternative paradigms most debates tend to be ideological rather than deeply sociological. I should think that if one wished to closely examine the nature of dialectical-materialist orientation in the sociological studies, one would once again encounter the two-fold problem of theory-building in sociology: one of near-impossibility of formalization and secondly, the metaphoric content of the structure of categories and their operationalization for research. This problem is equally shared by most so-called theorists of sociology. The paucity of space does not permit me at this stage to go into the metaphoric aspects of the dialectical-materialist theory. It would, however, be not far-fetched to state that in ways that it has been applied to the study of the Indian reality, its nature too has been more metaphoric. than formal.

An important implication of the metaphoric nature of theories in sociology is their deep anchorage in ideology. When formal-logical closure of propositions, concepts and their internal relationships remains inadequate, there is always scope for allusions of values and motives to individual scholars in their work which is largely extraneous to the requirement of theory. It is my impression that such ideological allusions though relevant in the context of evaluation of the relative power and relevance of a theoretic metaphor should be appreciated only at an appropriate level. A simplistic method is that of debunking an individual scholar's work by invoking his social conditioning. It is forgotten that social conditioning ceases to be sociologically relevant if it does not have collective structural character. The conditioning only at the level of personal deprivation or, 'trouble', as C. Wright Mills noted, does not become a matter of sociological inquiry, but an 'issue', a collective deprivation does constitute such a subject matter. How does such a social conditioning influence the choice of paradigms and metaphors, is a relevant proposition. Ideology operates rather normatively also at the unconscious level in the inscription of cultural norms in linguistic structure. This is the form in which a deeper level of ideology exists in social science vocabulary. It is this element particularly which further renders theoretic efforts in sociology largely metaphoric.

2

Evolution of Society

A sociological perspective has two distinctive advantages: first, it views nationalism as a social process and not as a formal structural construct. It treats nationalism with a degree of methodological elasticity and portrays it at various levels of its functioning in a dynamic international setting. Secondly, sociologist's attempt is always to examine a social process in terms both of its intrinsic character and also as an element in the general forces of social transformation in society. Instead of taking an isolationist view, sociology attempts to offer 'explanation' wherever it can, in a broad historical and culturally specific setting. It offers a blending of micro-history with macro-history and of theory with practice in society. No doubt, such effort has its hazards, specially of stepping into terrains unknown. It might also lead to over simplification of issues that are far too complex. Yet, a sociological treatment of nationalism in India may be useful for two basic reasons: first, its conceptual formulation involves issues which are common to Indian social sciences viz the Western origin of its categories and their relevance, We have had a long debate in sociology on this question and shared experiences may have some validity. Secondly, sociologists in India have been engaged in intensive observation and analysis of diverse social processes in society, particularly those related to values and social structure, which might offer new insights into the problems related to social framework of Indian nationalism.

We come across several distinctive conceptual formulations of Indian nationalism both by our own and foreign scholars. A dominant view, that of historians and sociologists, sees the rise of nationalism in the context of British colonialism and the distortions it created in social structure and ideology of our society. These distortions refer to class character of nationalist leadership and its social, cultural and economic policies. It is said, these colonial distortions contributed to the rise of communalism, partition of the country and persistence of communal politics even after independence. Yet it is recognised that colonial contact though subversive, generated social and economic forces that gave rise to nationalism and national movement in our society. In this approach, the study of relationship between social structure and cultural ideology forms a relatively weaker link. Its historiography draws heavily from policy framework and pronouncements of nationalist leadership and other agents involved in the Indian national movement in order to construct a social morphology of nationalism. It focuses upon macro-historical processes, their intricate movements, their filter-down effects and patterns in society. The basic tension between nationalism and communalism, its linkages with class structure, the role class structure plays in the power structure, and the evolution of secularism as an ideology after independence are analysed at a general level. It does not, however, examine these issues, as a sociologist or social anthropologist does, in the context of micro-historical processes and their given normative framework in the social structures, such as caste, community, family, kinship, locality, region and belief system, etc. The indigenous cultural traditions are not examined closely in formulating social contexts of communalism and secularism and their implications to Indian nationalism. It is not able, therefore, to establish fully the linkages between the top and the subterranean levels of mobilization of nationalist consciousness and its structural tensions. Without fuller understanding of such linkages a sociology of Indian nationalism remains inadequate.

Participants

We have come across contributions of some historians and social scientists that show sensitivity to the problems of linkages. They find macro-historical analysis of nationalism and national movement in India to be dominated by elitism either of liberal or marxist variety. Such historiography of Indian nationalism suffers according to them, by colonialist-elitism or bourgeois nationalist elitism, an 'ideological product' of the British rule in India. They suggest an alternative model for understanding national movement and nationalism which derives its inspiration from structuralism theory. The model proceeds through constructing a series of binary opposites such as elite versus subaltern, vertical versus horizontal mobilization, formal (cautious) versus spontaneous sources of movement and to delineate national movement as a dialectical process. The national movement and the ideology of nationalism according to this view suffered in India from structural cleavages between the 'mass mobilization' on horizontal lines and its vertical mobilisation by elite nationalist leadership. The mass movement was located in principles of kinship, caste, class and territory, it was spontaneous in making and aimed at social resistance against exploitation. Its mobilization was not based on formal ideological or legalistic strategy, and it could change course and operation in midstream. The national movement led by elite leadership made use of such subaltern mobilizations selectively. The subalternity could not forge national movement all by itself. Yet the elite leadership, it is held, did not help forge these movements into a united front for social mobilization, due to its own class ideology. It created a structural hiatus in nationalist mobilization for large scale social transfor-mation. This hiatus and the failure of our nationalist leadership according to this view, constitutes the problematique of Indian nationalism even today.

This viewpoint recognises the role of linkages between the pan-Indian and local mobilizations in the formation of political consciousness but its characterization of these linkages through notions of 'brokerage' or 'collaboration' neglects the cultural basis of such interaction in the social structure of our society. The notion of linkage is defined in rational-utilitarian terms and is devoid of cultural content. It is evident also from an assumption in this thesis that local mobilizations enjoy total autonomy or that they have a *sui generis* existence. Moreover, this view on Indian nationalism overemphasises particularistic manifestations of social and cultural forces denying pan-Indian national consciousness.

Its 'collabora-tionist' notion of linkages between mass movements and British imperial administration, unconsciously promotes a 'pupil's pro-gress' model of nationalism in India. The structural dissociation between the mass and the elite levels of national movements in this thesis is extended into a dichotomy between Eastern and Western social and cultural systems, and ideologies of nationalism.

This view abounds in the writing of several scholars on political culture and political system in contemporary India. Focus is on 'factional' characteristics of Indian political culture, its roots are primordial principles such as caste, kinship aid religion. The segmentary features of society are enlarged as if these were the general principles of Indian social organisation and its cultural pattern. The particularistic features are universalised without taking into consideration social institutions which serve as links between local and national levels of functioning. Despite there being some awareness of limitations of such approach to understanding pro-cesses in Indian society, the tendency to hold to these views continues.

It is true that social institutions and groups at local levels in India enjoyed autonomy from elite traditions, but this autonomy was relative. Indian society through ages provided for organic linkages of these micro-institutions with the macro-organisations, such as economy, civilization, polity and administrative institutions. The dichotomy as posed between 'vertical' or elite levels of social and political mobilization and 'horizontal' or mass levels was not absolute. For example, horizontal mobilization of caste on vertical lines into 'caste association' used to take place long before Independence. The tribes differentiated into caste like social formations. Even the comprehension of caste distinctions through ritual purity and pollution would have been impossible without a civilizational model of 'varna' with a pan-Indian extension of meanings and symbols. Otherwise, caste is only a regional entity. Comparative studies of folk cultures in geographically disparate regions show extensive commonalities of symbols, meanings and cultural contents across regions.

We might reiterate the historical role played by interstructural autonomy of basic social institutions in Indian society. The institutions of social stratification, political administration and values and beliefs in their relative autonomy provided flexibility of responses to forces encroaching upon from the outside. These could be forces of colonialism, alien cultural contacts or contemporary processes of modernisation. This relative autonomy of basic social institutions continues even today, but its quality is undergoing fast transformation. In traditional India, caste panchayats could in large measure conduct internal self-administration, avoid appeals to state administration for judicial settlements, since caste enjoyed stability and strength with support from other institutions such as economy, technology and belief systems. Yet in the past also these regional cultural traditions had a sustained and institutionalised interaction with pan-Indian institutions. Professor N.K. Bose in his study of the geographical background of Indian culture, identifies several such institutions which provided linkages between local and national institutions in the past; these include: traveling mendicants, traders, story-tellers, craftsmen and artists. They came from all castes, low and high. The pilgrimage centres, fairs and festivals provided yet another nodal points of such interlink ages. Professor Bose concludes: 'Although India was, by and large illiterate, yet there were built up certain mecha-nisms by means of which common intellectual and emotional elements of culture were brought to the door of the most distant communities, isolated either by geography or the promotion of social separatism (Bose: N.K.: 1977:6).

The autonomy of grass-root social institutions has been over-played in total disregard of linkages among these also as a device to under-rate the forces of unity in the Indian society and its civilization possibly as a measure of colonial or imperial policy of the British administrator turned social scientists. In such writings, concepts such as 'caste', 'tribe', 'village', 'community', 'family and kinship' were defined as segmentary entities, often analogous to their socio-historical equivalents in the European society. The emphasis was on showing how each of these entities affirmed the principle of segmentation and autonomy rather than being parts of an organic whole. The element of discreteness was over and the linkages, both social and cultural, which bound these entitles into an organic system of social structure and civilization were neglected' (Singh, Y. 1986:1).

Pace of Development

Localism and nationalism are social processes in continual interaction in all societies that have passed beyond the elementary stages of segmentary social organisation to civilization. This stage of societal evolution is achieved through advancement of civilization, a long drawn process of growth in economy, technology, political institutions and intellectual and artistic creativity. A civilization society has to build up linkages with local or mass level institutions, and communities to sustain itself economically, techno-logically and ideologically. Nationalism is a process, a product of historical conjuncture of social forces through which the linkages are not only established or expanded but also qualitatively streng-thened. Nationalism is, therefore, not a finished product, nor a formal structure or normative model but an organic historical process through which civilization societies strengthen themselves by qualitative differentiation from within and their superior integration organically, within a territorial boundary. Often it is the formal notion of nationalism and its ideology that turns it into a monstrosity that all civilized societies must avoid. Nationalism as a social process evolves towards maturation as Louis Dumont suggests: 'nationalism refers to the nation as a tendency inspired by its existence or as the aspiration to build up a nation' (Louis Dumont: 1976:47).

For nationalism as a process, aspiration is as important as achievement. The studies on France, the first European nation, show that movement from provincialism to nationalism was often a fractured and painful process. In 1864 an inspector of education, touring the mountains of the Lozere, asked the children at a village school: 'In what country is Lozere situated?' Not a single pupil knew the answer. 'Are you English or Russian?', he demanded. They could not say. This was in one of the remoter parts of France, but the incident illustrates how Frenchmen gradually became aware of what it was that distinguished them from other men. The French nation had to be created' (Zeldin Theodore: 1980:3). Eighty three years later, in 1951, an opinion poll revealed the persistent hold of provincialism, and ambivalence towards the culture of the capital 'Paris' was strong. Only 42 per cent of the provincials (as opposed to 79 per cent of Parisians) knew who J.P. Sartre was-others described him variously as a street, a deputy, a painter and a dress designer' (quoted in Zeldin T: 1980:3). A publication in 1934 about France said that 'the clan and tribe still survive in small towns and in the countryside. People entrenched themselves in their little properties with their petty interests, and petty grievances... mistrustful of young talent... oblivious of the great problems of the world (Ch. J. Million: 1934; quoted in Zeldin T: 1980:34).

Without in depth sociological historiography the western nationalism has come to present itself as a mythical model for Indian society and its many scholars. As deeper studies of its nationalism and national identity become available one gets more realistic assessment of the questions of nationalism and national identity. Writing in a publication of 1979 on France, Theodore Zeldin says: 'When I examine the forces working for the creation of more uniformity and unity in the country, I find the growth of a sense of national identity to be superficial, despite the imposition or adoption of a common language, and of common ways of thinking and talking which seem to distinguish Frenchmen from all other people (Zeldin Theodore: 1979: viii). According to Zeldin, French national identity is the creation of classes and politicians. It was reinforced by the policy of education and the existence of army. Not class struggle but urge for social mobility, competitive-ness and anxiety dominated the personal behaviour of the people in this process. Zeldin notes how: 'By 1966 less than half (44- per cent) of metal workers in large factories said that for them the capitalist was the enemy; in small firms only 12-15 per cent held that view (Zeldin T: 1979: xi).

We have made these references not to pass value judgment on provincialism or nationalism but to illustrate that movement towards nationalism in any society is a process in which counter pulls of antagonistic tendencies remain active in accordance with the conjuncture of historical and social forces. Humans get their maximum succor from their private life world and primordial ties. Hence nationalism should not mean in any society the total aboli-tion or death of regional or provincial cultures or group identities. Our hypothesis is that neither the structure nor the normative construct of society could offer us sufficient measure of nationalism in a country. Its strength, more latent than manifest, lies in the linkages that bind these structures and norms at various levels into a super organic whole which has great plasticity and, there-fore, endurance. The movement from particularistic ties of loyalty to principles of nationalism and national identity is governed by emergence of social forces that trigger the process of moder-nisation.

A modernisation hypothesis is probably implicit in most debates on nationalism in developing societies. The relevant question is whether the model of modernisation in terms of which nationalism in these societies is analysed, is itself adequate or not. Most western models of modernisation suffer from futurological fallacy, and historical analogues are proposed from western experiences without much regard for differences in basic values, history and social structure. Professor I.P. Desai made a perceptive remark in this context when he said that, we should see the work of academicians abroad in terms of its relevance to what we are thinking and doing. It should not be other way round as it has been in the past' (Desai I.P.: 1981: 56).

Most Indian academicians we find today are sensitive to this question. They have continually endeavoured to formulate conceptual and theoretical responses to this problem. The dilemma they face is about evolving a conceptual frame through which complex linkages between nationalism and modernisation in India, that are grounded empirically in primordial and provincial structures and values, could be explained through universalistic concepts and categories that are also sensitive to historical specificity of the Indian process of nationalism. In simple terms, the question is: can tradition be modernized? Or, would the 'cunning of reason', the Enlightenment ideology of which nationalism is an off-shoot ultimately triumph and imprison nationalism in the iron cage of universal history? To many scholars both in India and abroad answer to this question poses crucial problems of nationalism and modernisation. A large number of them, however postulate opposition between tradition and modernity and between provincialism and nationalism, as conceptual dichotomies. Our contention is that tradition, modernity, or provincialism, nationalism should not be seen as strong normative structures but as social processes. The impregnable wall that isolates and divides them is semantic not real.

The structuralist theory in sociology and social sciences has encouraged the tendency among both the marxist and non- marxist scholars to postulate social, economic and cultural parameters of nationalism, modernisation and development, etc. in logical sets of opposites or in binary terms, where linkages between them are tenuous not real, syntactical not historical. Consequently, analysis of nationalism under such theoretical impulses fore-closes the possibilities of constructive reciprocity and interaction between tradition and modernity, between nationalism and provincialism and between equality and hierarchy. Louis Dumont in his treatment of questions of communalism and nationalism in India articulates this dilemma when he says that in India, 'elements such as people and territory, normatively stressed on one side, are found as *empirical and undifferentiated* datum on the other. The orientation to ultimate values shows a more drastic and complex difference. On the traditional side, the ultimate values are found in the conformity of each element to the role assigned to it in the whole of being as such. In the modern society, they are found in the concrete human indivisible element, which is taken as an end in itself, and as the source of all norms, rationality and order; in other words, the Individual. As history shows transition is difficult, and has given rise to intermediary forms' (Dumont L: 1964: 70). Louis Dumont recognises the significances of *interaction* between tradition and nationalism or even the existence of intermediary forms. His doubt about a smooth or even successful transition to nationalism in traditional societies is based on the diversity of the two worldviews one hierarchical, that is Indian and the other individualistic, that is western, of which nationalism and modernisation are products.

One might easily notice elements of historicity and formalism in the views expressed by Dumont and others who approach the question of nationalism as opposition between tradition and modernity. In operational terms, this opposition exists in the dualism of what is defined as, rational' and 'basic' or fundamental in the value system of societies. Indian society is supposed to be rooted in fundamental value system of hierarchy, and its transition to nationalism or modernisation is thwarted due to lack of primacy of rational values in social life. The limitation of this reasoning rests in its non-recognition of the fact that in real life rational values have a tendency to co-exist with basic or fundamental values. The social, political and economic processes of change in India illustrate this fact. The challenge in India is not of the transition from tradition to modernity but of the modernisation of Indian tradition.

Historical experience of nationalism even in the western societies shows that crucial factors which contributed to institutionalisation of nationalism and to their modernisation were primarily through rational technological changes. The basic values or the religious worldview of western society only accommodated these transformations. The growth of one has not led to the obsolescence of the other. The relevant question, however, which makes a material difference between successful or not so successful transi-tion to modernisation of which nationalism is a historical byproduct is how successfully rational principles are applied for the growth of society.

The Indian experience in this context clearly indicates that rational values have been widely imbibed in the uses of technology in public and private life. All sections of people covet for careers in sciences and professions. Pragmatism in political, economic and social life, is widely pursued, often uncrossing limits of principles or moral standards. In practical life, be it agriculture, trade, industry, transport or other services, adoption of modern utilitarian or rational values is common. So, if measures of nationalism and modernisation are acceptance of rational values, Indian society is well on the way to this goal. These values, however, co-exist with traditional basic values and worldview.

Instead of replacement there is adaptive synthesis of the rational with the traditional values and beliefs. Largely, this is how it should be. But this process of adaptive change sets into motion also counter-tendencies or negative social forces which not only serve as impediments to modernisation but also threaten the processes of nationalism and national integration.

These counter-tendencies emerge from the sharpening consciousness of social and economic inequalities among groups in society. Modernisation has set into motion a process of social restructuration in our society. The traditional society was based on a relative evenness in the dimensions of social, economic, and political status of people at an integrated, though lower level of social order. The rational and basic values of society were integrated together due to relative stability of the former, represented pre-eminently by technology. The process of modernisation upsets this balance in society. The rational or utilitarian values not only far outweigh the basic moral values of society, but expand faster and have higher degree of intensity. This coincides with emergence of high information society. In India, political participation, mass media, education, social mobility and increasing incidence of migration have intensified the awareness of social and economic inequalities. Continuous inculcation of values of consumerism and ostentatious life style of privileged sections has negative effect upon people in general. The modern means of communication make consciousness of social inequalities carry sharper edge which distorts the perception of a rational order of society. This creates imbalance in the means end relationship in the pursuits of life chances.

Violence, communalism, cartelism and regionalism erupt symbolising these distortions in means end relationship in pursuits of social, economic, political and cultural objectives. The process of modernisation enlarges opportunities which adds to the strength of the middle classes, professional groups and political functionaries. These new classes are products of social restructuration and social mobility. A substantial segment of these new classes climbs to higher status through dynamic pathways. Ironically, this process also creates pauperization in rural areas, marginalization of peasantry and urban migration of the rural poor. Not all the underprivileged people that emerge in this process have subaltern identity, as not all new social climbers have commitment to rational utilitarian ethos. We witness all over the country today this process, where resentment of underprivileged is coming face to face with cussedness and arrogance of the dominant classes. Provincialism and cominualism are products of this environment. If the emer-gence of new middle classes consolidates the processes of Indian nationalism by widening and strengthening the societal linkages in the system, the linkages of territory, administration, resources, market, technology and culture, it is also sharpening the divide between privileged and underprivileged that reinforces tendencies towards communalism, regionalism and counter-nationalism. The Constitution of our republic does not envisage only legal rational order. It encompasses it in the basic values of socialism, secularism and democracy. Strengthening linkages in the social system sponsored by the needs of the dominant classes in society may not achieve these goals, and may lead to fractured modernisation. History tells us, to be wary of nationalism that is a product of such process.

It leads to brutal application of state power for repression of underprivileged in society. Solution lies in a model of modernisation that is consensual and aims at vigorous pursuit of goals of social justice in society. This alone will strengthen the roots of nationalism in our society.

3

Social Issues

The Indian Social Structure and cultural pattern are characterised by unity as well as diversity. Historically, India has been hospitable to numerous groups of immigrants from different parts of Asia and Europe, but the culture of each group has undergone enough change over the centuries to become an integral part of the Indian mosaic. The institution of caste may be mentioned as a typical example of the paradox that is Indian society. Each caste stands for a way of life that is to some extent distinctive, but at the same time the castes of a region form part of a single social frame-work. It is important to note that caste is found not only among the Hindus but also among the Muslims, Christians, Sikhs, Jains and Jews. Caste is ubiquitous, and this has resulted in an ideology tolerant of diversity.

National Integration

Factors making for diversity are apparent even to the casual observer. The population of India is racially diverse, containing elements from six main racial types: the Negrito, the Proto-Australoid, the Mongoloid, the Mediterranean, the Western Brachycephals, and the Nordic. All the great religions of the world are represented in this country. The tribal groups enjoy varying degrees of contact with one or the other of the great religions. The major literary languages alone number fourteen. Diversity is seen in the patterns of rural as well as urban settlements, commu-nity life, forms of land tenure and agricultural operations. In kinship, marriage rites and customs, inheritance, and the general mode of living, there are striking differences between groups.

Diversity is, however, only one side of the picture. There are unifying factors as well. India is a political entity, every part of which is under the same Constitution. The process of unification developed as several great rulers Asoka, Samudragupta, Akbar brought large parts of the country under their power; but it was only during British rule that India became for the first time a single political entity.

The concept of the unity of India is inherent in Hinduism. There are sacred centres of Hindu pilgrimage in every corner of the land. Certain salient aspects of Sanskritic culture are to be found all over the country. India is the sacred land not only of the Hindus but also of the Sikhs, Jains and Buddhists. The Muslims and Christians, too, have several sacred centres of pilgrimage in India. The institution of caste cuts across diverse religious groups and gives them all a common social idiom.

The declaration of India as a secular State provides one more evidence of the tolerance of diversity which has been characteristic of Indian history from its beginning. The process of economic development ushered in by the Five Year Plans and the spread of egalitarian ideals have brought about revolutionary changes in the Indian pattern of social life. A single government and a common body of civil and criminal law, a developing economy, and a secular approach to public life and problems are now providing substance and reality to India's claim to be a nation.

New Developments in the social structure may be discussed under the following heads: (i) caste in modern India; (ii) changing rural and urban life; and (iii) changes in the position of women.

Dr. Bailey's study, *Caste and the Economic Frontier* (1958), provides a good example of the kind of changes which came in the wake of British rule. In Bisipara, a village in Khondmals in Orissa two non-landowning castes, made money because they could get a monopoly of the profitable trade in hides and liquor. It would have been polluting for the higher castes to handle liquor or hides. Of the two castes one was able to raise itself up in the hierarchy by Sanskritising its ritual and way of life; the other, found that untouchability came in the way of its mobility.

Caste vs Profession

The dissociation between caste and occupation is greater in the towns than in the rural areas, and much greater in the big, industrialized towns. A number of occupations have come into existence in the big cities and these are, to some extent, "Castfree". For instance, several castes, including Brahmins, are found driving taxis in Indian towns.

The policy of giving preference to Harijans in appointment to Government posts has helped in breaking the traditional association of that caste with agricultural labour, sweeping and leatherwork. In one taluk of Mysore State, for instance, a majority of the teachers in the primary schools are Harijans.

While the association between caste and traditional occupation has been disturbed to some extent, the fact that high castes had a literary, commercial or military tradition has resulted in their dominating the liberal professions the higher posts in the government and the army, and the new commerce and industry. At the other end, the urban proletariat consists, by and large, of the "lower" castes. The Chamar repairs shoes in a small shop, or works as a labourer in a shoe factory, the Dhobi in an urban laundry, the Darzi in a tailor's shop, the Nai in a "hair-cutting saloon" and so on. There is a modicum of continuity between rural and urban hierarchies. Opportunities for social mobility are greater in cities than in villages. An industrious, shrewd and lucky Charnar may in course of time become an owner of a small shoe factory and the Dhobi of a big laundary.

The idea of hierarchy is central to caste. The customs, rites and way of life were different among the higher and lower castes. The dominant caste punished those who encroached on forbidden ground, but the process could not be stopped. This adoption of the symbols of higher status has been called Sanskritisation. The Lingayats of Mysore Sanskritised their way of life over eight centu-ries ago. In recent times, Sanskritisation has been widespread both spatially as well as structurally. The Ilavalls of Kerala, the Smiths of South India. the Ramgharias of Punjab, the Chamars of Uttar Pradesh and many other castes have all tried to Sankritized their way of life liquor and forbidden meals are given up. Sanskritic ritual is increasingly adopted and there is an increasing demand for the services of a Brahmin priest at wedding, birth, funeral rites and *sraddha*.

Wave of Modernity

On the other hand, the higher castes, especially those living in the bigger cities, are undergoing a process of westernisation. Westernisation, like Sanskritisation, is a blanket term, it includes Western education as well as the adoption of Western ways of life and outlook. It also implies a degree of secularization and rationalism and in these two respects it stands opposed to Sanskritisation. In certain other respects, westernisation helps to spread Sanskritisation through the products of its technology—newspapers, radio and films.

In some exceptional cases, the lower castes and tribes are being westernised without undergoing a prior process of Sanskritisation. Again, Sanskritisation occurs generally as part of the process of the upward movement of castes while westernisation has no such association. In fact, unlike Sanskritisation, Westernisa-tion is more commonly an individual or family phenomenon and not a caste phenomenon, though some groups (Kodagus) and some areas (Punjab) may be said to be more Westernised than the others. Again, some groups may be more westernised in the sense that they are highly educated, whereas some others may be westernised in their dress, food habits and recreation.

Hypergamy, a manifestation of the hierarchical aspects of caste, is becoming less popular in certain parts of the country. Kulin hypergamy has largely disappeared. A movement is afoot among the Nayars to marry within caste and stop giving girls in *sambandam* to Nambudri men. Correspondingly, Nambudri leaders look down upon *sambandam* and encourage the younger sons to marry Nambudri girls. In Gujarat, however, hypergamous marriages continue to be popular with Patidars and Anavils, though perhaps not to the same extent as before.

We have already commented on the importance of pollution in maintaining the structural distance between the various castes. Pollution rules are much less strictly observed in cities than in villages. In fact, in certain areas of urban life pollution has ceased to have any application. People mix freely in factories and schools, and very few bother about the caste of fellow passengers in train and buses. In cities pollution is being increasingly confined to the house, to women and to ritual occasions.

In older days the higher castes regarded contact with the lower castes as polluting, and the latter were also subjected to some disabilities. For instance, the lower castes were not allowed to build tiled houses, wear the clothes which the upper castes wore or take out wedding processions in streets inhabited by high castes. Punishment for an offence varied according to the caste of the persons who committed it and against whom it was committed. Mahatma Gandhi roused the conscience of educated Indians about the practice of untouchability. Apart from the injustice, educated Indians realized the political dangers of trying to deny basic conditions of decent living to large numbers of people on the ground of birth in a particular caste. It is this awareness that has led to the adoption of various measures in Independent India to put an end to untouchability and to enable the Scheduled Castes and Tribes to advance to the level of the high castes. The grosser expressions of untouchability have disappeared in the cities, but in rural areas it still holds sway. The economic emancipation of the Harijans and their increased migration to urban areas are necessary for the complete eradication of untouchability.

The British not only introduced a new body of legal ideas including that of equality before law) but also new procedural methods. Some of these were not understood by the litigants, the bulk of whom were illiterate. The language used in the higher courts was English and there was a hierarchy of courts, the higher court occasionally reversing the decision of the lower that deepened the mystery of the new legal processes. Justice seemed to the peasant a gamble in which the rich had a better chance than the poor, they hired the cleverer lawyers and moved from one court to another. The British lawcourts greatly reduced the power of the panchayats, but the latter continued to function. Even today people take a variety of disputes to the elders and abied by their decision. Occasionally, a case pending before a law court is withdrawn and submitted to the panchayat.

Overall Development

In the last few decades, with the great improvement in communications, castes have shown a tendency to extend the area of their operations. The settlement of an intricate caste dispute or the defence of a caste interest might call forth a meeting of the representatives of the concerned caste from fifty or more villages. Sometimes, several endogamous *jatis,* all ,belonging to the same level (e.g., all the untouchable *jatis* in an area) might come together to fight for a privilege or a right, while to decide an accusation of adultery with a person of another caste the elders of a single endogamous unit or the two concerned units may come together. Castes have shown much organizational ability in meeting the challenge of new social, economic and political situations. This brings us to the functions of caste in modern India.

The new activities which castes have undertaken may be considered under four heads: reformist and philanthropic educational economic and political. One of the results of British rule was to make sensitive and intelligent Indians critical of their own society and some of its institutions. Many political leaders of all-India stature were also earnest social reformers. Meetings of castes such as Kayasthas took place and passed resolutions on a variety of matters. Caste newspapers, journals and conferences had as their main aim the safeguarding of the interests of the caste in the context of the new situations which British rule had brought about. In the towns, there come into existence caste hostels, hospitals, banks, orphanages, co-operative societies and organizations undertaking a variety of charitable tasks for a particular caste. Matters such as the age of marriage of girls, girls education, high dowry, widow remarriage, high cost of wedding and funeral cere-monies and many other matters were discussed in caste conferen-ces. Concessions and privileges in education and appointment to Government jobs were demanded for the caste from the Govern-ment. On the one hand, there was an attempt to argue that a particular caste was backward and that concessions were necessary to enable it to catch up with the advanced castes. On the other hand, the Sanskritisation of the customs, manners and way of life of the caste was advocated to claim a high place for it in the ritual hierarchy. Backwardness was claimed in a secular context and a high status in a ritual context.

Some Indian towns have hostels for the locally important castes. The great peasant caste of Okkaligas of Mysore, for instance, collect during the harvest a grain contribution from every landowner in the Mandya and Mysore districts, and this is sent to Okkaliga hostels in towns. Scholarships have been endowed for which only members of a particular caste are declared eligible. Allover India even the middle-range castes have realized the importance of education and consequently there is keen competition to secure opportunities for education at all levels for members of their castes. Nowadays, State Governments discourage caste hostels and give grants only to "cosmopolitan" hostels.

Castes with a literary tradition were the first to take to western education, and this naturally meant that they dominated the liberal professions and higher posts in the Government. These castes did not exploit the new commercial opportunities because of an initial resistance against trade. It is only when the kind of jobs they preferred became very difficult to secure that they entered trade and commerce. Even the traditionally commercial castes could not trade in certain articles, we have already mentioned how in Orissa two low castes made money out of trading in liquor and hides, articles which the high castes would not handle. On the other hand, Brahmins in South took to restaurant-keeping not only because cooking was their traditional occupation but also because food cooked by them is acceptable to all. In Mysore. the Lingayats also took to hotel-keeping since food cooked by them is acceptable to most non-Brahmin castes.

We have already mentioned co-operative societies formed on the basis of caste. The Saraswat Housing Colony in Bombay is an example. The Nattukottai Cettiyars of South India, a trading caste, have built a co-operative banking organization. There are other caste banks in South India—the Vysya Bank, Kaniyara Bank and Mandyam Bank are instances.

We have earlier mentioned that British rule set in motion a number of forces which facilitated the horizontal organization of castes. This was specially true of the lower castes which felt that the higher castes, thanks to their education along western lines, had obtained a near-monopoly of the higher posts in the Government of the liberal professions, and of positions of power in local self-government. The British admitted their demand for concessions and privileges as reasonable. In the former Bombay State, for instance, castes were classified as backward, intermediate and advanced and the first two were given preference in appointment to official posts. They were also given representation in local self-governing bodies.

In Madras, the Justice Party was founded in 1917 to promote sectional interests. The party co-operated with the British to form the government in the Madras Presidency under the Government of India Act of 1919. At this time the Congress was fighting the British. In the inter-war period the Congress, under Mahatma

Gandhi's leadership, succeeded in winning the masses to its side, and in the 1937 elections it swept the polls in large areas of the country, including Madras. The Justice Party suffered heavily. This did not mean that "casteist" parties suffered a permanent defeat.

The Dravida Kazagam was created to promote the exclusive interests of the Southerners. The Dravida Munnetra Kazagam owes its birth to personal and ideological differences between the leaders of the Dravida Kagzam. The D.M.K. seems to be more alive to economic issues than the D.K. It is certainly more popular than the D.K. It won 50 seats in the Madras Legislative Assembly at the 1962 General Elections.

The gradual transfer of power from the British to the Indians has been accompanied by an increased activity of caste in the political sphere. In its simplest manifestation this shows itself as the tendency to vote for a man of one's own caste, other things being equal. Nowadays, all political parties try to put up candidates belonging to the locally preponderant castes. The Communist Party of India calls this "social base", and makes sure that the candidates it puts up have a "social base".

The Caste Factor

Caste considerations influence politics in other ways as well. In Maharashtra the Konkanastha Brahmins were the first to become westernised and they dominated the political arena for several decades. There was also a non-Brahmin movement in Maharashtra, and in the early years of this century, the Maharaja of Kolhapur played a leading part in it. In 1948, a large block of the Maharashtra Congress left the party to form the Peasants and Workers Party. According to Miss Maureen Patterson, this was "both an attempt to protest against what was considered the overtly 'capitalistic' domination of the Congress and to bypass what was claimed to be continued Brahmin control over positions of leadership in the Maharashtra Congress Organization". Selig Harrison writes that the rivalry between the two dominating land-owning castes, Kammas and Reddis, "is only a modern recurrence of a historic pattern dating back to the fourteenth century"t. In 1955, the Kammas were predominantly in the Communist Party while the Reddis were in the Congress. Even during the "violent phase" of the Andhra Communist Party, Kamma landlords were spared by the Communists, while the other landlords were not. In the Mysore Congress today, rivalry between the Okkaligas and the Lingayats is a well known fact, and it influences in one way or another every important decision. The opposition of the Mysore Okkaligas to the formation of a Kammas-speaking State inclusive of North Karnataka, Coorg and South Kanara was due to their fear of domination by the Lingayats, the largest single caste in the new State.

It is not only in the South that caste finds expression in politics. Gujarat, Bihar and Uttar Pradesh show evidence of caste activity in political parties and elections. The 1957 elections provided positive proof of the active part played by caste. In March 1957, the Congress Working Committee expressed its deep alarm at the rise of communal, caste and subcaste feelings in the country.

The new opportunities which we have referred to increased caste consciousness and inter-caste competition. In South India, this was accompanied initially by anti-Brahmin sentiments. In other parts of the country there was opposition and hostility to the caste or castes which enjoyed a dominance in government jobs, professions, and commerce and industry.

Nowadays, in the South, there is a struggle between the locally dominant castes for a larger share of power and pelf. The process of democratic decentralization *(Panchayat Raj),* and Community Development and allied programmes have all benefited the locally dominant castes and not the poorer and smaller castes. In fact, the position of the latter has worsened because of increased pressure on land. The Harijans, for whom the Government is trying to do a great deal, feel that they are far from being equal, economically or otherwise, to the high castes. They have been pressing for the continuation of constitutional safeguards for a further period of six years (till 1970). The high castes, on the other hand, resent the privileges given to the Harijans.

The land reform measures have increased the tension between landowners (generally belonging to high castes) and tenants. Even within a caste, they have set the poor against the rich. The attempt by the Harijans to assert their rights has often resulted in fighting, bloodshed and arson. The anti-Brahmin riots in Mahara-shtra after the assassination of Mahatma Gandhi, the rioting in Ramanathapuram in Madras in 1957 and the clashes elsewhere between the Harijans and the high castes provide evidence of the underlying tensions in rural areas.

We have earlier made the point that there is a broad coherence between the caste hierarchy and the economic heirarchy, and this coherence continues to exist in the towns and cities. Where there is inconsistency between ritual and economic status, two consequences are possible: if the ritual status is high while the economic status is low, the gap between the two can exist for a long time. But when the economic status is high and the ritual status low, the latter tends to adjust itself to the former. Such a tendency has been inherent in the caste system for a long time.

It is true that industrialization and urbanization weaken the hold of pollution ideas. Western education has, resulted in the spread of a liberal, democratic and secular ideology among the Indian intelligentsia. The advent of universal adult suffrage abolishes the distinction between high and low as far as voting is concerned. The Congress, Communist and Samyukt a Socialist Parties have all accepted the creation of a "classless and casteless society" as their ultimate goal. But the formulation of a goal is not the same thing as making a sustained, and systematic effort to realize it. Neither the traditional institutions nor the ones created under the British rule show a consistent movement towards egalitarianism. What is now coming into being is a new type of stratification in which caste and class are mixed up in an inexiticable tangle.

Hope and Aspirations

It must be stressed here that the formulation of the goal of a "casteless and classless society" by the principal political parties is an important event. The measures undertaken to abolish untouchability constitute a definite advance towards a more egalitarian society than before. The various measures designed to help the Backward Castes have enabled at least the middle-range dominant castes to come up. But it is also true that the latter have a vested interest in keeping down the Harijans and other low castes who supply them with tenants and agricultural labourers. Devolution of power has added to the power of the locally dominant castes and this has enabled them to collar the benefits of Community Development and other rural welfare programmes. Indian society today is stratified along the lines of caste as well as class. The desire to bring about an egalitarian society is no doubt there; but it needs a systematic programme of action spread over a long period of time if inequalities have to be reduced appreciably. The task of transforming the most rigidly stratified society in the world into an egalitarian one is indeed Himalayan.

Rural society is undergoing changes and they may be considered under the following heads: industrialization; urbanization; and political and administrative changes.

During British rule, Indian economy became a "colonial" one geared to subserve the needs of the developing British economy. The beginnings of industrialization also occurred during British rule. These facts adversely affected some artisan castes and especially the weavers and Potters, many of whom were faced with the prospect of joining the growing ranks of landless labourers and tenants or migrating to towns. Villagers became increasingly dependent on nearby towns for many goods and services. The growing of commercial crops such as cotton, jute, tea, coffee, indigo and tobacco brought cash to the village and made village economy and society sensitive to changes in the external demand for these commodities. In those villages where the growing of commercial crops became the major concern, *jajmani* relationship tended to disappear.

When the new economic opportunities benefited the higher castes, the gulf between them and the lower castes widened still further. When they benefited the lower castes, the latter tried to move up in the hierarchy and this increased caste consciousness.

Traditionally rival patrons competed with each other for land, clients and women. With the establishment of British rule, seeking the favour of officials became very important. Nowadays, patrons compete with each other to start rice and flour mills, operate bus lines, and become *sarpanch* and secretaries of co-operative societies. Urban political leaders cultivate rural patrons for votes at elections.

Over the last hundred years migration from villages to towns has been steadily increasing. The "push" factor has been, probably more important than the "pull" factor in this: the' increased pressure of population on land has driven the most vulnerable section of rural population, the poorer tenants and labourers, to the cities and plantations. (*"Dry"* or non-irrigated areas have been more vulnerable too such pressure than "wet" or irrigated areas.) For instance, the textile mills of Bombay have attracted large numbers of Mahars, a Harijan caste of Maharashtra as also Muslim Julahas (Weavers) from Uttar Pradesh. The towns also beckoned the higher castes who saw in them the means of obtaining western education, without which well-paid and prestigious jobs could not be secured. The trading castes and the artisans migrated into towns in search of new opportunities.

The city not only provides employment but also it changes the way of life of the rural people living in its hinterland. Nearby villagers take to dairying, poultry-keeping and marketgardening to supply the urban demand for milk, fruit and vegetables. The villagers make use of the medical, educational and recreational facilities available in the city. More money circulates in the nearby villages, and villagers get increasingly urbanized and westernised.

Political and administrative changes introduced in recent years have had important effects on the rural social structure. Most important of these are the various land reform measures including the abolition of *zamindari* and *inamdari* and the Tenancy Reform Acts giving the tenant a greater share of the produce and protec-ting him from, exploritation by the land-owner. Restrictions have been imposed on the area of land a person may own. *Panchayat Raj* has been introduced in most States of the Indian Union. Universal adult franchise has given the underprivileged groups new political opportunities and a sense of power.

Before Independence, even educated Indians in the towns used to invest some of their savings in arable land. Urban gentry having *pied-a-terre* was a common phenomenon. But the land reform measures have resulted in discouraging urban people from investing in land. Even the bigger rural landowners have come to realize that it is risky too own too much land. Savings are being diverted into other channels, and the ceiling scare has resulted in the formal and only formal-partitioning of family land to circum-vent possible legislation. Land is now passing into the hands of owner-cultivators. A landbased but urban living intelligentsia will fairly soon become a thing of the past.

The enhanced power given to village panchayats, the abolition in some places of the hereditary principle in the holding of village offices *(e.g.*, headman and accountant), and the Untouchability Offences Act, 1955, are all beginning to change village life. The changes will probably be more radical in the near future. The

Community Development Programme which now covers most of rural India, has made some impact on the rural population: it has made them aware of the fact that a new nation-wide organization has come into existence with the avowed aim of helping them to change their lives and economy.

Though the Portuguese built the first town *(e.g.,* Cranganur) on the Western model in India, it was during British rule that the Western-type town became a familiar phenomenon. Four types of towns came into existence: ports, cantonments, administrative capitals, and industrial and commercial centres. Frequently, the British urban pattern was superimposed on a traditional town. Examples of such cultural schizophrenia are Bangalore, Poona, Ahmedabad and Delhi. In Bangalore, for instance, the traditional part of the town with its narrow, congested streets and even narrower lanes leading off them offers a perfect contrast to the cantonment with its broad and straight roads, bungalows, parks and playing fields. Again, social life in the traditional part of the town differs from social life in the cantonment.

The ports of Calcutta and Bombay have developed into huge, sprawling cities. They are an unprecedented phenomenon in India's social history. People have migrated to them not only from all parts of India but also from different cultural groups, and this has resulted in a rich and diversified social life. That a certain amount of tension should occasionally show itself between these groups, and that sometimes personal and group frustration is translated into hatred of a group, are not at all surprising. What is indeed surprising is that they are living together in peace most of the time.

During the last sixty years, several industrial towns and cities have come into existence. Some of them have literally sprung up in jungles where previously tigers roamed. India's first steel town, Jamshedpur; today employs a large number of Santhals, the, tribal inhabitants of that area. Now the tribes not only work in the factory but live in close relationship with groups which come from different parts of India and speak different languages. Bhadravati in Mysore State has also developed into a steel, cement and paper town in an area which was tiger-infested even as recently as the forties. In Independent India, three new steel towns have emerged. Bhilai in Madhya Pradesh, Rourkela in Orissa and Durgapur in West Bengal. These factories have not only brought. prosperity but are altering the social landscape of the areas. Regions which were only recently backward, economically and culturally, are being pitchforked suddenly into prosperous, urban and cosmopolitan social life.

The manufacture of steel is not the only industry around which towns are being created. Sugar, paper, chemicals, fertilizers, textiles, and mining and dams provide other nuclei. Social life in the new industrial towns is different from social life in cities which grew around or near extant and traditional towns. In the former, the civic hierarchy shows a tendency to follow the factory hierarchy. The town is nothing more than a place where the factory workers live when they are not working. (There are, of course, small shopkeepers and others who are ultimately dependent upon the factory). As in these towns the factory-employees live in houses built by the employers, they cannot choose their neighbours. Thus, in a textile factory near Mysore, a Brahmin may have a Harijan or Muslim or Christian for a neighbour. In Neyveli, there are seven types of houses according to different income-categories. The lower income levels tend, however, to overlap somewhat with the lower castes, and to this extent even the new towns tend to perpetuate traditional distances between higher and lower castes.

By far the most common are the "mixed" towns: the capital which is also a centre of trade and has a well-known temple or two, the commercial town which is also an important railway junc-tion and houses a big university and so on. In such a city, there is usually a "core" consisting of people who have lived in it for a long time and whose way of life is different from that of the immigrants. Usually the "core" inhabit the older parts of the town while the immigrants occupy the fringe. The residential pattern of the older parts of the city shows a close relation to language, caste and religion. Even in a city such as Bombay residence is associated with these factors. Tulu-speaking Billavas holding lower posts in offices and restaurants live in the Fort area; Matunga and Sion are areas inhabited by Tamil Brahmins and Nayars - holding white-collared jobs; Maharash trians live in Girgaum, Dadar and Shivaji Park, while Gujaratis live in Bhuleshwar, Matunga, Santa Cruz and Vile Parle. Muslims live in Masjid Bunder and Goan Catholics in Marine Lines, Mahim and Bandra. Parsis are concen-trated in Dadar, and a few other areas. Marine Drive, Malabar and Cumballa Hills are on the whole comopolitan and affluent, while industrial workers are concentrated in Paret, Worli and Cotton Green. Immigrants at lower economic and educational levels tend to gravitate to areas where their caste-fellows and language-speakers live.

In the smaller towns and cities, segregation is recognized to occur on the basis of caste. (Caste in the sense of *jati* usually also means linguistic and religious homogeneity). Caste enters into urban life in other ways too. In the rural areas, members of different castes are tied together by patron-client and economic ties while members of the same caste are driven by economic competition. In the towns this dependence between members of different castes is absent. The result is an increase in horizontal solidarity at the expense of the vertical. Cities are centres of caste consciousness. There is intense competition for securing educatinoal facilities and Gavernment jobs. Economic competition and frustration increase inter-caste tension. Where one or the other caste speaks a different language or comes from a different region, inter-caste tension may assume the form of inter-regional tension.

In understanding urban social values, it is relevant to consider the way Indian cities have grown. Usually, several villages exist on the fringe of all Indian city. As the latter expands, these villages are sucked-in and the villagers lose their land. They take to new occupations such as selling milk, factory-work, domestic service and tonga-driving. The sucked-in villages present a striking physical contrast at the other areas of the city. Socially, the villagers, espe-cially the older people, are rural in their habits and outlook. Their attitude to work, leisure, recreation, ritual, etc., is different from that of the people in the other areas. This difference often results in tension: for instance, the educated and upper class citizens in a fashionable area may value silence and privacy, while the rustics do not mind noise and do not care for privacy. Again, the former are hygiene-conscious while the latter have no conception of hygiene. There are areas in Indian towns which are socially more or less rural. This is minimal in big cities such as Bombay.

Modern urbanization differs from traditional urbanization in important respects. Industrialization, which is a potent source of urbanization, has come to India from the West, and in particular from the British. It was cantact with the British and the study of English that led Indians to be critical of many of their customs, manners and ideas. The English-educated in the cities are partly westernised in their way of life, in their dress, manners, furniture, in the language they use and in the books they read. More important, it is these sections which have to some extent rejected traditional values and institutions. Such rejection is associated with education, income and of course, urban residence. In the highly westernised sectors of Indian society in the big cities, caste, pollution, extended kin connections, ritual and astrology seem to play a minimum part though it is not as "minimal" as it may seem at first sight. Industrialization also means the development of what Weber calls "rationality". It means the development of discipline, punctuality, time-consciousness, hard work and acquisitiveness-attitudes which tend to increase production and profits, which in turn cantribute to capital-farmation. It leads ta greater industrializatian. So, once the people are an industrial axis, there is no going back. Their attitudes contrast in same ways with those of villagers.

Indian urbanism is, however, not the same as western urbanism. B. F. Haselitz remarks, "Ahmedabad resembles much more the Manchester of 150 years age than a modern city." This may be so in the way Ahmedabad's industries are organized and in the progress of civic consciousness, but it shauld not be forgotten that the culture of Ahmedabad is quite different from that of Manchester. Social life in the latter city has never been regulated by caste and all that it implies. But ethnic affiliation is important in western cities. In the United States of America, for instance, the Whites, Negroes, Chinese, and others tend to live in distinct areas of the city. In the older European cities, Jews were forced to live in ghettos. In modern England, West Indians and East Indians are beginning to occupy distinct areas of cities. But caste is not the same as membership of an ethnic group.

Again, caste and religion tend to cut across the lines of class. A poor man may live next door to a rich man because both belong to the same caste. We have already referred to the existence of wards in urban areas, each ward being homogeneous in its caste composition. In many Indian cites, non-vegetarians are excluded from some parts because the residents have a religious objection to meat-eating.

In the matter of sanitation, Indian towns leave much to be

desired. This is partly due to the fact that Indians carry over their rural sanitary habits to urban areas. But, as we have said earlier, the educated and high-income groups living in the biggest cities are far more urbanized than the poorer and less educated people living in the small towns. Just as there is a continuum between rural and urban life in India, there is a continuum between urban life in India and in the West. This should not be taken to mean, however, that there are no cultural and other differences between India's highly urbanized sections and people living in western cities.

It is a popular belief that urbanization, industrialization and westernisation have secured for Indian women an increased measure of freedom. This may be true of women of the highest castes but not necessarily of the others. For instance, women of the lower castes have the right, given to them by custom, to marry again if widowed. Divorce is also permitted by custom. The income from the sale of dairy products goes to women. The ornaments and money of a woman pass on to her daughters after her death. In some parts of the country, a portion of the ancestral land is held for the maintenance of a widowed mother, and is redistributed after her death.

It may be recalled that among the matrilineal castes on the west coast of India and among the Khasis of Assam it was the women who inherited the ancestral estate. Among the matrilineal Bants women are also heads of households. Among the patrilineal Nambudris, after the passing of the Nambudri Act of 1933, women had equal rights with men in the ancestral property.

It is only among the high castes in towns and cities that women lead a narrow, secluded and pollution-ridden life. Indian intellectuals coming from the urban high castes have written chiefly about this section, and it has been assumed in this connection that when rural people become rich, their women acquire the disabilities of high caste, urban women. This is one of the results of the process of Sanskritisation.

During the last hundred and fifty years, Hindu reformers worked hard to remove some of the disabilities of Indian women, especially those from the high castes. Sati was abolished in 1829. The age of consent for girls was raised to ten in 1860. The Child Marriage Restraint Act of 1929 laid down fourteen as the minimum age for girls. The evil effects of child marriage were publicized by reformers for decades before legislation was passed. The Hindu Marriage Act of 1955 raised this minimum to fifteen.

Upper-caste Hindu reformers also conducted propaganda in favour of widow marriage. Reformers in Bengal and Maharashtra led the rest of the country in this respect. It was due to their efforts that the Widow Remarriage Act was passed in 1856. The Indian Divorce Act, 1869, enabled marriages entered into by Christians to be dissolved. Under this Act, a husband was entitled to divorce an adulterous wife, while the wife had to produce evidence of an aggravating circumstance such as desertion or cruelty in addition to adultery on the part of the husband. (Act is pending before the Parliament to consolidate the marriage law applicable to Christians.

Until 1954 when the Special Marriage Act was passed, a marriage solemnized under the Special Marriage Act of 1872 was also governed by the Indian Divorce Act, 1869. The 1872 Act was passed to enable Brahmos to solemnize marriages according to their own ritual, discarding the rules laid down by the *sastras.* The Special Marriage Act, 1872, did not apply to Hindus, Christians, Muslims, Buddhists, Jains, Skills, Parsis and Jews. But a large number of Hindus and others appeared before the registrars and declared that they did not profess anyone of the above religions, and married under the Act. Subsequently, a Privy Council decision held Brahmos to be Hindus and to be governed by the marriage and inheritance laws applicable to Hindus. The Act was amended in 1923, and made applicable to Hindus, Buddhists, Sikhs and Jains.

The Hindu Marriage Act, 1955, includes provisions for divorce. We have already mentioned that Islam provides for divorce. Parsi and Christian (except Catholic) marriages may also be dissolved.

European, and especially Christian, criticism of Hindu polygamy created in some educated Indians a desire to introduce legislation to put an end to it. The first attack on it was made in the Special marriage Act, 1872. In the forties, a few States including Bombay attempted to declare bigamy an offence. The Hindu Marriage Act of 1955 makes bigamy (both polyandry and polygamy) an offence. The Special Marriage Act of 1872 also legalized marriage between members of different castes, but the partners were required to renounce their religion and membership of their joint families as a prior condition. An amendment of the Act in 1929 did not remove all the drawbacks. The Hindu Marriages Validity Act was passed in 1949 and under it a marriage between two Hindus could not be deemed invalid on the ground that the parties belonged to different castes. This Act was repealed by the Hindu Marriage Act 1955, under which parties to a marriage need not be identified according to caste.

In the matter of property, the widow, daughter and mother of a Hindu are now heirs, with full and unfettered rights over their share of lite property. In the Mitaksara school, however, the son's right by birth in the ancestral property continues to exist. This means that the female relatives only take equal shares in the dead man's share of the ancestral property, whereas each son of the dead man has a share equal to his father's.

In several parts of India, big temples had attached to them "dedicated" women who perfonned a variety of tasks: they sang and danced before the deity on certain occasions, perfomed certain routine menial tasks in the temple, and looked after the comfort of pilgrims, sometimes even catering to their sexual needs. Indian public opinion was roused against these temple servants (called devadasis or basavis) in the first few decades of this century. The Bombay Devadas Prevention Act X of 1934 and the Madras Devadasi (Prevention of Dedication) Act XXXI of 1947 declared this institution illegal.

The problem of prostitution as well as immoral traffic in women has roused the indignation of reformers an along. Several States have passed legislation to stop or reduce trafficking in women and limit prostitution.

Between the passing of laws which intend to improve the position of women and their translation into practice, there is a gulf which needs to be bridged. In rural areas, girls are often married when they are less than fifteen, and widow marriage and divorce are still rare among the upper castes, especially Brahmins. Among the higher castes living in towns, the age of marriage for girls has gone up owing to a variety of factors. economics as well as social. Unmarried girls aged twenty or more are to be found in many upper-caste homes in towns. Again, the rich and westernised Hindus living in cities no longer view widow marriage and divorce with horror. It is in this section that intercaste as well as inter-regional marriages are beginning to occur. The laws

Governing inheritance will probably be more observed than laws regarding age at marriage. The economic interest of people will make them seek the enforcement of inheritance law by resorting to law courts.

Apart from legislation, the social, economic and political changes will have occurred in the last sixty years have contributed greatly to the mancipation of women. The education of women, migration into towns, the weakening hold of caste and the demand for dowry are some of the factors. Mahatma Gandhi drew women into the Nationalist Movement, and during the Civil Disobedience Movements of 1930 and 1942, thousands of women left the shelter of their homes to disobey laws, face *lathi* charges and enter jails. In 1937, when the Congress contested elections, scores of women stood for election to the Provincial Legislative Assem-blies. One of the successful candidates became a Minister in a Province. With the achievement of Independence, several women became, Governors Ambassadors, Ministers and Parliamentary Secretaries. Hundreds of educated girls are employed as clerks *grama sevikas,* teachers, sales girls, typists, officials, doctors and research scientists. What is even more significant, women in the, rural areas now serve as members of panchayats and occasionally even as preaidents of panchayats.

Difficulties Ahead

With the emancipation of women new problems have arisen. Educated young women find the traditional type of marriage not quite to their liking. But new institutions which enable young men and women to come together and know each other have not yet been evolved. Educated girls find it difficult to live with their parents-in-law, obeying the mother-in-law at every point. They desire separate homes. When girls marry late, the conflict between competing loyalties to natal and conjugal homes becomes acute. Conflict between home-making and seeking a career also occurs. The stability of marriages can no longer be taken for granted. The changing values of women force men to change their values also.

4

Social Hierarchy

The caste and class both, have been debated from narrow ideological standpoints. One extreme view, for example, is that Indian society can be best studied from a 'caste model' or 'caste perspective'. Caste is viewed as an overarching ideological system which pervades over all aspects of social life of Hindus in particular and of other communities in general. One of the implications of such a view is that caste is basically an infrastructural basis of Indian society; and occupation, division of labour, rules of marriage, interpersonal relations etc. are super-structural in nature as they emanate from the ideology of caste. A very pertinent question is: Whether caste is a normative system, or a system of actual social-structural relations? Perhaps the answer would be both yes and no. In certain arenas caste adheres to its normative sanctions whereas in some others caste groups and their members have taken up activities which have no traditional sanctions of the caste system. The crux of the matter is: what do we mean by caste system? It is a very complex and complicated system. One finds that members of a caste compete with each other; and they are also found co-operating with each other. Class-based distinctions within the caste are found in a pronounced form. Members of a caste in a given village can sometimes be representative of India's class structure. While observing all the pertinent rules of marriage members of a caste may still give premium to class-status in matrimonial alliances.

Caste refers to inequality in theory as well as in practice. Dumont considers inequality based on the caste system as a special type of inequality. 'Ideas and values' are considered by Dumont as basic for knowing actual and observable behaviour of the people. For Dumont, therefore, the idea of the pure and the impure is basic to the understanding of caste. This idea is the basis of hierarchy in Hindu society. Dumont's main concern is with the traditional social organization of India from the viewpoint of values and ideas. He constructs an ideal type of the caste system based on ethnographic and indological research materials. Madan upholds Dumont's view that hierarchy is a 'universal necessity'. Society in India has remained static; change in society has taken place, but the change of society is absent.

The basis of understanding of caste system as an empirical reality is to locate caste groups as *jatis* in a specific rural/urban context. Caste is seen as a status group in these contexts. It is a source of placement in the social set-up. But at a macro-level, caste is also a means of identity. At this level it is not a functioning reality of informal, day-to-day relations. Caste does not become a basis of marriage between a Tamil Brahmin and a Kanyakubja Brahmin of Uttar Pradesh. But still a Tamil Brahmin and a Brahmin from Uttar Pradesh can always have a sense of belonging to the same stock and even may co-operate for common good of the two in situations of crises and challenges. Is caste an interest group? Can common interests bring together men of different castes from various regions and states more smoothly than those of the same caste? Caste is certainly a resource, but its resourceability varies from caste to caste depending upon the status of a given caste in a given area. Caste identity/membership has become a liability for the members of upper and middle castes in recent years because a certain percentage of jobs, seats in parliament and state legislatures and admissions in institutions of higher learning have been reserved for the 'weaker sections' of Indian society.

The view that caste and class are polar opposites is not correct. Both have been inseparable parts of India's social formation, hence the study of their nexus, continuity and change. The view that recent processes of change have given way to a change from caste to class in Indian society is also not quite tenable and convincing. Caste is a very complex system as it is not simply a system of power relations and economic activities for namesake. If it gets weakened in one aspect, it also gets strengthened in an other with certain alterations, additions and accretions. Therefore, what we need is to study the dynamics of this complexity of the system. One obvious inference is that there is caste-basis of class and class-basis of caste, hence both are cause as well as conse-quence of one another. There is a class basis of rituals, pollution-purity and other apparently non-material aspects of social life. We may give an example of some associations. Jat Sabha is not a simple caste association; in effect it is a peasant's organization. Kisan Sabha is not a simple peasant's organization; it is very much an association of castes engaged in agriculture, particularly of Jats in northern India and their counterparts in other states. The same logic applies to the Vaishya Sabha, Kshatriya Mahasabha, Bhooswami Sangh etc.

It is a myth that caste is mainly a rural phenomenon, and class is found generally in towns and cities. We may cite here an example of caste-elections in Jaipur. The annual elections of Khandelwal Vaishya Mahasabha were being held at the time of one of my visits. To my utter surprise in the heart of the city, opposite to the Central Reserve Police Lines on the Station Road, hundreds of cars, jeeps, auto-rickshaws and two-wheelers were parked and an equally large number of vehicles were plying around, all engaged in the elections. At least 50 to 60 stalls were installed for electioneering on both sides of the road. Traffic was diverted and the police pickets were also posted to watch/control the situation. It was not only a show of casteism, but also of factionalism within the caste. Why all this show? What elected people would get out of this by spending thousands of rupees on these elections? One should seriously take up these questions to understand caste-class nexus in urban India. We know that there is no uniform pattern of caste structure in actual terms throughout India. The same can be said about class structure. Both caste and class bear ideological contents as conceptual elements. Both have substantive elements as existential and mundane schemes of relations. There are thousands of castes in India with different names and nomenclatures, but there are only about five or six classes throughout the country. The number of castes or classes is not so important in determining basic relations—

social or econo-mic or both. More important is that these apparently distinct bases of social division in Indian society are not realistically very different from each other. There are numerous middle classes which are not directly related to production processes, they are an offshoot of the modern Indian state apparatus.

In India, class-struggle is also in effect caste-struggle and *vice-versa*. Separation of the two seems to be superfluous and mechani-stic. An anomological plea that the two are different as they refer to 'social' and 'economic' realities cannot be accepted because it has been proved with ample substantive support and evidence that caste and class are found not as separate entities. For example, caste mobility movements are also class mobility movements, both manifestly and latently.

We suggest that the frame of reference and the metho-dological device for studying India's social formation should com-prise dialectical reasoning, structural processes, historicity, and ideological (cultural) and political consciousness. The goal is not really to study the totality of social formation in the literal sense of the term, but to discern both the dominant as well as the not-so-dominant elements of a given situation. The dominant causality would certainly mean ascertaining whether the causation is mainly social or economic or political etc. or it is a certain combination of these or/some other factors and forces.

Basic Problems

Undoubtedly, due to multidimensionality and complexity of the caste system, one encounters numerous difficulties in giving a precise definition of caste. Structural aspect of caste is explained by accepting it as a general principle of stratification. Caste as a cultural system is understood in terms of prominence of ideas of pollution-purity and notions of hierarchy, segregation and corpo-rateness. Caste is also viewed as a 'closed system' of stratification, whereas Beteille considers caste system as both 'closed' and 'open'. He finds that caste is becoming increasingly 'segmentary' because of the emergence of differentiated structures in India. These analytic variations hinder a common definition of caste. However, these variations also explain the fact that caste is like all other systems of stratification in some ways while it is quite unique in some other respects. Caste is not really a very flexible system, yet a caste permits mobility in certain areas to its members. A given caste is guided by norms of the caste system, hence inter-caste dependence; but a given caste has also its autonomy in regard to observance of its practices, rituals and protection of its rights in relation to other castes. In fact, caste has adapted itself as it has confronted innumerable varied situations, forces and constraints. Caste has evolved simultaneously in several directions and adjusted with ideologically antagonistic systems. It has not allowed the emergence of an alternative system of stratification and social relations though it has undergone significant changes from time to time. There is no point, therefore, in enumerating features and functions of the caste system with their descriptions as done by Risley, Ketkar, Senart, Hutton, Funiivall, Sherring, Ghurye, etc. Caste has been eulogized as a positive and functional system in the writings of the British ethnographers and some Indian scholars. Srinivas notes that even today agricultural production requires cooperation of several castes. The use of the caste idiom is quite widespread. Even Marx related the Asiatic mode of produc-tion to the stability of the caste system in India. Similarly, Maine considered caste as an illustration of a non-contractual 'status-society'. Dumont and Bougie thought of caste as an ideological system of a unique nature. Such a view was earlier held by Hocart. Weber too considered caste as a system of status stratification. None of these views and explanations offers a properly diagnosed understanding of the adaptive capacity and dynamic nature of the caste system. They explain caste basically as a cultural system implying that significant structural changes have not occurred in the Indian society due to its stable character and cultural dictum.

It has been inferred that a 'caste model' of Indian society has emerged as a result of implicit and explicit ideas and values. Beteille blames Dumont in particular for encouraging a 'caste view' of Indian society. 'Caste model' as viewed by Beteille does not provide an analysis of material interests along with the study of ideas and values. There is a dialectical relationship between the two, and Dumont and Pocock's notion of 'binary opposition' is far from the notion of 'dialectics' as given by Marx. Beteille also suggests that economic and political conflicts occur with a certain degree of autonomy of their own, hence they could be studied independent of caste and religious beliefs and ideas. Caste model would not permit such a path of understanding. The view that castes co-operate with each other is also a misconceived one. Non-antagonism and hierarchy both are nomological constructions. In reality defiance and conflict among castes are not uncommon. Leach's understanding that co-operation refers to caste and competition refers to class is naive and unconvincing. Not only families of dominant castes compete with each other to extend patronage to the lower castes for maintaining their dominance, but the lower caste families too compete to seek favours from the families of the dominant castes. Such a competition is really not a new phenomenon. Even feuds were quite common among the Kshatriyas and Brahmins for seeking power over a territory in ancient and medieval India. Leach's view that caste was simply 'caste' and a 'class-like situation' emerged only when the patrons started competing with each other ignores the fact that inter-caste conflicts and revolts by the lower castes against the upper castes have been a historical fact.

There are two serious but erroneous consequences of upholding caste as a unique, closed and corporate system of social ranking: (i) caste and class are polar opposites; and (ii) 'caste view' could explain everything in India. Srinivas' concept of dominant caste and his collection of essays on caste, Mathur's book on caste and ritual, Marriott's studies on caste, and Kothari's works on role of caste in India's politics are some of the notable examples of the 'caste view' model. Emphasis in these studies has been singularly on the hegemony or over-determination of caste by cultural/normative criteria rather than economic and political. However, in late sixties and seventies, 'multiple criteria', 'levels of caste dominance' and 'levels of mobility in caste system, structural processes of change and downward mobility' were discussed with a conscious intent to counter the falsity of the culturological concepts like dominant caste, pollution-purity, sanskritisation, westernisation, etc. Some of these studies also repudiate the over-emphasized significance of the concepts of 'reference group' and 'relative deprivation' in analyzing social mobility in the caste system in India.

Those who draw a sharp line between caste and class observe that the two are different forms of social stratification. The units ranked in the class system are individuals, and those ranked in the caste are groups. D' Souza draws a simple and mechanical distinction between caste and class obviously guided by the American notion of class. In other words, class for D' Souza is a result of what he calls objective rating of positions based on certain attributes. Here D' Souza refers to the rigidity-fluidity dimension of social stratification implying class as a case of fluidity and caste as referring to rigidity. Description of caste through the concepts of status rigidity and immutability, organic solidarity and functional interdependence, *Homo Hierarchicus* and pollution-purity; and description of class by the ideology of individualism, competition and equality, are grossly erroneous. Caste as a system of social stratification represents a semblance of rigidity and fluidity, co-operation and competition, holism and individualism, organic and segmentary divisions, interdependence and autonomy and inequality and equality, etc., The genesis of these polar charac-teristics lies in the notion of superiority of the non-caste western society. These are 'analytic' explanations of caste, hence 'historic' and experiential contents are lacking in these writings. No static and abstract model of caste or class would help in the under-standing of Indian society.

Not only caste has been thought as antithetical to class, but the notions of both caste and class have been guided by the experience of alien situations. Weber's notion of 'status group' has been equated with 'caste group', and his notions of 'class,' 'class situation' and 'market situation' have been found relevant for studying class in India. The other observation is that caste is 'real' phenomenon, whereas class is a category, an attributional construction. We may state that if caste is a 'real' phenomenon, class is also equally 'real' and empiric, if not more. Both caste and class are real and empiric in the same situations and human transactions. Both are interactional and hierarchical, and one incorporates the other. Another fallacy is to bestow 'class' only the Marxian meaning for studying the Indian society. What about 'unity' and 'harmony' among the patrons and clients, landlords and tenants, the upper caste 'haves' and the lower caste 'have nots', etc. These also refer to contradictions and consequent conflicts between the powerful and the lesser ones. Power is not a zero sum reality in Indian society as the Marxists would perhaps think of it. Thus, to reduce the totality of social relations to two simple layers, namely, the top and the bottom would be too crude a way of understanding the multi-layered and intricate social formation of Indian society.

Since caste incorporates class and class incorporates caste, neither 'caste view' nor 'class view' alone would explain the totality of India's social reality. Researches by Stein, Panikkar and others have shown that a perfect congruence between caste, class and power never existed in the pre-British India. Mobility and migration were quite normal activities particularly resulting from warfare for acquiring powers and revolts against the atrocities committed by the rulers and upper caste priests. In recent years, land reforms, adult franchise and certain constitutional provisions have brought about incongruities in summation of statuses. Since 'caste view' has been given unwarranted and undue emphasis, it is quite appropriate to make a note of 'class view' of Indian society. Kosambi analyzes the Aryans in the post-Rig Veda period from the point of their economic formation. Thapar, Habib and Desai have analyzed class character of Indian society in ancient, medieval and modern India, respectively. Lamb reports prevalence of class relations as early as 600 BC in India. Material and cultural traditions existed in a congruent form, and class transformation had been a vital fact in the form of new kingdoms, settled agriculture, trade, cities and banking and guild organizations. Desai's approach is, however, more of a doctrine rather than an empirically relevant frame of reference. Caste inheres an underdeveloped but poten-tially explosive class character. Desai also analyzes character of the Indian State from the Marxist point of view and calls it 'capitalistic' in its essence and reality.

Both caste and class are real dimensions of India's social formation, hence inseparable from each other. Class is not simply a conceptually abstracted category. It is not a construct based on certain attributes or indices, operationally arrived at. Classes of landowners, landless labourers, traders and moneylenders are not abstractions, but they are existential structural components of India's class structure. Interactional ties (both conflict and co-operation) between them refer to their life-situations. Caste and class nexus is highlighted by Gough in her analysis of mode of production as a social formation in which she finds interconnections of caste, kinship, family and marriage with forces of production and production relations. The Marxist ideologues Namboodaripad and Ranadive consider class relations as domain assumption in the treatment of caste and kinship in India. Even *varna* and *jajmani* systems have been explained in terms of class relations and mode of production. A 'class view' of social structure and social relations is found in the analyses of several others including Djur-feldt Goran and J. Lindberg, Singh, Thorner, Saith and Tanakha and Bhardwaj and Das.

Caste and class represent to a large extent the same structural reality. Singh rightly comments on caste and class nexus: "The situation corresponds to a 'prismatic' model of change where traditional sentiments of caste and kinship undergo adaptive transformation without completely being 'diffracted' into classes or corporate groups. Classes operate within the framework of castes." Caste conflicts are also class conflicts as the gap between the upper and the lower castes is also the same that one finds between the high and the low classes. Castes also function as classes as they are geared for performing their class interests. Therefore, common class consciousness among the members of a caste is mainly due to their common economic deprivations. Caste associations, particularly in urban context, perform economic and political functions for the benefit of their respective members. Thus, castes are more of interactional groups rather than attributional constructs. Mencher finds caste as a very effective system of economic exploitation of the lower castes. Precisely due to this, the upper castes (in the garb of exploiting classes) have not allowed emergence of class consciousness among the lower classes as they feared a threat to their entrenched status in India's social structure.

The Milestones

Marxist notions of class and class-conflict have become hallmarks of the studies of India's agricultural and urban-industrial structures. Marx himself stated about caste and traditional ethos of village communities in his two articles on India in 1853 in the *New York Daily Tribune* (1951). Initially, Marx thought of Asiatic mode of production by which he meant absence of private property in land and static nature of economy due to a certain tie-up between caste, agriculture and village handicrafts. However,

Kurian observes that the analysis of Asiatic mode does not deny the role of class contradictions and class structures. India's pre-capitalist economic formation was neither classless nor static. Social relations and exploitation were based on both caste and class side by side. Now it is viewed that different forms of communal societies, forms of slavery and bondage, and feudal relations have existed in different combinations in the same areas at the same time.

Two questions are relevant for a discussion on class: (1) How to analyze the class structure in Indian society; and (2) what is class-caste nexus and its ramifications and inter-relations in each region? The purpose of discussing these questions is not to accept or reject the Marxian approach for studying Indian society, but to understand the concept and reality of class in Indian context, and how it has been different from or similar to the concept and reality of caste. Rudra while analyzing the class composition of the Indian agricultural population observes that there are only two classes in Indian agriculture, one of which is termed 'the class of big landlords', the other 'the class of agricultural labourers'. These two classes are in antagonistic contradiction with each other, and this contradiction constitutes the principal contradiction in Indian rural society. Similar to Rudra's view is the view held by Desai. Rudra and those who adhere to his view do not accept the view that class differentiation in terms of agricultural labourers, poor peasants, middle peasants, rich peasants, landlords, etc. exists today and even existed in medieval India. Rudra's view is that Indian agriculture has capitalist relations and capitalist develop-ment, hence two classes—'haves' and 'have nots'. State in India has assumed property norms of capitalist society as the axis of developmental strategy. One of the implications of this formulation is that the frame of reference which applies to the rest of the world also applies jolly well to the Indian society. The other infe-rence is that the dominant causality in Indian society is 'economic' in nature in all situations and contexts.

Kosambi accepts modes of production as the basis of understanding of class relations, but does not accept the hypothesis of 'economic determinism' and universal application of Marxism as a monolithic frame of reference and a method of study. Con-cepts specifically relevant for studying Indian society could be evolved from its historicity and experience. Mukerji and Thorner, for example, have used indigenous concepts drawing from agrarian relations and Indian's cultural heritage. Even Patnaik who uses notions of mode of production and differentiation of peasan-try rejects a mechanical acceptance of Marx's model of study. She observes that several modes of production co-exist in India, and there has been a limited and distorted development of capitalism. Lin makes a reference regarding interpenetration and integration of pre-capitalist and capitalist relations.

Dandekar examines nature of class and class-conflict in Indian society. Five major classes in India, according to Dandekar, are: (1) pre-capitalist (cultivators, agricultural labourers and household industry); (2) independent workers in capitalist society; (3) employers; (4) white-collar employees; and (5) blue-collar workers. The main classes today in India can also be referred to as: (1) agrarian, (2) industrial, (3) professional, and (4) business and mercantile. The emergence of these classes in modern India cannot simply be explained by the Marxist approach. Dandekar states that large-scale industry and monopoly capitalism have not been seen fully in terms of their implications in India. Marx did not see that capitalism would change due to trade unions and collective bargaining power of workers. Class antagonism is the kernel of Marxism, but class harmony is also a fact of life, and multiplicity of classes in-between the haves and the have nots, cannot escape our attention. There is a 'middle class' inevitably in all societies, and it has a class higher and a class lower to it—this has not received Marx's serious attention. Proletarian is pro-pertyless, but he has also a chance for embourgeoisiement, and this is not stated by Marx. In India strikes by wage-earners is a very common feature, and they include those earning from Rs. 200 to Rs. 2,000 per month, hence wage-earners (proletariat) are a heterogeneous category. About fifth-sixths of the total workforce are left out by the Marxian yardstick. Indian State, being a welfare state, is the largest employer today. Is the Indian State a capitalist, exploitative and oppressive agency just like an industrialist or an employer of wage-earners? About 10 million workers are engaged in small-scale industries and family-owned concerns, and these workers generally do not witness class antagonism and strikes. The organized labour in India is one-ninth of the total workforce. Can we accept the Marxian approach in toto in view of these vital facts mentioned by Dandekar? Besides these points, overlapping of class, caste and occupation, and elite conflict, pressure groups and factions, influence of middle classes, and prevalence of mixed classes like 'gentleman farmers' are some other important points to be taken into account for a serious analysis of India's class structure.

The Disparity

Gough has analyzed conflicts and litigations based on economic inequalities between different castes. The 'mix' of caste and class in East Bengal, class genesis of caste structure in Bengal, and changes from caste to class by Misra, Beteille, Miller, and Kolenda have been reported, but none of them have studied resurgence of caste in the new situations with its multiple facets. Some scholars have undertaken a class analysis of India's social formation considering caste, religion, family and politics as subservient to class relations. However, Harris and Omvedt have analyzed class relations as a dominant causality within which they explain caste and other cultural aspects in Indian society. They have objected to the culturological determinism as advocated by Srinivas, Dumont and several others of their persuasion. Parvathamma, while commenting on Srinivas' *Remembered Village,* writes: 'In all the writings of Srinivas, the Brahmin-non-Brahmin values are juxtaposed." Hierarchy based on pollution-purity remains intrinsic to Srinivas' thinking in regard to all aspects of human life even if it is actually not so pronounced. However, Bailey incorporates both cultural and structural dimensions in the definition of caste. Class as an analytic notion is used by Beteille, Bhatt and Aggrawal as they draw a distinct line of demarcation between caste, class and power. Methodological device is the main concern of these and other sociologists in drawing a distinction between caste and class. Emergence of grades within a caste has also been referred as class-like change within caste. Hypergamy within caste endogamy always refers to status distinctions based on economic position and parental heritage, and therefore, class grades have always been there as part of the caste system itself. Class is not a result of the new forces of change which have affected the caste system. Changes are in the traditional caste and class relations and not in caste alone paving way to emergence of class relations. Thus, classes are found as part of a system of social stratification in the same way as castes are rooted in the Indian society. There is no universal and monolithic nature of class, class relations and class conflict. There are certainly objective criteria of class identification and determination of class position. A class is certainly a concrete unit of interaction with other units.

Caste in India is mistakenly projected as a system of harmonic relations. Caste inheres numerous problems related to economic domination and subjugation, privileges and deprivations, and 'conspicuous waste' and bare survival. Class relationships are treated as domain assumption in the treatment of caste and kinship in India. *Jajmani* system can be explained in terms of class relations and the mode of production. Klass hypothesizes that class exchanges women, whereas caste system exchanges goods without exchanging women. According to Klass, India has ecosystems in which people have different modes of life and within these systems caste adapts itself to nature and economic conditions.

Some empirical studies reveal a high concentration of socially backward castes among tenant cultivators. The study by Reddy and Murthy shows that as many as 73 per cent of the pure tenant-cultivators belong to the backward castes, and of the owner-cum-tenant cultivators 70 per cent belong to these backward castes. The backward castes tenant-cultivators are predominant in the small and medium size groups. The socially backward castes in Andhra Pradesh consist of Settibaliji and Harijan, and the socially advanced castes consist of Brahmin, Kapu, Devanga and others. Thus, most of the tenants of small and medium size belong to economically and socially depressed castes and pure rent-receivers except 12 per cent belong to the dominant castes. Mukherjee cites the example of caste riots to explain the unidimensionality of caste, class and religion. He writes: "Caste riots are frequent in those areas where the castewise 'social' deprivations are manifestly correlated with the classwise economic deprivations, such as in Bihar, Maharashtra, Tamil Nadu, etc." According to Mukherjee, these caste contradictions are due to inherent class contradictions in the caste system. Vagiswari observes that the Harijans have proletarianized between 1950 and 1970, while the non-Harijans have improved their economic standing during the same period.

The *dalits* have been attacked, murdered, their women-folk raped and put to indignities. Sinha observes that it is 'class war' against Harijans, and not atrocities. In another despatch to *Economic and Political Weekly,* Sinha observes that "in the villages of Bihar, the rise of a rich peasant class has driven agricultural labourers of all castes—Chamars, Dusadhs, Kurmis, Yadavas, Bhumihars, and so on, to forsake their caste organizations and fight along trade union lines." This shows that 'class war' cuts across caste lines. But the fact that a Harijan or Chamar agricultural labourer cannot simply be equated with his Brahmin or Bhumihar counterpart because the two have the same position in the class structure. The real situation in post-independent India is that a class of rich peasants from the backward castes is at the top of class hierarchy. This class is struggling against the social and political domination of the upper castes. The backward classes received encouragement for accelerating their struggle against the upper castes during the Janta government regime in Bihar. The upper castes are upper class in overall sense of the term and the lower castes are lower class. The backward classes are at intermediate level in the caste hierarchy and so is their position in class structure. The Janta rule brought about a shift in the structure of dominance in Bihar having implication for the political economy of the state. Brahmins lost heavily their political dominance. A study of a village in Andhra Pradesh as mentioned earlier shows that the four tenurial categories, namely, pure tenants, owner-cum-tenants, pure rent receivers and owner-cum-rent receivers are concomitant with caste divisions. Most of the tenants of small and medium sizes belong to economically and socially depressed castes, viz., Settibaliji and Harijan, whereas the dominant sections (big size) of all the tenurial categories belong to socially advanced castes, viz., Kapu, Brahmin and Devanga.

The incidents of massacre, loot and rape of scheduled castes in Belchi, Agra, Pantnagar, Marathwada and Bajitpur, among other places, show the role of the caste system *vis-a-vis* class struggle and class organization as reported by Atyachar Virodhi Samiti. The Samiti investigated the nature and extent of repression of scheduled castes in Marathwada in Maharashtra. The SCs were also poor peasants and agricultural labourers. The specific oppre-ssion and exploitation of women among the rural poor both sexually and as a class, particularly of the *dalit* women, have been highlighted in the report by the Samiti. The findings and observations of the Samiti on Caste are quite meaningful as caste is seen as a relation of production. The following points may be noted:

(1) The caste system functions as an extremely effective method of economic exploitation. The dominant class also acquires political power and social prestige which further perpetuates and consolidates caste hierarchy. Thus, caste hierarchy reflects ownership of land, and economic hierarchy is closely linked with social hierarchy.

(2) Caste determines a definite relation to the means of production and subsistence specially in rural areas. Caste riots reflect conflict of class-interests.

(3) Caste also refers to the relations of production as it controls the access of groups and individuals to the conditions of production and to resources and provides the social framework for politico-ritual activity.

(4) Ambedkar rightly observed that "the caste system was not merely division of labour, but also a division of labourers." However, caste prevents labourers from being a class-for-it-self, hence caste as an ideology.

(5) Caste and religion are used to perpetuate a particular class structure.

(6) Caste persists as a part of feudal ideology.

The view of the Samiti seems to be apt for our discussion on the caste and class nexus, its continuity and change: "Caste is one of the most important aspects of Indian society. It represents a specific form of oppression at the level of relations of production. To say that there are only class issues, nothing like questions pertaining to caste, is totally absurd, because of the material reality that caste divisions beyond purely 'economic' classes yet persist. So issues around specific caste questions must be taken by all the progressives and leftists, *dalits* and *non-dalits* and organizations." The reality today is of caste oppression and class exploitation in India and particularly in villages. A report from a village in Punjab by Singh shows that farm workers are Harijans and rich farmers are Jat Sikhs. The principal demand of the village workers is an increase in the wage rates. The big and middle peasants are united in opposition to the agricultural labourers. Thus, both class and caste are found inseparably in the tense situation. Convergence of caste and class has been reported in Gujarat by Bose against reservation of seats for post-graduate medical courses, and in Bihar against for reserving 44 per cent of government jobs for the backward classes. Scarce resources and employment opportu-nities are the main cause of caste-class convergence. The Mandal Commission for Backward Classes was faced with the problem of caste and class convergence. It thought that caste and class hierarchies went together, and therefore, caste was considered as the basis of determining backwardness of a given member of society. Again, in the context of Bihar, Das observes that apparently the phenomenon of caste is found in its virulent form, but to ignore the concept of class is to undermine the concrete conditions of the state. Caste is not a simplified entity as it would have only non-class social elements. Class is not an abstract, mechanical construct; it is a politico-economic concept, it refers to an active process and not to a catalogue category. A 'class analysis' of Bihar situation even in terms of expressions through caste idioms is essential."

Classes are found in India in caste idiom. A Marxist explanation of this statement is quite relevant here. Caste should be analyzed in regard to its nature, its material basis in history and in the present, and its role in politics. Which castes are the ruling ones, and which ones own land and capital, employ wage-labourers and extract surplus. Caste divisions hamper progress and unity among the oppressed classes. According to this view, all classes are defined by the relations in which the various sections of society are found related to the means of production, and castes are a carryover of feudal class divisions. The Annual Number of *Economic and Political Weekly* of 1979 is specially devoted to "class and caste in India" employing a 'class view' of caste and not *vice-versa*. The titles in this volume include "Dialectics of Caste and Class Conflicts", "Caste and Class: An Interlinked View", "Caste Conflicts versus Growing Unity of Popular Democratic Forces", "Caste, Class and Property Relations", "Caste and Class in Maharashtra", "Class and Caste in Tribal Movement", "Caste, Class and Economic Opportunity in Kerala: An Empirical

Analysis", "Caste and Class in Bihar", and "Class and Jati at Asthapuram and Kanthapuram." All these studies report caste and class nexus, use of caste, class and religion for gaining political power, emergence of an elite class in every caste, an interlinked view of caste and class, realization of caste idioms in power game, role of caste in agrarian and social movements, etc.

Different Opinions

Extreme viewpoints have been expressed about caste and class. One such view is that the two are polar opposites and antithetical to each other. The other view is that caste represents ideational and normative aspect whereas class refers to basic economic relations.

We have discussed in the present paper the nexus between these two systems of social stratification in terms of their continuity and change. Our analysis shows that there is a caste basis of class and a class basis of caste. A given caste association, for example, is not simply an organization of the members of that caste group, but it is also an organization of unskilled workers or potters or traders etc. Structural aspects of caste, namely, economic and political dimensions, etc. have remained underestimated, whereas the cultural aspects such as pollution-purity and rules of marriage, etc., have been over-emphasized. We have stated that a wholesome treatment of both structural and cultural aspects of social stratification could provide a deeper understanding of India's social formation as the two are, in fact, inseparable from each other. Both are conceptual constructs as well as empiric phenomena. Thus caste and class represent to a large extent though from different angles the same social reality. Classes function within the contexts of castes. Caste conflicts are also class or agrarian conflicts. The rifts between the upper and the lower castes to a large extent correspond with the conflicts between the landowners and the sharecroppers or agricultural labourers. Hence, an over-emphasis on either ideological or on structural aspect would provide an incomplete view of social reality.

French scholar, Louis Dumont is an expert in the domains of sociology, social anthropology and indology. He has written on Hinduism, caste, kinship, kingship in ancient India, and social and political movements in modern India. Dumont's writings are rooted into French tradition, and he has written his magnum opus—*Homo Hierarchicus* for the French-speaking people. *Homo Hierarchicus* is a study of the caste system and its implications for Hindu society and allied groups. Its French edition was published in 1966, and the English edition appeared in 1970. *Homo Hierarchicus* is literally speaking, opposite of *Homo Acqualis,* in other words, 'homo hierarchicus' is opposite of 'equality'. A commentator observes: "By taking this approach, Dumont rejects the ethnocentrism of western sociology, which has usually viewed caste as the ultimate form of social distinctions found in egalitarian societies. He insists instead on viewing India on her own terms, as a society based on different principles for which new sociological concepts are needed." Dumont has been praised for making most profound and important contributions to the study of Indian society. He has the clarity of thought, crudity of scholarship and lucidity in writing. Leach states that Dumont is possibly one of the most important sociological thinkers of his generation. Dumont's book is the most important theoretical treatise on caste. A dis-cussion on hierarchy, ideology and observation, problem of com-parison, change, ideology of caste, pure and impure, division of labour and egalitarian society, etc. is given in a highly scholastic manner. Madan writes: "*Homo Hierarchicus* is an unusual work in its conception, design and execution."

Caste Factors

The first question that Madan asks is: How does Dumont define caste? Dumont observes that the western scholar's definition of caste as a type of social stratification is socio-centric. He makes it clear that caste cannot be interpreted and understood from the point of western ideas of egalitarianism, individualism, and pre-eminence of politics and economics in society. Dumont is an Indianist at the core. Caste stands for inequality in theory and practice both, but it is not simply an opposite of 'equality'. The inequality of the caste system is a special type of inequality. Dumont admits that the idealist or intellectualist orientation of the French tradition is dominant in his understanding of sociology, hence the study of ideas and values. Dumont writes: "The ideas which they (the people) express are related to each other by more fundamental ideas even though these are unexpressed. The caste system, for example, appears as a perfectly coherent theory once one adds the necessary but implicit links to the principles that the people themselves give." Thus, Dumont adopts the methodology of structuralism in his analysis of the caste system.

One finds stress on the role of ideology in moulding human behaviour, hence a close tie between sociology and indology in Dumont's works. The notion of the fundamental opposition between the pure and the impure like Bougie is the hallmark of Dumont's analysis of the caste system. Bougie defined caste system much before Dumont in terms of hierarchically arranged hereditary groups, segregation, and interdependence. Dumont recognizes significance of these three mutually entailed 'principles', but they are based on the fundamental principle of the opposition between the pure and the impure. Dumont calls it 'a single true principle'. 'This opposition underlies hierarchy, which is the superiority of the pure to the impure, underlies separation because the pure and the impure must be kept separate, and underlies the division of labour because pure and impure occupations must likewise be kept separate. The whole is founded on the necessary and hierarchical co-existence of the two opposites."

Thus, hierarchy, as defined by Dumont in terms of the superiority of the pure over the impure, is the most important notion in Dumont's approach to the caste system. As such hierarchy is independent of other biological inequalities and the distribution of power. Hierarchy is, in fact, the principle by which the elements of a whole (society) are ranked in relation to the whole. Here Dumont becomes a sort of 'functionalist' like Talcott Parsons and Kingsley Davis. Since religion provides a view of the whole, caste hierarchy tends to become religious in essence. According to Dumont, hierarchy is the relationship between "that which encompasses and that which is encompassed." Madan remarks that "such a perspective helps us to obtain a holistic view of the system and to overcome the dualism of opposition."

Dumont analyzes "the traditional social organization of India from the point of view of theoretical comparison." Dumont's approach seems to be the construction of a model of the traditional caste system in an ideal form. He does not concern himself much with the social formation of present-day India. Dumont does not provide a history of the caste system. However, he uses historical data and indological sources in the formulation of his model for the understanding of the caste system. According to Madan, Dumont's method is of a theorist. His analysis is both deductive and dialectical. He calls his method as an 'experiment'.

Use of ethnographic materials is found in abundance in Dumont's method. He uses it in two ways or at two levels. Firstly, his major concern is undoubtedly with ideology, that is, with a system of 'values and ideas', but Dumont realizes that ideology is not everything. Ideology encompasses the whole of social reality, but cannot explain everything. Likewise, observation of actual behaviour can reveal everything. To understand this 'residue', ethnographic materials have been used to confirm nexus between ideology and observation. Secondly, Dumont uses ethnographic materials to elucidate or qualify various aspects of the main thrust of the book.

The Ranking

Dumont writes that the castes teach us a fundamental social principle, namely, hierarchy. The opposite of equality is hierarchy and not inequality. According to Dumont, hierarchy is an indispensable element of social life everywhere, but it is more so in case of India as it is very well affirmed. The caste system is a system of ideas and values, a formal, comprehensive rational system, a system in the intellectual sense of the term. The foremost aim is to understand this intellectual system, this ideology. Castes are related through a system of oppositions, a structure, in terms of the opposition between the pure and the impure. Thus, Dumont introduces the notions of 'system' and 'structure' in terms of ideology and relations between the pure and the impure castes.

Upholding his view about primacy of 'values and ideas', Dumont focuses on *the differentiation between status and power, and the subordination of the king to the priest,* in Hindu society. Hierarchy involves gradation, but it is distinct from both power and authority. Dumont states that hierarchy refers to 'religious ranking' and classifies 'things' and 'beings' based on their dignity. Therefore, hierarchy is an all-embracing, comprehensive concept. Hierarchy and *varna* are found to be in consonance like *varna* and *jati.* Hierarchy, in fact, encompasses both *varna* divisions and caste system. However, the connection between hierarchy and power remains problematic. Hierarchy cannot give a place to power without contradicting its own principle. Realizing the tie between purity and power in 'actual situations', Dumont gives a place to power without compromising with his main argument. Both 'interaction' and 'attribution' are present in a situation where ideology and power co-exist. Based on his main plank of thought, Dumont analyzes *jajmani* system and regulation of marriage, and commensality, un-touchability and vegetarianism, etc.

Theory and Practice

Dumont discusses the confrontation of ideology and observation as most important aspects of his method of study. In regard to actuality of caste, Dumont analyzes territory, power, village dominance, and ownership of wealth, and their mutual relationship. These are referents of fact and not of theory or ideology. Realizing the ontological basis of caste, Dumont discusses dominant caste, factions and economics. He concludes that just as religion encompasses politics, so politics encompasses economics within itself. However, Dumont clearly states that religion is supreme, and politico-economic domain is subordinate, and further econo-mics remains undifferentiated within politics. This clearly shows Dumont's preference for culturological determinism.

Let me quote from my earlier work about the essence of Dumont's approach to the caste system. The following points are important:

1. In the caste system we have to do pre-eminently with religious ideas connected with purity.
2. The caste system can be understood when we realize that it is permeated by essentially religious conceptions and further that these religious conceptions are based upon a social apprehension of the pure and the impure.
3. In order to understand the distribution of occupations in India we have to go to beliefs of a religious nature.
4. It is above all religious ideas rather than economic values which establish the rank of each group.

5. These religious values commingle with elements of power and form a composite system of social stratification, which Dumont calls 'Kingly model'. The Kingly model, according to Dumont, rests upon the mutuality and interdomination between the principles of *Kshatriya* or power and *Brahman* or the priestly normative order. Both are, however, rooted in the religico-ritualistic order of the caste system.

However, this does not mean that Dumont is immune to empiricism. The source of authority such as the village panchayat, caste panchayat, caste jurisdiction, and ex-communication are discussed in this chapter. Clearly Dumont gives premium to ethnographical evidence as against ideology. But the basic principle is that of hierarchy to understand authority and dominance. Dumont is not able to resolve the dilemma whether caste encompasses power or power encompasses caste. If the latter is right, *dharma* (ideology) becomes subordinate to *artha* (power), and if the former is upheld as super-ordinate, the ruler becomes subservient to priestly order. However, in the final analysis, Dumont upholds ritual or religious power (hierarchy) superordinate to politico-economic power.

Practical Difficulty

Dumont considers Indian and western societies as logically opposite cultural types. But this does not mean that in the western society there was nothing but the individual, and in the Indian society nothing but the collective man (caste). More important is to see whether the caste system could have existed and survived independent of its contradictions. In fact, both collectivity and man were operative in Indian society in a particular way, and hence adaptability of the caste system. However, Dumont is unable to come out of his ideological leanings. He says that caste should be deemed to be present only where the disjunction between status and power is present and where castes exhaust the entire society.

Social Power

Dumont poses the question: What is the caste system becoming now-a-days. Dumont answers that contemporary literature on caste overestimates and exaggerates changes. The overall frame of society has not changed. There has been change *in* the society and not of the society. The only significant change, according to Dumont, is in the organic (traditional) interdependence between castes; now different castes have become segmentary competitive groups. Dumont calls this process 'the substantialization of caste'. Most noticeable changes in the caste system are juridical and political, socio-religious reform, westernisation, growth of modern professions, urbanization, spatial mobility, and the growth of market economy. Dumont admits that change doer not mean replacement, it means a 'mixture' or a 'combination' of traditional and modern features.

Madan holds the view that *Homo Hierarchicus* is a most impressive achievement and shall long remain a basic work for Indianists. Dumont, unlike Maine, does not consider caste as "the most dangerous and blighting of all human institutions." Dumont also does not defend caste like Bougie, Hocart, Senart, Hutton etc., but his treatment of caste amounts to its defence and perpetuation. Dumont considers caste as worthy of serious study. *Homo Hierarchicus* is neither a historical work nor a stock of available ethnographical information. Madan writes: "His is essentially an essay in methodology. He seeks to construct a model to help us understand the caste system." Further, Madan praisingly writes: "What I find most valuable in Dumont's approach to the understanding of caste is his attempt to seize its specificity: he preserves it by 'typifying' it and does not dissolve it by 'classifying' it."

Nothing is more important to Dumont than the ideology of caste itself. Nothing can be studied without ideas and values. All aspects of caste and even of entire gamut of social relations can be studied only from the ideational point of view. Therefore, Madan's view that *Homo Hierarchicus* is an essay in methodology is not quite tenable. His (Dumont's) method of study follows from the ideology of caste itself, and so is in the case of ethnographic data he pours into *Homo Hierarchicus.*

Negative Aspects

A sociology of knowledge perspective would ask clearly for (i) the 'fit' between theory, method and data; (ii) the ideologizing influences on the understanding of Indian society; (iii) the construction of reality in Indian context; and (iv) the specificity of Indian, sociology different from that of the western countries. These questions have not been clearly formulated by Dumont as he has been overwhelmed by the nostalgia of French tradition in sociology, and the uniqueness of Indian society. Dumont thus equates indology or culturology 'for a sociology of India'. Two questions follow from this position of Dumont: (1) Is it not an attempt toward academic indoctrination of scholars interested in the study of Indian society?, (2) Is it not Dumont brings in the ideas which would reinforce and relegitimize India's caste system?

While commenting on Iravati Karve's book—*Kinship Organisation in India,* Dumont and Pocock have suggested that Karve should choose between sociology and culturology. Why Dumont ignores this suggestion in his own case? He projects his eclectic indology and part-ethnography as sociology proper in India's case. Bailey rightly observes that Dumont and Pocock's is a 'Very odd kind of inverted ethnocentrism." Their view is more of an assertion than an evidence. Saran's view is no less culturological than that of Dumont, but Dumont calls Saran's view as 'cultural solipsism', a Hindu sociology. Dumont is also disdainful of the Marxist approach. While commenting on Desai's book—*Social Background of Indian Nationalism,* Dumont writes: "More than university thesis, it is an overgrown political pamphlet clad in a university gown." Thus, Dumont is critical of both culturological and Marxist approaches except his own approach which he considers very specific and unique one. Dumont can blame Saran for wrong 'hypothetical deductive reasoning', 'irrelevant quotations', and for his 'neo-Hindu creed', to Desai for his 'doctrinaire dogmatic Marxism', but why he (Dumont) gives such an enormous premium to culturology and caste system and its allied institutions—remains an open secret. Why India's caste system becomes a datum for Dumont to develop a global sociology? Dumont is too naive a scholar if he thinks that India does not have differences, differential interests, conflicts, exploitations, etc. He lacks in elementary education about India. To think that they are prevalent but do not become the data for sociological enquiry compounds Dumont's scholastic ignorance. Dumont's polemics would not really provide a clear frame of reference, a method of study, and relevant data for understanding the fast changing character of India's caste system.

Even Madan, an ardent admirer of Dumont, raises a few questions about Dumont's model of traditional Hindu society. For example, it is not clear at what point of time the caste system as portrayed by Dumont crystallized. His (Dumont's) manner of citing literature is not very helpful in this respect. It seems after the crystallization of the caste system, all further change was ruled out. Madan pointedly asks: (1) Is it not Dumont's method, then which makes him play down the element of change? (2) Is he (Dumont) not setting up too narrow a definition of change? Dumont writes: "A form of organization does not change, it is replaced by another; a structure is present or absent, it does not change." Most of the changes in India take place in politico-economic domain and since this occupies a secondary place in Dumont's scheme, they remain generally unnoticed to Dumont.

Now a few more criticisms of *Homo Hierarchicus*. Berreman accuses Dumont of presenting a 'distorted image' of the caste system based upon 'limited, biased, albeit scholarly, sources of evidence.' Dumont, in fact, puts forth his model independent of the body of indological and ethnographic literature. Leach points out that to assess the value of a model in view of 'facts' is wholly erroneous. No model is a replica of reality. Dumont's model has explanatory power through its principle of *hierarchy*. Other commentators have suggested instead of the dichotomy of pure-impure the more inclusive dichotomy of the sacred and the non-sacred. Along with the notion of hierarchy, the notions of reciprocity and equality, and contradiction can be useful in understanding of the caste system. Dumont's use of the structuralist approach, his emphasis upon the *specificity* of the caste system, and 'typification' have come under severe attack.

The value *of Homo Hierarchicus* remains immense in spite of the criticisms we have listed above. The wide acclaim it has received and the controversy it has created speak volumes for Dumont's scholarship and involvement in understanding of the caste system. Madan writes: *"Homo Hierarchicus* is a work complete in itself and must be judged as such." "What distinguishes this work from the usual social anthropological discussions of caste is that it does not proceed from field-work to a model of how the system works. Instead it begins with a cardinal explanatory princi-ple—hierarchy—and boldly sets out to build a model thereon, throughout maintaining the position that theory or ideology overrides and encompasses ethnography. A conscious and single-minded preoccupation with the ideology of complementarity and separation leads Dumont to ask fundamental questions about Hindu society and about the structuralist method."

5

Rapid Growth

Various studies on social stratification in India reflect the same theory, method and data which we find in regard to the studies on other aspects of Indian society. Social stratification is a very sensitive field of study. The people, the researchers and the government agents (leaders and bureaucrats) are parts of the system of social stratification. The people are divided into different caste, class, occupational, professional and power groups or categories. The researchers are part of these divisions and study of social stratification by them may bring in subjectivity in understanding of positions of others *vis-a-vis* their own positions. The government has a policy about the nature of social groupings and categories of groups and relations between them. The criticisms of the government are that their policy and action have been at variance; that the rich are becoming richer and the poor are becoming poorer; and that the inequality is 'officially' institutionalized; and this speaks about the nature of the ruling classes and power elite. Thus, social stratification is a field of study which demands a critical analysis from the point of sociology of knowledge. Theory, method and data are the three main concerns in this paper.

A large number of studies on 'caste' have been brought out during the past half a century. A few studies have been published on 'class', particularly in the seventies. Some scholars have focused on the three 'orders', namely, social, economic and political in their studies on social stratification taking clues from Max Weber and P.A. Sorokin. Our objective is not to provide a chronology of the studies on caste, class and social stratification. Our main aim is to analyze these studies from the point of their theory, method and data.

Yogendra Singh has analyzed the studies on social stratification and social change conducted in the 1950s and 1960s from the viewpoint of sociology of knowledge. In a recent study, Singh analyzes the studies on social stratification conducted in the 1970s. It would, therefore, be desirable to give a brief resume of Singh's analysis of the studies on social stratification published in the fifties, sixties and seventies.

Major Issues

The issues in the sociology of social stratification relate to questions of theory, structure and process of social stratification. "The theory of social stratification implies a set of concepts, propositions and assumptions that are verified and validated and constitute an explanatory system." Singh observes that studies on social stratification rarely reach the formal level of theory. The two well-known orientations in the studies on social stratification are of 'functional' and 'conflict' theories. Singh refers to a couple of attempts made by sociologists towards a synthesis of the functional and the conflict theories. He observes: "Now the increasing tendency is to analyze social stratification from a pluralistic conceptual frame by treating both conflict and consensus as two dimensions of the same reality." But Singh does not make this statement in regard to the studies on social stratification in India. Referring to Hans Zetterberg's distinction between the 'prepositional' and the 'dimensionalistic' theory in sociology, Singh mentions 'status, wealth, power' approach to the study of social stratification as this corresponds to the 'dimensionalistic' theory. The 'theory' of social stratification thus refers to 'why' of social stratification.

The 'structure' of social stratification could be seen in two ways: (i) the nominalist, and (ii) the realist. The *nominalism* refers to role or status as the unit of social stratification. Davis and Moore and Parsons (the well-known functionalists) consider 'positions' and 'roles' as the units of social stratification. Certain 'attributes' are the basis of classification of roles and positions. Social classes, elites, status groups or castes are taken as units in the *realist* frame of analysis. The processes of social stratification are seen as "changes in the differentiation, evaluation, ranking and rewarding patterns." Accretion, transformation and replacement are the consequences of the processual nature of social stratification. The questions which Singh has posed in regard to theory, structure and process of social stratification are as follows:

(1) What theoretical assumptions have guided studies in social stratification in India?

(2) How far have the functional or dialectical (conflict) theoretical postulates been used either for analysis or selection of problems in social stratification?

(3) Which are the major structural foci in social stratification studies, and has the focus been comprehensive enough to cover most strategic structural units or components of the system of stratification?

(4) Has the focus been biased for historical or other disciplinary reasons towards studies in a specific or particular direction?

(5) Have these studies been sociologically relevant?

(6) Do these studies focus upon the most strategic processes of social stratification?

(7) Have the studies highlighted in a representative manner the processes of social stratification, their causes, consequences and impact upon the overall social order and change in the Indian social system?

Singh analyzes 'caste system and social stratification', 'scheduled castes and social stratification', 'class structures and social stratification', 'agrarian class stratification and change', and 'elites and social stratification' in India in the first trend report published in 1974. The studies in the fifties and sixties have been grouped under these headings.

In *Sociology of Social Stratification in India-II,* Singh provides a sharper analysis of sociology of knowledge perspective about social stratification. The headings are evidence of the concern for the sociology of knowledge perspective. The main points are: 'ideological debate', 'changing theoretical orientations', 'structuralist approach', 'structural-historical approach', 'Marxist analysis of social stratification', 'other social sciences and stratification', 'social stratification in non-Hindu communities', 'tribes and scheduled castes', and 'sociology and social change'. These points compared to the points in the earlier trend report are definitely indicative of change in the theoretic orientations and themes of study in social stratification. Singh clearly exposes the sociology of knowledge perspective for studying social stratification in India.

New theoretical and substantive issues in the studies on social stratification in the seventies have come up due to self-awareness of Indian sociologists. New social situation and evaluation of the national ideology of social stratification have led to the emergence of self-criticism and search for relevance among the Indian sociologists. Singh identifies the following new trends in the studies of social stratification:

(1) increased debates on the ideological moorings of concepts and theories;

(2) efforts to re-schematize conceptual systems and their presuppositions in the light of shifting paradigms;

(3) the new substantive concerns in stratification studies; and finally

(4) fruitful convergence of multidisciplinary interests, both substantive and theoretical, in the studies of social stratification.

The colonial background of the methodological and theoretical legacy of social sciences was attacked along with sociological positivism of the West. The quest for indeginization of paradigms and for relevance became a focal point of attention among Indian social scientists. A broad framework of sociology of knowledge was rooted into experiential reality of Indian society and its historicity. The shadow of colonialism and positivism has been haunting Indian sociology for a long time. Why its harmful impact is realized in the seventies and not in the fifties and the sixties is a question to be examined carefully. Concepts and frameworks given by the British scholars during India's colonization and by the American social scientists in the fifties and sixties have led to perpetuation of colonization, academic and intellectual dependency and mystification of knowledge. A serious 'rethinking' is required. It is not true that all the sociologists and social anthropologists were influenced by American sociological positivism or British functionalism. Iravati Karve's work on kinship, I.P. Desai's study of family, A.R. Desai's study of nationalism and some other studies remained unaffected by western theoretical and methodological thinking. However, departments of sociology at the universities in Delhi, Jaipur and Chandigarh have had the imprints of such influences.

The crux of the ideological debate is that the concepts, frameworks and paradigms which have dominated the academics are being challenged, refuted and revised or replaced. Mencher suggests that caste be studied from 'upside down' rather than 'top down' perspective. Use of historical material is emphasized by Saberwal. Sharma pleads for structural-historical perspective accepting Indian society as a 'social formation', The bias of the upper caste and class sociologists in their studies has been highlighted. An alternative perspective is offered in the form of a shift of emphasis. Caste model of Indian society is being questioned. The question of evolution of caste and class in India is again looked at afresh by Myrdal, Klass, and Sinha. Arguments of Srinivas and Dumont for 'sociology for India' are considered not only irrelevant but also harmful. They are blamed for putting wrong priorities and emphasis in sociological studies.

Ideologial Basis

Yogendra Singh classifies the theoretic concerns in the stratification studies of the seventies as: (i) structural-functional, (ii) structuralist, (iii) structural-historical, and (iv) historical-materialist or Marxist. During the fifties, there was dominance of the structural-functional theory of stratification. Towards the end of the fifties, structuralism and Marxism emerged in the studies of social stratification. In the seventies, the historical perspective was adopted by both Marxists and non-Marxists. Before we take up the studies on social stratification for our analysis, it may be noted that the evolution of approaches to stratification cannot, in fact, be characterized only by structural-functionalism in 1950s, struc-turalism and Marxism in 1960s, and structural-historical (both Mar-xists and non-Marxists) in 1970s. Structural-historical perspective was adopted by A.R. Desai, a noted Marxist in 1940s; structuralist view could be seen in the 1950s in the writings of Bougle, Dumont and Hocart. The 1950s and the 1960s were dominated by struc-tural-functionalism (both American and British) and structuralism (both British and French). Structural-historical perspective has ideological overtones of both borrowed and modified Marxism and indeginization in the form of a reaction to Marxist perspective and rejection of western positivism and culturology. Even today, there are people engaged in studies from the viewpoint of western positivism, culturologism and orthodox Marxism.

K.L. Sharma divides the studies on stratification into two categories: (i) the studies on caste stratification; and (ii) the multi-dimensional studies. The studies in the first category are by Kroeber, Weber, Mutton, Ghurye, Hocart, Myrdal, Dumont, Leach, Srinivas, Dube, Bailey, Lewis, Mayer, Mathur, Majumdar, Marriott, etc. These sociologists and social anthropologists have focused on caste as the sole institution of social ranking. What is known as 'caste model of Indian society' is their theoretical perspective. Caste is treated as an extreme form of class or as a closed community. Some others have given premium to socio-religious and ritualistic considerations. The ideas related to pollution-purity and religion are treated as the basis of caste ranking. 'Elaboration' of caste ranking has also been compared in various zones of India. None of these studies refer to the phenomena of class and power. They, in fact, consider caste as synonym with social structure. These studies were carried out in 1950s and in the first half of the sixties.

The multidimensional studies on social stratification do not consider caste as an all-inclusive basis of social stratification. Economic position, style of life, education, occupation and personality attributes are evaluated for assessing a person's rank in his community or caste. Beteille refers to the emergence of 'differentiated institutional structures of various kinds' and 'case free' areas. Later on he explains the necessity for studying 'ideas and interests'. One finds a shift in Beteille's emphasis from 'caste-oriented'studies to 'class-oriented'studies of stratification. Bhatt's study of caste, class and politics and Aggrawal's study of caste, religion and power also emphasize the multidimensionality of social stratification. However, studies by Gough and Ramakrishna Mukherjee are different in their theoretic orientation compared to the studies by Beteille, Bhatt and Aggrawal. Gough and Mukherjee look at caste from a class point of view with Marxist disposition. But, it is clear that even in the sixties 'caste alone' view was questioned. Sharma's study of six villages in Rajasthan in the sixties highlighted the role of ascription, units of ranking, dimensions of stratification, ideological bases of stratification, factors of change in stratification and its emerging patterns. Both 'structural' and 'cultural' perspec-tives were used to facilitate analysis of caste, class, caste and class consciousness, occupational and social mobility, power structure and value-orientation. Land tenure systems, land reforms, *Pancha-yati Raj,* educational achievements, occupational opportunities and networks were studied in particular in view of the multidimen-sionality of social stratification and limitations of the 'caste model'.

The studies of social stratification in the fifties and the sixties were guided by structural-functionalism and structuralism barring a few studies which had variants of structural-historical perspective. Yogendra Singh observes that the basic premises of structural-functional studies have implied a *systemic teleology* based on the Brahminic or 'hierarchical' model of caste society, harmony or consensus as the system state from which change, differentiation or fission was studied emphasised on a micro-structural or communitarian scale of reality. The caste system would not change. It would absorb all tensions and changes generated by polity and economy. 'Summation of roles' was its basic feature, hence consensual ideology. Historicity was a casualty in these studies of caste system. However, the structural-functional studies in 1970s have shown two tendencies: (i) deeper substantive and theoretical concerns in respect of processes of change, and (ii) increased diagnostic orientation.

The notions of social mobility advanced by Srinivas have been examined afresh. Downward mobility, proletarianization and bourgeoisification as processes of structural change have been reported. Relations between caste and class, caste and religion, caste and tribe, etc., have also been questioned. Dumont and Srinivas have ideologized (in their differing characteristic styles) resilience of the caste system and its principle of hierarchy. Bailey, Kolenda and Miller refer to changes in the caste system from its 'organic' nature to its 'segmentary' character, but hold the view that caste continues to be the focal point of hierarchial relations in Indian society.

Let us take up a few studies from the viewpoint of their theoretical positions. Srinivas' emphasis on the role of religion in the Coorg society is clearly an extension of Radcliffe-Brown's functionalism. Srinivas observes that everything could be seen in terms of pure and impure. The entire life is organized around religion. Thus, it is the social organization of religion that encompasses everything else. Srinivas does not look at village polity, economy, consequences of religion on people's existence as the points necessary for investigation.

Srinivas perspective has inspired several scholars for undertaking their doctoral researches on similar lines. However, some students of Srinivas have differed from him. Beteille's study of social stratification in a village in Tamil Nadu may be cited here. Beteille poses the question: "What is the central theme of the study here presented?" He answers this question by saying: "Broadly speaking, our concern is with the phenomena of caste, class and power with their changing relations." Beteille refers to 'caste-free' areas. He writes: "The social system has acquired a much more complex and dynamic character, now there is a tendency for cleavages to cut across one another." "The hierarchies of caste, class, and power in the village overlap to some extent, but also cut across." Beteille justifies his use of the concept of 'class' as he finds "the differentiation of institutional structures". Weber's notion of class is found useful to understand emergence of market economy. Beteille's perspective is also evident when he states that "there is a very little preoccupation with purity, pollution, and rituals in general." This is a qualitatively different position compared with that of Srinivas. Beteille not only treats caste, class and power as abstract categories on the pattern of 'class, status and party' as given by Weber, he also finds diversity at empirical level between economic, social and political distinctions among the people.

The problem with Beteille's formulation is not that distinctions are not there, but *a priori* acceptance of Weber's theory and its implicit ideology creates problems in proper understanding of social reality in a village of Tamil Nadu. Methodological individualism, *Verstehen* or interpretative understanding and rationalism (or psychologism) are fundamental bases of Weber's trio (class, status and party). These are neither stated nor exemplified by adopting certain research strategies. Surreptitious adoption of Weber's schema is evident in Beteille's study. Diversity between Indian village and German society (which was basis of Weber's formulation) is overlooked. Application of Weber's approach for studying social stratification by Beteille implies a contradiction between theory and method.

There are two more studies, one by P.C. Aggarwal and other

by Anil Bhatt, which may be treated along with Beteille's study discussed above. Aggarwal also does not formulate his theoretical proposition like Beteille; however, we can perceive it from some of the statements and data reported in Aggarwal's book. Let me also mention that Aggarwal's book is more of a village monograph rather than a study of social stratification based on caste, religion and power. He has studied the Meos of Mewat with a holistic perspective. Meos are a Muslim community. Structural-functional orientation is implicit as Aggarwal gives a detailed account of the region, people, village, caste system, economic life, family and kinship, religion, life cycle rites and political organization. Some historical glimpses have also been provided. Participant observation and unstructured interviews were used for gathering data. Scaling technique was also used in analyzing data. Integration of Meos with the wider society and with the Hindus was also investigated.

Though Aggarwal uses ethnography as a methodological device, his emphasis is on the understanding of social structure of the Meos in Chavandi Kalan, a village in Alwar district of Rajasthan. Aggarwal concludes that ritual status is insignificant in social ranking. Unequal distribution of power and economic resources is the crucial basis. However, Aggarwal's study lacks an understanding of 'class relations' among the Meos. Thus, only inferentially, we consider Aggarwal's study as structural-functional, but in form as the title suggests, it is more of a Weberian study.

A clear exposition of theoretical formulation is found in Bhatt's study of caste, class and politics. He states that the objectives of his study are: (i) to compare and correlate ascriptive, socio-economic and political dimensions of social stratification; (ii) to study the interaction between traditional social structures and modern democratic politics; and (iii) to examine the extent to which the traditional model of social stratification in India obtains today. The model of social stratification in traditional India is that of 'summation of statuses'. All aspects become subservient to the basis of this model. The implications of this model are that caste encompassed all other aspects; there was no differentiation within the caste groups; it was a homogeneous but complex social organization; and there were non-antagonistic strata. Thus, the traditional India had closed, highly hierarchical, combinative, non-competitive social stratification. Bhatt writes: "For my purpose, the first view serves as a benchmark in contrast to the democratically ordered society envisioned by the constitution of Independent India." Like 'comparative polities', Bhatt uses the phrase 'comparative social stratification'. The writings which are cited by Bhatt are of Robert Dahl, L. Rudolph and S. Rudolph, Bernard Barber, McKim Marriott, Neil Smelser and S.M. Lipset, M. Tumin, A.C. Mayer, F. Barth, Andre Beteille, F.G. Bailey, Rajni Kothari and S. Verba and N. Pie, etc. in support of his structural-functional perspective.

Bhatt puts the question: "Can India realize this new order in such a deep-rooted and pervasive traditional social structure?" In view of this question, Bhatt explores relationship between society and politics. "Social system is conceptualized as a larger system and political system as its sub-system." Bhatt's conceptual framework conceives of society as a separate and larger system instead of an aggregate of interacting sub-systems. Such a framework considers social structures as independent variables and political factors as dependent variables. Bhatt's study is an 'ideal' illustration of structural-functionalist positivism. Analysis of the pattern and degree of relationship between caste, class and politics, the degree of status congruence, the extent of socio-economic and political inequalities, the degree of internal differentiation, the impact of caste status on socio-economic and political positions and conversely the impact of democratic political structures on processes of the caste system reveals the notion of 'whole' and 'parts' relationships. We shall refer to methodological and substantive aspects of this study later on it this chapter.

Different Strategies

Victor S. D' Souza applies the structural-functionalist-positivistic approach to the study of social stratification. His study of Chandigarh and analysis of caste and class emphasize the significance of the continuum of the rigidity-fluidity dimensions and the individual and his properties as the units of analysis rather than castes as endogamous groups. Class and individual as the bases of social stratification in place of caste and group are consi-dered significant in the present context. In his study of Chandigarh, D' Souza considers educational, occupational and income hierarchies as predominant features of urban social stratification. These are significantly related with each other. A scale of prestige is constructed based on these variables. Following L. Warner and Richard Centres, D' Souza classifies classes as upper, middle, working class and lower class based on the prestige of individual members. The data are based on survey method and attitudinal responses. This approach is generally known as 'attributional' approach.

A crude application of structural-functionalism is found in Rajni Kothari's book *Politics in India.* Kothari and Bhatt provide a similar perspective, however, their data-base and research strategies are not the same. Kothari analyzes politics at macro-level based on secondary sources, published researches and other materials. Bhatt's study is rooted into typical American sociological positivism, hence a comparative study based on sampling and questionnaire from four states of India. Structural-functionalism in Kothari's study is evident from the following statements taken from the first chapter of his book:

(1) India is a relatively open political system, hence no congruent development. Discrepancy between ideal and real creates inequalities including the political ones.

(2) The social system in India provides a key to political stability. Any change in power relations should be seen in this perspective as well.

(3) The traditional political culture seeks to incorporate into its womb the best elements of the culture of the modern world, without destroying the age-old traditions and diversities.

(4) Thus, Indian society operates still largely as apolitical society.

(5) Politics in India is preeminently the politics of *integration,* e.g., structural continuity exists in the sphere of power.

Kothari refers to the processes of 'nation-building'. He writes: "What is being stressed is the increasing political orientation of social interests, in which the political process provides the inclusive setting within which these interests are found to interact." However, this perspective of Kothari has been belied even before this was published. The elections of 1967 witnessed defeat of the Congress in more than half of the states. Of late, the emergence of regional forces and culture of politics in Tamil Nadu, Andhra Pradesh and Punjab have also falsified the basic tenets of Kothari's thesis. What was not accepted said by Selig Harrison about the emergence of regional forces perhaps could be accepted after the recent Akali movement and the emergence of Telugu Desham in Andhra Pradesh.

Kothari uses the vocabulary of American 'functionalists' in particular without any sort of inhibition or objection in both *Politics in India* and in his 'Introduction' to *Caste in Indian Politics.* I cite a few statements to show the conservatism of functionalist approach *vis-a-vis* of Kothari. "Politics is a competitive enterprise, its purpose is the acquisition of power for the realization of certain goals, and its process is one of identifying and manipulating existing and emerging allegiances in order to mobilize and consolidate positions." Politics is mass based. Politics must strive to organize through such a structure (caste structure). *Politicization of caste* is necessary for modernizing India. Politics is an instrument for a group to consolidate its position. Kothari accepts an American author's view—*the democratic incarnation of caste.* Caste has the *secular aspect,* it has the integration aspect, and the *aspect of consciousness.* These aspects led to the *modernization* of India's polity. Let us quote again: "Finally the politicization of caste makes for outward looking, upward moving orientations and as this results in the phenomenon of multiple memberships and overlapping identities, the result is highly secular for the polity as well as the society at large." This not only speaks of theoretical, methodological and epistemological apriorism and determinism, but also reveals an utter lack of understanding or realization of historicity of Indian society and polity. Kothari does not debate the relevance or irrelevance of the functionalist perspective before accepting it for studying Indian society. He does not compare it with alternative perspectives and frameworks. The quite acceptance of a theoretical perspective smacks of an academic conspiracy and ideological propaganda. We leave the debate at this point.

Let us now make a brief mention of two books, namely, F.G. Bailey's *Caste and the Economic Frontier* and T.S. Epstein's *Economic Development and Social Change in South India.* Both of the studies focus on social change in village. Since the structural aspect of change is duly taken into account, it would be relevant to make a reference about them. Bailey looks at the caste system in a village in Orissa under a new economy. The new frontiers are economic, political and administrative. Transfer of land from the ex-landowners is a significant fact which makes land a market commodity, and other occupations which were tied with landlordism also become part of a market situation. Bailey gives details about new economy, land transactions, services and trade. He writes: "The mercantile economy has impinged on the system of agriculture, because those who profited as merchants, traders and earners of salaries invested their money in land." Bailey puts three questions: (1) Why did they do so? (2) What made it possible for them to buy land? (3) What has been the effect of the redistribution of land on the social structure of the village? These questions support the position which Bailey took about Dumont and Pocock's position regarding Indian sociology. Bailey looks at 'culture' from the perspective of 'structure'.

Epstein's study also emphasizes on social change, but from a comparative perspective. Epstein follows by and large Bailey's line of research. The main argument of Epstein's study is that a structural innovation (irrigation) consolidates village economy, but it restricts social change, namely, migration, contacts, education and politicization, etc. Conversely, a lack of such an innovation results into widespread social change without corresponding economic development. Epstein's study of two villages in Karnataka from this structural perspective provides us details about crops, houses, landholdings, livestock, family incomes and expenditures, market networks, etc. This study also like that of Bailey focuses on changes in the traditional social structure and hierarchy in the village community.

Levi-Strauss structuralist principle of complimentary dualism or logical principle of opposition as a fundamental feature of human mind is applied by Louis Dumont in his study of hierarchy and marriage alliance. Pure and impure, consanguinity and affinity are examples of this logical dualism. These also refer to the notion of hierarchy. Graded statuses are entrenched into all spheres including kinship. Dumont sees inter-caste, intracaste and intra-familial ranking as projections of the same intellectual and ideological principle. Dumont emphasized necessity of looking for *cultural meaning* of affinity and consanguinity. The structuralist stance of Dumont is clearly seen in his assertion that it is hierarchy which is pervasive principle of Hindu society and the caste system is only one expression of it. There is hierarchy of principles and values of occupations, food and clothes, and also of 'bride givers' and 'bride takers'.

It is this thinking of Dumont which he had about Indian society in 1950s that found its fuller expression and exposition in his subsequent writings in *Contributions to Indian Sociology* and in *Homo Hierarchicus.* Yogendra Singh observes that the pivotal notions of structuralism are: *ideology, dialectics, transformational relationship and comparison* in regard to social stratification as particularly found in Dumont's *Homo Hierarchicus.* The basic tenet of caste system is 'hierarchy'. The opposition between pure and impure defines its binary tension, its dialectics. Dumont observes that "hierarchy also inheres the relationship of 'encompassing' and being 'encompassed'."

Dumont's theoretical perspective is clear in the statement: "I think that this view of the duality as one of form and content is mistaken, and that hierarchy, especially in its exemplary Indian form, teaches us a better way of looking at it." Dumont makes three points about this:

(1) A hierarchical relation is a relation between larger and smaller, or more precisely, between *that which encompasses and that which is encompassed.* "The duality that plagues us is not one of form and content but that of the *encompassing and the encompassed."* The duality is real in so far as *we come to know* the two kinds of aspects in a different way: (i) basic values related to kinship, caste, status, etc., and (ii) political or economic aspects as observed in actual situations.

(2) Opposition is found between the orientation to the whole *(holism)* and the orientation to the element *(individualism).* Caste represents the holistic orientation and equality refers to the individualistic orientation. The 'whole' is something religious (or philosophical), while 'economy' is a matter of the individual. The division of labour in the Indian village is not an economic fact; it is a holistic (religious) fact.

(3) The third point refers to ritual status and power. The king as sovereign is the high priest and the ruler in one person. It is a fact. But *in principle,* the priest and the king are absolutely distinguished—the priest is highest in status even if he is dependent materially. Thus, priesthood encompasses rulership; and at the same time these 'twin forces' together encompass all the rest.

Dumont's conception of social change or the principle of transformational relationship is moulded by his frame of reference. He observes that there has been change in the society and not of the society. Dumont postulates that *comparison* is possible within a cultural type, it is also possible within such types. He does not emphasize on the uniqueness of a society. Comparison is possible between logically opposite types, hence comparison of India with West and *vice-versa.*

Dumont's structuralist view on India's social stratification in terms of pure and impure or binary opposition (encompassing and encompassed) is found lacking theoretically as well as substantively. The 'pure' is found in the 'impure', and *vice-versa.* Gould's concept of 'contrapriest' explains the fusion of purity or priesthood in the 'impure' or 'untouchable'. In a symposium on Dumont's *Homo Hierarchicus,* it is suggested by Veena Das and Veena Das and J.P.S Uberoi that the pure and impure are fused in many rituals. It is suggested that the dichotomy of 'sacred' and 'non-sacred' and the notion of 'reciprocity' would be more appropriate for analyzing caste system in India.

Dumont's structuralist perspective lacks a conception of history. His view also suffers from the neglect of the politico-economic dimensions of Indian reality. However, Dumont makes a clear distinction between the substantivist and the structuralist modes of thinking. He draws a distinction between dialectics and hierarchy, contradiction and complementarity. Pure and impure are not of a dialectical nature; they are complementary opposites. Singh observes that Dumont's view has created a high self-consciousness among Indian sociologists about the study of caste and class in India.

Another Dimension

There are a few studies in which differentiation, evolution and change in caste and class over a period of time have been focused. We could say that the emphasis in these studies could be seen as on caste, caste and class, class alone, again caste, and now caste and class as parts of social formation. Besides sociologists and social anthropologists, historians and economists have taken up studies from structural-historical perspective particularly of the agrarian and industrial stratification, and mode of production in agriculture *vis-a-vis* rural class structure. Mortan Klass and S.

Sinha have analyzed once again the origin and evolution of caste system in India. The continuity of caste system has been possible mainly due to support of economic factors and internalization of the hierarchical norms among people. The question of origin of caste has also been raised by the Marxists, namely, S.A. Dange, B.T. Ranadive and E.M.S. Namboodaripad. They all look at caste as an institution based on exploitation of the lower castes by the upper castes. Mencher sees caste as a form of class. The non-Marxist scholars do not treat caste as a super-structural entity, whereas the Marxist scholars treat it as a superstructural phenomenon. The latter are certainly not correct, but the former also should not ignore the role of economic factors in the evolution and resilience of caste system.

Studies of social and agrarian movements have been undertaken with structural-historical perspective by M.S.A. Rao, Rajendra Singh, P.M. Mukherji, K.L. Sharma, and of caste and class relationship by Satish Saberwal, S. Sivakumar and Chitra Siva Kumar. All of them have emphasized the element of *time* and the influences which economic, political and ideological forces had upon caste and class. These studies are 'historical', but they are different from those of historians as they have studied neither the remote past nor the immediate present in *detail* based on primary sources. Most of these studies are of contemporary period and cover a vast canvas. They refer more to 'levels' and 'break-throughs' for getting insights into the emergence of the present structures. Thus, the historically oriented studies give emphasis to the understanding of the present by conducting field studies. Singh also shows his preference for structural-historical approach, but he has not conducted an empirical study based on this approach.

Yogendra Singh outlines the main features of Marxist analysis of social stratification as follows: "The treatment of stratification in Marxist theory has distinctive features: it is systematic; it is dialectical; it treats structures (stratification) as historical product; it locates historical forces in the mode of production, reflection of the specific nature of man which under certain historical conditions creates contradictions of classes; it is essentially evolutionary and develop-mental, since mode of production and the relationship that it gene-rates are endowed with dialectical quality of self-transformation." Mode of production is the key of the Marxist theory of social stratification.

Systematic studies based on this approach began with A.R. Desai's study of 'nationalism' in 1940s, but more of such studies have been taken up recently as a reaction to the studies based on structural-functional and structuralist approaches. Singh refers to the studies by J. Pathy, P.K. Bose, Hira Singh, D.N. Dhanagare, D. Gupta and Kathleen Gough. The mode of production debate highlights the issues related to the nature of agrarian class structure and differentiation of peasantry. These studies refer to the forces and factors of class polarization, exploitation, bourgeoisification of the peasantry and pauperization of the rural working class. Thus, the basic concern is the study of origin, structure and change in caste and class in India. Caste and kinship are analyzed from a class point of view. Caste is not treated as culture-specific system, but a reflection of class relationships.

Now we may refer to a few illustrative studies from the point of their conceptual framework. While analyzing the social and economic structure of rural India, Bettelheim writes: "Throughout its existence, the colonial system grafted new legal ties and property rights into the existing framework of production." The laws created privileged social classes and also enforced the *status quo*. Bettelheim analyzes rural class structure in the post-independence period in view of Zamindari, Mahalwari, Ryotwari and Jagirdari systems of land tenure. Borrowing from D. Thorner, Bettelheim analyzes *mazdoors, kisans* and *maliks*. The change is seen towards *capitalism*. In the same way, Bettelheim analyzes India's industrial structure, the bourgeoisie and capital, the proletariat and the petty bourgeoisie, and the nature of Indian State. A similar analysis is found in a collection of essays by A.R. Desai.

In a recent study of a village in Tamil Nadu, John Harris discusses the issue of capitalism and peasant farming. He uses the Marxist approach with a difference. Harris writes: "I argue that the expanded reproduction of capital in agricultural production is subordinated to that of merchant and finance capital, in a form of economy like those described by Marx as 'intermediate' forms of capitalism. The process of 'differentiation of the peasantry is thus 'blocked' both because of the character of the economy and by the ideological structures of caste and kinship which reinforce the existing relations of production and the power structure." Thus, Harris examines the question of relationship between caste and mode of production. Control of land by members of a caste is considered as a decisive determinant of 'dominance'. Harris finds that class of rich peasant-merchant-moneylenders came to dominate both agriculture and trade, and this is shown up in the dominance of the members of the same caste in both agriculture and trade.

Some of the essays in a recently edited book *Land, Caste and Politics in India* by Gail Omvedt clearly show that caste is not merely a cultural category. Atrocities on Harijans, movements of Dalits, unity moves among the Kulaks, and that the dominant castes are less of castes and more of classes—have amply shown class genesis of the social relations among people. Omvedt writes: "Class should be basically defined in terms of the *social* Marxist concept of the social *relations of production.*" Omvedt feels that "caste is not only form but also concrete material context." The Indian feudal social formation was actually based on a *caste, feudal mode of production.* Castes and classes are found in a mix, and both have 'feudal' and 'capitalist' forms and affect each other, hence a social formation perspective. Omvedt agrees with Cough's classification of the pre-British South Indian society into five major classes: (1) the state class; (2) the state servants, (3) commodity producers and merchants, (4) peasants, herders, fishermen and attached village servants, and (5) agricultural and menial slaves. The last could be called *dalit* labourers. The first four classes are seen as equivalent of four *varnas,* and the fifth with the untouchables.

In a recent article, K.L. Sharma writes: "The understanding of caste and class demands an approach which has: (1) dialectics, (2) history, (3) culture, and (4) structure as its essential features." Dialectics does not mean binary tension, it refers to change through time as a result of contradictions. History gives an account of levels and events in the structure of society. Culture refers to the norms which define the patterns of relations. Structure is seen as a product of dialectical, historical and cultural forces. Therefore, caste-class polarity is a misplaced one. The idea of change from caste to class is a wrong perception. Caste as an ideology is a dangerous move and perhaps so is the case with 'class alone' perspective as the basis of study of Indian society. However, no serious studies have been carried out by sociologists and other social scientists considering Indian society as a social formation *vis-a-vis* social stratification.

Practical Application

Indian sociologists and social anthropologists have not been quite sensitive to research methodology and field of study. Broadly speaking, they have been swept (barring a few exceptions) by currents of theory and method in the western countries. Even if it was not the case at an early phase of Indian sociology, a large number of sociologists followed the methods of study adopted by a few leading sociologists of that period. Thus, one could say that indological survey, participant observation and historical methods (or techniques) have dominated sociological researches in India. A clear link between a method of study and a given theoretical perspective has generally remained vague in a large number of researches. Thus, the theoretical perspectives adopted by Indian sociologists have not remained rooted in Indian social reality. The methods of study have remained unrelated to these perspectives. The methods have been adopted mainly due to two reasons: (i) the notion of scienticism has compelled a researcher to accept a particular method; and (ii) convenience of accepting a method of study. We hardly find any study on social stratification which explains the correspondence between its theoretical perspective, method of study and data.

Beteille's study of caste, class and power in Sripuram village of Tanjore district in Tamil Nadu is based on intensive field-work (participant observation). Beteille writes: "I did my field-work in Sripuram while living with people as one among them. I was permi-tted to live in the *agraharam* in a Brahmin house—a privilege, as I was often told, never before extended to an outsider and a non-Brahmin. I dined with the Brahmins and had access to most of their houses. I was perhaps the only non-Brahmin ever to have sat and eaten with the Brahmins in Sripuram on ceremonial occasions. I was identified with the Brahmins by my dress, my appearance, and the fact that I lived in one of their houses."

Beteille admits that his identification with the Brahmins was not an unmixed blessing. The non-Brahmins and Adi-Dravidas took Beteille like as one of the Brahmins of the village. Consequently, he could not elicit properly the required information about the non-Brahmins and the Adi-Dravidas. The reason for staying in *agraharam* as given by Beteille is: "Had I lived with the non-Brahmins the Brahmins would not have moved freely with me. Had I lived with the Adi-Dravidas, the *agraharam* would have been un-accessible. I chose to live with the Brahmins for practical reason and also because this gave me an opportunity to gain some insight into the literate cultural tradition of the region."

Beteille admits certain limitations of his study. "Had I lived with the Adi-Dravidas this study would perhaps have had a different focus." The other point is that "the study is qualitative in its character and emphasis." The village has not been understood "in quantitative and statistical terms." Beteille says that he has understood the village's social life "from within, in terms of the values and meanings attributed to it by the people themselves." It is mentioned by Beteille that his status as a resident of *agraharam* was curiously ambiguous one of 'outsider' as well as 'insider'. As Beteille claims it gave him the advantage of both insider and outsider. He writes: "My field-work was not done in a very planned or organized manner. I did not enter the field armed with a battery of hypotheses." Beteille feels that formulation of hypotheses "would have done more harm than good." Beteille writes in an article that "in adjusting oneself (Beteille himself) to a stratified community one learns much about the nature of stratification itself." The points raised in the article—"The Tribulations of Field Work" by Beteille are the same which he makes in his study of caste class and power. Some observations given by P.N. Mukherji on participant observation in the form of criticism of Beteille's view may be mentioned below.

Mukherji formulates three questions: (1) By what criteria does the researcher select his community or small group for study? (2) Does the researcher enter the field first and then let the investigation lake 'shape' or does he approach the field with a clearly formulated plan of investigation? (3) What indeed is the method of participant observation, and how are we to assess its utility in the Indian context? Our interest is in the first two questions more than the third one. Simply an interest to understand a community's social life cannot be the basis for an extensive study. Also some knowledge about the people cannot be the basis of an insightful investigation. The point is that some research objectives are always thought of beforehand. However, our concern is still more for the second question and we tend to agree with Mukherji's observation on that question. We, like Mukherji, do not agree with Betride's statement that he went to Sripuram without a definite preference for any particular aspect of its social life; that he did not have an interest in the problem of social inequality. Beteille's assertion that he got interested in the study of social inequality after seeing the marks of stratification in virtually every sphere of life. The danger in acceptance of Beteille's position is that it is not the cognitive understanding of society and explanations about society that determine our interests of research, but it is the observation of field that determines the object of study.

A number of questions could be raised about Beteille's method of study. Why did he not plan his field-work? Was his village a unique one? Did he not have any idea of a village in India? Did he not read Max Weber or Karl Marx before conducting the present study? Did he relate his data with the formulations of Weber in particular and of Marx and others in general after field-work? Beteille perhaps knows about these questions relating to his study. There is no connection whatsoever between the 'battery of hypotheses' and 'concepts' which he has formulated (may be after he completed his field-work) and the method of study. Beteille's study lacks required *historical* perspective. The formula-tions of Weber and Marx would demand a historical understanding of caste, class and power. Beteille has also ignored (perhaps unwittingly) the ideological implications of Max Weber's conceptual framework. The ghost of Marx was the basis of Weber's distinction between class, status and party. Where was such a ghost before Beteille? However, it is true that analysis of rituals and religion finds a negligent place in Beteille's study of Sripuram, but it is not clear whether it was consciously planned to chase the ghost of Louis Dumont's binary opposition of pure and impure or Srinivas' emphasis on the study of religion in Rampura. Certainly, Srinivas' impact on Beteille is seen in the advocacy of participant observa-tion, but Beteille is unable to relate it with Weber's theory of social stratification and its implicit ideological moorings.

K.L. Sharma's study of the changing rural stratification system has been guided by 'a battery of hypotheses'. He expresses his concern for scarcity of multidimensional studies of social stratifica-tion. His study raises questions about 'caste' as an overreaching stratification, vertical or pyramidal arrangements of caste groups and caste (or group) as the unit of social ranking. Sharma questions the thesis of 'corporateness' about social ranking and social mobility. He uses both structural and cultural criteria in understanding of social stratification.

Emphasis on comparison based on variables such as economic conditions, geographical factors and cultural distinctiveness along with land tenure systems is the hallmark of Sharma's-study of social stratification in six villages of Rajasthan. The study is based on census and enumeration method, sampling, interview, case study, secondary data, and historical records. Participant observa-tion alone is not the standpoint of Sharma's study. Since the study was based on a well-thought of plan, these techniques were found useful for gathering a variety of information. The study provides a 'mix' of qualitative and quantitative analysis of social stratification.

Anil Bhatt's complaint is that ethnographers and social anthropologists have made 'qualitative'studies of single villages or single or multiple castes and communities. They do not provide quantification, but have a tendency to generalize or typify their limited observationsand studies. Generalization and quantification are closely related. A large part of Bhatt's study is based on quantitative data gathered through survey research and deals with macro-national and regional levels of social stratification. He talks of 'degrees' and 'amounts' instead of 'generally', 'approximately' and 'mostly', etc. in his analysis of data. Bhatt deals with individuals as members of a caste, caste as a group in relation to other castes and the caste system as a dimension of social stratification in relation to socio-economic and political dimensions. He has collected large-scale data in more substantive and relevant contexts. Bhatt writes: "I have tried to be very explicit in relating the evidences to the theory." Perhaps Bhatt has done more justice to Weber's conceptualization than Beteille in regard to substantiation, unit of study and range of analysis.

There are a few village studies based on information collected by questionnaire. Computerization of data has also been reported in village studies. Techniques of scale analysis have been applied. In several studies, interview schedule has been used for data collection. However, most of the studies on social stratification concerning rural India are based on participant observation, interview and case study method. Studies of social stratification relating to urban India are based on survey method and questionnaire.

Let us now discuss briefly the Marxian method of study. The essence of this method is that the explanation comes from the conditions and structure of social reality. Marxian approach is a historical explanation. It takes into account the course of events over a period of time in a given society in regard to class relations among the people. It is an evolutionary approach. Some have called it emancipatory and hermeneutic in nature. For studying social stratification in the British period, A.R. Desai has analyzed economy, agriculture, handicraft industries, means of transport, modern education, political and administrative set-up, class structure, role of press, social and reform movements etc. The perspective is dialectical-historical. Bettelheim's study of caste and class structure in post-independence period uses the same approach. But, between the two, Desai does more justice with Marxist approach and method of study.

The variants of the Marxist theory and method of study are found in the studies of D.P. Mukerji, Kathleen Gough, Gail Omvedt and Ramakrishna Mukherjee. As we know that Mukerji has analyzed Indian tradition from the Marxist approach, but he collected a different sort of research material compared with that of Desai and Bettelheim. He was more interested in understanding of the cognitive and meaning structures which formed Indian tradition than the concrete classes itself. Gough and Omvedt consider caste as an important aspect of Indian society, and the study of caste along with class structure and mode of production is characterized by this method. Gough has done this in her recent studies of South India, and Omvedt has done this in her recent studies of *dalits* in Maharashtra. Mukherjee has combined historical and census data with the data relating to the present class and caste structure in his study of rural society in Bengal. Several other sociologists with Marxist and non-Marxist dispositions have used historical method in their analysis of caste and class and agrarian movements. Among the non-Marxists (or even anti-Marxists), Dumont is one who combines the method of indology, abstracted empiricism and pseudo history in his well-known study—*Homo Hierarchicus*.

The method of study largely determines the nature of data in a given study. As we know, a large number of studies on caste have used ethnographic accounts prepared by the British officers. Some others have used scriptural texts as source of their analyses. Historical accounts and studies are found as data in some studies. However, in the post-independence period, generation of data by sociologists and anthropologists in both rural and urban areas has been a pronounced practice. This has been done through field studies based on techniques such as survey, interview, observation and case study.

The main problem is still to find out a proper connection between theory, method and data. Field studies with the use of research techniques such as survey, interview and observation and some statistical devices became so fashionable that researchers remained 'unarmed' or 'unaware' about the intrinsic connection between theory, method and data. In other words, the false notion of making a study scientific simply by adopting these techniques of research has created innumerable problems. Secondly, the notion of 'science' in social sciences has been distorted by imple-menting it in a vulgarized and unrealistic way. However, such a problem is seen more in the case of 'commercialization' of social research. It is this sociology of knowledge perspective, which is lacking, that is, sensitization about nature of theory and its implications for method and data.

6

Practical Aspects

A number of points are there, which have so far remained un-clarified in regard to the nature of caste and class in India. Some misconceptions are: Caste and class are polar opposites; caste is being replaced by class; caste is a rural phenomenon where-as class is found in urban-industrial settings; caste is an ascriptive system while class is based on the achievement principle; caste is a closed system and does not permit mobility for its members where-as class is an open system and allows mobility for its members; India has/had a caste system, hence a 'caste model' for studying Indian society and the West has/had classes, hence a 'class model' for studying western societies. However, these notions are rooted in the historicity of Indian society and its culture including British and post-independence academic colonialism.

The other points refer to the debate regarding approaches to the study of caste and class in India. The various approaches can be classified as: (i) interactional versus attributional; (ii) struc-tural versus cultural; and (iii) Marxist versus functional. These approaches have been borrowed from the West, and are clearly reflected in the studies of social stratification in India. Rural versus urban stratification, corporate vs. individual mobility, caste versus class relations, and ritual versus secular hierarchy are found as main issues in most of the studies on social stratification. The studies range from the study of caste or class alone to caste and class, caste and power, class and power, and caste, class and religion. I wish to analyze these issues in view of the available studies on caste and class from the point of theory, method and data. Both caste and class have been analysed in terms of theory, structure and process. Earlier Singh (1974) made this observation about social stratification in India. There is no epistemological apriorism in this sort of exercise. The studies can be seen from the point of their requirements as well as from the point of caste and class relations in India.

Ideal Setup

A certain conception of 'model' of traditional Indian society has emerged. This model has/had implications for studying Indian society. The main features of this caste model are: (i) it is based primarily on the ideas held or expressed by certain sections of society and not on the observed or recorded behaviour of people; (ii) it attaches a kind of primary and universal significance to caste as this has been conceived in the classical texts; (iii) the entire system is viewed as being governed by certain more or less explicitly formulated principles or 'rules of the game' ; and (iv) the different castes which are the basic units in the system are conceived as fulfilling complementary functions and their mutual relations as being 'non-antagonistic' (Beteille, 1969).

No doubt, the 'caste model' brings into focus some of the significant features of the traditional Indian society, but it fails on two counts: (i) when it is made too general it can be applied to almost every society and therefore does not tell us very much about the specific properties of any society; and (ii) when it is made too specific it fails to take into account certain crucial features of economic and political life (Ibid.). Beteille observes that the model has been more systematically elaborated by Dumont as it is concerned essentially with ideas and values. It has failed, however, in providing a proper place to material interests in social life. Beteille argues a case for the study of material interests along with the study of ideas and values in terms of the dialectical relations between the two. But Beteille does not offer a 'class analysis' of Indian society as an alternative to the caste model. In fact, Beteille suggests a sort of modification of the caste model by putting an emphasis on the study of economic and political conflict with a certain degree of autonomy for the economic and political activities of inter-caste relations. However, he points out that it would be wrong to consider India as a 'caste society', and the United States as a 'class society', and Europe as an 'estate society'.

Beteille denies the validity of a sociology of values and ideas. He emphasizes the role of material interests in the studies of traditional society and culture in India. Beteille takes a clue from Leach (1960), Bailey (1963), and Dumont (1970), who have offered a 'caste model' of Indian society. The essence of the views of Leach, Bailey and Dumont is that caste is a non-competitive system, the castes are 'non-antagonistic'strata. Leach (1960) writes: "Wherever caste groups are seen to be acting as corporations in competition against like—groups of different castes, then they are acting in defiance of caste principles." Competition refers to class and cooperation refers to caste. This is really a very erroneous view about both class and caste, and more so about the under-standing of caste in India. Western scholars (including Leach) look at the caste system from the viewpoint of class in western societies. Leach refers to castes as groups which co-operate and do not compete. Leach finds competition within the 'dominant caste' and not between the dominant caste and other castes. The latter would refer to a class situation, and the former to a class-like situation without affecting the caste system. The idea of non-antagonistic strata has come from Ossowski (1963) who refers to the Polish situation in terms of status gradations and not as classes based on antagonism.

Thus, the western notions of class as well as non-antagonism have been used for analyzing the structure of Indian society. The historicity of Indian society is the real casualty, and reductionism has been the hallmark of 'caste model'. Everything is reduced to the all-pervasive principle of caste hierarchy. However, factually, this was not the situation in ancient, medieval and British India. Migration, mobility and defiance have been reported in historical researches (Thapar, 1974; Panikkar, 1955; Stein, 1968; Habib, 1974; and Desai, 1948). These researches have been ignored by anthropologists and sociologists perhaps due to British colonialism and an overwhelming impact of American and British social science research.

British ethnographers have defined caste in terms of its assumed or real functionality to Indian society and culture. The salient features given by them (including some Indian sociologists) are that a caste has a common name, common descent, and the same hereditary calling and communitarian living (Risley, 1969). Ketkar (1909) mentions hereditary membership and endogamy as the most striking features of the caste system in India. Senart (1930) writes: "A caste system is one whereby a society is divided up into a number of self-contained and completely segregated units (castes), the mutual relations between which are ritually determined in a graded scale." The uniqueness of the system is prominently emphasized in the above definitions of the caste system. Furnivall (1939), Hutton (1946) and Sherring (1974) observe that the caste system is 'functional' for Indian society. Furnivall applauds the 'pluralism' of the caste system. Hutton speaks of its functions for the individual, community and society as a whole. Sherring refers to cleanliness and order and a bond of union among Hindus promoted by the caste system. Ghurye (1950) refers to six features of the caste system and upholds endogamy as its essence.

Other students of Indian society have also provided a view which either refers to the uniqueness of the caste system or they have viewed it from the viewpoint of their own society. Marx (1945) related the (Asiatic) mode of production to the stability of the caste system in India. Maine (1890) referred to caste as an example of a non-contractual 'status-society'. Senart (1930), Hocart (1950), and Dumont (1970) have emphasized ritual criteria and pollution-purity as the bases of Hindu society. Weber (1947) considered caste as a system of 'status groups' based on the otherworldly doctrines of Hinduism.

Sinha (1974), in a report on caste, notes the following trends:

(i) Speculative theories about the origin of the caste system have practically been given up.

(ii) The bulk of the work on caste is done by the method of social anthropology on the basis of a study of multi-caste villages.

(iii) Considerable interest is shown in these studies on an understanding of the adaptability of the caste system to view situations and forces of changes.

(iv) Study of inter-ethnic status ranking is done through an analysis of data collected through a rigorous methodology.

(v) Literature on social mobility in the caste system has grown in abundance and improved in quality.

(vi) The concept of hierarchy based on the binary polarity of purity-pollution has received much attention.

(vii) There is a felt need for interregional comparison.

(viii) The comparability of caste beyond Indian society has been examined.

(ix) The emergent non-caste phenomena are left unana-lyzed because of the obsession with caste.

(x) The number of scholars interested in the study of caste has grown considerably.

Sinha does not reflect upon caste and class polarity, the 'caste, class and power' approach to stratification, and caste as a cultural or structural phenomenon (Sharma, 1977). Sinha also ignores the analysis of the entrenchment of caste into politics, education, industry and ethnicity. A sociology of knowledge perspective would demand an understanding of theory, structure and process of the caste system and this is lacking in Sinha's trend report. Sinha considers caste basically as a cultural phenomenon. "The cultural system of caste thus naturally promotes an infinite variety of stable crafts and ritual styles" (Sinha, 1967). Sinha further observes: 'The social and cultural systems of caste thus segment the total society into many Jati groups committed to particular britis and styles of life, arranged in a social hierarchy defined in terms of the cultural value of the purity and impurity of these occupations and styles of life" (Ibid.). Sinha's plea for combining structural and cultural perspectives on caste stratification will not stand the test of validity in view of his clear preference for considering caste as a cultural phenomenon.

Thus, the studies on caste aimed at the legitimacy and justification of the caste system itself. Caste was pronounced as an all-inclusive and encompassing functional system. The 'pluralism' of caste was glorified with the intent of establishing British rule on a sounder footing. This was an exercise in befooling the Indian people and the leaders of various castes and even intellectuals. At the same time, the scholars of the West glorified the class system with a view to establishing the superiority of western society and culture (Sharma, 1980). "Class was considered as an open system, the individual was given freedom of movement under the system, and achievement was the essence of the system. In contrast, the caste system was considered as a closed system, the individual could not move up in the hierarchy, and it was a system based on ascription. Caste and class were polar opposites, caste was considered a feature of an archaic society like India, and class was considered a characteristic feature of the industrially advanced achievement-based western society" (Ibid.). This clearly shows that the western scholars (mainly American and British) tried to establish their hegemony by academic propaganda.

MacIver and Page (1967) do not define class strictly in the economic sense. They refer to 'status' as the basis of what they call 'social class'. Marshall (1934), Parsons (1954), Davis and Moore (1945), Bottomore (1964: 148) and Centres (1961: 27) define class either in terms of 'status' or in psychological terms (attitudes and consciousness). The quintessence of the definitions of caste *vis-a-vis* class is that caste is found in India and class is a feature of the western world. The important point is that caste is used as a double-edged weapon, namely, keeping it intact by declaring it as a 'functional' system, and by pronouncing its inferiority or subordination to the class system of the West. Two consequences followed from this academic propaganda:

(i) the indoctrination of social scientists in terms of theorization, methodology and field studies; and
(ii) legitimation of British hegemony and the superiority of their understanding of Indian society. Consequently, social science research in India in the fifties and the sixties was clearly directed by the western social scientists and was patterned in terms of their perspectives.

Literature on caste was produced in abundance in the fifties and sixties. The emphasis was on the overwhelming role of caste in Indian society, caste ranking and mobility in the caste system. Some writings also dealt with class in India. A brief resume is given here. The higher castes revolted against any attempt to challenge their status and power, and the lower castes were content with their lower status, believing that it was due to their *karma* (Prasad, 1957). Srinivas's collection of essays on caste (1962) and his earlier essay on caste (1959), Mathur's book on the role of caste and ritual (1964), Marriott's study of caste and kinship in Central

India (1960), and Kothari's edited work on the role of caste in politics (1970) are some of the important studies on the theme.

Dube (1955) writes that the main criteria for the ranking of castes are ritual and not economic. Srinivas's work on religion and society among the Coorgs of South India (1952) is also an attempt towards caste ranking based on the criterion of pollution and purity. Marriott's essay (1959) is on the criteria of caste ranking whether they are 'interactional' or 'attributional' or both. Later on Marriott (1965) has used the concept of 'elaboration' for examining the rigidity and flexibility of the caste system in five regions of India. Mahar (1959) and Hazlthurst (1968) have referred to multiple criteria for caste ranking. Dube (1968) and Gardner (1968) refer to 'levels' of caste dominance and highlight the role of the individual in caste mobility and refute the utility of the concepts of 'dominant caste' and 'sanskritisation' as advocated by Srinivas. There are other studies in which 'structural mobility' has been noted. Sharma (1969,1970,1974,1980) discusses stresses in caste stratification, modernization and rural stratification, and bourgeoisification, proletarianization, downward social mobility and levels of social mobility in village India. He also discusses the crystallization of class relations in the countryside.

A number of studies on caste mobility have been reported by Majumdar (1958), Silverberg (1968), Lynch (1968) and Singer (1968). Silverberg, Singer and Cohn have brought out several studies on caste and mobility in their edited volumes with particular emphasis on the relevance of concepts of reference group and relative deprivation, etc. Saberwal (1976) discusses mobility among the Rampurias of a Punjab town who belonged to the lower stratum but took up trade and commerce as their main occupation. Berreman (1979) has published his essays on caste written over a period of two decades. The emphasis in Berreman's essays is that caste-based inequalities in India are not different from race-based inequalities in the United States of America.

Gough has highlighted the class basis of the caste system in India. She refers to conflicts and litigations between different castes in a Tanjore village (1960) based on economic inequalities. The mix of caste and class in East Bengal (now Bangladesh) is referred to by Ramakrishna Mukherjee (1957). Bose (1967) refers to the class genesis of the caste structure in Bengal. Changes from caste to class are noted by Misra (1960), Beteille (1969), Miller (1975), and

Kolenda (1978). But none of them deny the resurgence of caste in the new situation. A class analysis of Indian society in general and the caste system and village community in particular is found in Desai's edited work on rural sociology (1978) and in his book on Indian nationalism (1948), and in Bettelheim (1968), Harris (1982), and in an edited work by Omvedt (1982).

Novel Structure

Caste is a unique system; it pervades the whole of Hindu society in India; and it is an encompassing system. These are the views upheld by Bougie, Srinivas and Dumont in particular and several others in general. Bougie (1971) writes: "To sum up on these points: hereditary specialization, hierarchical organization, reciprocal repulsion: as far as any social form can realize itself in its purity, the caste system is realized in India. At the very least it penetrates Hindu society to a level unknown elsewhere. It plays some part in other civilizations but in India it has invaded the whole. It is in this sense that we may speak of the caste system as a phenomenon peculiar to India." Srinivas (1952) following Bougie, notes the preeminence of religious values in the caste system. The religious values among the Hindus centre in the ideas of pollution and purity. Bougie follows Hocart in regard to the role of rituals in the caste hierarchy. However, Hocart (1958) finds that religion encompasses power, hence the priesthood is not 'absolute' in nature. Relations between Brahmin and Kshatriya are defined in terms of a certain reciprocity, namely, the Brahmin represents the 'religious' authority and the Kshatriya enjoys 'political' power.

Srinivas notes various types of purity and impurity among the Coorgs of South India. Ritual impurity, normal ritual status and ritual purity form a hierarchy based on the notion of pollution and purity. Normal ritual status is the one which a person normally enjoys: it is a mild form of impurity. However, Dumont and Pocock (1959) discard the expression of 'normal ritual status'. Hierarchy based on pollution-purity does not include 'mildly impure', it includes only 'pure' and 'impure'. Ephemeral purity or impurity after purification do not guide inter-caste relations. Ritual purification or impurification is a generalized phenomenon among all Hindus.

However, Srinivas feels that the concept is absolutely fundamental to the caste system. Sanskritisation is the only way to remove impurity or to minimize it. While commenting on a book by Srinivas (1976), Parvathamma (1978: 91) writes: "In all the writings of Srinivas, the Brahmin-non-Brahmin values are juxtaposed." Hierar-chy based on pollution-purity remains intrinsic to Srinivas's thinking in regard to all aspects of human life, even if it is actually not so pronounced. That sanskritisation can also cause tensions and contradictions manifestly or latently is overlooked by Srinivas. His main emphasis remains on dominance and solidarity. It is not only Srinivas who has heavily endorsed 'Brahminical'sociology, several others including Dumont (1970), Marriott (1955) and Singer (1968) have emphasized disproportionately the pheno-menon of caste in Indian society. Pollution-purity, religion and rituals are the central foci of their studies. Today, social structure is not considered beyond the parameters of the notions of pollution-purity, hierarchy and dominance.

Compared to Leach, Dumont and Srinivas, a different view is provided by Bailey (1963). Bailey refers to three types of definitions of caste. These are: (1) the 'rigidity' type; (2) the 'cultural' type, and (3) the 'structural' type. The first type of definition is found inapplicable as it refers to status immobility, hence 'analytic'. The second type is found 'useful' as it refers to religious ideas, namely, opposition based on purity and pollution and hierarchy. The pollution-purity opposition implies (i) hereditary specialization, (ii) hierarchy, and (iii) opposition of parts. Caste as a system based on beliefs and ideas becomes a closed unique system of social stratification. The third type of definition refers to exclusiveness, exhaustiveness and ranking as the 'structural' criteria of the caste system. The 'cultural' criteria limit comparison and the structural ones facilitate cross-cultural comparison.

Thus, according to Bailey, caste is a unique system so far as its cultural criteria are concerned, and it shares certain features with other systems of social stratification so far as structural criteria are concerned. Bailey disapproves Dumont's view about caste as he considers it in terms of 'finality' and 'completeness'. Bailey considers Dumont's definition of caste 'analytic' rather than 'synthetic'. The latter refers to the existence of the caste system at the micro-level. The analytic statement tends to become axiomatic. However, Bailey also accepts the analytic statement of Dumont as the starting point of his analysis. Bailey does not refer to 'class analysis' or inherence of class in caste. Like Leach and Dumont, Bailey's view also refers to 'organicism' ; competition and equality are not found in the caste system. Bailey's attempt at formulating a 'compromised definition' of the caste system is not different from the understanding of the caste system provided by Dumont, Leach and Srinivas.

Thus, ultimately, Bailey also tends to formulate an 'analytic' statement about the caste system, and in effect, not so different from that of Dumont and Srinivas. Bailey fails to recognize the historicity of the caste system which brings to light innumerable adaptations and contradictions faced by it. For Bailey, the caste system is an inviolate system, hence closed and organic in nature. Inviolate systems are found in simple societies, or in relatively insulated enclaves of complex societies. Caste is also seen by Bailey as an organizing principle of competition, and not the one by which politico-economic groups are recruited. Castes are not corporate or organic political groups, hence caste is a closed segmentary stratification. 'Segmentation' refers to change from organicism. However, such a conception of change does not explain the change of the caste system. Segmentation does not lead ultimately to equality or castelessness. Bailey's notion of change in caste is thus based on a sort of false consciousness about change (Sharma, 1980). Increasing segmentation does not mean emergence of class-based relations, and the latter do not mean equality or egalitarianism. Singh (1968: 170) observes that Bailey's analysis is based on a static and abstract model of caste, and on the same type of 'analytic'statements as those of Dumont. Beteille's notion of the emergence of 'differentiated structures' (1966) also does not provide a class-view of social stratification or/of the village community.

The Strategies

Marriott (1959) was the first to make a reference to the 'interactional' and 'attributional' approaches to the study of the caste system. Later on it was exemplified in great detail by Singh (1974) in a trend report on social stratification. Marriott is the one who has promoted 'culturology' by studying Indian tradition and the interaction between what he calls 'Great Tradition' and 'Little Tradition'. Marriott's study (1955) substantiates the interactional approach to the study of Indian society in terms of the relations between 'Sanskritic' and 'oral' traditions. The study of relations between higher and lower castes in basic to the 'interactional' approach. However, this approach has also been vigorously applied by Marxist scholars to the study of class relations in village India.

Emphasis in the 'attributional' approach is on 'order' rather than 'relation'. The configuration of elements constituting a system of hierarchy is the essence of the attributional approach. The attributes are, for example, income, occupation, education, positions of power, etc. These attributes have sufficient measurability, and they facilitate construction of categories such as upper, middle and lower. Thus, an attempt is made to work out the indicators of status, and the variations are measured on different types of scales and indices. The 'composite status' of individuals is worked out. 'Corporateness' of status is ruled out as the individual's attributes are the basis of constructing the 'order'.

That caste is not an exclusively cultural system is the view held by D' Souza (1967). Caste and class are different forms of social stratification. Groups (caste groups or *jatis)* are ranked in the caste system, whereas positions are ranked in social stratification (particularly with reference to class stratification). The ranking of endogamous groups and not endogamy as the rule of marriage, is the hallmark of the caste system. D' Souza's contention is that changes in the caste system have brought about changes in the properties of individual members. A 'hereditary group' might continue in the caste system as a 'class'. This fact explains the similarity between caste and class. In fact, D' Souza emphasizes the significance of the continuum of the rigidity-fluidity dimensions in regard to both caste and class. Thus, the individual and his properties are the real units of analysis rather than the endogamous groups.

D' Souza decisively concludes that class is replacing caste, and the individual is replacing the group. A certain place for the individual as a unit of status, and a certain level of social mobility at that level are the basic assumptions of D' Souza's formulation. Even if the role of the individual and the fact of social mobility are admitted, class would not take the place of caste inspite of the fact that caste has undergone significant changes. It would be untenable to infer that change is taking place from caste to class, from hierarchy to stratification, from closed to open system, and from an organic to a segmentary system of social stratification

(Sharma, 1977; 1980). Singh (1968) rightly points out that a 'prismatic model' of change is suitable where traditional segments of caste and kinship undergo adaptive transformation without completely being 'diffracted' into classes or corporate groups. Thus, class segments operate within the frame of caste categories with a new sense of identity, and they also violate caste norms, hence contra-dictions. Caste has been a dynamic system full of adaptations, accretions, contradictions and transformations, hence resilience and change.

Having realized that caste alone is not the totality of social stratification and that caste is not being replaced by class as the two are not necessarily antithetical to each other, Beteille (1965), following Weber's trio of 'class, status and party', analyzes patterns of social stratification in a Tanjore village in terms of 'caste, class and power'. Beteille is not quite clear about the phenomenon of class. He says that "classes are categories rather than groups," but he contradicts this statement when he writes that "by class we mean a category of persons occupying a specific position in the system of production" (1965). The first statement has the overtones of the Weberian notion of class and the second has those of Marx's conception of class. However, Beteille by no means intends to provide a Marxian analysis of social stratification, nor he does justice to Weber's ideas of rationalism and *verstehen*. Beteille's study, therefore, also falls short of the 'attributional' or 'interactional' criteria of social ranking.

In fact, it is Anil Bhatt (1975) who has done more justice to the attributional approach in studying social stratification. Bhatt's trio comprises 'caste, class and politics.' He observes that social stratification in India has deviated considerably from the traditional caste model. Caste does not encompass economic position and political power. A caste is internally differentiated in terms of class and power of its members. Thus, Bhatt finds status incongruence, relative openness, mobility, and competition as the salient features of the emergent system of social stratification. Bhatt has relied on secondary data and attitudinal responses. It is more of a 'formalistic' approach and does not go into actual details regarding the functioning of institutions related to caste, class and power. Aggrawal (1971) and recently Chauhan (1980) have also followed the viewpoint adopted by Beteille. There is no doubt that Beteille has presented a new approach to the study of social stratification in

India, but without realizing the incongruity between the his approach and the method of his study (Sharma, 1980).

Whether caste is a cultural aspect of the Indian tradition or a structural form was discussed in a symposium (Reuck and Knight, 1967) in which Myrdal, Leach, Dumont, Berreman, Sinha, Cohn, Mayer and Tambiah participated along with some others. I have already referred to the view that caste is considered a cultural aspect of the Indian tradition. Dumont, Leach, Srinivas and Marriott consider castes as corporate groups, found exclusively in Indian society, particularly among Hindus. Beteille and Bailey partly agree with this view; however, D' Souza and Bhatt clearly advocate the application of an attributional approach (class approach in a non-Marxian sense). Caste as a cultural phenomenon is seen as a system of values and ideas. Srinivas's (1966) notions of sanskritisation and westernisation are examples of 'intrasystemic' or 'positional changes.'

Caste as a structural phenomenon is considered as a part of the general theory of social stratification. Earth (1960) writes: "If the concept of caste is to be useful in sociological analysis, its definition must be based on structural criteria, and not on particular features of the Hindu philosophical scheme." Barth considers caste in general as a system of social stratification. The principle of status summation seems to be the structural feature of caste stratification. In other words, caste should label not a particular social system but a general social sub-system. Opposition, segmentation and hierarchy are universal criteria of social stratification, and are expressed in different cultural idioms including caste. Berreman (1967) also refers to three universal elements of all castes, namely, stratification, culturalism and interaction. Harper (1968) and Nadel (1957) have expressed the view that caste stratification is one of the various forms of social stratification.

As we have stated earlier that D' Souza (1967) draws a polar distinction between caste and class, but he does not consider caste as an exclusively cultural system. D' Souza's main concern is that changes in the caste system are ultimately brought about by changes in the properties of the individual members. The emphasis in D' Souza's view is on the significance of the continuum of the rigidity-fluidity dimensions to the understanding of both caste and class.

Leach (1960) also refers to emergence of 'caste grades' as class-like changes in the caste system.

Studies on caste mobility refer to the structural dimension of caste stratification. Thapar (1974), Panikkar (1955) and Stein (1968) refer to caste mobility in spatial and status contexts rather than in the context of rituals. Bailey (1957) and Epstein (1962) also consider economic factors responsible for changing inter-caste relations. Kothari (1970) mentions caste as a variable in politics in independent India. Singh (1974) analyzes caste in terms of cultural and structural factors and considers it as a 'structural-particularistic' type of social stratification. The essence of the structural approach is that caste should be seen in terms of a system of 'relations' between different castes, and structural factors bring about changes in the vertical and horizontal gradations in the caste system. Mencher (1974) analyzes caste from a Marxist (also structural) point of view. She considers the exploitation of the low castes and the prevention of the formation of classes as the two main features of the caste system. Thus, caste is, in fact, a system of class relations, and at the same time, its functioning idiom does not allow it to operate as a class system.

Fruits of Revolution

Class in India is generally seen as a consequence of change in the caste system and not as a concomitant and co-existent system inseparable from caste. Several questions can be raised about the studies of caste hierarchy and social mobility. For example, why did Srinivas and his associates often study caste structure, positional changes, village community, and family life and kinship; and why did they leave out the studies of class relations, vertical mobility, urban community, industry and formal organizations from their sociological purview? Culturology is given primacy over the structural perspective in the understanding of the caste system in most studies carried out by Srinivas and his followers. Structural changes are visualized only latently and that too due to sanskri-tisation and westernisation. Emphasis on the study of social mobility in terms of upward movement in the caste hierarchy further legiti-mizes the culturological approach to the study of society and culture in India. The concepts of dominant caste and sanskritisation remain central to this view. Corporate mobility and the study of the social and cultural aspects receive greater attention instead of mobility at the level of family and individual and economic and political aspects. Resentment, opposition and conflict in the study of inter-group relations remain inactive notions.

Dube (1976) and Singh (1979) both realize that the concepts of caste and class have been basically 'western', and therefore, ignore the historicity of Indian society in their formulations. Indigenization of social science paradigms would ensure a proper input of historical substance in the concepts and theories related to Indian society. Both Marxist and non-Marxist scholars (Thorner, 1974; Saran, 1962) have pleaded for the use of native concepts and categories, respectively. D.P. Mukerji (1958) has argued vehemently for making the Indian tradition as the sole basis of analyzing social change. Desai (1948) has strongly opposed to the application of the non-Marxist approaches. Srinivas has been blamed for an inappropriate application of British structural-functionalism by Mencher (1974) and Saberwal (1979).

Caste has been taken as synonym with the social formation of Indian society and therefore class is treated as an alternate system to caste. However, the fact is that neither does caste refer to the totality of social formations nor is class the polar opposite of caste. Studies such as caste and class (D' Souza, 1967); caste, class and power (Beteille, 1965); caste, religion and power (Aggrawal, 1971); and caste, class and politics (Bhatt, 1975) do not provide a corrective to the 'caste alone' approach. These studies are rooted in the falsity of the western dichotomy of tradition and modernity and the trio of 'class, status and party' (Weber, 1947). They do not incorporate the experience of Indian society into the concepts of caste, class and power, hence inadequate in rescuing us from these alien concepts and theories.

Class in India has existed along with caste and power. Caste incorporates class and class incorporates caste in the Indian context. Neither the 'caste alone' view nor the 'class alone' perspective can help in a proper and fuller understanding of Indian society. It has been noted that there was never a perfect congruence between caste, class and power. Mobility and migration were quite normal activities in ancient and medieval India. However, Bailey, Beteille and Bhatt give the impression that a congruence prevailed between caste, class and power in the pre-independent India, and land reforms and politicization have brought about incongruities and caste-free areas.

Historians of the Marxist disposition have realized that there is an intertwining of caste and class in India, but they prefer to look at caste from a class point of view. Kosambi (1956) makes a class analysis of the Aryans after the Rig Veda. Thapar (1974), Habib (1974), and Desai (1948) have also done a class analysis of Indian society. According to Desai, caste inheres in an under-developed but potentially explosive class character. In another study, Desai (1975) has analyzed the Indian State from a class (Marxist) point of view. But class does not necessarily mean openness, mobility and a combination of certain attributes as generally perceived by western social scientists and their followers in India. Castes have been functioning as classes for all practical considerations. Class relations are as old as caste relations or even older than caste relations. Lamb (1975) reports the prevalence of class relations as early as 600 B.C. in India. Material and cultural traditions existed with a sort of congruity, and class transformation had been a vital fact in the form of new kingdoms, settled agriculture, trade, cities and banking and guild organizations.

The non-Marxist scholars in general have relied on analytical abstractions in the form of statistical-mathematical indicators or analytical topologies (Singh, 1981). D' Souza (1975) treats class as a conceptually abstracted category. Class does not exist as a community like caste. Class is defined operationally in terms of certain indices. D' Souza applies the attributional approach to class purely in terms of constructing an 'order' comprising upper, middle and lower class categories. The following points have been made about classes in India:

(1) Classes are not found as a system of stratification in the same way as castes are rooted in the Indian society.
(2) Class is not a universalistic phenomenon of social stratification.
(3) There are no objective criteria of class identification.
(4) It is not clear whether class is a category or a concrete unit of interaction with other units.

One could affirm that these points have been put forth in order to prevent a class analysis of Indian society. Caste has created numerous problems of a class nature related to economic domination and subjugation, privileges and deprivations, 'conspicuous waste' and bare survival. However, these problems have not been taken up as central concerns of social research. Pollution-purity and the encompassing power of caste have been taken up as a positive dimension of the caste system. The usual pretension is that class antagonism, class consciousness and class unity are not found as Karl Marx had seen, hence no class analysis. However, this is not true. Caste is a system of harmonic relations from a particular perspective only, it is also a system of opposition and antagonism from another perspective, and the latter has not been taken up seriously.

The mode of production and class contradictions are essential features of the Marxian approach to social stratification. Gough (1980) considers the mode of production as a social formation in which she finds interconnections of caste, kinship, family, marriage and even rituals with the forces of production and production relations. Gough's study of Thanjavur explains the emergence of a new bourgeoisie, the polarization of the peasantry, and the pauperization of the working class due to historical transformations in the mode of production. The totality of contradictions in social stratification can be seen through the contradictions in the mode of production. Marxist ideologists like Namboodaripad (1979) and Ranadive (1979) consider class relationships as a domain assump-tion in the treatment of caste and kinship in India. Even *varna* and the *jajmani* system can be explained in terms of class relations as they are embedded in the mode of production (Meillassoux, 1973). Others who have used the mode of production as the framework for analysis of class relations in village India are: Djurfeldt and Lind-berg (1975), Heera Singh (1979), Thorner (1969), Saith and Tanakha (1972), and Bhardwaj and Das (1975).

The main classes today in India are: (i) agrarian, (ii) industrial, (iii) business and mercantile, and (iv) professional. Contradictions can be found between various classes in terms of continuance of the old classes and the emergence of new ones at the same time. Industrial, business and professional classes characterize urban India, and landowners, tenants, sharecroppers and agricultural labourers are found in the countryside. These classifications have ideological overtones. The classification comprising landowners, moneylenders and labourers does not refer necessarily to class antagonism. But the other classification comprising the bourgeoisie, capitalist-type landowners, rich peasants, landless peasantry and agricultural labourers necessarily refers to class interaction, dependence-independence and conflict as the basic elements of class structure.

Theoretical Orientation

Approaches to the concepts of caste and class bear ideological contents. The methodology and data used in the studies of caste and class provided legitimacy to these approaches. Caste was treated not as a 'social formation', but as an encompassing institution which encompassed all other aspects of Hindu society. However, caste, in fact, was more than a 'ritualistic' mechanism, and it could face a variety of forces and constraints due to its all-inclusive character. If it were simply a ritualistic arrangement, it would have crumbled down long ago due to its very cumbersome nature. The social formation of Indian society comprises class, ethnicity, power, religion and economy along with caste. All these aspects of the social formation are incorporated into each other. They provide an understanding of the historicity of Indian society including that of caste and class. Indigenization of the concepts of caste and class must come from the realization of such a formation and the totality of its historicity.

The approaches such as the functional, dialectical, psychological and structuralist are inadequate for explaining the historicity of the Indian situation as they are rooted in the experience of the situations that are unfamiliar with India's historicity. Issues relating to caste and class were raised and debated elsewhere and subsequently passed on to Indian scholars through the mechanism of the academic hegemony of western scholars. Whether caste is a cultural phenomenon or a structural aspect, whether it should be studied by participant observation or by using survey method, whether it should be treated as the sole representative institution or class, power and religion should also be studied, whether 'caste alone'should be studied—have been raised by western scholars and later on taken up by their Indian counterparts with the tacit understanding of promoting certain ideas upheld by them. We must examine carefully why structural-functionalism has become so popular, why participant observation is regarded as a sacrosanct technique of research, why Redfield's notions of 'little community' and 'peasant society' or Marriott's notions of Little and Great Traditions and parochialization and universalization have gained currency. One view is that the Brahminocentric sociology produced by Srinivas is due to such indoctrination by these academic forces.

In an earlier study, Singh (1974) provides a paradigm of social stratification in the light of cultural versus structural and particular versus universal characteristics. The types that emerge from these criteria are: (i) cultural-universalistic; (ii) cultural-particularistic; (iii) structural-universalistic; and (iv) structural-particularistic. This paradigm is based on Parson's analysis of social structure. Singh's analysis shows relevance of the structural-particularistic type for analyzing social stratification in India. However, Singh does not provide reasons for the suitability of such a classification. Nomology is the obvious reason for Singh's scientism. However, in a recent study, Singh (1981) provides another classification of the studies on social stratification carried out in the 1970s. The main theoretic concerns are: (i) structural-functional; (ii) structuralist; (iii) structural-historical; and (iv) his-torical-materialist or Marxist. I have already referred to some of the studies which have been analyzed under the rubric of these approaches. Caste is the central concern of all the researchers including the Marxists.

Caste is an all-inclusive institution and it subsumes class relations. Any departure from caste is treated as incongruence between caste, status, wealth and power, hence the emergence of class relations. Such a view is known as the structural-functional. Change within the caste (sanskritisation), resilience and consensus are the hallmarks of structural-functionalism. Dumont is the most well known proponent of structuralism. The pivotal notions of this approach are reflected in *Dumont's Homo Hierarchicus* (1970). Singh (1981) points out ideology, dialectics, transforma-tional relationship and comparison as the salient features of Dumont's study of caste. For Dumont, hierarchy is ideology, and hierarchy implies ranking based on the notion of purity-impurity. The opposition between pure and impure refers to binary tension or dialectics. Pure and impure imply exclusion as well as inclusion in regard to caste hierarchy. Hierarchy also refers to the relationship of the 'encompassing' and the 'encompassed'. The 'pure' encompasses the 'less pure' and so on. This applies to all the sections and aspects of society. Thus, change is in the society and not of the society.

Dumont's view falls short of all those points which have been indicated in regard to structural-functionalism. In addition to these points, Singh (1981) comments that Dumont's structuralism suffers both theoretically and substantively. Gould's notion of 'contra priest' (1967) also negates the dichotomy or binary opposition between the pure and impure. The lower caste men also function as priests, hence they become pure. But they remain impure being lower in the caste hierarchy. The implication of Dumont's treatment of caste is that caste and class are in binary opposition. Singh's (1981) comments on structuralism are as follows: "The structuralist's treatment of dialectics is dissociated from history. History, indeed, links essence to existence, form to content, superstructure to infrastructure and theory to practice. Devoid of such a sense of historical conjecture structuralism amounts to a set of conceptual schema, devoid of a basis in evolutionary changes in society. Its transformational relationships being a historical abound in tautologies."

In a study, Klass (1980) has raised the question of origin of caste. Klass projects a paradigm of the possible development of the caste system. The main idea is that clans exchange women, whereas the caste system exchanges goods without exchanging women. The explanation given by Klass is that India has developed ecosystems in which people have different modes of life, and the various human groups (corporate groups) would have a minimum of intercourse and not exchange women with outside groups. Thus, corporate groups form marriage circles. Klass relates caste with physical force and economic power. However, the corporateness of caste groups is equated with their egalitarian character, and this might be historically and substantively incorrect.

The understanding of caste and class demands an approach which has such as: (i) dialects, (ii) history, (iii) culture, and (iv) structure. Dialectics refers to the effective notions which bring about contradictions and highlight relations between unequal segments and men and women. Thus, it does not simply mean binary fission in the cognitive structure of Indian society as perceived by structuralists in terms of pure and impure. History provides a substantial account of the conditions of human existence. It is not a conjectural construction based on mythology, scriptures and ideations. Culture defines the rules of the game, the nature of relations between the haves and the have-nots. Thus culture does not include only cultural practices, rituals, *rites de passage,* etc. Structure is a product of dialectical contradictions, historical forces, and a certain 'formation'. Once it has emerged, it becomes a sort of force in determining the course of history, the nature of contradictions and the evaluational standards. Thus, structure refers to relations between social segments at a point of time as a historical product and as an existent reality.

Dialectics, history, culture and structure refer to a combination of theory, structure and process about the social formation (both caste and class) of Indian society. Together they explain the historicity of Indian society from the point of its genesis. The debates today are: whether changes in caste and class are 'transformational' or they are 'replacements', whether caste is 'closed' and class is 'open' ; whether caste is 'organic' and whether class is 'segmentary' ; and whether caste is replaced by class. These are questions which have come up quite often as the idea of 'social formation' has not gained currency in our understanding of caste and class. The obse-ssion of considering caste and class as polar opposites has prevented us from thinking of caste and class as dimensions of the historicity of India's social formation.

Several scholars have denied the 'congruence' version about caste, class and power in the ancient India. They have conclusively established that social mobility existed in ancient and medieval India. The *jajmani* system was never completely 'organic' in practice. The idea of the contrapriest exposes the hollowness of the concepts of hierarchy and pollution-purity. In the place of sanskritisation, westernisation and dominant caste etc., it is necessary to study downward mobility and proletarianization, upward mobility and embourgeoisiement, urban incomes for the rural people and the migration of the rural rich to towns, and rural non-agricultural income and mobility etc.

Caste has inhered in class and class has inhered in caste for centuries in the Indian context, and Indian society continues to have this inseparable mix even today. Role of caste and class in elections is an evidence of this mix. However, caste operates as a 'marriage circle' in a different way from the way it functions in other arenas. Hypergamy explains the role of status and wealth within caste. Class-like distinctions within caste and caste-like styles within a class are part of the people's life situations. 'Class' has been an in-built mechanism within caste, and therefore, caste cannot be seen simply as a 'ritualistic'system, and class cannot be seen as an open system as it has often been influenced by the institution of caste. In order to go deep into such a phenomenon the structural-historical perspective becomes inescapable.

7

Family Issues

The traditional literature of pre-British India, including the Vedas, Smritis, Epics, Purans as and other literary works, and Buddhist and Jain literature, provides information on the religious, social and political life of the Hindus. The source material is not all of the same kind, nor equally rich in all sectors of social life. In the field of marriage and kinship, however, the material is more copious than in some others, but a few limitations of the data need to be mentioned. It is obvious that the material covers only the Hindus, and among them only the higher castes. This latter fact has been frequently ignored; worse still the institutions and beliefs of the "twice-born", and especially the Brahmins have been interpreted to be the institutions and beliefs of all Hindus. Thus, the ban on divorce and widow marriage has been unquestionably assumed to hold good for all whereas it hords good only for the "twice-born" castes. Again, it is assumed that the rules governing marriage, adoption, inheritance, inrer-caste relations, etc., were observed by everyone, everywhere, while it is likely that the degree of observance varied from one section of the society to another and from one part of India to another. Intensive field research carried out in recent years in different parts of India has thrown a great deal of doubt on the picture which Indologists had presented to the scholarly world about Indian society. It is now seen that this represented a book view and an upper caste view, and that the reality was far more complicated and diversified.

While there is much variation between different groups in the customs and beliefs regarding marriage and kinship, the institution of marriage itself is common to all. It is well known that marriage is an essential duty for all Hindus. It is a sacrament, and among the "twice-born" castes religious considerations are espe-cially prominent in making marriage obligatory. A son is thought to be necessary because he performs periodical rituals, including the annual *Sraddha,* which keep the dead ancestors out of a hell called put. Marriage enables the individual to enter the second stage of *garhostya* (householdership), and through its ritual the husband and wife perform five great sacrifices to the creator *(Brahma),* ancestors, deities, elements, and fellow human beings. Among the *non-dvija* castes, however, marriage has a more secular character. In the rural areas a son is essential to cultivate the family land and to look after the parents in their old age. Even among the *dvija* castes, the secular importance of marriage is considerable, often huge dowries being paid to the groom.

Table : Median age at Marriage of those Married up to Age 52.5

Country	*Females*	*Males*
Egypt	19.4	25.2
Canada	21.1	24.11
U. S. A.	20.4	23.2
Japan	23.1	25.8
India	14.5	20.0
U. K.	21.9	25.2
W. Germany	24.7	27.4
France	22.6	26.0
Guatemala	18.69	22.88

Marriage among Muslims is a contract, which a man and a woman enter into by mutual agreement, but rituals are performed on the occasion of marriage. A sermon (khutba) sanctifies the contract before the parties announce their acceptance of it.

Early marriage is still common in India though the marriage age has been going up in the last few decades among the urban and educated sections. The median age at marriage in different countries is given in Table below:

It is seen that India has the lowest median age at marriage both for females and males. The highest median age at marriage is registered by West Germany.

Table : Mean Age at Marriage of Religious Groups in India

Religious Groups	*Female*	*Male*
Hindus	12.5	19.7
Jains	13.1	20.5
Muslims	13.2	21.0
Sikhs	15.0	22.5
Christians	17.1	23.9

There are significant differences between the various religious groups and castes in the matter of age at marriage. Dr. Agarwala observes, on the basis of census data for the 1891-1931 period, that Christians have the highest mean age at marriage (17.1 for females and 23.9 for males) followed in order, by Sikhs, Muslims and Hindus. Dr. Agarwala also states that women of the Harijan castes have the lowest mean age at marriage followed respectively by Brahmins, and Warrior (Kshatriya) and Trading (Vaisya) castes, except in Mysore, Madras and Kerala where Brahmin women have the lowest mean age at marriage. The same pattern is found to prevail for men also. A caution must be entered here about the above generalizations for different *varnas*. It includes innume-rable *jatis* speaking different languages and also differing from each other in several other respects. Thus two Brahmin groups from different parts of the country differ from each other in impor-tant respects the marriage age of Brahmin girls in South India has gone up strikingly since the thirties. Even within the same linguistic region, two *jatis* belonging to the same *varna* may differ from each other in custom, ritual and way of life.

The Hindu Marriage Act of 1955 prescribes the minimum age of marriage as 18 for boys and 15 for girls. But this law is not strictly enforced. This is specially true of rural areas where the marriage age for girls is usually lower than 15.

Institution of Marriage

Attempts were made to classify Hindu marriages as early as the beginning of the Christian era. Manu classified them into eight forms : *Brahma, Daiva, Arya, Prajapatya, Asura, Gandharva, Rak-shasa* and *Paisacha*. The *Asura* and *Paisacha* forms were both regarded as unlawful. Commentators coming after Manu accepted the eight-fold classification though they evaluated the relative merits of each form differently. Generally, the first four forms were regarded as good or merit-conferring. The above classifica-tion was apparently an "ideal" one and not the outcome of an analysis of different forms of marriage obtaining among different sections of early Indian society.

Monogamy, polygamy and polyandry all occur amongst Hindus. Here it is necessary to distinguish between what is permitted and what is practised. Until the passage of the Hindu Marriage Act in 1955, every Hindu was in theory free to marry a number of women. In fact, however, a very small percentage of Hindus were polygynous. The barrenness of a wife or her failure to give birth to a son was generally the reason for taking a second wife. Among some trading to warrior castes, a wealthy or powerful man took a second wife. Among the higher castes monogamy prevailed, the ideal of having only one wife *(ekapatnivrata)* being as old as the *Ramayana*.

That applies to the Jains also, but they have no religious necessity for a son; Muslims are permitted to take four wives each, provided all are treated as equal. Again, the actual incidence of polygamy among Muslims is small; only the wealthy and powerful occasionally take a second wife. Christians are forbidden to take a second wife.

Polyandry-the custom of having more husbands than one is even less common than polygamy. A few Kerala castes practised polyandry until recently and it is not unlikely that it still continues to be practised to some extent in remote places. The Todas and Kotas of the Nilgiris, the Khasa of Jaunsar Bawar (Dehra Dun District) and a few other North Indian castes also practise polyandry. There are two forms of polyandry, fraternal and disparate. In the fraternal form, the husbands are brothers, while in the disparate, the husbands are not related to each other. The Nayars of Kerala formerly practised disparate polyandry, whereas in the Cis-Himalayan region the fraternal form is practised even today.

In the latter area the eldest brother has more rights in the wife than his younger brothers. Amongst the Todas, it is the eldest brother who marries a girl but the younger brothers also have access to her. The eldest brother performs a ceremony with a bow and arrow in the seventh month of the wife's pregnancy and this makes him the legal father of the child. In fact, he is the father of all the children born subsequently till another brother performs the bow-and-arrow ceremony. The Todas formerly practised femafe infanticide and this meant that there were fewer women than men. With the' abolition of infanticide, women became more numerous and the Todas began to combine polyan-dry with polygamy.

Leviratic alliances occur among the Ahirs of Hariyana, some Jats and Gujars and several other castes in Uttar Pradesh, the Kodagus of Mysore, and among some Muslim castes. In a leviratic marriage, a man is obliged to marry the widow of a brother, and the children born to the new couple are their own, whereas in levirate proper a man has sex relations with his brother's widow to continue the dead brother's line. In the leviratic alliances mentioned above it is customary for the widow to marry the husband's younger brother, and not the husband's elder brother, though the latter is not unknown. Sororatic alliances, *i.e.*, the marriage of a widower with his wife's younger sister occur in South India and probably in other areas as well.

A widower is permitted to marry in all religious groups but that is not true of a widow. Widow remarriage is permitted among Muslims, Christians and Parsis. Among the Jains, local and caste custom determines the question. For instance, among the lower Jain castes of the Deccan, widow remarriage is common. Though it is allegedfy forbidden among the Jain Baniyas of the former Central Provinces, it occurs frequently among them.

Widow marriage is common among the Hindus of the "lower" castes. But when a low caste wants to move up in the hierarchy, it imposes a ban on such marriage as also on divorce. The widespread belief that widow marriage is prohibited in Hinduism is an example of the way in which a Brahmin institution is mistaken for the institution of all Hindus. The Hindu Widows Remarriage Act, 1856, 1egalized the remarriage of Hindus of all castes.

Hindu marriage is in theory a sacrament and irrevocable. Actually, divorce is practised among *non-dvija* castes in every part of the country. It was particularly easy among the matrilineal Nayars even as recently as sixty years ago. The husband had to supply his wife with oil and cloth at three calendrical festivals and his failure to do so was regarded as a sufficient ground for divorce. Divorce is also permitted among tribal folk. The Khasis, for instan-ce, allow divorce for adultery, barrenness and incompatibilitly. Consent of the elders, and occasionally of the local panchayat as well, is a necessary condition for the grant of divorce.

During 1940-48, several provinces and States passed laws permitting divorce for Hindus. The Hindu Marriage Act of 1955 allows divorce for incurable insanity, incurable and virulent leprosy, and venereal diseases in an acute form. Presumption of death, conversion to another religion, assumption of *sanyasa* and adul-tery also provide grounds for divorce. A wife is entitled to sue for divorce if her husband commits rape, sodomy or bestiality.

Divorce is allowed in other religious groups also. There are two forms of divorce among Muslims: divestiture (*khul*) and dis-missal *(talaq.)* .In the former, divorce is the result of friendly agree-ment between husband and wife, and *mehr* (dower) has to be returned by the wife to her husband. In *talaq,* the husband has the right to dismiss his wife by thrice repeating the dismissal formula. The wife's right to demand divorce is conceded by the *Quran ('Hadith')*. The dissolution of Muslim Marriage Act, 1939, enables a Muslim wife to seek the dissolution of her marriage on certain grounds.

In most societies there are rules, positive as well as negative, regarding the selection of spouses. The positive rules lay down whom a person may marry, while the negative rules lay down whom he may not marry. Thus endogamy and hypergamy specify the groups in which a person is expected to find a bride, while exogamous rules prohibit him from marrying in certain groups. Endogamy and hypergamy are both intimately related to the caste structure. A man has to marry within his subcaste or *jati*. *Varna* affiliation is not as significant as *jati* affiliation for purposes of endogamy. For the vast majority of the people, however, the endogamous unit consists of a series of kin-clusters living in a fairly restricted area. In South India the preference for marrying people related in specific ways as also the absence of a ban on marrying members of one's own village, results in restricting the field of marriage socially as well as spatially. Village exogamy as well as, the ban on the marriage of cross-cousins, which are features of North India, extend the field. This is further accentuated in the Ganga valley where the village which receives girls in marriage regards itself as superior to the villages which supply girls to it, and therefore refuses to give its girls in return to the latter. Two factors which limit the field in the North should also be mentioned: the tendency to marry into villages not farther than 12 or 13 km away and to confine material links to a few kin-groups.

Endogamous *jatis* also exist among Sikhs, Jains, Christians and Muslims. The Syeds, the aristocratic Muslim caste, are, divided into endogamous groups. Sometimes the endogamous group is so small that it includes only the extended families of a man's parents. Such a group is called a *kufw,* while the maximal endogamous group is called *hiradari.* Among some Gujarati castes there is strict spatial delimitation of the endogamous field.

Hypergamy occurs in different parts of India: among the Brahmins of Bengal; Anavil Brahmins and Leva-Patidars of Gujarat; Rajputs in Gujarat and Rajasthan; Marathis of Maharashtra, and Nayars, Kshatriyas and Ambalavisis of Kerala. Hypergamy tends to occur where the structural gulf is narrow in fact it may be said to occur among the different sections of a single caste rather than between castes which are widely separated. The custom of high caste Nayar women having *sambandam* with Nambudri Brahmin men is perhaps an exception to the rule, but *sambandam* is not exactly marriage. This is related to the tendency to minimize the husband's and father's role, an important feature of the Nayarkinship system. Not all Nayar marriages are hypergamous. It may be noted here that in the traditional literature of India hypergamous *(anuloma)* marriages are permitted while hypoga-mous *(pratiloma)* marriages are prohibited. According to the latest legislation, all inter-casre marriages, whether of the hypergamous or hypogamous kind, are valid.

In Bengal, the Rarhiya Brahmins are divided into three *jatis,* Kulin, Bansaj, and Srotriya. The last mentioned are sub-divided into Suddha Srotriya and Kasta Srotriya. The Kulins are the highest among the three *jiitis* and Kulin bridegrooms are in great demand.

A few decades ago, the demand for Kulin men was so great that they could (and did) demand huge dowries from the parents of girls who sought to marry them. It also gave rise to polygamy among Kulins.

Leva-Patidar hypergamy is more intricate than the Kulin hypergamy. The Patidar of Charotar are divided into the people of the twenty-six, twelve and finally six villages respectively. The women of the first group may marry men in the first, second and third groups, while the women in the second group may marry men in the second and third groups, and the women in the third group only men in the third group. This means that there is a great demand for men in the third group. Huge dowries are paid to Patidar bridegrooms.

Educated Indians are critical of the institution of hypergamy, and especially of the large dowries associated with it. The classical form of Kulin hypergamy has disappeared, while the Nayar practice of entering into *sambandam* alliance with Nambudris is on its way out. But Patidar hypergamy continues to flourish.

Exogamous rules are complementary to endogamous rules and they prohibit marriage between members of the same group. As mentioned earlier, in North India, high caste Hindus regard the village as an exogamous unit. Girls born within the village are called "village daughters" and they do not cover their faces before local men, whereas girls who come into the village by marriage do so.

Two other kinds of exogamy have to be mentioned: *sagotra* and *sapinda*. Gotra-exogamy applies in its fullness to all the "twice-born" castes. These castes have a tradition of descent from certain sages who are believed to have lived in the remote past, and two persons claiming descent from the same *gotra-rsis,* even when they came from different linguistic areas, were forbidden from marrying each otter. It may be added that several ambitious non-Brahminical castes have either claimed descent from traditional *gotra-rsis* or have invented new *gotras.* The Lalgayats of Mysore have *gotras* which are quite different from the Brahminical *gotras.* Gujars, Ahirs, Jats and other castes in villages near Delhi have *gotras* but these are also different from Brahminical *gotras.* Often, a non-Brahmin caste which was divided into exogambus clans, with each clan claiming descent from a plant or animal, changed the totem names for *gotra-rsis.* The Hindu

Marriage Act of 1955 legalizes marriage between members of the same *gotra*.

The marriage of *sapinda* relatives is prohibited among Hindus. The term *sapinda* has two meanings: (1) those who share the particles of the same body; and (2) those who are united by offering balls of cooked rice *(pinda)* to the same dead ancestors. Hindu lawgivers vary in defining the kinship group outside which marriage may occur. Gautama takes an extreme position, prohibiting seven generations (called "degrees" in Hindu law) on the father's side and five on the mother's. But several others have narrowed the circle to permit the marriage of crosscousins; *i.e.,* descendants from the same pair of grandparents may marry, so long as they are not parallel cousins. The Hindu Marriage Act of 1955 bans marriage within five generations on the agnatic side and three on the mother's side. But it permits the marriage of cross-cousins where this is customary.

The observance of pollution at birth and death marks off the members of a kin-group, patrilineal as well as matrilineal full pollution obtains among the closest relatives; and who the closest relatives depends on the form of the kinship system. Broadly speaking, patrilineal relatives are regarded as closer than affinal or cognatic relatives among patrilineal: castes; and matrilineal relatives are regarded as closer than patrilineal relatives among matrilineal castes.

The patrilineal joint family is an important exogamous unit among most Hindus. The enormous amount of attention bestowed on *sagotra* and *sapinda* exogamy has served to obscure this simple fact. In some parts of South India, the institution of domestic deity *(mane devaru, vittu perumiil)* serves to define the exogamous unit in the absence of known genealogical links. The institution of surname serves a similar purpose in certain other areas, though identical surnames are not always evidence of the existence of agnatic or matrilineal relationship.

With Christians and Muslims, the elementary or nuclear family is the exogamous unit. Outside of it, marriages are possible. Moplah Muslims of North Malabar live in matrilineal units and among them the matrilineage is the exogamous unit. Lineage exogamy also exists among the Muslim Gujjars of Jammu and Kashmir.

Sub-caste endogamy does obtain among Muslims, even though it is not as rigid as among the Hindus. Castes at either end of the scale appear to be more particular about observing endogamous rules than the middle-range castes. For instance, generally speaking, a Syed marries another Syed, and a Shaikh another Shaikh. Sometimes, however, a Syed man may marry a Shaikh girl but a Syed girl would not normally marry a Shaikh boy. This would be against the rule of hypergamy which is occasionally practised. Hypergamous marriages occur particularly among converts to Islam from Jat and Rajput castes. Castes which consider themselves mutually equal, such as the artisan castes, inter-marry among themselves. But then castes which are considered equal in one area may be regarded as unequal in another. In Eastern Uttar Pradesh, the Darzi (Tailor) and Julaha (Weaver) are regarded as mutually equal and inter-marry, while in the western part of the State the Darzi regards himself superior and does not inter-marry with the Julaha.

The Sikhs are generally endogamous, though hypergamy does occur occasionally among castes with a tradition of hypergamy (e.g., Jats) prior to conversion. The Jewish sub-divisions, mentioned earlier, are endogamous. Among Parsis, the Dasturs (priests) accept girls in marriage from the non-Dastfirs but do not give their girls to the latter.

We have already mentioned that in South India marriage with some relatives is preferred. In the Marathi-Telugu-Tamil and Kannada speaking areas, marriages with the cross-cousin and cross-niece are preferred. Descendants of the siblings of the same sex are paralleled cousins to each other, while descendants of the opposite sex are cross-cousins to each other. Similarly, a man is parallel uncle to his brother's children and a cross-uncle to his sister's children. Among the higher castes, however, marriage with the father's sister's daughter is not popular. But marriages with the maternal uncle's daughter and cross-niece are both preferred and such preference finds expression in ritual and custom. Horo-scopes may not be consulted when a relative is being married. Among Telugu Komatis (traders) there is a strong obligation to marry the mother's brother's daughter or elder sister's daughter. The marriage of near kin helps to mitigate the conflict between mother-in-law and daughter-in-law and thereby strengthens the patrilineal joint family.

Among the matrilineal Nayars marriage with the mother's brother's daughter is preferred. In the Nayar kinship system, while the maternal uncle is the actual or potential head of the *tarawad"* his own children are in his wife's *tarawd*. The marriage of a man's daughters with his cross-nephews helps to continue in the next generation the link which has been forged in bis generation between the natal *tarawd* and his conjugal *tarawad,*. Likewise, the son's marriage with his maternal uncle's daughter continues the bond between his natal *tarawikf* and his mother's brother's Conjugal *tarawad*. The net result is a model in which three *tarawd* are continually linked with each other through kin marriages. Marriage between a cross-uncle and niece, so favoured in the other regions of South India, is forbidden among Nayars, since the maternal uncle is in *loco parentis* to his nieces {and nephews). Preferential marriage with the father's sister's daughter occurs among the matrilineal Giros in Assam.

South Indian Jains prefer cross-cousin marriage, and the Jaids of Karnataka even practise cross-uncle-niece marriage. Muslims show a preference for marriage with the father's brother's daughter. Among the Syrian Christians of Kerala, and several other groups in South, as well as North India, the exchange of brother and sister is often practised: X marries Y's sister and Y in turn marries X's sister. "Exchange marriage" circumvents the obligation to pay dowry. "Exchange marriages" occur among the Kannadigas though they are not approved.

A traditional marriage is more the concern of two groups of kindred than of two individuals. Each kin-group has an interest in the marriage and its continuance. The head of the household and his wife take the initiative in finding the bride or groom. Among the higher castes and especially the Brahmins, the parents of the girl go in search of the groom while among the lower castes it is the other way about. Among the former, a dowry has often to be paid to the bridegroom. The Nambudris of Kerala, the Cetpyars and Brahmins of the Tamil country, the Patidrs of Charotar in Gujarat and the Rajputs are among those who pay high dowries. The dowry system has extended to the lower castes also. Among non-Hindus, the Syrian Christians of Kerala, Sikhs and Jains pay dowry.

In rural North India, the Barber acts as match-maker for non-Brahmin castes. Brahmin priests may also perform the role of intermediaries. In Bengal, the *Ghafaks* were professional match-makers. The preference for marrying certain relatives in South India reduces the need for the services ot a professional match maker. The urban middle classes have started using the advertisement columns of newspapers to secure brides and grooms.

The matching of the horoscopes of the boy and girl, the exchange of gifts between the two parties, and elaborate ritual are all features of the traditional type of marriage. And the kingroup of the boy and girl have an important say at every stage of the marriage. It is only among the westernised and urban sections of Indians that the boy or girl has a dominant voice in the choice of partner. Inter-caste and inter-regional marriages are becoming increasingly frequent among them.

Rites are a very important part of marriage and they show great variation not only from one region to another, but also within a single region on the basis of religion, sect, caste, income and rural-urban residence. The sacramental character of Hindu marriage is particularly evident among the 'twice-born" castes and especially the Brahmins. The marriage rites include the ritual of engagement *(niscitartha)* , the fixing of an auspicious day and time *(muharta)* for the wedding ceremony, the reception of the bridegroom by the bride's parents *(kaszyatra* and *varapaja).* The formal seeing of the bride *(mukhadarasana),* the mutual garlanding of bride and groom, the giving of the bride to the groom *(kanyadana),* clasping of the bride's hand *(panrigrahana),* circumambulation of the sacrificial fire *(agniparirnaya),* the offering of parched grain to the sacrificial fire *(lajahoma),* and walking the seven steps *(saptapadi).* We have only mentioned the main items of ritual which form the core round which is built an ela borate complex of rites. The rites and accompanying hymns are taken from the Vedas, Grhya Sutras and Smritis. The existence of a ban on the use. of Vedic mantras in the weddings of the lower castes has led to the adoption of *mantras* from the Puranas, to accompany Vedic rites. Every wedding, whether Brahmin or Harijan, also includes ritual performed exclusively by women.

Weddings also mean processions; the feasting of relatives, castefolk and villagefolk, fireworks; and sometimes dancing by women of the Courtesan caste. Formerly, among the landowning and trading castes, marriage rites continued for three to five days and involved considerable expense. A recent tendency, among the

Westernised sections, is to reduce the ritual to the minimum. An opposite tendency may be seen among the more prosperous of the lower castes; they are adopting Sanskritic ritual and custom in order to move up in the hierarchy.

It is necessary to stress that the Sanskritic and sacramental elements are minimal in the wedding ritual of some "low" castes and tribes. Among some Kerala tribes marriage "ritual" consist in nothing more than the exchange of new cloth between the bride and groom. Even among a high caste like the Nayars, the exchange of clothes mutual garlanding and circumambulation of lighted lamps constitute marriage. (We are excluding from our consideration the elaborate pre-marital ritual of *talikattukalyanam).*

The increasing Sanskritisation of the "low" castes has made marriage ritual more complex among them, and has often necessitated the employment of a Brahmin or Sanskritised non-Brahmin priest. For example, the Ilavans (TIyans) of Kerala, traditionally toddy-tappers, have accepted Sanskritisation of customs and rituals, including wedding ritual, under the leadership of the late Sri Narayana Guru. In the Punjab the Arya Samaj has been an agent of Sanskritisation, and in Gujarat the Swaminarayan a movement has played a similar role. It is interesting to note that the most Sanskritised castes at the top are reducing ritual and becoming more Westernised.

The marriage rites of the two Jain sects, Digambara and Svetambara, are identical in important respects. They are on the whole similar to Hindu marriage rites, and vary in some respects from region to region. The main rites are engagement *(vagdana,* promise), the presentation of jewellery by the groom's father to the bride *(pradana)* the giving of the bride to the groom *(kanyadana or varana),* the groom clasping the bride's hand *(panigrahana)* and the seven steps *(saptapadi).*

Muslim marriage rites show some variation on the basis of sect and region. Among the high caste Sunni Muslims in Uttar Pradesh, marriage negotiations begin with a mediator approaching the bride's kin on behalf of the groom's kin. When the proposal is accepted, the sum to be paid as *mehr* to the bride is agreed upon and a date fixed for the wedding. The groom's kin send sweets to the bride's kin. On the wedding day, the groom's party goes in procession to the bride's house. The bride's parents make gifts of clothes to the groom who puts them on. When a represen-tative *(vakil)* of the groom goes to the bride, accompanied by two witnesses. After obtaining the bride's formal consent, the party returns to the groom to secure his consent. The *kazi* then recites a passage in which are mentioned all the famous marriages in the Islamic tradition. A prayer follows and then the *vakil* goes with the witnesses to the women's quarters where the marriage is confirmed.

The Shiahs differ from the Sunnis only with respect to the ritual in Which the formal consent of the bridegroom is sought and obtained. Two *mudjtahids* (priests) stand facing each other, one representing the bride and the other the groom, and one asks the other whether the party he represents. has given consent.

Converts to Islam from Hinduism retain some of their pre-conversion rites. Blunt noted in 1931 that several Muslim castes employed a Brahmin priest to fix an auspicious day and time for wedding ritual. Muslim Bhats, for instance, first celebrate marriage in the Hindu way and then in the Islamic way.

Converts to Christianity also retain some of the customs, of their former castes. For instance, the South Indian Hindu rite of tying the *tali* by the groom to the bride is also an essential part of the marriage ritual of the Syrian Christians of Kerala.

The Special Marriage Act, 1954 provides for secular, civil marriage which may be dissolved by mutual consent. The Act applies to all Indian citizens who choose to avail themselves of its provisions, irrespective of religious affiliation. Civil marriage enables persons to avoid the expense of traditional weddings.

Reformers and writers on Indian economics have deplored the huge cost of weddings, especially among the peasantry. The amount of money spent varies according to income, caste, region, rural-urban residence and the extent of westernisation. Generally, among the patrilineal high castes, marriage means heavy expense for the bride's kin. Large sums of money, gifts of jewellery, furniture, vessels and clothes have to be offered. In some parts of the country there is a "tariff" for grooms based on education, the kind of job held, and the amount of ancestral wealth. Among some castes, however, not only is there no dowry, but the groom's kin have to incur more expenditure than the bride's kin. Among the Okkaligas (Peasants) of Mysore, for instance, the groom's representatives have to state at the marriage agreement ceremony the details of the jewellery and clothes they are going to give to the bride. A similar situation obtains among the Marathas.

Before the Indian rural economy became monetized to the present extent, the various castes which contributed to the work of the wedding were paid in grain and cooked food. Also, ostentatious display on the part of the lower castes was not encouraged by the locally dominant caste. Nowadays, the lower castes imitate the higher freely. In several parts of India, relatives, neighbours and friends of the bridal party are required to make cash contributions, which have to be returned when a wedding takes place in each donor's household.

Close Relationship

The sucia institution of marriage ensures the children born of it a recognized and legally sanctioned position in society. Where marriage is monogamous, the husband and wife become the nucleus of a domestic group. A domestic group consisting of a man and his wife and unmarried children is called an elementary or nuclar family. The elementary family is widespread over the world, either by itself or as a part of a wider group.

It is not only in a polyandrous or polygynous marriage that the elementary family is part of a wider domestic group. Often a group of married brothers and their wives and children are found to live under a single roof under the authority of the eldest brother. Or the domestic group consists of a man and his wife, his married sons and their children. Domestic groups which are bigger than the elementary family, and often include two or more elementary families, are termed joint or extended families. They may be patrilineal, as in most parts of India, or matrilineal as among the Nayars of Kerala or the Khasis of Assam. Several joint families descended from the same ancestor, and acting together on certain occasions form a lineage.

In several parts of the country people live in lineage groups. Large lineages were probably more frequent during the nineteenth century than they are today. The members of the lineage lived under the same roof, or in a group of neighbouring houses, held property together, and ate together. Such a lineage formed a coparcenary, every member (male in the case of a patrilineage and female in the case of a matrilineage) having a share in the ancestral property. Among some groups, including the Nayars, Nambudris and Kodagus ancestral property was traditionally impartible. Over a hundred years ago, village headmen in Bundel-khand periodically redistributed the arable land among the lineages of the dominant landowning castes. The same was true of the Pathans of the North-West Frontier Province. In the Thanjavur District it was common for arable land in a village to be owned by members of a patrilineage who were called *pangali* (sharers).

The matrilineage of the Nayars is called *tarawad* and it consists of all the descendants, .in the female line, of an ancestress. A Nayar household may include a woman, her brothers and youn-ger sisters, her children, and her sisters' children and her daughters' children and her sisters' daughters' children. The Nayars are not a single caste but a group of castes divided into high and low, and some of the high caste Nayars owned land while the others held land on the twelve-year *Kanam* lease from those (Nambudris or Kshatriya Nayars) with a superior title to land. These lessees in turn sublet land to tenant cultivators on a three-year tenure.

In pre-British Kerala, Nayars formed the soldiery of the Zamorin of Calicut, the Rajas of Cochin and local rulers. Nayar men either remained in the villages, looking after land, or stayed in a prince's court as soldiers. Except in North Malabar a Navar girl was not required to leave far her natal home on marriage. She cantinued to stay with her sisters, brothers, mother and mother's brothers and sisters. The husband was only a visitar and the children born of the marriage were regarded as members of the mother's natal *tarawd*. The oldest living male was the manager of the *tarawiad* and it was his duty to look after its praperty which was cansidered impartible. The members lived in the ancestral hame, situated an the ancestral estate, which included a sacred serpent-grave *(kavu*) and even crematian ground. The *tarawad* was a carparatian which continued in perpetuity.

Nambudri Brahmins lived in patrilineages which were called *Warn*. The Nambudri house, like the Nayar house, was situated on the ancestral estate, and near it were the serpent-grove and crematian ground. The Nambudris were landowners and their land was leased to Nayars an *Kanam* tenure. Land was considered impartible, and impartibility was ensured by the rule of primogeniture. Only the eldest san was permitted to marry a Nambudri girl and the yaunger sons had liaison *(sarnbandam)* with girls belonging to the higher Nayar castes. The yaunger sons visited their partners at night and the children born of the union became members af their mather's *sons.* The Nambutdri *illam* cansisted of a man, his wife or wives his children, and his younger brothers. Sometimes the *illam* included his oId parents or his eldest son's children.

The *okka* af the Kodagus resembled the Nambudri *illam.* It cansisted of all the descendants, though males only,of an ancestor and their wives and children. The oldest living male was usually the head of the *okka.* The *okka* hause was situated on the ancestral estate, and until 1840 land was regarded as impartible. Just as primogeniture helped to ensure the impartibility of land, the institution af leviratic alliance helped to contribute to the unity of the *okka.* The members of an *okka* regarded the spirits of dead ancestors *(karanavar)* with reverence and periodically prapitiated them.

Among the paarer and uneducated folk in rural areas, the residential groups generally tend to be small, being confined to members of the elementary family and one or two other relatives. In this section of the population, the falpily group holds together during the father's lifetime, partition being usual after his death. Among the richer rural folk and among the urban-educated, jaint families tend to be more frequent. A joint family consists of a man, his married sons and their wives and children, and his unmarried daughters. A joint family may persist even after the father's death, the eldest on becoming the head in place of the dead father. Occasianally a widowed sister or daughter and her children may be part of the joint family. An affinat relative of the head may also be living in a joint or elementary family.

The members of a joint family live under the same roof, eat from the same kitchen, perform their rituals together, and their common expenses are met out of the income of the ancestral estate. Every joint family has a manager who takes decisions on behalf of all. Every male member has a vested interest in the ancestral property. Some joint families are big, having as many as twenty or thirty or more members, while others are small. In the former case, it is usually found that members of three different generations are living together. In the latter, the joint family may cansist of an elementary family and one or two additional relations such as a younger unmarried brother or sister or niece of the head of the household.

A joint family loses members through marriage of its girls and through death, and gains members through marriage of the boys and through birth and adoption. Sometimes a woman returns to her natal joint family after the death of her husband. A joint family splits up into canstituent elementary families when partition occurs. But partitian is a periodical process, the elemen-tary families resulting from partition in time developing into joint families. Joint and elementary families are parts of a single cyclical process and failure to perceive this fact has resulted in much misinterpretation of facts.

The camposition of a joint family depends upon the mode of descent and the pattern of residence general to a group. Descent may be patrilineal or matrilineal or cognatic, and residence may be virilocal (staying with husband) or uxorilocal (staying with wife) or neolocal (both moving to a new house). Matrilineal descent does not always mean uxorilocal residence. In North Malabar descent is matrilineal but residence virilocal. A womao moves into her husband's house after marriage and the children born of the marriage stay with their parents till they reach adulthood and then they move into their mother's natal *tarawad.* The composition of a *tarawad.* in North Malabar may be similar to that of a patrilineal joint family, but the juridical rights of the members living in it are entirely different.

Virilocality is the general rule in India, and this is not confined to Hindus but extends to Muslims, Christians, Sikhs and Jains. The wife joins her husband soon after marriage and the latter generally lives with his own parents and brothers. It is only later, after the death of the parents, that the brothers separate from each other. Even this may not happen and the brothers may decide to stay together. Among the poorest groups and the lowest castes, the family breaks up soon after the parents' death. Among the highly westernised and urban sections, neolocality is coming to be the rule. But the establishment of a new home does not mean the severance of ties with kin-groups of the husband and wife. Kinship connections are recognized on both the sides and a close relative on either side may live with the couple. It may be added here that in recent years spatial mobility has increased considerably and young men have jobs away from their natal towns. This means that in urban areas there are many families which are seemingly elementary.

The female members of a Nayar *tarawad* receive their husband at night, while the male members go to their wives. So there is variation in the diurnal and nocturnal compositions of the Nayar *tarawad*. The custom of visiting wives and choice of place of residence is a complicated matter. Nowadays, in urban area patterns of residence are changing towards virilocality if not neolocality.

The Khasi of Assam are also matrlineal but the pattern of residence obtaining amongst them is somewhat different from that amongst the Nayars. Marriage is followed by matrilocal residence which lasts till a child is born, the couple then moving into a new house. But if the wife is the youngest daughter of her mother, the couple continues to stay in the wife's natal household permanently. A form of ultimogeniture seems to prevail amongst the Khasis. Among the Garos also, residence is uxorilocal.

While the composition of a household is usually determined by the particular principle of descent and the type of post-marital residence obtained in a caste, the bilateral principle finds greater recognition than is commonly thought. A household may include not only patrilineal relatives such as two full brothers, their wives, their children and unmarried sisters, but also the brother or sister of a wife of one of them. In a matrilineal household, on the other hand, increasing recognition of the bilateral principle may result in the parents of either the husband or wife residing with the couple. It may be added that among the urban and educated sections of the population the household consists of the husband, wife, their children and a relative of the husband, or less frequently a relative of the wife. These households are justifiably considered as part of wider kinship groups elsewhere. In big cities like Bombay and Calcutta high rents act as a limiting factor on the size of the household.

In the traditional Hindu joint family the senior male, either father or eldest brother or son, was usually the head of the household. It was his duty to look after the property, meet the expenses out of the income of the ancestral estate, and clear the debts. He was expected to keep the estate in good order and manage the resources carefully. The education of the younger members, the marriage of adults and the expenses of funeral ceremonies for the dead were all legitimate charges on the ancestral estate. The head of the household was the manager of the joint family corporation and as such he wielded much power and authority. The members, were expected to obey him in all matters. Even today in rural areas the head of the household tells everyone, including the adult members, what they should do during the course of the day. The head is respected in proportion to his impartiality and concern for the common good of the family.

General principles of the social structure, such as differentiation on the basis of sex and age, regulated relationship between members of a joint family. Differentiation on the basis of sex resulted in intensifying social interaction among members of the same sex and correspondingly weakening interaction between the different sexes. A married girl, for instance works in the kitchen with her mother-in-law and sees her husband only at night. In Western Uttar Pradesh, to give an instance, the house of a rich landowner comprises two parts; one, where women cook and sleep; the other, consisting of a raised platform and a room or two, where the men meet their friends and smoke the *hukka*. Cattle are parked in the men's *coupal*. At caste or village dinners men and women dine separately; women take their turn after the men and children.

Age is another operative principle, the younger members being required to show respect to the elder. In formal greeting, obligatory on ceremonial occasions, the younger person is expected to place his head on the elder's feet. The distinction on the basis of age cuts across the distinction on the basis of sex, a young man is expected to salute and take the blessing of an old female relative. When an exception is made, it only serves to emphasize the rule. Among the Kodagu, while generally young people have to show deference to the old, a wife must salute her husband's younger brother by touching his feet, even when he is younger than her. Formerly there was a general preference for leviratic marriage among the Kodagu, the younger brother often became the husband of his elder brother's widow. And as between husband and wife, the former has to be treated as superior.

Respect for age resulted in power and privilege being concentrated in the hands of elders. Generally the male head of the joint family was the oldest living agnate, and the female head, his wife. The one exercized authority over men, the other over women. Difference in generations meant only an accentuation of age difference. But sometimes, thanks to early marriage, a man is younger than his elder sister's or brother's children. In such cases there is a conflict between the two principles.

We have already described the relations obtaining between the head of the joint family and the other male members. Where the head is the father of the older male members, his authority as head is reinforced by the general rule which requires sons to obey their parents and especially the father. When the eldest brother succeeded to the father's position as head of the joint family the younger brothers had to obey him as they did their father. The position of the eldest son as the future head of the family marks him off from the other sons who are taught to respect him from an early age. This is specially true of the richer sections and higher castes. It is to be noted, however, that this transfer of authority from father to eldest son is only partial. Here is one of the reasons why families generally split up after the father's death.

Ideally, the children in a joint family are the children of all the male members of the parental generation, and discrimination by a parent in favour of his own children is regarded as reprehensible. The different units of the joint family pose a potential threat to its continuity, and as long as the joint family exists the units are subordinated to the bigger entity.

The relation between women members in a joint family is frequently one of conflict. The mother-in-law and daughter-in law relationship is celebrated in folklore for the intensity of its conflict. Relations between a woman and her husband's sisters, and between her and her husband's brothers' wives, are also conflict-ridden. The basic fact of rivalry between brothers (or sons) and the conflict between women lead to the splitting up of the joint family. In North India, a man has a friendly and even joking relationship with his elder brother's wife and a formal one with his younger brother's wife. In South India, a man treats his wife's younger brothers and sisters with familiarity. The relation between a man and his parents-in-law is a farmal one and only gradually, with the lapse of time, does it become less formal.

Nowadays, traditional patterns of behaviour are yielding place to new ones over a wide area. For instance, educated daughters-in-law do not obey their mothers-in-law as completely as before. There is a wide cultural gulf between the old-fashioned mother-in-law and the educated daughter-in-law and this, as may be expected, is a constant source of friction.

The principle of differentiation on the basis of age and sex: holds good in matrilineal systems also. Respect is paid to older relatives and strict segregation is the rule between the sexes. The women confine themselves to a particular part of the house. Sisters have an "avoidance relation" with their brothers (including parallel cousins) and especially the eldest brother, the future head *(kara-navan)* of the matrilineal household.

Uxorilocality, polyandry and easy divorce in the traditional kinship system of the Nayars were all intended to strengthen the sibling bond and weaken the conjugal bond. The head of the *tarawad* was expected to treat his sister's children as his own and be indifferent to his own children. The changes which have occurred in recent years have strengthened the father's position at the expense of the maternal uncle's.

A joint family is bound together by periodic propitiation of the dead ancestors. Among Brahmins this happens at the *srsddha* ceremony where a man propitiates his dead father's or mother's spirit *(pitru)* by offering it *pinda*. The dead person's parents and grandparents are also propitiated at a *Sraddha*. Among non-Brahmin castes ancestor propitiation takes different forms. Highly Sanskritised non-Brahmin castes, including the Ksatriya and Vaisya, perform the *sraddha* ritual. On the west coast of India, groups with a developed lineage system such as the Nayar and Coorg have elaborate ancestor propitiation in which the spirits of the dead "possess" low caste oracles. Where lineages are not so developed, all the dead ancestors are propitiated collectively on a particular day. A favourite period for the propitiation of ancestors is the fortnight preceding the *Dussehra* festival, known as *pitripaksh* (ancestors' fortnight).

In many parts of South India, a joint family or lineage has a tradition of worshipping a particular deity. Vows are made to this deity in times of trouble, and the first tonsure, the donning of the sacred thread, and the marriages of the members of the client-family are celebrated in or near the deity's temple. Srinivasa of Tirupati and Subrahmanya of palni are two well known deities, who have innumerable families attached to them.

Another important bond is pollution. When a member of a joint family or lineage dies, pollution has to be observed, the maximum period being ten days for the upper castes. Birth also results in pollution up to a maximum of ten days for the upper castes. The pollution group always includes the members of the joint family, patrilineal or matrilineal. It may be noted that the bonds created by the worship of family deities and ancestors and by the observance of pollution persist even after a joint family has split up into its component units or are residing in different places.

The political, economic and ideological forces that were released during British rule brought about certain changes in the joint family system. Large kin-groups, in rural areas at any rate, hiid been confined to a few landowning high castes. Residence in the same village, absence of economic differentiation between the different members of the joint family and the difficulty of getting the caste or village panchayat to agree to partitioning the joint family had been factors which kept the institution as a growing concern. British rule altered that situation. The new economic opportunities which came through the link-up of the local economy with a much wider one increased monetization; and greater opportunities for trade and increased spatial mobility due to the building of roads and railways led to the emergencc of smaller kin-groups. The rapid growth of population with the resultant pressure on land was felt especially at the lower levels of the rural economic order. The Hindu Gains of Learning Act, 1930, declared that property acquired by a Hindu as a result of his education was his personal property, even though his education was paid for by his joint family.

While the forces mentioned above certainly operated against living in big joint families, it must be remembered, that the rural poor probably always lived in kinship groups which were not very much bigger than the elementary family. Living in big joint families is generally associated with wealth from land or trade or industry. It seems likely that the family pattern of the rural poor did not undergo as serious a change as that of the comparatively rich. Even among the latter, the cost of education and increased mobility did contribute to strengthening joint family links. The earners in a joint family often made higher education possible for the younger members even when they themselves were unedu-cated. Residence away from the natal kin-group removed the stresses and strains of day-to-day living, while increased communi-cations kept the links alive. This is borne out by recent studies supporting the conclusion that the urban family is larger than the rural family.

Even if figures for urban areas show a dwindling in the size of the family, it does not necessarily mean that the joint family system is breaking down. Urban families are frequently not autonomous entities but only limbs of bigger families situated elsewhere. Any crisis in the parent or offspring family will be faced as a common problem. Weddings, funerals and other ceremonies are usually celebrated in the "parent" household. There is occasional transference of persons from one to the other family.

Heredatory Factors

Generally speaking, in the matter of succession to a traditional office, the rule of primogeniture is observed. That is, the eldest son of the incumbent of an office succeeds to it on the death of the latter. The eldest son becomes priest or headman or village watchman in the areas where those posts are hereditary. Sometimes the office may be split up like property among the sons of the office-holder. In parts of Gujarat, for instance, the hereditary headmanship of a village rotates among the different branches of a lineage each of which has a share in the office. The principle of splitting up a hereditary office is not, however, as widespread as primogeniture.

Among the matrilineal Nayars, the managership *(karanavan)* of the *tarawad* passes from maternal uncle to nephew. Among the matrilineal Khasis, the office of the priestess of the matrilineage devolves on the youngest daughter *(kakhadduh)* of the incumbent.

All Hindus are patrilineal, with the exception of the Nayan and Bants and other castes on the West Coast and Khasis and Garos of Assam. Muslims, excepting the Moplahs of North Malabar and Christians, excepting Khasi converts, are patrilineal. All Jains, Buddhists and Sikhs are patrilineal. But even among the patrilineal groups some movable property is given to daughters and this property shows a tendency to devolve matrilineally. *Stridhana,* gifts made to a bride (in contrast to the dowry), devolve eventually on her daughter. Again, the fact that women (until recently) did not inherit immovable property in patrilineal households was compensated for by their possession of rights in two households, natal and conjugal. Among the matrilineal Nayars, on the other hand, the women inherited the immovable property while the men managed the *tarawad* property.

Patrilineal Hindus were (and still are, to some extent) governed by two main schools of law in the matter of succession and inheritance, *viz.*, the Mitaksara and Dayabhaga. Founded by Vijyanesvara and Jimutavuhana respectively, they flourished in the 11th-12th centuries A.D. There were other schools which varied slightly from the Mitaksara. The Mayakha school is followed in Bombay, Gujarat and North Konkan; the Mithila school in Bihar; and the Varanasi and Madras schools in their respective areas. We shall confine ourselves only to the chief differences between the Mitaksra and Dayabhaga schools. The Dayabhaga school is followed in Bengal and Assam. Under the Mitaksara, a son has a vested interest in his father's ancestral property from the moment of his birth. The father cannot alienate any part of the ancestral property to the detriment of a minor's interest. Buyers hesitate to buy ancestral property when the seller has a minor heir. Under the Dayabhaga system, however, the father is the absolute owner of his share and the presence of a minor son does not constitute a bar to alienation. The term *sapinda* refers in the Mitaksara school to all relatives who are bound by ties of flesh and blood (particles of a single body), while in the Dayabhaga it refers to relatives bound by the ritual offering of funeral cakes. This difference results in certain non-agnatic kin being given preference over agnatic kin in the Dayabhaga school: the sister's son, father's sister's son and father's father's sister's son are included in the list of heirs and take precedence over some agnates.

In the matrilineal system of inheritance, a person inherits froin his maternal uncle and not from his father. Amongst the Nayars the father has no obligation to maintain his wife and children who belonged to a different *tarawaq* from his property descended from a mother to daughters. The men only managed their sister's or mother's property. The Marumakkawiyam Act of Malabar, 1933, gave the children of a man the right to inherit his self-acquired property. (A similar Act had been passed even earlier in Travancore and Cochin.) Even the self-acquired property of a man did not, however, go to his son's children but to his daughter's children. Until 1956, when the Hindu Succession Act was passed, there were two systems of inheritance in Malabar: the *tarawaq* property which devolved matrilineally, and the self-acquired property which devolved on the children of a man and his daughter's children. The Hindu Succession Act and the Hindu Adoptions and Maintenance Act, 1956, make the husband legally responsible for the maintenance of his wife and children.

All Muslims, excepting matrilineal Moplahs, are governed by the Shariat Act of 1937. Under Islamic law, the mother, wife and daughter are the three female heirs. The maximum share of the mother is one-third and the minimum one-sixth, depending on the existence or otherwise.of other heirs. The share of the wife is one-fourth or one-eighth, depending on the absence or presence of a child, or child of a son. The wife is also the owner of the *mehr* given to her at wedding. She is also entitled to be maintained by her husband. The daughter is a primary heir like the son. Her share fluctuates, depending upon the number of surviving children. The daughter's daughter, however, does not stand on a par with the son's daugter.

The Hindu Succession Act of 1956 governs the inheritance of Hindus, Buddhists, Sikhs and Jains. It applies to both matrilineal as well as patrilineal groups. According to this Act, the property of a Hindu dying intestate devolves on his sons, daughters, widow and mother. But in the Mitaksara school the shares of the female heirs extend only to the share of the deceased in the coparcenary property. Another change introduced by this Act is the inclusion of the mother in the same category of heirs as the widow and children of the dead man.

8

Caste Factors

The first literary traces of the caste system are to be found in the *Rig-Veda,* where three groups are mentioned: *Brahman* (Priests), *Kshatriya* (Kings or Rulers), and *Vaisya* (common people). The *Purusukta* hymn, however, speaks of four classes originating from four parts of the body of the creator. These classes, *Brahmana, Rajanya, Vaisya* and *Sudra,* are referred to in later literature as *Chaturvarna.* The term *varna* does not seem to have been applied to these classes in the earliest literature, except to contrast the fair *Arya* with the dark *Dasa.* The initial distinction of people into two *varnas* later developed into three *(Brahman, Kshatriya,* and *Vaisya)* and finally into four. The occupations of the first two *varnas* are clearly stated to be priesthood, and administrative and military duties, respectively. But the duties of the Vaisya and Sudra are not very clear. The village headman was usually a Vaisya, and Sudras were servants. The *Vaisya* cate-gories do not, however, exhaust the various occupations practised in Vedic India. The *Rig-Veda,* for instance, mentions several occupa-tions by name—chariot-builder, goldsmith, barber, physician, leather-worker, potter, merchant and others. The question arises whether these occupations referred to endogamous *jatis* as we know them today. It is not known how they fitted into the *vaisya* framework.

The post-Vedic period saw the growth and consolidation of the power of the Brahmins. Brahmin writers continually discussed and defined the duties and rights of each caste and its place in the hierarchy. The relation which these writings bore to the empirical reality is not clear) Justifications and rationalizations of the hierarchy were also produced during this period. In the *Bhagavad-Gita,* for instance, the caste system is sought to be justified on the basis of the ideas of *gyhna, karma* and *dharma.*

The 6th century B.C. saw the rise of Buddhism, which is believed to have questioned the basis of the caste system itself. Some scholars, however, have said that Buddhism on its social and political side was chiefly a Ksatriya movement against Brahminical supremacy.

Post-Vedic Brahminical writers continued their attempts to systematize and codify inter-caste relations. The idea of pollution was elaborated to define the distance separating the castes. Violations of caste rules were punished either by the village panchayat or the panchayat of the locally dominant caste or by the king.

The Bhakti movement with its long history contained elements which ran counter to caste ideology. The Bhakti saints came from all castes, including the Harijans. It appears as though the path of *Bhakti* offered a way out of the tyrannies of the caste system, and as the Bhakti saints commanded respect from everyone, the movement itself served to stress the worth of an individual irrespective of his caste affiliations. The origins of the Bhakti movement are traced to the Krsna-Vasudeva cult in the first century B.C. The Saiva (Nayanar) and Vaisnava (Alvar) saints of the Tamil country, the Haridasa and Lingayat saints of Karnataka, Vallabhacarya and his followers in Gujarat, Chaitanya in Bengal, and Tulasidas, Surdas, Kabir and Radim in the North, were all representatives of the Bhakti movement. The movement was more or less continuous in Indian history, and it spread right across the sub-continent. It may not be too fanciful to regard it as a protest, in the realm of religion, against the division of human beings into high and low castes.

The Lingayat movement, which came into existence in Karnataka in the 12th century A.D., rejected many ideas of traditional Hinduism, including *karma,* ritualism and caste. It also emphasized the necessity as well as the dignity of labour. The movement attracted converts from all castes including Harijans, but over the centuries it became a congeries of small, endogamous *Jatis.* The followers of Kablr (Kabirpanthi) also became a caste.

Caste even survived conversion to Christianity and Islam. During the last century there came into existence the Arya Samaj in Punjab and the Brahmo Samaj in Bengal. These movements, as well as the Ramakrishna Mission, represented a shift towards the liberalization of caste.

Major Factors

We shall now consider the main features of caste before it was deeply affected by recent changes. Those changes, which present a quite different picture of the Indian social structure today are discussed in the last pages of this chapter.

The features of caste prevailing through the past centuries may be described under nine heads: hierarchy; endogamy and hypergamy; occupational association; restriction on food, drink and smoking; distinction in custom, dress and speech; pollution; ritual and other privileges and disabilities; caste organization and caste mobility.

The essence of caste is the arrangement of hereditary groups in a hierarchy. The popular impression of the hierarchy is a clear-cut one, derived from the idea of *varna,* with Brahmins at the top and Harijans at the bottom. But, as a matter of fact, only the two opposite ends of the hierarchy are relatively fixed; in between, and especially in the middle regions, there is considerable room for debate regulating mutual position. In a dispute over rank each caste would cite as evidence of its superiority the items of its dietary, the other caste groups from which it accepted or refused to accept cooked food and water, the ritual it performed and the customs it observed, its traditional privileges and disabilities, and the myth of its origin. The fact that mutual position is arguable, if not vague, over great areas of the hierarchy permits social mobi-lity. Mobility, it may be noted, is not a recent phenomenon. Even in the traditional system it was possible for a caste to move up. The Raj Gonds of Central India, for instance, successfully claimed for themselves the rank of Ksatriyas on the basis of their acquisition of political power. At the coronation of Shivaji, Brahmin priests declared him a Ksatriya. Not infrequently the claim of a caste to a higher rank is not conceded. Thus, the Smith group of castes in South India have claimed to be a twice-born caste and call themselves Visvakarma Brahmin. The other castes resent this and even the Harijans do not accept drinking water from a Smith. The Lingayats consider themselves superior to the Brahmins but others do not accept their claim.

Disputes regarding mutual position occur even at either extremes of the hierarchy. In Kerala, Nambudris consider themselves superior to Tamil Brahmins, and among the Nambudris those who have a hereditary right to study the Vedas claim superiority over the others. Again, there are very low groups among the Brahmins. No caste, including the Harijan, will accept cooked food or water from the Marka Brahmins of Mysore. Likewise, the Vatima Brahmins in the Tamil country and the Tapodhan Brahmins in Gujarat are considered as inferior.

All Caste Hindus regard Harijans as being at the bottom rung of the ladder. But the category of Harijans is not homogeneous. In each linguistic area there are a few Harijan castes which form a hierarchy. The leather-working Chamar in Uttar Pradesh considers himself superior to the Bhangi, a sweeper. The Kannada Holera places himself above the Madiga; he proudly stresses the fact that he does not accept even water or betel leaf from either the Smith or the Marka Brahmin.

Islam proclaims the idea of equality of all those who profess the faith, but in India it has been characterized by caste. Muslim caste differs in some respects from the Hindu caste system; there are no ethico-religious ideas justifying the hierarchy or regulating inter-caste relations through ideas of purity and pollution; there are no *varna* categories. What we have is a hierarchy formed by several *jatis*.

In Uttar Pradesh, *Muslims* who have a tradition of foreign ancestry (Iran, Arabia) are called Shurafa or Ashraf and are considered to be the highest. After them come converts from high-caste Hindus, such as Rajputs. Next come occupational castes such as the Weaver (Julaha), Barber (Nai), Cotton Carder (Dhuniya), Potter (Kumhar) and Oilman (Teli). Last come the Sweepers. Among the Ashraf, the Syeds rank as the highest.

The Moplah (Mappilla) *Muslims* of Kerala are also divided into castes. The Thangals, claiming descent from the Prophet's daughter, Fatima, are at the top; next to them are the Arabs, descendants of immigrants from Arabia. The Pusalars, said to be recent converts from the Fisherman caste, occupy the third position while the Ossans, who are barbers, are at the bottom.

Equality is a tenet of Sikhism also, but that has not prevented the existence of castes, including Brahmins, among Sikhs. Sikhs are broadly divided into Sardars and Mazhabis, the former consisting of higher castes and the latter of Sweepers. The Sardars include Jar and Kamboh (landowners), Tarkhan (Carpenter). Kumhar (Potter), Mehra (Water-carrier), and Cimba (Washer man). The first two castes regard themselves as superior to the others. The Mazhabis, not only came from a low caste but Were converted to Sikhism later than the higher caste groups. In some parts of Punjab there exist the Sansi (Shepherd) who were for merly included among the "Criminal Tribes"; Sansi converts to Sikhism rank even lower than Mazhabis.

There are three divisions among Indian Jews: Beni-Israel, Cochin Jews and Baghdadi Jews. The Beni-Israel are to be found principally in Mumbai. They are divided into groups, *Gora* (White) and *Kala* (Black), the former being considered higher in rank. The Cochin Jews are divided into similar White and Black groups, and there is a third division called Meshurarim comprising the descendants of Cochin Jews and their slave concubines; the Meshurarim, who are decended from a White Cochin Jew, claim superiority over those descended from a Black Cochin Jew. The third Jewist- group, the Baghdadi, are later immigrants, and are found in Mumbai and Calcutta.

Caste divisions occur among Indian Christians, Catholics as well as Protestants. The Syrian Christians of Kerala, the earliest converts to Christianity in India, claim to have been recruited originally from Nambudri Brahmins and Nayars, and caste distinctions are conspicuous among them. Caste restrictions are rigidly observed among the Christians of the West Coast. A Catholic Brahmin from Maharashtra would marry none other than a Catholic Brahmin. Some West Coast Christians have migrated to East Africa and their descendants try to marry within their particular sub-caste.

Conversion does, however, weaken pollution ideas, and social life among Christian converts is more free than among Hindus. Again, all over India, caste restrictions are far less meticulously observed today than they were a few decades ago. Social institutions are changing, and this affects all social groups, though in varying degrees.

Professional Grouping

The hereditary association of a caste with an occupation has been so striking that it has occasionally been argued that caste is nothing more than the systematization of occupational differentiation. Even though a caste is not only associated with an occupation but has a limited kind of monopoly over it, it is not true to say that every member of the caste practises that occupation exclusively. This kind of association is suggested when, for instance, the term Kumhar is translated as Potter, and Dhobi as Washerman. But, generally speaking, most castes also practise agriculture in addition to their traditional occupation. A Kumhar may be an agriculturist in the monsoon months, and a trader in grain for a brief period after the harvest. Often, the artisan and servicing castes do not have an adequate income from their traditional occupations and they therefore work on land, either as tenants or as casual labourers. It could be argued that, in the context of a growing population, the occupational aspect of the caste system would have broken down completely if the surplus in the artisan, trading and servicing castes had not been either absorbed in agriculture or able to migrate to other areas.

Traditionally, agriculture (used broadly to include even mere landownership) was a common occupation for all castes. The profession of arms was also practised occasionally by the non-Ksatriya castes, including Brahmins and the locally dominant peasant groups.

To associate a caste invariably with a single occupation is an oversimplification. Even "agriculture" can mean a variety of things: landownership, tenancy and labour. Each may be practised exclu-sively or in combination with the others. Sometimes cultivation includes processing the grown crop into a sale able commodity. Thus, the cultivation of sugarcane, except when grown for a factory, includes the processing of cane into jaggery and its sale to a middleman. Again, different members of a family may have different occupations. All Women cook and they may also take some part in agriculture. Women of the artisan castes may in addition participate in the caste craft.

Occupations are also classified into high and low, those practised by the high castes being regarded as high. Manual labour is looked upon as low, and certain occupations like swine herding and butchery are considered to be polluting.

Among Muslims, only artisan castes such as the Teli, Darzi, and Julaha are associated with traditional occupations. Priests tend to come more from the Syed and Shaikh castes than from the others. Among the Sikhs, the traditiODaloccupation is often practised along with agriculture. Jats are generally landowners, while the Mazhabis are agricultural labourers. Sikh Tarkhans are Carpenters. An occupation which is indispensable every where except among the Sikhs is hair-cutting. But the Sikh Nai renders other services: he clips the nails of his patrons; he carries news of birth, marriage and death. He is also a masseur.

An individual in a caste society lives in a hierarchical world. It is not only the people who are divided into higher and lower groups, but also the food they eat, the dress and ornaments they wear, and the customs and manners they practise. In India's dietetic hierarchy the highest castes are usually vegetarians and teetotallers. Even in meat there is a hierarchy. The highest non-vegetarian castes eschew chicken, pork and beef. Wild pork is superior to domestic pork, since the village pig is a scavenger. Eating beef in rural India means eating carrion and it comes accordingly under a double ban. Liquor is prohibited to the high castes.

Elaborate rules govern the acceptance of cooked food and water from another caste. Food cooked with ghee, milk or butter is called *pakkii* food and may be accepted from inferior castes. (Higher castes buy sweets from the *Halwai* because he is supposed to be cooking them with ghee.) *Kaccii* food, on the other hand, is food cooked with water and it may be accepted normally only from one's own or equivalent or superior castes. When two castes are contending for superiority, they stop accepting cooked food and water from each other. Sometimes, a very low caste refuses cooked food or water from a high caste. We have already mentioned the instance of the Kannada Holeya. The explanation of these usages lies in the history of inter-caste relations in the area in question, and in particular, in the attempts of individual castes to raise themselves up.

There are exceptions to the general restrictions on the acceptance of food and water. Food or drink which has been sanctified by being offered to a deity in a temple may not be refused, even though the cook is from a low caste. The cooks in the famous Jagannath temple at Puri are Barbers by caste. Significant regional variations also occur. Further, women tend to observe restrictions more strictly than men, and the old more strictly than the young. Among the highly westernised sections in the big cities, such restrictions are minimal.

In North India, *hukka* smoking offers an index of castcstatus. Castes which may share, *on* occasions, a single *hukka* are equals. Thus Jats and Ahirs may smoke from the same *hukkii.* Sometimes the Lobar (Blacksmith) and Khan (Carpenter) are allowed to smoke from the same *hukka* as the Jat and Ahir. The Nais (Barber) like many other castes, have their own *hukka.*

Muslim castes freely accept cooked food and water from one another. Such restrictions regarding food and drink as obtai-ned among Muslims are common to them all. As for the Sikhs, Sardars have reservations about *kaccii* food cooked by Mazhabis, but accept liquor brewed by them.

Each caste has a culture which is to some extent autonomous: there are differences in dress, speech, manners, ritual and ways of life. The higher castes wear fine clothes and gold ornaments while the lower castes wear coarse material and silver ornaments. The speech of the higher castes is refined while that of the lower castes is rugged. Traditionally, the lower castes were prohibited from taking on the dress, ornaments and customs of the higher, and the offenders were punished by the village panchayat.

The concept of pollution plays a crucial part in maintaining the required distance between different castes. A high caste man may not touch a low caste man, let alone accept cooked food and water from him. Where the two castes involved belong to either extreme of the hierarchy, the lower caste man may be required to keep a minimum distance between himself and the high caste man. In Kerala, a Nayadi had to keep 22 m. away from a Nambudri and 13 m. from a Tiyan, who himself had to keep 10 m. away from a Nambudri. A few decades ago, in most areas of South India, there were rules which laid down what parts of a high caste man's house the other's could enter. The rules of pollution, at least so far as inter-caste relations were concerned, were more clearly elaborated in South than in North India.

There is a broad line between Caste Hindus and Harijans in the matter of pollution. The village barber and washerman will not serve Harijans, and the latrer have to provide for these services from among themselves. Harijans have to take water from a lower end of a river canal than the high castes and they may not use the Caste Hindu well.

The breaking of pollution rules results in the higher castes becoming "impure", and the latter have to perform certain purificatory rites *to* regain their normal status. Where the breach of the rule is serious, as when a high caste person eats food cooked by a Harijan or a high caste woman has sex relations with a Harijan, the offender may be thrown out of caste irrevocably.

The idea of pollution is present among the Sikhs. The Mazhabis have a well of their own everywhere, and in rural areas they may not be allowed to enter the houses of Sikh high castes beyond the cattle-yard.

The culture of each caste is to some extent peculiar to itself, and this is related to the fact that the lower castes are barred, at least in theory, from taking over the customs and rituals of the higher castes. Only the "twice-born" castes are entitled to study the Vedas and perform rituals in which Vedic mantras are chanted. Traditionally, the Brahmin was exempt from capital punishment and his land was assessed at a lower rate. These restrictions and disabilities operate fully against the Harijans they may not use Caste Hindu wells or enter temples and teashops. In some parts of the country they were prohibited from entering the high caste streets. The high castes also kept away from the Harijan ward of the village.

Among the Sikhs, Mazhabi wedding parties are not accommodated in gurdwaras as they are regarded as impure. Among Muslims, however, lower caste groups are not Subjected to disabilities. The Christians on the west coast of India observe caste restrictions: there are separate pews for the Brahmins and the Harijans in some churches, and very rarely, even a separate church for the Harijans.

Villagers are subject to the two-fold control of caste and village panchayats, (Caste panchayats, however, are not well developed among Brahmins.) When the disputes concern law and order in the village, for example, setting fire to someone's hayrick, grazing cattle on another's land, stealing fuel or vegetable- it is reported to village elders who may levy a fine on the offender or subject him to corporal punishment or declare a boycott against him. In a marital dispute the council of the concerned caste is the proper body to adjudicate. But the village council may take a hand in the dispute. Where a man is accused of having sex or commersal relations with a member of a lower caste, his own caste or the council of the locally dominant caste, or the village council might be called upon to adjudicate. Punishment may include a fine, temporary outcasting and fine, or permanent outcasting. Re-admission to caste requires that the offender undergo purificatory ritual, express his regret to the caste assembly, and give avdinner to the caste. Occasionally an offender may be re-admitted to caste after having been outcasted for a decade or two.

Many Muslim castes, excepting the *Ashraf* and *Shaikh,* have councils like Hindu castes. Generally, a caste council deals with all questions concerning trade, morals and religion. Sometimes a caste may not permit its members to take up an occupation considered less honourable than its traditional one.

Life in Rural Areas

We have given a brief description of the genetal features of the caste system and we shall now show how it actually functions in the context of the village community. Inter-caste relations at the village level constitute "vertical" ties. They may be classified into economic, ritual, political and civic ties.

The castes living in a village, or a group of neighbouring villages are bound together by economic ties. Generally, peasant castes are numerically preponderant in villages and they need the Carpenter, Blacksmith and Leather-worker castes to perform agricultural work. Servicing castes such as Priest (Brahmin as well as non-Brahmin), Barber, Washerman and Water-carrier cater to the needs of everyone except Harijans. Artisan castes produce goods which are wanted by everyone. Most Indian villages do not have more than a few of the essential castes and depend on neighbouring villages for certain services, skills and goods.

In rural India, with its largely subsistence and not fully monetized economy, the relationship between the different caste' groups in a village takes a particular form. The essential artisan and servicing castes are paid annually in grain at harvest. In some parts of India, the artisan and servicing castes are also provided with free food, clothing, fodder and a residential site. On such occasions as birth, marriage and death these castes perform extra duties for which they are paid a customary sum of money and some gifts in kind. This type of relationship is found allover India and is called by different names: *jajrnani* in the North, *bara balute* in Maharashtra, *mirasi* in Chennai and *adade* in Mysore. The relationship between a *jajrnan* and his *kamin* is unequal, since the latter is regarded as inferior. Though primarily an economic or ritual tie, it has a tendency to spread to other fields and become a patron-client relationship. The relationship is generally stable, and usually inherited. The right to serve is hereditary, transferable, saleable, mortgaable and partible. Thus, for instance, the right to officiate as priest to high castes living in some sixty villages in the Mysore district is shared among the different branches of a single Brahmin lineage in Bannur.

The *jajmani* system bound together the different castes living in a village or a group of neighbouring villages. The caste-wise division of labour and the consequent linking up of different castes in enduring and pervasive relationships provided a pattern of alliances which cut across the ties of caste. The modern "caste problem" is to some extent the result of the weakening, in the last fifty years or more, of these vertical and local ties and the consequent strengthening of horizontal ties over wide areas.

Caste was related to the exercise of differential rights in land. At the top were the castes who were either absentee or non-cultivating owners. Next came the cultivating tenants (not infrequently owning a little land as well), and at the bottom of the hierarchy came the landless labourers. There was regional variation in this matter. Kerala, for instance, had a chain of intermediaries between the owner and the actual cultivator. There was more or less perfect congruence between caste hierarchy and differential rights in land in Kerala. At the top of the hierarchy were the

Nambudri Brahmins who were non-cultivating owners *(jenmi)*. The "high" Nayar castes were the non-cultivating lessees of Nambudri land on twelve-year leases *(karzam)*. The agricultural labourers, both tied and free, came from the lower castes like Ceruman and Pulayan and from the Panan tribes. In Punjab, however, there was a lack of coherence between the agricultural and caste hierarchies, Brahmins being the cultivating tenants of Jat landowners. But, in both areas, agricultural labourers came from the Harijan castes. In some parts of Punjab and Uttar Pradesh, only a few castes snowed a direct concern with land and agriculture, the owner cultivators being either Jats, Ahirs and Rajputs (Thakurs) or Gujars, while the agricultural labourers were mostly Chamars.

The existence of a high degree of congruence between caste and agricultural hierarchy meant that the stratification ran deep, economic stratification strengthened ritual stratification and *vice versa*. This enabled the landowners to exploit the tenants as much as they could-rack-renting, eviction and forced labour were usual features of rural life. But where the tenants' caste was higher than that of the landowner, and particularly when a tenant was also the landowner's priest (as was sometimes the case with the Brahmin tenant of a Rajput landowner), exploitation had to be much less extreme.

In pre-British India, in many parts of the country, the lower castes were serfs or slaves, either attached to the land and liable to be transferred along with it, or attached to the landowner and liable to be sold by him. The economic forces released under British rule *(e.g.,* the starting of tea and coffee plantations, and of factories and railways) enabled the law abolishing slavery to be translated into reality. But even now the agricultural hierarchy have been mixed up in different ways and degrees with the caste hierarchy in several parts of India.

The relationship between master and servant is another type of bond which often cuts across caste, and more rarely, even religion. The terms and conditions of this bond vary from region to region. A common form is the advance by the master of a loan which is worked off by the servant in the course of two or three years in the master's house. Frequently, before the expiry of the period, the servant takes another loan which results in prolonging his servitude. It is not unusual to come across families linked with each other for generations by ties of master and servant. In some parts of the country, like Mysore, there was until recently a traditional bond as of master and servant between the landowning castes and the local Harijans. The obligations involved were only a few duties on occasions such as marriage and death. The payments were also traditionally fixed.

The relationship between landowner and tenant, master and servant, creditor and debtor, may all be subsumed under a single category-patron and client. This relationship is widespread and crucial to the understanding of rural India. Voting at elections, local and general, is influenced by the patron-client tie.

Ritual occasions, e.g., life-cycle ceremonies, festivals and fairs, require the co-operation of several castes. Life-cycle ceremonies are somewhat more elaborate for the "twice-born", especially the Brahmin castes. Certain rituals which are common for all the castes occur at birth, a girl's puberty, marriage and death. Thus when a son is born to an Abu or Thakur, a Bhaksorin (Harijan) woman helps in the delivery and a Bhangi beats a drum before the house in which the birth occurred. A Brahmin casts a horo-scope, while the village barber acts as a messenger and also serves food at the feast. These services are paid for by gifts in cash as well as kind. In Kerala, the Washerwoman gives freshly-washed clothes to her high caste patrons after the termination of birth, menstrual and death pollution. In rural Mysore there is a saying that eighteen castes have to come together at a wedding: the Harijan servants cut the wood, whitewash the house and clean the grain; the Barber not only shaves the groom but provides the wedding band; the Washerman supplies the washed cloth for the bridal pair to walk on; the Potter provides the utensils and ritual pots, the Carpenter puts up the wedding *pandal;* the Goldsmith makes the ornaments; the Oilman supplies the oil; the Brahmin acts as priest; the dancing girl threads the *tali,* the trader supplies several articles; the Shepherd provides a woollen thread which is tied as *Kankan* round the wrists of the bridal pair, and so on.

Several castes are also required to co-operate in the performance of calendrical festivals, and festivals of village deities. In the case of the latter, the castes may come from more than one village. Thus, Bannas from Malabar dance at the festivals of some

Coorg village deities. The festival of a village deity always involves the co-operation of several castes, and frequently a few of these castes come from neighbouring villages.

The temple organization itself needs the coming together of several castes. In Kerala, for instance, the head priest of a Sanskritic, vegetarian and teetotal deity is a Nambudri Brahmin. A few Nayar castes have the task of washing the vessels and cleaning the temple. The Ambalavasis perform a variety of tasks and they make gar-lands, assist the chief priest, provide music. There is a caste of story-tellers attached to the temple. In temples to non-vegetarian deities, a member of the Pidarar caste is the priest. Low caste dancers get possessed by the deities, and sing and dance in that state.

It may be taken as axiomatic that all the local castes are involved in the festival of a village deity. Even the Harijans have important duties, such as beating the drum, carrying messages, and removing the leaves on which the villagers have dined.

In many parts of India, villagers believe (or at least believed until recently) that the goddesses Mari, Kali and Sitala presided over epidemic diseases such as smallpox, plague and cholera. An outbreak of one of these diseases was attributed to the wrath of the village goddesses and their propitiation followed. The priest was usually a member of a non-Brahmin caste and occasionally even a Harijan. Members of all castes including the Brahmin sent their contributions in cash as well as in kind to the ritual propitiation. The fact that occasionally a Harijan or other low caste priest catered to the religious needs of all, including the highest castes, affected the quality of inter-caste relations.

Sometimes the ties of ritual stretch even across religious cleavages. A Sikh farmer may go to a Brahmin priest to find out an auspicious hour for starting ploughing operations. Until *forty* years ago, Brahmin priests officiated a life-cycle ritual in Sikh homes. In recent years the Akali Movement has enjoined religious self-sufficiency on the Sikhs, and the Sikh Granthi is increasingly acting as priest at Sikh weddings. The Sikh priest may come from any caste except Mazhabi. Sikhs and Hindus attend festivals in honour of Pirs (Muslim saints). In Mysore a Muslim peasant may vow to Madesvara that he will give a money-offering if his cow calves, or if it is cured of a disease. However, the tendency to religious and even sectarian self-sufficiency has gained strength in recent years.

The functioning of the village as a political and social entity brought together members from different castes. First, there was the traditional village panchayat which, though run by the locally dominant caste, usually included a few representatives from the other castes. The available historical evidence points to the existence of vigorous communities in South India in the panchayats of which members of every caste took part.

Every village had a headman usually belonging to the dominant caste. The accountant was always a Brahmin in South India. Every village had a watchman and messengers and town-criers. In irrigated areas, there was always a man to look after and regulate the flow of water in the canals feeding the fields. The headman and accountant collected the land taxes with the aid of the Harijan village servants.

The village council performed a variety of tasks, including the maintenance of law and order, settling of disputes, celebration of,. festivals and construction of roads, bridges and tanks.

In many parts of rural India there exist castes which are locally numerically preponderant, own the bulk of the arable land, occupy a fairly high position in the ritual hierarchy, and wield power over the other castes. Examples of such castes are Jats, Ahirs and Rajputs in the North, Patidars in Central Gujarat, Marathas in Maharashtra, Kamma and Reddi in Andhra Pradesh, Limgayat and Okkaliga (Vakkaliga) in Mysore, Vellala and Gounder in Chennai and Nayar in Kerala. Sometimes the dominance of a caste is decisive, all types of power being concentrated in it. At other times, however, the different elements of dominance may be distributed among several castes. In the first instance, the dominant caste wields great power over the others, while in the second there is likely to be a balance of power among the powerful castes. It should be noted in this connection that the maintenance of law and order in rural areas even now depends to some extent upon the leaders of the dominant caste. They are the people who can punish errant individuals and ensure the maintenance of the caste codes. When a caste is politically or economically dominant, its religious position tends to fall in line with its secular position.

The Sikhs as a whole are dominant in many parts of Punjab and Sikh Jats are dominant among the Sikhs. Similarly, in parts of Kerala, the Syrian Christians and Moplahs are dominant. In Mallhabad Tahsil in the Lucknow district there are villages in which Pathans are dominant.

The village community consisted of hierarchical groups, each with its own rights, duties and privileges. The castes at the top had power and privileges which were denied to the lower castes. The lower castes were tenants, servants, landless labourers, debtors and clients of the higher castes. There was competition among the former to be clients of the rich and powerful patrons while the latter wanted to have as many clients as possible. The patrons had duties towards clients and vice versa. The caste system together with the inequalities of landownership produced a deeply stratified society, but that did not prevent the village from functioning as a community. Conflict and co-operation went together. There was economic conflict between masters and servants, landowners and tenants, and competition between members of the same caste. The struggle for higher status between structurally neighbouring castes also produced conflict. And in recent years the lower castes have shown an increasing desire to free themselves from the control of the locally dominant caste. This has been assisted by political forces operating from higher levels.

9

Practical Aspects

The social scientists in India are well conversant, at least, with the apparent character of western theories and methods of study as they have amply used them in their analyses of Indian society. However, it is still an open question whether they have done so consciously, knowing well about their implications or have done so without a proper awareness of their deep-rooted implications—ideological, political and material. Even a cursory look at literature on social stratification shows that theories and concepts used by Marx, Weber, Durkheim, Sorokin, Pareto, Dahrendorf, Centres, Warner, Hollingshead, Mills, Dumont, etc., have been freely used by Indian scholars for studying social stratification and mobility without weighing their relevances. It has been more an exercise in sophistry and super-fluousness than in genuine sociological research and understanding. If a question is posed about the relevance or otherwise of the Marxian and Weberian concepts and theories in the Indian context, I would prefer to maintain that both are partly relevant and partly irrele-vant. However, about the dichotomous, trichotomous or the continua concepts, one would discover more of irrelevance than relevance. The concepts such as *vertical* and *horizontal mobility, reference group* and *sanskritisation* are partly useful and partly futile.

Fundamental Issues

The concepts of 'integration', 'conflict' and 'social mobility' have been at the centre of a large number of studies on caste, class and status-emulation in Indian society. Lack of 'indigenization' in these studies has been pointed out as a major drawback. The superiority of the western social sciences in the understanding of western societies is accepted by way of using it in the studies of Indian situation. I am not against accepting or borrowing explanatory models, concepts and methods from western social sciences, but one must ascertain their application in terms of time and space. Transnational and regional variations and historical-ideo-logical moorings are basic to any scientific and objective study of social inequality.

A *sociology of knowledge* view of social reality is the foremost requirement for studying social stratification. Such a view is missing in most of the studies which emphasize either caste or class to the exclusion of each other. The protagonists of caste studies show a bias for its continuance and functionality (Hutton, 1963; Furnivall, 1939; Senart, 1930). The advocates of class studies have different ideological upbringings and look at everything from the point of class alone (Desai, 1948). A combination of concepts with analytic synthesis may ensure a deeper and realistic understanding of social stratification in India. These are concepts of culture, structure, history and dialectics (Sharma, 1982). Normative standards, social relations, specificity and levels of change in regard to social strati-fication can respectively be explained by these concepts. One can have a vision of social formation of Indian society or of a part of it by using the concepts of culture, structure, history and dialectics.

Marx gives us a call for the application of historical-dialectical materialism; Weber impresses upon us the value of Using *verstehen;* Durkheim advocates the use of sociological positivism; Parsons advances the cause of structural-functionalism; and Popper declares that historicism is a poor method—a misconception, hence, the relevance for his brand of positivism (Sharma, 1983). We have been influenced by all of them at different points of time and in different contexts and sometimes in contradiction to each other in our attempts to understand Indian society. Therefore, the most important question continues to be: How to understand Indian social reality in an effective manner? Is there a congruence between theory, method and data in regard to the present studies on social stratification? This question could be posed even at the general level of the nature of sociology in India, but I do not intend to dwell upon this paper.

Whatever Louis Dumont (1970) might say about *caste as a method* of studying Indian society, he does support caste system and its allied sanctions. For him, caste is 'social', as religion is 'social' for Radcliffe Brown and Durkheim. Dumont approvingly quotes from Hocart, Senart and Hutton, who have advocated for continuity of caste system by emphasizing the functions of caste system for individual members, for caste as a group, and for the entire Indian society or state (Hutton, 1963). Such an advocacy during the British days had led to the promotion of their colonial interests in India. However, this view of theirs stands contradicted when they make a sharp distinction between caste and class. Class is considered as a characteristic feature of the western society and the latter is characterized by its emphasis on democracy, individualism and openness. On the contrary, caste, as a core-feature of Indian society, is defined as an archaic institu-tion lacking in democracy, individualism and freedom (Sharma 1980). Such a dichotomous perspective on the part of the western scholars easily exposes them to the blemish of ideological particularism. They also have many camp-followers among the Indian scholars who have borrowed these deceptive and one-sided models deliberately and sometimes unwittingly. Dumont (1957, 1958, I960, 1966) criticizes Saran's view as 'cultural solipsism', reactionary, obscurantistic and Hindu chauvinistic, but under the cover of 'external view', comparison and objectivity, Dumont brings in a mystic hallo around the caste system. Why Dumont accepts India's caste system as a datum for his under-standing of all the rest? Why does he consider caste as a cultural form of social inequality? Is inequality based on racial criteria not of an extreme form? Continuance of monarchy in England or depriving women from contesting election for presidentship in USA are equally retrograde and archaic practices, but Dumont forgets them conveniently, not declaring them as 'extreme' type of institutions.

Thus, the question is not of preferring one approach against another. The question is also not of studying 'ideas' or 'relations' or both. The question is rather of studying social inequality and its ramifications—historically and contextually. The relevant questions to be posed in this connection are: (1) How far studies of social stratification have incorporated the historicity of Indian society? (2) What are the approaches, methods and techniques of research in regard to social stratification? (3) Where did they originate and how the experience behind their origination is different from the experience of Indian social reality? (4) What measures have been taken to ascertain a *priorism* of these tools of understanding? Does it not mean accepting them as academic cults? I shall refer to these questions while analyzing some selected though well-known studies of social stratification.

The Strategies

This is not to suggest that since functional approach to social stratification has been in vogue for long enough, therefore, dialectical approach should be accepted now. It is also not to make a plea for a synthesis of the two approaches so as to have a pluralistic or multidimensional approach for studying social stratification. I do not wish to assert that in the studies so far 'consequences' of social inequality have been emphasized more than its causes and processes, and therefore, the trinity of theory, structure and process should be studied now. More important than these endeavours would be the one which recognizes the historicity of Indian social stratification, and accordingly seeks to identify its present character. Why functional or dialectical approaches, either individually or in synthesis, are recommended for the understanding of social inequality in India since neither of these has emanated from the experience of social inequality in India? None of the theories and concepts of social stratification can be applied in any context without knowing their ideological moorings. Their presuppositions need to be analyzed in terms of new forms and expressions of social inequality in divergent social situations. *Particularism* of theories and concepts under the garb of their *universality* should thus be uncovered.

The structural-functional theory of social stratification dominated in the 1950s. Congruence between caste, class and power was found in the village community. Division of labour among various castes in a given local situation was found desirable.

Corporate character of caste groups was analyzed with regard to intra-caste and inter-caste relations. Structuralism and Marxism as explanations of and approaches to social stratification acquired prominence in the 1960s. Dumont is the spokesman of structuralism. Marxism has been advocated by A.R. Desai and Charles Bettel-heim. However, in the 1970s, the historical perspective has been accepted by the Marxists as well as non-Marxists in their studies of social stratification. The non-Marxist adherents of structural-historical perspective have given more emphasis on indigenization of Marxist approach with an emphasis on understanding of Indian society in relation to its historicity (Singh, 1974, 1981).

Caste as the singular institution of social ranking was the characteristic argument during the fifties and sixties in the studies of Hutton, Ghurye, Hocart, Bougie, Myrdal, Leach, Srinivas, Marriott, Lewis, etc. All of them have treated caste as coterminous with the entire gamut of social relations and thought it to be an all-inclusive basis of social stratification (Beteille, 1969). Multi-dimensionality of social stratification is emphasized in the sixties and seventies in the studies conducted by Beteille (1966), Bhatt (1975) and Aggarwal (1971). Class and power along with caste are treated as economic and political dimensions of social inequality and hierarchy. Ramkrishna Mukherjee (1957), Gough (1960) and Mencher (1974), however, look at caste from a class point of view. Mencher feels that caste be studied from 'upside down' rather than through 'top down' view. In fact, caste is treated by all these scholars as a system of economic relations rather than merely as a system of ritual hierarchy. In my own study, I applied both structural and cultural perspectives to understand social stratification in six villages of Rajasthan (Sharma, 1974). Not only I could identify the structure of social inequality in divergent social settings, I could also analyze the ideological basis of social stratification, factors of change and social mobility, levels of caste and class consciousness, power structure and value orientations in my attempt to examine the relevance of 'caste' model to the study of Indian society.

Theory, method and data are generally in complementary alliance. Functional approach to the study of caste implied that it was a useful institution and it would not change, and also that it would adapt itself to meet the challenges and exigencies of a variety of situations. Caste was found as an adaptive and pragmatic system performing as an interest group for its members (Kothari, 1970). In such studies, however, several significant structural processes such as proletarianization of the *ex-zamindars* and bourgeoisiefication of the ex-tenants and *raiyats,* which have affected caste structure, have been ignored (Sharma, 1973). In fact, normative and cultural aspects of caste have received more attention through analysis of sanskritisation and westernisation (Srinivas, 1966). It also seems relevant here to recall that a couple of studies have comprehended contemporary changes in the caste system as a movement from its organic nature to its segmentary character, from its closedness to openness and from its emphasis on corporateness to individualism (Bailey, 1957; Miller, 1975). The central message of all these studies is that caste is continuing but bases of its continuity and forms of its functioning are quite different now from what they were four decades ago.

An overview of the studies on caste by the Indian sociologists suggests that we are competing with each other in imitating approa-ches, models and methods used by the British and American scholars. A study of the role of religion among the Coorgs (Sri-nivas, 1952) is clearly an extension of Radcliffe-Brown's functiona-lism. Religion is *sui generis* for Srinivas. Caste and religion are intertwined, hence religion becomes the basis of caste hierarchy. Beteille (1966a), in trying to go beyond caste through his 'caste-class-power' analysis, is explicitly guided and inspired by Weber's triology of 'class, status and party'. Whether study of caste alone is sufficient or class and power should also receive adequate atten-tion is not a matter of concern here. No doubt application of Weber's trio is a step ahead of the application of the British func-tionalism to the study of caste system. Yet, the fact remains that in the understanding of Indian social stratification, structuralism. Marxism and positivism, along with their numerous variations, have been accepted more as fads than as relevant theoretical and methodological devices. History of social inequality has been the biggest casualty in regard to these approaches.

Social Factors

Beteille makes a distinction between caste, class and power on the pattern of 'class, status and party' as suggested by Max Weber (1970). The distinction between these three is justified by Beteille's observation of "the differentiation of institutional structures", and also because of the absence of "summation of statuses" (Beteille, 1966b; Bailey, 1963). Beteille also notes that there is a very little preoccupation with purity-pollution rituals in general. The problem is neither regarding application of Weber's approach to social stratification, nor is it in connection with incongruence between social, economic and political aspects of rural people. Instead, it is concerning *apriori* acceptance of Weber's theory and its inherent ideology. The theoretical core of Weber's formulation is constitutive of rationalism, subjectivity and objectification, whereas its substantive inspiration comes from his experience of Germany's political and economic situation. These points have not been kept in view while trying to understand the Indian situation through the application of Weber's frame of reference. Methodological appreciation of Weber's theory, namely, *verstehen* does not constitute a part of Beteille's research strategy. In fact, the research strategy adopted by Beteille is 'foreign' to Weber's theoretical apparatus. Hence, the contradiction between Beteille's approach and his method of study.

Anil Bhatt's study (1975) of caste, class and politics provides a clear theoretical exposition and a set of objectives. He has borrowed extensively from studies of 'comparative politics' and 'comparative functionalism', and in fact uses the phrase 'comparative social stratification'. His main focus is on the understanding of 'summation of statuses' between the contemporary social structure and politics. This he does by comparing the traditional Indian society with its contemporary setting. Quantitative analysis is his main source of objective understanding of social stratification. Generalization and quantification are closely linked. He has gone beyond 'village' in understanding social stratification, and also in avoiding ethnographic and anthropological-qualitative analysis. Through survey research, macro-national and regional-level analysis has been attempted. He writes: "I have tried to be very explicit in relating the evidences to the theory". However, one should also recognize that survey research is the most favourite technique of research for the American structural-functional positivists.

In most of the studies discussed above, a link between *theory* and *method* of study has remained unclear. Two reasons can be attributed to this vagueness: (i) tne notion of scientism associated with a *method* of study; and (ii) convenient acceptance of a particular method of study (Sharma, 1983). Beteille accepted 'participant observation' as a method of study with a view to stay in the Brahmin locality in the village. He did not plan his field-work before hand, and as he says, he did not have "a battery of hypotheses and concepts" prior to the field-work. But why? Is it that he had not read Marx and Weber prior to his field-work? But this does not seem to have been the case as all through his work, he extensively borrows from both, and clearly opts for Weber's approach to social stratification.

In my study (1974) of social stratification in rural Rajasthan, I began with 'a battery of hypotheses' which I have listed in the study. I also had a very clear awareness that empirical substantiation for these hypotheses required an application of a variety of research techniques and devices. Comparison was made based on several variables. Data were gathered from both primary and secondary sources. Historical details about the villages were also collected. A variant of qualitative analysis was thought necessary before launching upon the field-work in the six villages from three districts.

Invariably certain specific notions about social reality have guided studies of social stratification. Needless to say that most of these notions are inept to understand social stratification in India. Some of them are: caste is a rural phenomenon; class is found in urban centres; individual is the unit of social ranking in cities; group is the unit of status-estimation in villages; ranking is flexible in urban areas and rigid in rural milieux; achievement is the hallmark of urban people; and ascription is the essence of life in the countryside. Such notions have not only led to biased formulation of hypotheses, even empirical observations have been distorted due to such simplistic uncritical statements.

D' Souza's study (1967) of caste and class in Chandigarh no doubt highlights significance of the continuum of the rigidity-fluidity dimensions and of the individual and his properties as the units of analysis, but all this exercise is implicitly patterned on the notion of positivism of the structural-functionalist variety. His emphasis is on constructing 'order' of classes based on education, occupation and income. Concrete interacting social groups, such as professionals, businessmen, mill-owners, industrial workers, etc., have not been studied in situations of concrete interaction. Caste groups and forms of corporateness have also been left out from his study of Chandigarh. D' Souza is perhaps influenced by Warner's SES approach more than anything else.

In pursuance of the command received from the British government, their agents in India propagated that caste was a useful institution for Hindus in particular and for Indians in general. Furnivall, Senart and Button listed a couple of functions of caste system in the books they wrote on caste. Recently, some more western scholars have also lent support to this verdict inferentially through the findings of their studies (Marriott, 1965). They have stated that caste has a secular aspect. It has made people conscious and therefore it has had an integrating consequence. Kothari (1970) reports that one American scholar even talks of "the democratic incarnation of caste". According to some scholars, caste has even led to the modernization of India's polity. Kothari (1970b) accepts these statements and considers caste *apolitical*. In his study of politics, he uses the vocabulary of the American advocates of comparative functionalism.

Louis Dumont's *Homo-hierarchicus* is the most well-known exposition of structuralist perspective on social stratification. The pivotal notions of Dumont's structuralism as noted by Yogendra Singh (1981) are ideology, dialectics, and transformation. The basic tenet of caste system is 'hierarchy'. Hierarchy encompasses all aspects of life including binary tensions and dialectics of the opposition between 'pure' and 'impure'. Dumont's view in terms of binary opposition is wanting both theoretically and substantively, since 'pure' in actual practice is often found fused in the 'impure' and vice-versa in many rituals (Gould, 1967). Besides this, Dumont's structuralist view lacks a conception of history and analysis of politico-economic dimensions of India's social reality. To think of structuralism independent of empirical reality is Dumont's main concern. However, structuralism of such a variety in regard to the study of caste and its allied aspects has resulted into propagation of caste ideology and caste-based inequalities. Dumont has never bothered to see the hiatus between the rules of the game and the actual game played and enacted in a given context.

New Trends

A couple of studies on caste and class have taken 'change' as the focal point of analysis. Stratification as a process is now a well conceived notion. Structural-historical perspective is being applied by those who lay emphasis on the study of differentiation, evolution and change in caste and class in India. Modes of production in agriculture and industry in relation to caste and class have been discussed both by economic historians and anthropologists (Fryken-berg, 1969). The Marxists look at the origin or evolution of caste from the point of economic relations. Political activists like Dange (1949), Ranadive (1979) and Namboodaripad (1979) look at caste as a mechanism of exploitation in the hands of the upper castes. However, non-Marxists consider caste not as a super-structural entity, but mainly as a basic institution of division of labour and harmonic relations. Mode of production is the key to the Marxist theory of social stra-tification. But the mode of production and the differentiation of peasantry are old and familiar issuers (Sharma, 1983). To find them in Indian society, one does not have to borrow from Marx and Mao. Doing so would mean ignoring analysis of the traditional structure and processes of change affecting that structure. One could find uneven structures of landlords, peasants and tenants before the advent of the British rule in India. Over a time, the said unevenness of the traditional social structure has been trans-formed into a new one. Land reforms, green revolution, adult franchise, etc., have contributed to this unevenness in many ways. The essence of the Marxist method of study is that explanation emanates from the structure of social reality. Social reality is not static; hence, historical explanation. Marxist approach has also been called evolutionary, emancipatory and hermeneutic in nature. The problem does not lie in accepting its ethos, but in its transplantation in toto for studying Indian society. A.R. Desai's study (1982) is a well-known example of 'orthodox Marxism'. Other variants of Marxist analysis of caste, class and land relations are the studies by D.P. Mukerji(1958), Kathleen Gough (1980) and Gail Omvedt (1982). Gough, for example, employs a mix of anthropological method, history and Marxism in her study of agrarian relations in South India. Mukerji combines tradition, history and Marxism as the three main components of his study of modern Indian society, economy and polity. He calls himself a Marxologist and not a Marxian. Class is viewed as a sociological concept and Marxism is treated as a study of the history of entire process of alienation. Thus, Mukerji is one who has moulded and modified Marxism in view of the nature of Indian society—its tradition and history.

The problem, therefore, is first to identify the genesis of theory and method and then to explore its relevance for the study of social stratification. This inquiry also calls for understanding of the conscious motives of the researchers in applying these theories and methods. 'Researcher' is a very significant variable in social research, particularly in a developing country like India. Marxian, Weberian, structural-functionalist and structuralist theoretic orientations and methods of study have generally analy-zed here with a view to assess their relevance/irrelevance for a deeper understanding of social inequality in India.

In the studies of social stratification during the post-independence period, caste has been over-emphasized. Culturo-logical or indological dimensions have been predominant in the studies of caste and social mobility. Colonialism brought about social mobility affecting the caste system; this fact has remained unanalyzed to a large extent. In the wake of colonialism, economic and political domains were affected due to changes in land tenure systems, emergence of professional classes, migration, education, law and bureaucratic organizations, but the notion of class which has been akin to Indian society remained in the background. Western notion of class was propagated as a secular and demo-cratic concept of social relations. Class mobility was viewed as the opposite of mobility in the caste system. Simple facts such as class-like distinction within a caste, class considerations in hypergamy and coexistence of caste and class remained peripheral issues, whereas corporateness, pollution-purity and sanskritisation were over-emphasized. So much so that caste mobility at the level of individual, family and *jati* (group) has not been adequately analysed as corporateness of caste has overshadowed all other dimensions. Once again, downward social mobility (proletarianization) has not received much needed attention due to over-emphasis on upward social mobility. All these gaps could be filled up if theoretic orientations and methods of study could appropriately be suited for the study of Indian society. And this is possible only if theory and method could have their genesis in the rami-fications of social inequality existent in Indian society. However, indiscreet indigenization or nativism is not a good substitute for borrowed theories, concepts and methods of study.

10

Life in Villages

As a perennial problem social inequality is found universally in one form or other. Its prevalence is a part of human existence. On the origin of inequality among men the following questions posed by Dahrendorf remain pertinent: (1) Why is there inequality among men? (2) Where do its causes lie? (3) Can it be reduced, or even abolished altogether? (4) Or do we have to accept it as a necessary element in the structure of human society? These questions are, no doubt, ubiquitous, yet specific societies have shown differential patterns and expressions of social inequality. However, before we take up the case of social inequality in rural India in particular, it would be proper to analyze in brief the concept and perspective of social inequality.

Dahrendorf distinguishes between inequalities of natural capabilities and those of social position; and between inequalities that do not involve evaluative rank-order and those that do. Of these two pairs of distinction, Dahrendorf works out four types of inequality: (a) natural differences of kind, (b) natural differences of rank, (c) social differentiation of positions, and (d) social stratification based on reputation and wealth. In all the four types, 'individual' is evidently the focal point of status evaluation. Such a conception of social inequality, built on distribution of property, wealth, honour and power among individual members, would imply a certain ideological basis and a structural arrangement of people based upon those inegalitarian institutionalized norms. In the final analysis such a conception of inequality provides a logical legitimacy to social inequality, and to its functionality and inevitability. Based on such a plea social inequality is visibly found in the division of labour, differentiation of roles and, in fact, in differential evaluation of different tasks and roles assigned to or taken up by different members.

We start with a simple conception that social inequality is found in one form or other, but it is not necessarily functional and inevitable. Division of labour or differential expertise is functional, and it is this which is required too. One may reject this view by dubbing it 'idealistic' and 'imaginary', but all human societies have been striving for such a formation of social relations all through their existence. Another viewpoint is that social inequality is a multidimensional and dynamic aspect in the sense that its one pattern changes in part or full and another pattern emerges modifying or altering the previous one. There are two implicit points in this statement: (i) social inequality is not monolithic as wrongly conceived by some students particularly in the context of caste; and (ii) there has been a continuous (with variations in the magnitude) structuring and restructuring of social inequality.

In fact, it is erroneous to perceive inequality opposite of equality both in theoretical terms and empirical contexts. Inequality is a 'relational' phenomenon, that is, it is to be seen in terms of one another rather in an absolute sense. In a family its members are unequal in regard to their kinship—based statuses, but they are 'equal' as members of an intimate primary primordial unit. Family members are different from members of a formal organization. Even when there is 'unequal' distribution of work or assignment of duties and responsibilities, members of a family are treated as 'equal'. To evaluate social inequality in India from the point of organization of the western industrial society would certainly undermine the role of India's social structure, culture, history and dialectics. Of these concepts, the first two refer to structural and normative aspects, and the latter two refer to change and contradictions.

We may also state that there is no opposition between a structural analysis and a processual approach in the study of Indian society. These two together could explain the pattern of structuring of social inequality in a wholesome way. The dichotomy between the western industrial society and the traditional/backward society is also futile, and it is irrelevant to accept the former as a reference model for studying the latter.

We have no hesitation in accepting Beteille's view that a placement of people in layers (higher and lower) is inadequate for analyzing social inequality. There is a need for understanding the ongoing relations between individuals occupying different positions. But we notice some serious implications in what Beteille writes: 'The problem of social inequality is above all the problem of how people interact with each other, how they compete and contend, how some succeed in moving up while others are pushed down despite their resistance." We are aware that this formulation about social inequality is not specifically meant as such for studying Indian society, but formulations like this have quite often been used for analyzing Indian social situation without realizing the fact that it has emanated from the experience of modern western society. For example, if interaction among people is preordained by structural-social ties to a large extent, then competition would not become a pivotal aspect of social relations. There is nothing like a 'success theme' in the Indian society the way it is reflected in the above quotation. There is an implicit theoretical viewpoint which can be accepted only with some precautions. 'Rational' aspect assumes the element of volition which again is not quite a fact in India's context.

Statements about acceptance of western industrial society as a model for analyzing Indian society abound in the contemporary literature. Competition for status and power is more in modern industrial societies than in traditional agrarian societies. Individuals are units of social ranking in the western societies whereas groups and collectivities are the main basis of status and power in Indian society. Likewise these contrasts, continuity, ascription and cultural norms are said to be predominant in the Indian society, and change, achievement and material values overwhelm the western world. It has very often been stated that social classes are a feature of modern industrial societies. Even Aron's dichotomy between the *nominalist* and the *realist* conceptions of class in terms of 'individual' and 'collectivity', respectively, as the basis of class identification seems to be inadequate. The nominalist (psychological) basis is not independent of the realist (collective consciousness) in the Indian context as the two have been inseparable parts of India's social formation.

The question is: Is the notion *of Homo hierarchicus* synonym of India's caste system? Another question is: Are there no elements of *Homo aqualis* in India's system of social stratification? We do agree with Beteille that "the idea of hierarchy entails that of inequality...," but inequality does not necessarily mean 'hierarchy', that is, rigidity of high and low statuses. Rigidity of caste-based statuses is not more than that based on apartheid, estatehood and feudalism. Students of Indian social history have amply shown discontinuities, breakdowns, changes and contradictions in India's caste system in particular and in Indian society in general. Multi-dimensionality not only of India's social fabric but also of the caste system has already weakened the monolith of *Homo hierarchicus*. To accept *Homo aqualis* as ideological basis and also a fact of life of modern western industrial society is simply a myth, and to take it as a reference model for *Homo hierarchicus* in Indian society is perhaps a very serious ignorance (conscious or inadvertent) on the part of the students of Indian society.

Notions of both inequality and equality are built into the ideology and practice of the caste system. The position of priest speaks of superiority of ritual status, but the notion and practice of 'contra-priest' indicate the role of secular duties and obligations certainly with ritual umbrella. Relations between *jajman* (patron) and *kamin* (client) are not simply of higher and lower, superordinate and subordinate positions, but they also define rights and obligations of the lower sections along with the dominant castes. Therefore, we propose to cast a fresh look at the explanations of social inequality in rural India.

All not Equal

There are a number of approaches to the study of hierarchy and inequality. Following the Hegelian view, we would say that the 'world of things' is dominated by the 'world of thoughts'. "Hierarchy is the domination of thought, the domination of the spirit." Marx also considers hierarchy more in terms of an ideal form. Inequalitarian relations are determined by the existential conditions in a given society. The existential conditions as depicted by Marx are reflected in the following statement: "As individuals express their life, so they are. What they are, therefore, coincides with their production, both with what they produce and with how they produce. The nature of individuals thus depends on the material conditions determining the production." Marx simply does not speak of 'structure' of existential conditions, but also analyzes the process of change in these conditions.

Tribal ownership, ancient and state ownership, feudal or estate property ownership and capitalism are not only evolutionary stages but also, when put together, form the core of Marx's method for studying society and history. In each stage, Marx makes a mention about division of labour and distinctions between town and country, and, in fact, about nature of a socio-economic differentiation. Antagonism and contradictions are the causes of differentiation and change. The notion of basic structural change is an inseparable part of Marx's understanding of society and history as it is evident in his analysis of stages and groups of people in these stages.

Structuring of social inequality is a continuous process. Marx's view in this regard is: The social structure and the state are continually evolving out of the life process of definite individuals, but of individuals, not as they may appear in their own or other people's imagination, but as they really are, i.e., as they operate, produce materially, and hence as they work under definite material limits, presuppositions and conditions independent of their will." Further, he writes: "Consciousness can never be anything else than conscious existence, and the existence of men is their actual life process." "Life is not determined by consciousness, but consciousness by life."

We consider these eclectically taken statements from the *German Ideology* in the form of a method for studying social inequality. Men are seen by Marx (Engels) in their actual life process. The practical process of development of men is taken into consideration for understanding social reality. How social life is produced? What is its mode of production? What units are produced as a result of certain social conditions? What is the nature of social interaction between the groups produced through such an evolutionary process? We find a sort of answer to these questions in the following: "History is nothing but the succession of the separate generations, each of which exploits the materials, the capital funds, the productive forces handed down to it by preceding generations, and thus, on the one hand, continues the traditional activity in completely changed circumstances and, on the other, modifies the old circumstances with a completely changed activity." Thus, in fact, Marx visualizes continuity of tradition and emergence of modernity side by side. Structure of social relations is determined by the direction of change. Structure and process are, in fact, co-existent.

Another methodological perspective is given by Max Weber. Gerth and Mills write: "Much of Weber's own work is ofcourse informed by a skilful application of Marx's historical method." Weber criticizes Marx for an untenable monocausal theory, a segmental perspective and reducing the multiplicity of causal factors to a single factor theorem. However, Gerth and Mills comment that Weber's work may be seen as an attempt to 'round out' Marx's economic materialism by political and military materialism. Despite ideological and methodological differences between Marx and Weber, the two are interested in grasping the inter-relations, and in other words, the social structure itself. The principles of rationalization, depersonalization and routinization are key to Weber's thinking and understanding of society. The individual and his action as the basic unit are core of Weber's *interpretative socio-logy.* All forms of associations and institutions should be reduced to 'understandable' action. Thus, methodologically, Weber's theory of stratification is subjective. Gerth and Mills observe: "The nomi-nalism of Weber's method may be understood in terms of his attempt to avoid a philosophical emphasis upon either material or ideal factors, or upon either structural or individual principles of explanation."

Nadel works out a definition of 'structure' and based on that examines the relevance of the 'structural analysis'. "Structure indi-cates an ordered arrangement of parts, which can be treated as transposable, being relatively invariant, while the parts are them-selves variable." Nadel speaks implicitly of 'dynamic equilibrium'. The structure of a society in terms of 'network' or 'system' of relationships could be only a starting point for analyzing the process of change in the social relationships. Nadel writes: "It (structural analysis) enables us to present our data neatly, synoptically, and with some elegance." 'Time', 'reality' and 'function' are three cornerstones of the structural analysis. Therefore, the structural analysis is not just confined to 'the continuity' of a social life, its persistence and invariance; it accommodates the elements of 'time', 'variance' and 'changes' and even 'volition', hence a 'dynamic analysis'. Nadel agrees with Forte's view about social structure as "a sum of processes in time". All societies, therefore, combine necessarily structure and process (change). Ordering and reordering, and distribution and redistribution, imply both structuring and restructuring of social relations. In fact, there is no contradiction between structure and process, and the two are built into each other, and hence put limits upon each other.

Bailey, no doubt, unlike other researchers, discusses problems and methods of his study of Baderi village in Orissa. In his analysis of structure and system, Bailey seems to have made a claim for making a structural analysis of political change. He writes: "A structural analysis emphasizes the regularity, the continuity, the permanence of certain forms of social interaction, and of groups of persons. It also emphasizes system." For Bailey, the word 'structure' refers to a higher level of analysis of interconnections between various sub-structures. Compared to Nadel, Bailey puts more emphasis on coherence and continuity. For 'rationalizing' this view, Bailey states that at empirical level there is no antipathy between conflict and a structural analysis. But he also reiterates his 'structural-functionalist'stance by saying that the structure itself contains rules for the resolution of conflict, and conflict even plays a crucial part in maintaining the structure. Obviously, implication of such a view is that nothing transforms, replaces and displaces particularly in the Indian context. Caste, village community, its power structure and its linkages with higher levels are visualized as 'static'. Formulation of the structural analysis is guided more by the coloured colonial misconceptions rather than by the vigour and logic of the approach itself. If a society has not been 'static' or 'unchanging', or it has not been changing as per the perception of change of colonial rulers and some scholars (particularly the western ones), it is erroneous to start with a 'static analysis' of Indian society. Besides this, a 'dynamic analysis' is understood, again erroneously, as a result of some external factors which implies that all changes are from without and not from within. History of India's social formation is full of contradictions and changes ema-nating from within its structure and normative pattern. Therefore, Bailey's notion of structure as a higher level of analysis, in effect, is "a low level of generalization".

The Background

Along with the development of the order of the four ranks, namely, Brahmins, Kshatriyas, Vaisyas and Shudras, the development of state, law, religion, science and philosophy also took place in ancient India. Ruben holds the view that the structure of ancient Indian society can be described in terms of agrarian production and relations of different social strata to property, especially the soil. Thus, the rank-orders in the village community depended upon the quality of agricultural land and infrastructure for culti-vating it. However, Ruben does not seem to be right in assuming that the village community was stationary and inflexible. Guild *(sreni),* caste *(jati)* and devotion *(bhakti)* were later developments. Ruben also, along with some historians, prefers to characterize the Indian society by the Asiatic mode of production. He writes: "Thus, we may like to characterize Indian history as that of a society based on the Indian variant of the Asiatic mode of production with strong elements of slavery in antiquity and of feudalism in the middle ages, succeeded by capitalism which mainly came to India in the form of British colonialism till capitalist India became independent in 1947." Such a unilinear mode of change undermines variations within each of the elements of one stage into the next one. The hypothesis referring to replacement/displacement of social structure underlies such a process of evolu-tionary scheme.

Romila Thapar emphasizes two major aspects of the functioning of social groups and their mobility in the study of a society. She refers to pastoralism, settled agrarian economy, and an emergent commercial urban economy as features of Vedic, Mauryan and Gupta periods, respectively. She also observes that changes at the level of elite groups were most obviously brought about by foreign invasions and mitigations. The migrations affected status relationships and the rules of marriage. Thapar's view that ancient Indian society was not a rigidly structured society is based on the fact that a hierarchy of statuses was absent. The *varna* concept did not refer to an actual description of the social func-tioning, and therefore, Indian society was not a frozen one. There were periods of change which influenced social institutions and other domains of social life.

Thapar brings out a distinction between ritual status and actual status in terms of economic and political power. Despite a hazy line of demarcation between the two and the ideology of *varna-ashram dharma,* there were secular bases of social stratification. Rigidity of *varna* was weakened by the emergence of 'mixed castes'. Tribal identity and occupational identity paved a way for mixed castes. No doubt, ritual status was fixed, but change in its rigidity was brought about by improving it or by denying its importance. This was more of an ideological sort of change. There was mobility also in terms of actual status as it was not necessarily defined by and dependent upon the ritual status. Emulation of actual status required a change in the redistribution of society's resources. Also, the examples of tension between the ritual (Brahminic) and the actual (the Kshatriya) statuses have been brought to our notice by several scholars. However, it would not be correct to say that the two statuses were completely indepen-dent of one another. For example, caste system has performed innumerable functions including economic and political, and this is one strong reason for its continuity and change.

A study of social stratification based on evidence from Buddhist sources reveals two schemes of categorization of people: (i) *varna, jati and kula;* and (ii) a Brahminical division of society, namely, Brahmins, Kshatriyas, Vaisyas and Sudras on the one hand, and another based on non-Brahminical sources categorizing people into Kshatriyas, Brahmins and Grahapatis on the other. The Brahminical scheme uses *varna* and *jati,* and the non-Brah-minical categorization is based on the term *kula*. The latter represents "a division of society into the domains of power, ritual and the economy." In the Buddhist literature, the Kshatriyas are invariably enumerated above the Brahmins. Also tension is noticed between the Kshatriyas and the Brahmins. Buddha refuted the claim of Brahminical superiority. One finds a two-tier system of social ranking in the Buddhist literature. The system of social stratification is not as normative as portrayed in the Brahminical texts. Occupational divisions among the people were the basis of their identification. Thus, a system of stratification existed independent of the Brahminical scheme.

According to Kosambi, the essential relationship in India is not based on kinship. Production and mutual exchange of commodities and bonds of production hold society together. Caste was related to economic hierarchy and the two together paved way for feudalism. Feudalism was a form of social order. In the medieval period of Indian history, that is, from twelfth century till the advent of the British rule, basic structural changes occurred in the traditional Indian society. These changes comprised of the land tenure systems such as *iqta, mansabdari* and *jagirdari,* etc. which, in turn, brought about changes in the ruling class and the rural landed aristocracy. Below the rural aristocracy were big peasants. There was considerable stratification within the peasantry.

Nurul S. Hasan writes: "The Zamindar class played a vital role in the political, economic, and cultural life of medieval India." However, Hasan makes this reference in the context of their role in extracting the agricultural surplus, appropriation and control of rural economy. "At the same time, the separatist, localist, and parochial trends received powerful patronage from the *zamindari* class." The class of Zamindars was highly differentiated. Hasan classifies them into: (i) the autonomous chieftains, (ii) the intermediary Zamindars, and (iii) the primary Zamindars. The second and the third categories were found at the village level. Chaudhuris, Khuts and Muqaddams were intermediaries, and the primary Zamindars included the holders of proprietary rights.

Inequalities in the pre-British period existed in myriad ways. There were people who did not pay land revenue, and some paid only a nominal amount. There were others who paid the maximum. Such economic disparities were associated with caste hierarchy as well. The system of landgrants *(jagirs)* promoted creation of landed enclaves from among the ruler's caste and his kin groups. Some favourites, professionals, dancers and singers, and servants were also given *jagirs* in lieu of their services. The entire system became quite complex and inequalitarian. There were as many as *45 jagirs and* 175 taxes in the erstwhile State of Jaipur. The *jagirs* were arranged in a rank-order based on their size and revenue, and the Jagirdars enjoyed power and privilege in accordance with the ranks of their *jagirs*. Taxes were also socially patterned as they were imposed differentially in terms of caste ranks and other positions.

There were socially structured land control relationships in terms of the landlord and the tenant. But they were not monolithic as they were divided into innumerable strata. A social formation viewpoint explains that various landed strata were linked to definite socio-cultural and economic and political roles. Besides this, each caste group, for example, was differentially associated with other caste groups. A potter used to supply earthen pots to various families in the village community. He was treated as a *kamin* or servant by the Rajput landlords, but the 'untouchable' castes or even castes of 'equal status' could never treat him as a *kamin,* though like the Rajput landlords they were also his 'patrons'. Further, it would be wrong to assume that a potter was a *kamin* in all situations. He used to behave as a 'contra-priest' on the occasions of marriage etc. in the families of castes higher than his own. A contra-priest is a person who is required to perform certain ritual functions on auspicious occasions at the families of castes higher than his own caste. Thus, inequality and equality co-existed, and no caste, class and power groups enjoyed absolute power. The very nature of interdependence upon each other provided certain rights and privileges to all social groups. But these were certainly of an uneven nature.

Frykenberg's suggestion for formulating new theoretical models seems worth mentioning here. His two ideas are: (i) ideas of movement, namely, about process and causation; and (ii) ideas of structural relativity, that is, of dynamic relationships of social entities moving within a defined structural whole. Frykenberg considers ideas of structural relativity as intrinsic to the study of process and structure: 'The dynamic relationships of all social entities moving within a defined structural whole can hardly be analyzed without the invention of working models, some simple and some extremely complex." Land, labour and lord are appropriate elements according to Frykenberg. The British rule brought about drastic changes in the institutions of property, government and law, and these three significantly affected land, labour and lord, socially as well as economically.

Private ownership of land, land settlements, *zamindari* and *ryotwari* systems, centralization of governmental authority throughout the length and breadth of the country, bureaucracy, judiciary and new legislations changed the structural and normative patterns during the British period. Due to these changes, despite unwillingness of the British raj, the caste system became weak as a social hierarchy, and became stronger as a source of mobilization for social, economic and political gains. This process of caste mobilization for extra-ritual ends received further boost in the post-independence period due to adult franchise, elections, migration and education.

Both Cohn and Metcalf arrive at a similar conclusion in their studies of the eastern districts of Uttar Pradesh. Cohn writes: "Most of the Rajputs whose *zamindari* rights were sold continued to live as they lived before in their villages and *talukas,* dominating lower caste cultivators and offering sustained and at times effective opposition to auction purchases." Thus, change in status from *zamindari* to *ex-zamindari* or what Metcalf calls "from *raja* to landlord" could not substantially affect adversely their dominant position in Indian rural society. Change in legal status does not necessarily change the 'actual status' of the people.

This sort of hiatus between the ideal or expected change and the actual change and situation would not permit analysis of social change and mobility in terms of closed systems. Therefore, there is a need to go beyond the study of caste system and social mobility because social reality is much broader than what caste could encompass. Changes emanating from external sources, for example, during the British period, in terms of legislations, land tenure systems, technology, education and administration cannot be studied simply from a caste point of view. Unexpected or latent structural and cultural changes emerged during this period resulting into restructuring of hierarchical relations.

My own study of Rajasthan shows that the Jagirdars and Bhomias were allowed to retain best lands at the time of the resumption of jagirs. Some lands were not resumed at all. Jagirdars mobilized their caste association, namely, the Rajasthan Kshatriya Mahasabha, for allotment of *khudkasht* land, compensation and assessment of *jagirs* for land revenue. The government bowed to the pressure of the Jagirdars. The substantial tenants were able to manage transfer of large landholdings in their names depriving the smaller tenants of their due share. This was a significant step in structuring social and economic inequalities. The legal status was withdrawn but there was no corresponding effect on the actual status. Downward mobility was not a significant result of this legislation in several cases. Upward mobility was, however, quite a noticeable phenomenon in the case of tenants.

Social Organisation

We do not intend to discuss the patterns of social stratification in terms of caste, class and power as such in this essay. But a reference to Dumont's structuralist stance in regard to inter-caste, intra-caste and intra-familial ranking is not completely out of context. The principle of hierarchy not only applies to caste, but also to principles of values, occupations, food and clothes and bride-givers and bride-takers. Dumont looks for cultural meaning of affinity and consanguinity. In Dumont's *Homo Hierarchicus,* Yogendra Singh discerns four notions of structuralism: (i) ideology, (ii) idealistic, (iii) transformational relationship, and (iv) comparison. Hierarchy is an ideational notion; it pervades all aspects of Hindu society. Everything is seen in terms of 'pure' and 'impure', its binary tension and dialectics. Since pure and impure are parts of the same principle, they are complementary. But hierarchy is seen through the superiority of the pure over the impure. Dumont observes that there has been change in the society and not of the society, hence rules out a structural change in India's caste system.

Since we are interested in discerning change in the existing patterns of social inequality, we do not wish to go into the genesis of various approaches and methods of study of social stratification. It would be appropriate to lay hands on a few selected studies. Chakravarti discusses inequalities in rural India based on status, economic differences and power. The analysis of social inequalities in terms of these three spheres is based on the assumption that a lower status in one sphere is not necessarily accompanied by the same in the other two spheres. Of these three domains, caste status is fixed by birth. But it is to be seen how ritual basis of caste continues to play a decisive role in determining social, economic and political status.

Structural incongruities have certainly emerged in the post-independence period. Caste has become segmental entity as it has lost its 'organic' character. The pure does not encompass today the less pure or impure. In fact, if the "less pure has acquired strength in economic and political spheres, it encompasses to a large extent the pure". The nature of inter-caste relations is not so much valued today in terms of commensality as it is done in terms of wealth and power. Pollution-purity and untouchability have become more of casual rituals than a day-to-day reality. This is due to structural changes introduced in the countryside over a period of last four decades: Motivational factors or rational outlook have not brought structuring of social inequalities as much as the latter has changed values and aspirations of the rural people.

Two studies, one by Bailey and second by Epstein focus on structural change in the countryside. Bailey examines relationship between caste and new economy. As a result of the abolition of the traditional land tenure systems, new frontiers, namely, economic, political and administrative have taken land to market. Bailey analyzes new economy, land transactions, services and trade. The landlords have become ex-landlords, and the functionary and service castes have become landowners. The latter have taken their traditional produces to market and have earned profits which were not available to them in the traditional system.

Epstein's study reveals that structural innovation, namely, irrigation has brought about significant change in the village economy, but it has restricted social change by discouraging migration, education and employment outside the village. Lack of such an innovation has resulted into migration, education and employment in another village. Epstein analyzes structural change in two villages of Karnataka in terms of crops, houses, landholdings, livestock, family incomes and expenditures and market networks.

Social inequality is a structural and historical reality observable in diverse forms and in different contexts. Social inequality is, therefore, related to structure, ideology and behaviour of the people. Its consequences could be seen in terms of arrangement of the people and expressions of their life-styles and careers they pursue. Structure of inequality in a given society is generally found having dissonance between different dimensions. For example, the three dimensions of social inequality, namely, social, political and economic are not of the same magnitude in terms of pro-ducing inequalitarian relations, and therefore, these do not nece-ssarily correspond with each other having one-to-one relationship. Thus, social inequality may be pronounced in one specific domain, whereas in others it may not be of the same magnitude. Such a state of inequality is normally a result of specific structural conditions and processes of change. Men are, therefore, not equally unequal. Impact of inequality is also uneven. Even ascriptive bases of inequality such as age, sex and kinship statuses do not have a uniform pattern of social effects.

Social inequality is a very sensitive aspect of social life. The notion that a person is higher than someone else or that one has a realization that his position is superior to some other member of his village community makes it sensitive and evaluative. It is not psychological evaluation that matters so much. Such evaluations are based on differential possession of resources including house, household goods, property, education, lucrative job and political power. Since role of these factors in determining social inequality has increased, the role of ascriptive factors such as birth, sex, age and fictive status has declined considerably.

Fallers states that social inequality has both normative and structural phenomena. The normative aspect refers to evaluation, and the structural aspect refers to distribution of material resources and power. Berreman refers to a study of four dimensions of social inequality, namely, behavioural, interactional, material and existential. Social inequality is a lived-in experience and a stark reality. It is a relative phenomenon.

Let us illustrate the structural basis of social inequality from our field studies in Rajasthan. Brahmins are regarded high in ritual rank-order by other castes, but their influence and power in other domains depend mainly upon their economic and educational achievements. In one of the six villages we have studied Brahmins are dominant not because of their high ritual status, but because they enjoy dominant positions in economic and educational spheres. This is so to a large extent because being Brahmins they have more access to higher education and white-collar jobs than other caste groups. But it is not that all the families from among the Brahmins or even all the individual members from Brahmin families have such a privilege and opportunity. In another village, Brahmins have incongruity between their ritual status and economic and cultural (educational) achievements, and therefore, they do not enjoy power and dominance in the village community. Out of the remaining four villages, in one only Brahmins have considerable influence in the affairs of the village because of their better off economic and educational status. Thus, social inequality is a very complex phenomenon. It is not that high ritual status of Brahmins has become altogether redundant and insignificant. It is accorded importance on certain religious, ritual and ceremonial occasions, but it is ephemeral. A Brahmin priest becomes a commoner as soon as the particular episode is over. However, there are still some noticeable cultural and social distinctions between different caste groups particularly in regard to life-styles, performance of rituals and observance of some practices.

In regard to Rajputs, hierarchy based on the size of the *jagirs* is not closely associated with commensal and ritual bases of caste-based inequality. Norms in relation to pollution-purity and untouchability were never a significant element of the life-styles of Rajputs. They were always non-vegetarian and drinkers of alcohol, and their food habits made them to think that Brahmins and Banias particularly would observe norms related to pollution-purity and untouchability as they were vegetarian, teetotaller and performed rituals and worshipped gods and goddesses. Thus, theoretically, the Rajputs were number two in the caste hierarchy, but in practice they were number one in political sphere, and did not bother about their ritual rank as such. Generally, they were not engaged in gainful educational achievements. Because of the abolition of the *jagirdari* and *zamindari* systems, they have been affected severely. Now a good number of Rajputs are self-cultivators like their ex-tenants, and some of them today own much smaller landholdings than their own ex-tenants. A substantial number of Rajputs work as police constables and soldiers in Indian Army. Rajputs are one community which has witnessed a radical down-grading of their social status in the village community.

Conversely, the Jats who were tenants of the Rajput land-lords, have improved their status considerably in economic and political spheres. In the economic sphere, the loss of Rajput landlords has been the gain of Jat tenants as they have acquired substantial land-holdings. In the sphere of political power, they have taken maximum advantage of adult franchise and their preponderant numerical strength by arousing caste consciousness and mobilizing their members on the caste basis.

Thus, two obverse structural processes immediately after the first phase of land reforms created new cleavages within different caste groups and also brought about some 'levelling' effect on the structure of social inequality. Some of the Rajput families, though could not retain their traditional glory and power, tried to retain best lands, and diverted their savings and assets in economically gainful activities and enterprises. Similarly, the Jat cultivators who were substantially benefited by land reforms further consolidated their economic position by extracting maximum advantage of developmental schemes and facilities and by adopting new devices in the field of agriculture. Those groups and families which received a jolt could not recoup from that crisis, and have ended up with not only downward social mobility but also in some cases reached the level of pauperization.

Caste Factors

Dumont's structuralism and its application by several others to the study of India's caste system have led us to think that there exists the dichotomy of hierarchy and equality, and holism and individualism. Srinivas seems to agree with Dumont's approach to the study of social inequality. He writes: 'In short, there is, on the one hand, the syndrome of tradition, hierarchy and holism, while on the other hand, that of modernity, equality and individualism. There is no liberty in traditional societies for liberty can only be predicted of individuals and not of groups." The obvious confession is that Hindu society is hierarchical and the modern western society is egalitarian.

If we look at the Indian scene today, it is quite evident that individuals migrate to towns and cities for higher education and better employment. Srinivas writes: "Caste society is holistic and hierarchical and is inimical to individualism but in spite of this individualism surfaces in the *sanyasi* or renouncer, who transcends society." Srinivas and Dumont see individualism only in renouncing of the world and not in migration of a Marwari Bania from western Rajasthan to Assam, Bengal, Bihar, Tamil Nadu and Karnataka. A Rajasthani 'untouchable' labourer has been migrating to Delhi and Punjab for several decades for seeking employment parti-cularly in the years of drought and famine. Always a selected few have gone out of their native places for higher education and white-collar jobs. These are vital sociological facts of India's rural life in the context of inequality.

According to Dumont, the basis of the caste system is the opposition between the pure and the impure, but with increased, recession of pollution-purity syndrome, hierarchy does not conti-nue to be an ideology. There is also no combination of 'two forces', that is, Brahmins and Kshatriyas (status and power). The inter-mediate castes have extracted maximum economic benefits from green revolution, and political gains from adult franchise and elections because of their numerical preponderance and improved economic standing. Dumont and Srinivas both do not see any exploitation in the *jajmani* system, because it is not recognized as such as per the norms of the system. Exploitation of the *kamin* (functionary) castes and untouchables was not only clearly perceptible, but it was also highly institutionalized. Today, we have new forms of exploitation which are not clearly visible under the new systems of relations of production in agriculture and politics and elections.

We have discussed elsewhere that occupation, education, power and styles of life are the main aspects of change in social stratification. Distinctions based on these aspects are evaluated as the yardsticks of higher and lower status. There is no denying of the association of caste ranks with these aspects, but incongruities in them are indicative of weakening of the traditional social inequalities, and congruities speak of the continuity of caste groups or some families with fairly good economic position.

New forms of inequalities along with continuity of traditional inequalities in some measure in regard to various caste and class groups and families have emerged due to historical and cultural legacies and present-day distributive disparities. Class distinctions have even accentuated within the caste groups. Caste groups or some families have hindered not only emergence of class consciousness but have also created new enclaves of power and privilege. There is an undeniable element of casteness when only Harijan labourers are burnt alive, but at the same time this is also a case of class atrocity as the Harijans are generally poor, hence indulge in such inhuman acts.

Ownership, control and use of land in relation to caste partly become the basis of relations in rural India. Beteille identifies three forms of inequality: (i) between landlord and tenant; (ii) between landowner and wage labourer; and (iii) between large, medium and small proprietors. Issues related to agrarian structure and change are sharply focused in a study of the district Basti in Uttar Pradesh. The two main issues are: (i) the 'land grab' movement in 1970 by the poor and helpless peasants; and (ii) the structural and emergent factors resulting in the termination and failure of this movement. The questions raised by Rajendra Singh in this study are quite relevant for analyzing agrarian and social inequalities in the village community. These are: (1) How have various agrarian reforms affected caste, class and land relations? (2) Who have been the gainers and who the losers are of land as a result of these reforms? (3) What is their caste and class position today? (4) What is the impact of these reforms upon the emerging pattern of power structure in the district?

Explorations, to find answers of these questions, show that there was an increase in the number of Zamindars and in the growth of class solidarity among them. There was pauperization both of Zamindars and *mahants*. And finally, a strong lower middle caste rich peasantry emerged. We have discussed this process of change in terms of 'proletarianization' of the *jagirs* and Bhomias, and 'bourgeoisiefication' of the tenants in my study of six villages in Rajasthan. 'Downward'social mobility was quite perceptive in the case of a large number of landlord families.

Today, social inequalities in rural India cannot be diagnosed in terms of caste or class categories because of the very nature of social formation that has emerged in the post-independence period. Singh observes: "After examining the Basti situation, we find the inadequacy of class as well as caste. The agrarian society in Basti conforms neither to a class nor to a caste model." Class dichotomies and conflicts can be seen in the context of caste which mould the subjective perceptions of the people in the countryside. Since mobility has been both upward and downward simultaneously, it is evident that various caste and class groups are highly differentiated. The hypothesis that the rich are getting richer and the poor poorer is not correct in all cases. Omvedt endorses Singh's view that caste is not necessarily equivalent to class, but it very clearly puts some limits.

The idea of continuous hierarchies and discrete castes given by Dipankar Gupta refers to a commentary on Dumont's notion of caste as *Homo hierarchicus*. Gupta writes: "Any notion of hierarchy is arbitrary and is valid from the perspective of certain individual castes. To state that the pure hierarchy is one that is universally believed-in, or one which legitimizes the position of those who participate in the caste system, is misleading." Besides pollution-purity, distinctions and 'diacritical notches' are observed strictly in the caste system. Castes equally pure refrain from merging their identities. Distinctions related to pollution and purity do not systematically affect caste status. In view of these formulations, Gupta examines the *jajmani* system, sanskritisation, caste and politics and caste-class and social class. Inconsistencies and incongruities in behaviour of members of different caste groups in these spheres can be understood in terms of their discreteness.

The mode of production is a social formation in which we find interconnections of caste, kinship, family, marriage and even rituals with the forces of production and production relations. Social inequalities are seen by Gough in terms of the emergence of a new bourgeoisie, the polarization of the peasantry, and the pauperization of the working class. Namboodaripad and Ranadive analyze class relationships as a domain assumption in the treatment of caste and kinship in India. Even *varna* and *jajmani* systems are explained in terms of class relations and are found embedded in the mode of production. Caste is analyzed also in terms of physical forte and economic power. Castes operate as enclaves functioning parallel to ecosystems. Marriages take place within these ecosystems, hence these become operative caste boundaries.

We have analyzed the nature and patterning of social inequality from the point of both structure and process. Structuring of social inequality refers to 'structure in time'. Our analysis shows that there are both internal or historical contradictions and external influences along with structural and normative sources influencing inequality. Placement of groups, families and individuals in high and low positions based on wealth, property, occupation and education refers to structural sources. Normative sources refer to evaluative standards. These are applied differentially to various spheres such as social and cultural (caste), power and economy. We have analyzed the question: Whether these spheres of social inequality are independent of each other or they are inseparable aspects of the same social formation.

Neither caste nor class alone can be a sufficient approach for studying social inequality. In fact, we have examined that social and economic dimensions of inequality co-exist and are affected by each other. Upper castes have slided down in their status, and some of them have improved their position. Such a pattern is found almost among all caste groups. Thus, apparently equal groups are unequal in myriad ways and in their resourcefulness. Besides this, the social groups which occupied lower positions also enjoyed some rights and privileges.

Social inequality is structurally relational and relative phenomenon. Structural factors have brought about marked and manifest changes in the nature of social inequality. Ancient, medieval, British and contemporary periods in Indian history have shown role of these factors in terms of migration, invasions, warfare, land reforms, administration and education etc.

The caste system, which has been a pivotal infrastructure in shaping social relations, has not been 'static' and 'unchanging' as it is depicted in various writings. In fact, it has pervaded almost all aspects of social relations, and therefore, to see it as confined to ritual or religious phenomena would amount to undermining of its pan-Indian character. Both the contexts of caste, namely, historical and contextual, would permit us to know that the structural and the normative dimensions are inseparable, and therefore, a dichotomy of 'caste and class' or a trichotomy of 'caste, class and power' as forms of social inequality or as systems of social stratification bring out only a fragmented picture of India's rural social formation. A social formation point of view for studying social inequality is based on the understanding specifically of structure, culture, history and dialectics of Indian society.

11

Life in Cities

The criteria, used to understand urban-industrial social structure and stratification include the extent of closure or openness and the nature of deprivations and gratifications. Other criteria are: (i) the motivational structure, (ii) the opportunity structure, and (iii) the communication structure or the extent of 'visibility' of opportunity. Based on these sets of criteria of understanding urban-industrial social life, there are multiple references for an individual in urban-industrial milieu because a person is evaluated in terms of his/her attributes like education, income, occupation, style of life, etc. All these criteria are juxtaposed keeping in view the rural-agrarian social structure and stratification as opposite of the urban-industrial world.

'Rural' and 'urban' are certainly two distinct patterns of life because of the distinction between population living in these two settings, but these do not imply two different principles of social stratification. It becomes difficult to draw a strict line of demarcation between 'rural' and 'urban', and 'individual' and 'corporate' rankings. The rich and the poor are the same to a large extent in both the settings; the difference is mainly a contextual one. An individual is a part of his family, and a family is linked with a group, hence individual exists as a corporate entity to a considerable extent. Similarly, a village is part of its region, and the region is linked with civilization, hence village is part of a wider society and civilization.

A lot of changes are taking place in the countryside particularly in the caste stratification, agrarian relations and power structure, but rural social stratification has not transformed itself into urban stratification system. There are several common features of social stratification in the rural-agrarian and the urban-industrial settings as the same principles determine social relations in the two. The main difference is in terms of the extent of operation of a particular principle or a set of criteria/attributes. Caste, class and power are common to both the settings, but they differ in social life operationally because of the structural differences between the village and the town.

Blessings of Industrialisation

Urban industrial social stratification is characterized by 'professional' and 'working' classes to a large extent. Professionalism requires training to acquire skills for performing specific roles. It imparts values of rationality, objectivity and pragmatism. Professional classes reflect social and structural differentiation or changes from tradition to modernity in the fields of occupation, industry and economy. Emergence of professional classes becomes a measure of social mobility in the persisting social stratification. Naval'kha (1971) reports that as compared to other Asian countries the professional classes in India constitute a less significant proportion of all workers. Navalkha also highlights the uneven growth of professions revealing the pattern of recruitment process heavily biased in favour of the upper castes, urban dwelling groups and the metropolitan population. It is evident from several other accounts as well that caste is not a rural phenomenon alone and class is not simply found in urban India. Both have coexisted in rural and urban-industrial formations though in different forms and proportions.

Urban-industrial social stratification consists of the following classes:

(i) upper class

(ii) upper middle class

(iii) lower middle class and

(iv) working class

These classes are generally formed on the basis of 'income' and 'occupation'. However, it may be quite difficult to know the 'real income' from the apparent occupational status. D' Souza (1968) analyzes the 'bases of social organization' in the city of Chandigarh taking into consideration kinship, caste, class, religion and displaced or non-placed condition of the inhabitants. D' Souza finds that the educational, occupational and income hierarchies are significantly correlated with each other. But the correlation of each of them with the operational caste hierarchy is not significant. In a recent study, Mishra (1991) observes that the local institutions such as caste and kinship play a significant role in recasting the relationship between man and machine without dislocating the traditional social structure and also without affecting adversely the process of industrialization.

Theoretically, an industrial society is characterized by a very open view of status, role and power allocation. Open relationship, competition, radicalism, innovation and utilitarianism-rationalism are the main features of an industrial society. Relevant points regarding social stratification in industrial society are as follows:

1. What is the social background of the entrepreneurs and managers?
2. Does the hierarchy of the industrial elite correspond with the caste hierarchy?
3. Do the values of the pre-industrial society co-exist with those of the industrial society?
4. What is the relationship between the internal structure of the factories and the caste and class structure of the workers?
5. Do the industrial employers, municipal councillors, the benefactors and controllers of educational and religious institutions belong to the families which have become prominent in recent decades?

Studies of urban-industrial social stratification in India have come up mainly as a reaction to the studies of rural-agrarian relations, migration from rural to urban areas, social mobility and increasing number of urban-industrial towns. The studies by D' Souza (1968), Navalkha (1971), Sheth (1968), Saberwal (1976), Lambert (1963), Berna (1960), Sharma (1986), Sheth and Patel (1979), Raj Bala (1986), Sheobahal Singh (1985), Krishan Lal Sharma (1981), Singer (1972), Akbar (1990), and Philips (1990) impress upon the need to go 'beyond the village', and show how urban-industrial society and its components are constituted. Studies of urban-industrial social stratification have concentrated mainly on class and caste, occupation, income, education and class, social mobility and elite formation, professionals and working classes, middle classes, processes of social change and status-crystallization, dissonance and inconsistency, professional associations and trade unions.

A detailed annotated bibliography and analysis of trends in industrial sociology in India by Sheth and Patel (1979) and Patel (1985) examine the impact of society on industrialization and the effects of industrialization on society. Sociology of industrialization incorporates workers, supervisors and managers as the major human components along with trade unions, informal groups and owners of industry. Industrialization has fragmented the Indian society into 'classes' by weakening the caste system. The economic fragmentation created by industrialization has brought about both vertical and horizontal change, thereby a change is being registered in the persisting criteria of status-evaluation (Panini, 1986). Industrialization can transform life of the people, means of production, surplus labour, etc. Rubin (1986) writes: "And industrialization can produce the professional employments and affluent style of life to which urban middle and upper classes aspire."

The Background

The process of urbanization and industrialization though not necessarily unrelated are also not essentially concomitant in entirety. In the pre-industrial period, urbanization existed not only as an exclusive phenomenon, it was quite pronounced and was an ideal reference for a desired living. Based on the study of *Arthashastra* (C300-200 BC) and *Varna Ratnakara* (early 14th century AD), Jha (1988) finds 'urbanism' as a way of life in ancient Bihar. Besides provisions for water, roads, grounds, defence and other civic amenities, according to *Arthashastra,* there was a developed system of social ranking. The head of the city was called *nagaraka* (mayor). Below the *nagaraka* were *sthanikas* and the latter had *gopas* as their subordinates. There were also other functionaries and officials to look after various essential services. The administra-tive hierarchy was constituted independent of varna/caste ranking. Non-agricultural occupations, formal groups and impersonal relationship were the main features of urban social life. *Varna Ratnakara* provides, however, a vivid account of the lower castes, market activities, and artistic endeavours, ascetics along with a description of predominance of non-agricultural occupations, complexity and heterogeneity of population and preference for personalized relationship. These two valuable classical sources speak not only of the dynamics of urbanization, but also explain structural and cultural indices of urban life.

One can name several towns which had acquired a place of cultural and religious significance in ancient India (Rao, 1991). Many of these towns became known as centres of administrative and political activities. Naqvi (1968) classifies towns in medieval India into four categories: (i) capital cities (centres of administration, industry and trade), (ii) administrative centres with trading activities, (iii) pilgrimage centres, and (iv) specific-economy towns. However, our main concern here is to know about the people and the criteria on the basis of which they were ranked 'high' and 'low'. A subaltern study of a north Indian *Oasba* (small town) in the nineteenth century by Pandey (1984) shows that the community conscious-ness centered around the religious fraternity, class, *qasba,* and *mohalla,* and this cannot be explained in terms of today's social science vocabulary such as Muslim/Hindu, working class/ rentier, urban/rural, etc. Self-respect and human dignity were the main determinants of the community consciousness.

Despite the community consciousness rooted into a certain perception of honour and dignity people were *socially* differentiated into the following classes:

1. Zamindars
2. Weavers
3. Trader-moneylenders
4. Cultivating tenants
5. Labourers
6. Others *(halwais, pansaris,* beggars, etc.).

A comparative study of Bombay and Poona (1650-1900) by Meera Kosambi (1991) provides details regarding occupational structure, ethnic composition, languages, religious composition, age-sex structure, etc. However, Kosambi's study focuses mainly on the 'functions' performed by the two cities rather than on the system of social stratification.

Lipton (1982) argues: "Inequalities within rural areas also owe much to the urban-biased nature of the development policy." Rural-born doctors, teachers, engineers and administrators serve the urban population. Surpluses from rural areas are extracted out for the urban populace. But, in case of India, the urban-rural balance is not as disappointing as it is implied in Lipton's formulation. Green revolution has brought about a considerable change in agrarian stratification having implications for urban social structure. Urban social stratification in terms of capital/labour relation can be characterized by capitalists, administrators, professionals, labour aristocracy and large landowners. On the contrary, there are small farmers and tenants, landless agricultural workers and members of the informal sector in the countryside (Griffin, 1977). Byres (1981), however, finds 'rural bias' as the main hindrance in industrialization.

Two recent studies of sugar industry by Simon Commander and Ignatus Chithelen have thrown up enough evidence to show the emergence of a new pattern of social stratification. Commander (1985) writes about the sugar industry in North India: "The hub of the system was clearly agricultural and the divorce from the means of production characteristic of the factory system proper was never wholly engendered. Instead, the controls exercised by the *zamindar-khandasari* over labour, land and credit, which provided the basis of the system were, in many respects, antagonistic to a model of pure capitalism."

The assimilability of the non-capitalist features of economy with the capitalist system of production has produced a system of social stratification different from both the agrarian and the urban-industrial. The growth of regional markets and the development of modern transportation networks initially provided the requisite stimulus for the development of sugar industry. But the main factors were the ample reservoir of cheap, unorganized labour and money lending-debt-linkages which generated significantly high profit margins. However, the emergence of a rich peasant stratum in the early 1900s, and the spread of canal irrigation, coupled with financial support from a co-operative credit infrastructure, enabled the rich peasants to cultivate sugarcane in the Ahmednagar district of Maharashtra (Chithelen, 1985).

Stratification within Deccan peasantry in early 1900s contributed to the emergence of a rich peasant stratum placing them in a commanding position. By the mid-1900s, the distinction between the rich peasants and the mass of poor peasants had become distinctly clear. A rich peasant was one who had control and ownership of land as well as ownership and mastery of agricultural implements and techniques. The rich peasants also enjoyed independence and autonomy in the credit relationship. They were themselves lenders of money and suppliers of credit to others. By having control over debtors's crop as wells as lands, the rich peasants expanded their commercial links. These rich peasants belonged to the non-Brahmin upper castes of Maharashtra. They were earlier traditional cultivating elites or members of former royal families or *Inamdars* and other office-holders. A few low status caste groups like *mails* also rose to become rich peasants. Several factors including the spread of canal irrigation, co-operatives, legislations, favourable political milieu, etc. brought about socio-economic and political transformation of the peasantry having implications for change in the rural as well as the urban social stratification (Chithelen, 1985).

Prosperous Groups

The bourgeoisie/capitalist class is characterized by the following features (Hamilton and Hirszowicz, 1987):

(i) concentration and private ownership of the means of production;

(ii) a free market for the sale and purchase of commodities and services;

(iii) formally free labour sold in the market as a commodity;

(iv) the pursuit of profits by entrepreneurs for wages; and

(v) the division of society into two opposed and antagonistic classes as a consequence of the exploitation and alienation of the labour from the means of production.

The property-owning, entrepreneurial, capitalist-employer has emerged from a variety of sources including the decline of the feudal system. Along with the bourgeoisie the capitalist system has produced a *working class.* Marx's theory of the capitalist society is the theory of the commodity-producing society. Worker is treated as a *commodity* (Bottomore, 1985). Though Marx refers to bourgeoisie and the proletariat as the main antagonistic classes, he realizes the transition of society and the emergent role of the intermediate stratum situated between the workers and the industrial capitalists. He also realizes the increasing role of the managerial and ministerial classes and trade unions as a result of the transition from capitalism to socialism.

There is differentiation between and within the bourgeoisie, the petty-bourgeoisie and the working class. Class inequality is not simply 'economistic'. However, economic groupings in the form of classes and domination of one class over the other are found in all societies whether they are industrially more advanced or less advanced (Giddens, 1987; Godelier, 1978). Capitalist society has undergone the following changes over a period of its long journey (Hamilton and Hirszowicz, 1987):

1. Capital and industry are today controlled by professional salaried management due to growth of large joint-stock enterprises.
2. The class structure has diversified. Middle classes have grown enormously, particularly in the developing countries like India due to the new state apparatus.
3. The material standards of workers have improved considerably all over the world.
4. Power of the working class has enhanced greatly due to trade unions, civil liberty movements and democratization.

Planning in India, prior to her independence, aimed at overthrow of the colonial state structure and its replacement by an independent indigenous capitalist state structure (Mukherjee, 1978). The big capitalists, a large number of small traders and merchants actively supported the national movement opposing thereby the colonialist mercantalism and capitalism (Chandra et al., 1988). The Indian capitalist class had the following features:

1. The Indian capitalists had largely an independent capital base and did not act as junior partners of foreign capital or as compradors.

2. The capitalist class on the whole was not tied up in a subservient position with pro-imperialist feudal interests, either economically or politically.
3. It grew rapidly between 1914 and 1947, a period close to India's independence.

Rudolph and Rudolph (1987), among other features of the Indian State, list 'the marginality of class polities' as a major develop-ment in the post-1947 period. Capital and labour play a marginal role in Indian politics and policy because of the centrality of a third factor—the State. The Indian State has acquired the role of a defender and protector of the interests of the poor and the working class. There are also strong unions and organizations of the white-collar groups which in turn weaken both the bourgeoisie and the proletariat. Business has exercised some influence on the government but it has not been able to control it directly or indirectly.

The Industrial Policy Resolution of 1956 though reasserts the constitutional position that the 'common good' of the people and 'distributive justice' would remain the central concerns; the role of larger industrial houses and multinationals remains unaffec-ted to a large extent (Siddharthan, 1979). Associations formed by the capitalists have been used to promote economic as well as political interests (Mukherjee, 1978; Sharma, 1981). However, Desai (1984) considers the Indian State as an agent of the bourgeoisie pursuing the capitalist path of development. The state has been 'repressive' and 'oppressive' in nature.

Whether the Indian big bourgeoisie like the big landlords were a product of colonial rule or not is not a much relevant question for us. What is important here is that the Indian bourgeoisie was never a monolith, and its character was partly determined by the colonial rule and partly by the class character of the Indian National Congress, the movements launched by it and the fact of India's freedom and partition. The bourgeoisie is divided as it comprises two categories: (i) big comprador, and (ii) the small and medium national bourgeoisie (Ghosh, 1985). Because of the comprador character of the big bourgeoisie and latent tendency in the national bourgeoisie to follow suit have resulted into 'guided industrialization'. A similar historical account of the Parsi Seths regarding their roots, entrepreneurship, and comprador role is provided by Guha (1984).

Neo-Industrialists

Let us now take a note of the entrepreneurs and entrepreneurship. In a situation of new social dynamics new opportunities for economic activities are perceived for enhancement of one's economic and social standing. While presenting an integrated view of entrepreneurship, Tripathi (1985) deliberates on the entrepre-neurial process taking into account constellation offerees, entre-preneurial initiative, and change in constellation offerees. An entrepreneur is a person who finds a constellation of socio-political and economic forces favourable for venturing into one or other enterprise, and if he succeeds, he becomes socially and econo-mically distinct from those who remain out of such activities and from those who prove to be a failure.

Recent studies have shown that money-lending and trading were taken even by the landlords and substantial cultivating families in many parts of the country prior to independence. Today, entre-preneurial area is wide open for castes and communities which were earlier engaged in non-mercantile pursuits. There were 'pea-sant entrepreneurs', and there were upper caste manual and agri-cultural workers. Moreover, entrepreneurship is not confined to agriculture, business and industry alone. It has spread to the domains of medicine, science, government service, teaching, etc.

Interest in the study of entrepreneurs as a significant stratum in the scheme of social stratification is evident in some of the recent studies (Singh, 1985; Trivedi, 1991; Akbar, 1990). Singh's study shows that 39 per cent of the total entrepreneurs in an eastern Uttar Pradesh carpet manufacturing town were Muslims, whereas 56 per cent were Hindus, 3 per cent Jains and 2 per cent Sikhs. Banias, Muslims and to some extent Rajputs dominate carpet industry. A close tie is found between landownership, leadership and entrepreneurs by R.S. Singh (1985). However, about 75 percent of the rural entrepreneurs belong to three upper castes, namely, Brahmins, Rajputs and Bhumihars. In the city of Calcutta, Mahisyas, a peasant caste, have dominated the engineering industry surpassing both Brahmins and Kayasthas, mainly due to historically contingent factors after the Second World War (Owens, 1973). Trivedi's study of 250 tribal entrepreneurs explains emer-gence of new criteria of status-determination. Muslim entrepreneurs find no social values obstructing entrepreneurial growth (Akbar, 1990).

The Service Class

The pre-British middle classes comprised of the merchant, the artisan and the landed aristocracy having their roots in 'authoritarianism'. During the British period, the structure and complexion of the middle classes transformed due to a variety of factors and policy changes. The new middle classes included the businessmen and entrepreneurs, industrialists, landed people, educated groups, professionals, etc. The middle classes are basically trained 'service groups', and therefore, serve both the upper and the lower classes, though not making available their services in equal measure. The structure of the middle classes after independence has undergone a considerable change in terms of their size, functions and role mainly due to the nature and character of the Indian State. A brief sketch of some selected studies is provided below.

In the context of anti-reservation agitations in Gujarat, Shah (1987) writes: "The middle class has grown in size disproportionately with economic growth in Gujarat. While their aspirations have risen, they are unable to satisfy their needs and maintain the traditional status, and therefore, experience a strong sense of deprivation. This is specially true of the upper and middle caste members who are jealous of the new entrants from the traditionally low castes." For Shah, the middle class is a class between labour and capital.

The middle classes in India are a product of both capitalist development and the state. The anti-reservation agitations in Gujarat as understood by Shah imply a conflict-situation between the *entrenched* middle classes and the lower classes aspiring for the middle classes status by having access to lucrative white-collar occupations.

Elite formation in India (Navlakha, 1989) is largely determined by the traditional social structure (particularly caste), religion, language, networks, income, occupational background, education, family background, etc. The findings of this study show that select social positions are usually taken by persons from select social strata. This select group controls the positions of prestige, power and responsibility. Higher education is still under the grip of upper castes, hence it is 'status-stabilizer' (Jayaram, 1977) rather than an invader on status-rigidities. In four most prestigious institutions in Bangalore, despite a long history of reservations, 60 per cent Brahmin and 34 per cent Lingayat and Vokkaliga students were admitted to prepare them for higher professional and administrative careers, whereas only 4 per cent lower caste students found place-ment for this programme.

Navalkha's findings (1989) are quite revealing. As many as 81.3 per cent of the Hindu respondents hailed from upper caste groups (Brahmin, Kayastha, Vaishya and Kshatriya), 6.8 per cent came from the higher cultivating and other intermediate castes, and only 4.6 per cent belonged to lower castes. Further, 86.5 per cent of the respondents were of urban origin, 89.3 per cent were educated in modern educational institutions and 79 per cent of the respondents came from the highest advantaged stratum of the society.

Let us now take up a few studies of professions. A study of lawyers and law students in Pune, conducted by S.P. Sathe, Shaila Kunchur and Smita Kahikar (1982) and commented upon by H.K. Pranjape (1983) shows that the Brahmins dominate the profession both in terms of quantity and professional success. The proportion of lawyers from the backward classes is quite small, and most of them are recent entrants to the system. They also earn much less. However, women lawyers from among the back-ward classes are more as compared to Brahmin and other Hindus. The main reason given in the study is that it is easier to accept a backward woman lawyer as junior practitioner. Several studies in the field of sociology of law and legal profession have been conducted in the recent past. Notable among these are by J.S. Gandhi (1982), K.L. Sharma (1982, 1984, 1988), Upendra Baxi (1982), S.L. Sharma (1985), S.K. Lal (1988), Yogendra Singh (1989), and T.K. Oommen (1983). These studies provide sketches of stratification among lawyers and relations between lawyers, judges, *munshis,* touts and clients.

There are not many studies of technocrats, scientists and managers partly because of their considerable distance from administrative-political set-up and partly because of their style of work and way of life. Technocrat/engineer today combines management expertise with scientific know-how. An engineer with a degree of Master of Business Administration (MBA) has made a place of 'high status' in Indian society. Even an MBA without an engineering degree has much more job opportunity than those having skills in several other fields. Higher technical education provides a passport for a high-status lucrative job. The graduates of the Indian Institutes of Technology (IIT) enjoy more prestige, and they are more in demand than the graduates of ordinary engineering colleges. A large number of graduates of IIT, Bombay have gone abroad for better career prospects and work conditions (Sukhatme and Mahadevan, 1988).

The industrialists, technocrats and managers have to work in India under the politicians in particular, and to a considerable extent under the administrators (Bhattacharya, 1984). Managers and officers are organizing themselves through trade unions and associations (Ramaswamy, 1985). Hardly any literature is available on Indian scientists. Three articles in Lal et al. (1988), namely, by Sri Chandra (1988), Ramanama and Bambawale (1978) and Srivastava and Toha (1988) on India's scientists as professionals do not list any notable studies of scientists in India. Articles by Sri Chandra and Srivastava and Toha are in the form of preliminary notes without having any empirical bearing. However, Ramanama and Bambawale, based on their study of 780 scientists working in thirteen organisations, including universities, public sector and private sector undertakings in Bombay and Pune, report ambivalence and role-conflict as the main problems of the scientists working in all the three sectors.

The initial studies of medical profession have particularly emphasized social-structural and organizational aspects of the profession. Some of the recent studies too put more emphasis on the pattern of relationship between different segments of hospital as a social organization. Advani (1980), Chandani (1985, 1988), Mehta (1988) and Nagla (1988) have substantiated the exercise conducted in the earlier studies.

In the studies of managers, technocrats, scientists and medical doctors, high status of these professionals is taken for granted, and therefore, instead of knowing the actual social status, emphasis is put more on the formal criteria of social status.

In evaluation of formal positions like professor, reader and lecturer, non-formal criteria such as academic achievements, reputation as a teacher and scholar, cultural style of life, family background, etc. matter a lot. Since academic profession is accredited with a high degree of autonomy like the legal profession, informal criteria of status evaluation are valued in good measure along with the formal criteria like rank, income and office. The recent studies by Khanna (1988) and Bhoite (1987) only casually stress upon the stratificational aspect of academic community.

Rudra (1989) considers the emergence of the intelligentia as a ruling class in India in addition to the already existing two idling classes: one with base in agriculture, and the other with base in large industry. The intelligentia have become a member of the ruling coalition. The two traditional ruling classes have co-opted the intelligentia as a member of their fraternity. The intelligentia include the following:

1. All white-collar workers in the organized private sector, from managers and top executives down up to clerical workers.
2. All office workers in administrative services from top bureaucrats right up to lower division clerks.
3. Teachers (from the school to the university levels), doctors and nurses, lawyers and judges, engineers and architects in both private and public sectors.
4. Writers, journalists, artists and other skilled workers.
5. Professionals, politicians, trade union leaders, etc.

One common feature of all these middle classes is that "they do not themselves produce any values in the material product sense of value" (Ibid.). 'Members of this (middle) class therefore depend for their economic gains on the largesse of the other two ruling classes as well as the state" (Ibid.). However, there is no homogeneity among its members in terms of income, wealth and level of living. Very high inequality exists within the classes in respect of these criteria. Another commonalty is of 'social' nature, that is, they all can be regarded as a 'babu class', 'salaried people' or the class of people earning equivalent to the salaried class. One more point of commonalty among them is found in terms of 'culture and ideology'. The intelligentsia as a class have contradictions and conflict of interests with other classes, while the intelligentsia are considered as an ally and not as an adversary by the traditional ruling class.

Beteille (1989), while generally accepting Rudra's hypothesis regarding intelligentsia as a third co-opted ruling class in India, observes that intellectuals in India would not like to associate themselves with the exploiters of the masses—the workers and the peasants. Beteille suggests for seeking more empirical evidence before we arrive at some conclusion on the status and role of the intelligentsia (Ibid.). Main disagreement is expressed by Beteille about the concepts of 'class' and 'contradiction'. Beteille writes: "I maintain that contradiction is an inherent feature of all human societies whereas others believe that it is a feature of some or even most societies, but not necessarily all" (Ibid.).

Pranab Bardhan (1984) is also critical of Ashok Rudra's understanding of India's 'middle classes'. He writes: "Ashok Rudra underestimates the power of the professional class *vis-a-vis* the other two dominant classes. Compared to most western countries, the state is considerably more autonomous in India not merely in the political spheres but as a predominant *economic factor.* In some sense the state has captured the commanding heights of the economy, and sections of the professional class which run this gigantic machinery have thereby acquired powers which are not just of a junior partner in the ruling coalition. Further, because of the increasing social and economic interpretation among these classes, the conflicts among the classes in the dominant coalition are likely to decline" (1989). The public sector professionals benefit directly from all kinds of state subsidies and indirectly from the rental income earned by the state (Bardhan, 1984).

Middle classes are not direct rulers nor are they economic producers like the industrialists, workers and peasants. There is a marked lack of homogeneity among different middle classes. In fact, structural distinctions are quite marked even between the apparently equal/homogeneous classes. Some classes are not so important in people's eyes, yet they enjoy high prestige because of the autonomy of their professions and the networks which they develop simply as a by-product of their professional obligations. These points require further probing.

The Labour Class

For Marx the central issue was the understanding of the productive system in which the interests of the owners of the means of production and the wage-earning working class clashed. Marx always thought of ways and means for organizing the working class into a collective force to transform the capitalist system into a socialist society. Connections between social relations of production, social organization of the exploited classes and the state power formed the main basis of Marxian analysis. The growing social power of the organized working class was taken as a challenge to the authority of the state. Weber always emphasized on the problem of authority and legitimacy. 'Rational authority' was considered as key to the smooth functioning of bureaucracy and modern state.

Petras (1980), however, considers the notion of 'political legitimacy' as irrelevant issue or at best a derivative or subsidiary concern. "Different electoral regimes derive their legitimacy from different class reference groups and different balance of class forces." Power creates its own legitimacy. The organized working class itself becomes a power to reckon with, as it is embodiment of the class interests of the poor and the less privileged sections of society. An organized group representing its class interests becomes a 'political class' in its own right.

Studies of the Indian working class (Das, 1983) consider labour as a commodity, and the value of labour power as the basis of understanding the capitalist appropriation and exploitation of the surplus generated by the proletariat. According to Dev Nathan (1987), the working class can be divided into four broad sections:

(1) that which gets more than a family, i.e., more than the value of labour power;

(2) that which gets a wage about equal to the family wage, and can thus at a reasonable standard, cover the full cost of production and reproduction of labour power;

(3) that which is more or less able to cover the immediate costs of production of labour power, but has to depend on the non-capitalist sector in order to reproduce itself/ or has to depress its standard of living in order to reproduce itself; and

(4) the pauperized section that is not even able to meet the immediate cost of production of labour power. The composition of the working class is affected by two factors: (i) the caste, tribal or ethnic origin of the worker in the pre-capitalist sector; and (ii) the gender-based division of labour between male and female and the

> associated patriarchy. Thus, the working class is highly stratified within and in relation to the capitalist and the middle classes. The factors such as caste, ethnicity and gender create inequalities within the working class structure and therefore obstruct smooth sailing of the working class movement. The distinctions found within the working class structure ranging from the 'labour aristocracy' on the one hand and the 'pauperized labour' on the other explain the nature of economic stratification and its socio-cultural consequences on the workers.

Lieten's study (1987) of workers in multinational companies shows that a segment of the working class is able to command higher wages and can thus divide the class in a distinct manner. Such a structural divide within the working class hampers uniform class consciousness. The consciousness of the jute mill workers of Bengal (Chakrabarty, 1984) could not transcend their identification as a Hindu or a Muslim to have identification as a solid working class. Thus, all collective public actions of the workers were marked by inherent duality. The working class in terms of its socio-cultural composition is constituted of the urban poor living in slums and hutments, industrial workers (both men and women), textile workers, sugar industry workers, plantation workers, railway workers, cottage industry and informal sector workers, etc. The working class, despite these differences, is comprised of urban and rural poor both in organized and informal sectors of economy. This would mean that the poor are just poor, and therefore, it would be better if we understand them as such without under-mining this fact by using rural/urban, caste/class and caste/caste criteria (Joshi, 1979). Caste is not found as a major principle of social organization among industrial workers (Ramaswamy, 1979).

The Special Number of *Economic and Political Weekly* (1981) on "Indian Working Class: Some Historical Perspectives" contains papers on the following themes:

(1) Structure of the labour market in colonial India by Ratan Das Gupta.

(2) Labour legislation and working class movement: The case of the Bombay Labour Officer, 1934-37 by Dick Kooiman.

(3) Kanpur textile labour: Some structural features of formative years by Chitra Joshi.

(4) Growth of trade union consciousness among jute mill workers, 1920-40 by Ira Mitra.

(5) Industrial unrest and growth of labour unions in Bengal, 1920-24 by Sanat Bose.

(6) Tea labour in Assam: Recruitment and government policy-1840-80 by Suranjan Chatterjee and Ratan Das Gupta. Labour market, labour legislation, caste and class background of workers, class consciousness, work-ing class movements and their leadership are some of the issues taken up in these studies of the working class in India.

The 'industrial man' is not a monolith. Holmstrom (1984) discusses at length that 'industry' is primarily an inequalitarian system in terms of organized and unorganized labour sector, contract labour, labour markets, the working class conditions, workers'social worlds, the domineering role of owners, managers, superiors and leadership of trade unions. These distinctions based on gender (Mies, 1981) and nature of industrial or semi-industrial work (Bhowmik, 1980; Prasanneswari, 1984; Behal, 1985; Thomas Issac, 1982) have been taken as the main criteria of socio-cultural and economic heterogeneity of the working class, particularly in the analysis of working class consciousness, intra and inter-working class relations and relations of the working class with the owners and managerial and supervisory cadres of industry.

12

The Downtrodden

Some time ago, a nation-wide study of the educational problems of the scheduled castes and the scheduled tribes was undertaken. A lot of data about students at various levels of education in regard to their enrolment, drop-out, hostel accommodation, scholarship, performance, attitudes, aspirations, etc. were gathered through the 'conventional' techniques of *schedule* and *interview*. However, data were also collected from secondary sources, namely, census reports, reports of Scheduled Castes and Scheduled Tribes Commission and governmental reports. One of the serious limitations from which these studies suffer is that neither they have been rooted into the analysis of social structure nor they have any bearing on caste and class structure of Indian society. At the outset it may be stated that a proper study of social mobility among the scheduled castes must have its bearing upon social structure of 'caste society', that is, division of Indian society into caste and class groupings. Changes in the non-scheduled castes society would also have its repercussions on the structure of the scheduled castes. Therefore, a meaningful discussion would be possible if caste/class relations *vis-a-vis* scheduled castes are properly analyzed and all the 'ideological' points in the definitional and relational aspects of these two 'concepts', that is, caste and class, are discussed. What have been those conditions as a result of which several anti-Brahmin, anti-twice-born movements and other emulative movements by the scheduled castes have emerged? Self-consciousness among these sections could be a result of the inhuman and exploitative conditions in which the scheduled castes were forced to live for centuries. It is quite possible that factors external to the caste system were strong enough to loosen its rigid strings tied to the scheduled castes and other lower sections. In such a situation, it was perhaps wise for the upper castes to grant certain concessions to the lower castes, and make search for new avenues of status, honour and power. Social mobility among the scheduled castes should, therefore, be examined in view of their structural position in the caste system. Before we discuss the various viewpoints regarding caste and class, it is necessary to refer some points about social mobility. Regarding the social position of the scheduled castes in a village of Coimbatore district, Den Ouden points out the following questions:

> Do the scheduled castes comprise a recognizable category within the domain of regional norms and actual behaviour? To what extent do they constitute part of a more inclusive grouping in the eyes of the higher castes?
>
> Do the middle and high castes distinguish levels among the low castes?
>
> Do the low castes make similar distinctions?
>
> Is there a 'barrier of pollution' hindering or preventing the vertical mobility of the low caste?
>
> What sets the untouchable (and possibly sections within this category) apart from other castes?

Ouden rightly observes: "My principal concern was to identify and to interpret changes in the stratification system, to locate the causes of these changes and to evaluate their consequences for the low castes and their membership." Changes in caste rules structuring inter-caste relations may be of the following nature as observed by Ouden:

(a) Rules continue to exist but occur in the castes to which the rules refer.

(b) Rules continue to exist but situations formerly governed by these rules have declined in importance, some such situations are even disappearing.

(c) Rules lose stringency, weakened by new situations arising to which the rules hardly, if at all, apply.

(d) Rules become undermined by conflicting rules; more and more individuals conform to a new ideology and convert to new values and norms.

Ouden meticulously takes into account the role of caste hierarchy *vis-a-vis* 'caste relevant' and 'caste-irrelevant' roles. He also takes into account the role played by an individual in improving his position within the caste system. However, the question regarding caste and class, both conceptually and operationally, remains unanalyzed in Ouden's work. Therefore, first we will deal with the viewpoints and approaches concerning caste and class, and then our emphasis will be on the nature of social mobility among the scheduled castes *vis-a-vis* caste and class as systems of social stratification affecting it.

Scheduled Castes

Despite various difficulties in defining the caste system, a large number of sociologists, anthropologists, social historians and indologists have engaged themselves in the study of caste system at the neglect of the studies of class, political power, etc. Studies of caste have been innumerable. The main features of the caste system, according to these studies, are: a common name, common decent, hereditary calling, and homogeneity of caste members. Risely, Senart and Ketkar were among the early writers who studied caste exclusively as an Indian system. Later on, Furnivall, Hutton and Sherring in particular pleaded that caste system was 'functional' for the whole of the Hindu society. Even Marx's notion of the Asiatic mode of production and Maine's idea of caste as a case of non-contractual 'status-society' contributed to the stability and continuity of the caste system. Indologists such as Ghurye, Kapadia, Karve and recently Dumont have given caste system a renewed ideological strength rooted into India's specificity and cultural distinctiveness.

Singh observes that the abstracted and a historical detachment of caste from tribe, attribution of exaggerated autonomy to systems of religion and village community and the omission of the exploitative and alienative role of colonialism in India on its society and economy from most sociological analyses of its institutions, prove adequately the ideological foundation of such theorizing. Dube and Singh both realized that the demand for indigenization of social science paradigms now so widely voiced by social scientists in India is a product of such historical conditioning of concepts and theories. However, such a demand for indigenization of social science paradigms and schema is not a recent one only. Marxist scholars like Thorner pleaded for it in 1950s for a better understanding of agrarian relations. Even some non-Marxist scholars and indologists such as Karve and Saran made similar demands. However, reasons for them were different from that of Thorner. Mukerji made a vehement plea for making Indian tradition as the sole basis of analyzing social change. Desai realized the role of colonialism in Indian society, polity and economy, and felt that the Marxist concepts and paradigms could provide a fuller understanding of the Indian society. One of the criticisms against the lack of proper paradigms is the western education and academic socialization of Indian sociologists and social anthropologists. Srinivas has been accused of a wrong application of the British functionalism by Mencher, Leach and Saberwal.

Ideological contents have been predominant in the various approaches to the study of caste system. These elements were reflected even in the methodology and data which were used for substantiating the numerous explanations about the origin and functioning of the caste system. However, caste was never treated as a 'social formation', which also included components other than traditionally known as 'caste' components of Indian society. Some scholars for certain ideological reasons again equated caste with entirety of Indian social system. Whatever may be the reasons for stability and continuity of the caste system, the following formulation seems appropriate:

"My basic assumption is that the continuity of the caste system is a solid proof of its adaptive capacities. It has adapted to innume-rable varied situations, forces, and constraints. Because of its adaptability, caste has evolved simultaneously in several directions and adjusted with ideologically antagonistic systems, adjusting its principles whenever necessary. It has never paved the way to the emergence of an alternate system of stratification and social rela-tions, though the contents of its functions and other paraphernalia changed from time to time".

Sinha observes certain trends in regard to the studies of caste in India. These trends which refer to stability and change of the caste system could be taken for studying caste system as a part of a 'social formation' which certainly comprised of class, ethnicity, power, religion and economy along with caste. However all these aspects were webbed into each other should provide a proper understanding of the historicity of social formation of Indian society. Caste and class were parts of this formation in various ways. Such a perspective has not been formulated, nor a realization about indigenization of concepts and theories could provide the necessary understanding of Indian social structure as a social formation. As Singh has rightly hinted that historical and fragmented nature of understanding has been at the core of the studies of social stratification.

One of the serious limitations of the studies of social stratification is that caste has been considered as a logical opposite of the 'class'system. The class system has been thought of a basic feature of the western world. Beteille has outlined the basic features of the 'caste' model of Indian society while examining its usefulness as a scheme of analysis. Beteille's trio of 'caste, class and power' is an imitation of Weber's theory of social stratification, namely, 'class, statute and party.' The other Weberian adaptations are 'caste, class and polities' and 'caste, religion and power'. These adaptations have undermined the role of historicity of Indian society while accepting Weber's notions of rationality and historical specificity. Secondly, Weber's macro-analysis implied a certain method of study and research which has been neglected by Beteille, Bhatt and Aggarwal in their empirical studies of social stratification.

Caste and class are not polar opposites. Changes in caste and class have not occurred as 'replacements.' The view that "caste is changing into class", or change is "from hierarchy to stratification" or "from closed to open system" (the first implying caste and the latter referring to class) are not, therefore, true. At no point of time caste system was a 'closed'system, and class was not so 'open' system even in the western world. Therefore, the notions that class inheres mobility, openness and freedom to individuals are implanted in the minds of Indian intellectuals through western text-books and funding of researches. Caste was named by the western academics as a feature of an archaic society and characterized it by all those features which were just opposite to that of the 'class'system. Class has existed along with caste as an inseparable phenomenon. It is a different thing that caste has been a more 'elaborate'system of ranking in some regions than others, and similarly class-like relations have been more pronounced and visible among certain groups and in certain contexts than others. It is admitted by several scholars that caste incorporates the elements of class, and class has a cultural style of functioning in Indian society. Historians of both Marxist and non-Marxist dispositions have poin-ted out the co-existence of class relations with caste stratification. Therefore, the ideas that 'caste alone' could explain Indian social reality or that 'class alone' could explain Indian problems or both 'caste and class'should be taken as the basis of understanding of Indian society are not very relevant. Alternative to all these views should be the notion of 'social formation' which explains the totality of social relations from various viewpoints and at various levels in terms of historicity of the Indian society.

Borrowed approaches such as functional, dialectical, psychological and structuralism are inadequate to explain the totality of social formation and its dynamics. As we have pointed out earlier that the impact of western scholarship has been immense on Indian sociology. The two most popular views about caste are: (i) it is a cultural phenomenon; and (ii) it is a structural form of social stratification. Caste as a cultural phenomenon is mainly upheld by Dumont and Leach, and as a structural form it is upheld by Barth and Berreman. Caste as a cultural phenomenon is particularistic and Indian in substance, and according to the 'structural' view it is a form of general theory of social stratification.

It is true that systems analogous to caste are found elsewhere also, and it is also true that caste system is one of several stratifications found in other societies. Singh taking a clue from these two views formulates a paradigm of social stratification in view of cultural versus structural, and particular versus universal characteristics of social system. He suggests four types: (1) cultural-universalistic; (2) cultural-particularistic; (3) structural-universalistic; and (4) structural-particularistic. Singh does not indicate his preference for one of these types that resembles with the Indian situation; however, it seems that his view is nearer to the structural-particularistic category.

In a recent study, Singh categorizes the theoretic concerns in the seventies in the studies of social stratification as: (1) structural-functional, (2) structuralist, (3) structural-historical, and (4) historical-materialist or Marxist. These approaches are not discussed here in detail. However, some of the basic points in regard to caste-class debate could be mentioned. Class relations are subsumed by caste and any departure from caste in terms of incongruence between caste, status, wealth and power is considered as emergence of class relationships by the structural-functionalists. Structural-functional studies are characterized by mobility within the caste (sanskritisation), and norms relating to mobility are of a consensual sort. These studies lack historicity. However, in some studies, structural mobility (downward social mobility, namely, proletarianization and bourgeoisification, namely, upward social mobility) have been reported. Resilience is the main feature of caste, according to the structural-functionalists. Future of caste is seen quite safe as it is a localized system of social relations. Kolenda and others do not agree with the view that 'organic solidarity' existed in a congruent fashion at any time in the caste system. Bailey and Beteille assumed 'organic solidarity' in the traditional caste system. Not only Kolenda does refer to a point which goes 'beyond organic solidarity', several historians such as Panikkar, Stein and Thapar have pleaded that there was never perfect congruence between caste, class and power; and mobility and migration were quite normal activities in ancient and medieval India.

Another serious limitation of structural-functional approach is its reliance on analytical abstraction in the form of statistical-mathematical indicators or analytical typologies. D' Souza treats class as a category conceptually abstracted, hence class does not exist as a community unlike caste. Class is defined operationally in terms of certain indices. Marxists would accept this as a non-humanistic view of a system of social relations. It is considered as a 'Brahminicar or 'hierarchical' model of caste society. Leach has labelled Srinivas as the father of 'Brahminocentric'sociology. The 'dalitcentric'sociology or 'upside down' view has been advocated by Mencher, Parvathamma and several others in some recent writings.

Dumont's *Homo Hierarchicus* is the most significant representative of the structuralist approach to the study of caste system in India. Singh points out that pivotal notions of structuralism such as ideology, dialectics, transformational relationship and comparison have been brought in the analysis of caste stratification in India by Dumont. For Dumont, 'hierarchy' is 'ideology' and hierarchy implies 'pure' and 'impure' in regard to all sorts of social relations, hence binary tension or dialectics. 'Pure' and 'impure' are separate in all aspects as well together as parts of the theory of caste hierarchy. 'Hierarchy' also implies the relationship of 'encompassing' and the 'encompassed'. The 'pure' encompasses the 'less pure' or 'impure'. This applies to all the sections and aspects of society. Thus, according to Dumont, change is *in the society* and not *of the society.*

Dumont's view falls in the category of 'cultural-universalistic' type of social stratification. According to Singh, Dumont's structuralism suffers both theoretically and substantively. Pure and impure are fused together instead of being disjunct. The notion of 'contra-priest' by Gould also negates such a separation between the two at a substantive level. Dumont wrongly understands that tradition displies representation of structural relations irrespective of time, place and situation, and which might have changed disproportionately to the changes in the tradition. It is not at all a new idea that caste and class have been treated as binary notions by Dumont. All along the western scholars have done it for the reasons best known to them. Singh observes: 'The structuralist's treatment of dialectics is dissociated from history. History, indeed, links essence to existence, form to content, superstructure and theory to practice. Devoid of such a sense of historical conjecture structuralism amounts to a set of conceptual schema, devoid of a basis in evolutionary changes in society. Its transformational relationships being a historical abound in tautologies." Dumont's structuralism is no exception to these criticisms.

Structural-historical approach has been applied by both Marxists and non-Marxists scholars. The main emphasis is on structural orientation, historical evolutionary typologies and processual analysis of structures as social movements. The question of origin of caste has recently been resurfaced by Klass. Marxists such as Namboodaripad and Ranadive have made propositions about the nature of caste. The scholars of both the dispositions have not been able to prove their common thesis that social stratification in India has emerged from its ancient egalitarian character. Secondly, the view that from clan-like organization caste has emerged, is not factually tenable. On the contrary, class has emerged from inequalitarian system like caste due to recent change in it. To us, structural-historical approach does not refer to origin of caste or clan or class. It offers a new theoretic interest implying Indian society as a social formation with its different aspects having inter-linkages and inter-relationships which have evolved over the years due to their constraints and contradictions. This approach has not been applied earnestly by historians, sociologists and anthropologists. Singh is inclined to have a preference for this approach, but he has not analyzed the phenomenon of social stratification with such clear theoretic and methodological preparedness. Some studies of the social origin of equality/inequality have been undertaken but mainly as parts of the studies of social movements without having a direct bearing upon the structural-historical approach.

Marxist categories and concepts have been used in the understanding of national movement in India. The basic tenets of the Marxist approach refer to locating the historical forces in the mode of production and the contradictions of classes. It is essentially evolutionary and developmental and has a dialectical quality of self-transformation. Gough combines Marxist approach with the anthropological tradition of field-work. She considers mode of production as a social formation in which she finds inter-connections of caste, kinship, family, marriage and even rituals with forces of production and production relations. Her study of colonial rule in Thanjavur explains the emergence of new bourgeoisie, polariza-tion of peasantry, and the pauperization of the working class due to historical transformations in the modes of production. Totality of contradictions in social stratification could be seen through the contradictions in the mode of production. Thus, Marxists like Gough and even ideologies like Namboodaripad and Ranadive consider class relationships as the domain assumption in the under-standing of caste and kinship in India. Even *varna and jajmani* systems could be explained in terms of class relations as embeded in the mode of production. The mode of production framework has been put to test at the village level by Djurfeldt Goran and Lindberg, Heera Singh, Thorner, Saith and Tanakha, Bhardwaj and Das.

Caste-class congruence and/or incongruence has been examined in several studies of social movements. 'Caste feudalism' refers to class relations, or caste relations encapsulate class relations, or that caste relations are another name for class relations—are some of the recent expressions based on several studies conducted by social scientists in India.

There are four basic features for understanding caste and class relations and their transformations in regard to Indian society. These are: (1) dialectics, (2) history, (3) culture, and (4) structure. Dialectics does not simply refer to binary fission in the cognitive structure of the society. It refers to the effective notions which bring about contradictions and highlights relations between unequal segments and men and women. History is not again a conjectural construction based on mythology, scriptures and idealistic formulation, but it provides a substantial account of existent conditions of work and relationship; culture does not include just cultural practices, rituals, *rites de passage,* etc., it defines the rules of the game, the nature of relations between the haves and the have-nots and so on. Structure is no doubt a product of dialectical contradictions, historical forces, and certain rules of the game, but it becomes a 'formation' once it has emerged, and in return, becomes a sort of 'force' to determine in some way the course of history, nature of contradictions and the evaluational standards. Thus, structure refers to relations between social segments at a given point of time, but as a historical product and reality. Having these elements as the kernel of structural-historical approach, changes in caste and class structures could be considered as 'transformational' rather than replacements. All the debates regarding caste and class such as caste is closed and class is open, caste is 'organic' in its structure rather than 'segmentary', there is either caste or class, both caste and class are there, class is replacing caste, caste is weakening, class is emerging, etc. may be taken up with this perspective for a better understanding of social stratification.

Jajmani was never an 'organic'system in reality, though apparently it provided such an impression. The idea of 'contra-priest' even cannot undermine the hierarchy which is built into the *jajmani* system. It is necessary to understand the following patterns of change with a historical perspective:

(1) Downward mobility and proletarianization.

(2) Upward mobility and embourgeoisiement.

(3) Urban income for rural people and mobility in the village.

(4) Rural non-agricultural income and mobility.

Accepted Norms

Bougie writes: "To sum up on these points: hereditary specialization, hierarchical organization, reciprocal repulsion, as far as any social form can realize itself in its purity, the caste system is realized in India. At the very least it penetrates Hindu society to a level unknown elsewhere. It plays some part in other civilizations but in India it has invaded the whole. It is in this sense that we may speak of the caste system as a phenomenon peculiar to India." Srinivas, following Bougie, observes pre-eminence of religious values in the caste system, and these values centre around the ideas of pollution and purity. However, Hocart finds that religion encompasses power, hence priesthood is not 'absolute' in nature. Relations between Brahmin and Kshatriya are defined in terms of certain reciprocity, namely, the former represents the 'religious' authority, and the latter enjoys 'political' power.

Srinivas refers to various types of purity and impurity in regard to the Coorgs of South India. He writes: "Normal ritual status is the status which a person enjoys most of the times." Further, he observes: "Ritual impurity, normal ritual status, and ritual purity form a hierarchy. If a person in an impure condition touches another in a condition of either purity or normal ritual status, the latter becomes impure. If a person in a condition of normal ritual status touches another in a pure condition, the latter losses his purity and is reduced to normal ritual status. That is, normal ritual status is a mild form of impurity." Dumont and Pocock, however, observe: "We must discard the reassuring but unjustified expression of 'normal' ritual status." Normal ritual status, which is mildly impure is really outside the realm of the hierarchy of pure and impure in the context of the caste system in India. Ritual bath could eliminate such impurity and after the occasion is over, it could recur. Relations between castes in the caste system are not based on this sort of ephemeral purity or re-impurity after the purification.

Srinivas adds to the confusion that is also realized by Dumont and Pocock when he writes: "The concept of pollution governs relations between different castes. This concept is absolutely fundamental to the caste system." Srinivas further writes: "Some occupations are considered defiling because of the contact with some defiling object or other necessary to their practice. Swine-herding is defiling because swine defiles. Leather defiles, and consequently the making and repairing of shoes is an occupation of the untouchables. Finally, any occupation, however, remotely implying the destruction of sentient life in any form would be prohibited to the high castes." According to Srinivas, sanskritisation is the only way to remove impurity or minimize it. We may quote two points made by Dumont and Pocock about Srinivas' notion of pollution and purity among the Coorgs. One is that an object or a person is purer, or less pure (or of course more or less impure) than another. Secondly, a person or an object is impure in relation to one another, for example, when there is avoidable relationship between the two.

Srinivasian sociology is commented upon by Parvathamma: "In all the writings of Srinivas, the Brahmin-non-Brahmin values are juxtaposed." Hierarchy remains basic to Srinivas' thinking in regard to all aspects of human life even if it is not so pronounced or less existent. Srinivas does not try to analyze the tensions and contradictions which could be caused by what he calls 'sanskritisation'. His main emphasis still remains on concepts of dominance and solidarity.

It is not only Srinivas, Dumont, Marriott, Mandelbaum, etc. also have overworked on the themes of caste hierarchy, pollution-purity, religion, rituals and other allied aspects. Their impact on the younger scholars relating to the study of caste has resulted into the neglect of the study of social structure in totality as a social formation. The notions of pollution-purity, hierarchy and dominance have made a strong impact on the minds of scholars, reformers and political leaders as they do not see the social structure beyond these parameters. It is, therefore, necessary first to look into the measures taken for the welfare of the scheduled castes, and then to relate them to the reality of relations between the scheduled castes and caste-Hindus.

We are not comparing India's Dalits with Muslims or Blacks for the simple reason that they are a part and parcel of India's social formation at all the levels of its evolution and development. The Blacks have had never been part of the Whites and the same is true about India's Muslims and the tribes. We do not have to go into the genesis of the names 'untouchables', 'ex-untouchables', 'Harijans' or 'scheduled castes, '*dalits* which have been used for the lowest sections of Hindu society. Issacs makes a detailed reference to the beginnings and uses of these names for the scheduled castes of today.

To us, there are two patterns of social mobility among the scheduled castes: 57 (i) the welfare measures have brought about mobility among some selected sections of the scheduled castes, adversely affecting hegemony of the dominant castes in the fields of education and employment; and (ii) social mobility among the scheduled castes is also directly a result of certain socio- cultural movements which in turn has created anti-upper caste attitudes and awareness about their own low position. It is not that these two patterns are quite independent of each other. Since the scheduled castes were also a highly differentiated lot before Independence, that differentiation could be reflected in these broad patterns of social mobility among them. Certain sections of the scheduled castes have taken more advantages of the constitutional safeguards and welfare measures, hence they have more migration to urban centres, education and white-collar employment. The others who perhaps due to their earlier weak position among the scheduled castes had to choose the path of 'sanskritisation' for social mobility, and this created tensions without much benefits in concrete terms. Though latently 'sanskritisation' might have brought some benefits to the scheduled castes.

We have observed in an earlier article that the scheduled castes suffer today not only because of the imposed social and cultural disabilities but perhaps much more because of the imbalances created by the emergence of structural differentiation within them due to the policies and plans undertaken ostensibly for their uplift and welfare. The differential benefits received by the scheduled castes is a major reason for these continuing inequalities. The two patterns of social mobility on the one hand accentuate class-like distinctions among the scheduled castes, and on the other the demands of equality in relation to the mobile sections of the caste Hindus are not met. Data about Rajasthan in regard to enrolment, hostels and scholarships relating to SCs have amply revealed inter-district, intra-district, inter-caste and disparities.

The atrocities on Harijans and their exploitation by the dominant Hindu castes may be analyzed in view of the distinctions which we find among the scheduled castes *vis-a-vis* their relations with caste Hindus. All types of Harijans have not been equally victims of atrocities of the landlords, rich peasants and upper castes. To say that it is a situation of total class war between caste Hindus and Harijans is not a correct observation. The relations between caste landlords and Harijan labourers are quite intriguing.

The institution of untouchability is not functioning in a wholesome way. Its pollutional aspect has receded, but its reflections are seen quite effectively in economic and social relations. Untouchables have changed along with the changes in structural and cultural aspects of Indian society. The areas of untouchability and non-untouchability have become crystal clear in recent years. Like caste resilience, untouchability has more or less disappeared. It is not that caste has withered away with all its class-like character, and untouchability has been continuing and *vice-versa*. Since caste in the garb of class remains a pivotal force to a large extent, untouchability refers to a situation of exploitation, suppression and powerlessness of the wretched of the earth. Naturally, the exploiters are the well-off caste Hindu landlords and big peasants. Hari-jans or untouchables may not be doing today what they were forced to do a couple of decades ago, but the Harijans remain under the economic and social hegemony of the landed interests.

Constitutional Support

Article 46 of the Constitution of India provides: "The state shall promote with special care the educational and economic interests of the weaker sections of the people and, in particular, of the scheduled castes and scheduled tribes, and shall protect them from social injustice and all forms of exploitation." In view of this clause several provisions have been made for the reservation of seats for the scheduled castes in the states of union and in the parliament and reservation for jobs and services at various levels.

Further, Article 17 declares: "Untouchability is abolished and its practice in any form is forbidden. The enforcement of any disability arising out of untouchability shall be an offence punishable in accordance with law." In pursuance of these constitutional provisions, several programmes have been undertaken for the uplift of the scheduled castes.

The question is: "How close to equality are scheduled castes?" Chandi Das reviews the achievements of social welfare programmes for scheduled castes for two decades and finds that their position compared to that of the non-scheduled castes is still very inferior as regards titles to land as well as size of landholdings.

He further writes: "Their depressed position is reflected again in their economic and social mobility. Their rates of urbanization and education, compared to those of non-scheduled castes, are low. And their economic poverty is poignantly underscored in the fact that, as between districts which are at the same level of development, the average per capita income of those with a higher proportion of scheduled castes is much lower." A similar observation is made by Ramaswamy. The policy of preferential treatment of scheduled castes has been in practice for over two decades, but has barely scraped the surface of the problem. Even in the urban areas only a fraction of the posts in the administration which are reserved for them is actually filled. The same is the case in regard to completion of formal education even upto secondary level.

In regard to educational opportunities for the scheduled castes, Premi observes that new inequalities are creeping up among the scheduled castes themselves. She writes: "Mere existence of facilities does not ensure their optimum use. Awareness and acceptance are essential for utilization. To maximize the use it is necessary to generate better awareness. More publicity is needed to ensure the wider use of the facilities and to find out the reasons for the poor use". Premi arrives at the following conclusion:

(i) Education among the scheduled castes may not filter down as expected.

(ii) Equal access for unequal groups is not true equality.

Chauhan observes that the spread of education among the scheduled castes has created social classes among them on lines parallel to those existing in higher society. Chitnis concludes that the scheme of post-matric scholarship is neither equitably distributed not optimally used. Caste patterns within the scheduled castes determine differential distribution and utilization of scholarship and other amenities. Ramaswamy, in another article, reconfirms unevenness among the scheduled castes independent of the imbalances created by education and other measures for their welfare. She writes: 'In terms of social and economic status, there are clear differences among the scheduled castes. There is a well recognized hierarchy among them. Not all of them are untouchables, even among those that are, there are degrees of pollution. There are also religious cleavages among the scheduled castes." Each one of the scheduled castes is aware about its identity among themselves, and at the same time is conscious of their shared status as scheduled caste.

The realization that unevenness exists among the scheduled castes has led to the exploration of what is popularly known as 'scheduled caste elites'. Harold's *India's Ex-untouchables,* Saberwal's *Scheduled Caste Elites of Punjab,* Sachchidananda's *The Harijan Elite* and Deshpande's *Scheduled Caste Elites and Social Change* are some of the most well known titles on this theme. Issacs interviewed 50 educated persons from the scheduled castes; Saberwal added eight more, that is, he interviewed 58; Sachchidananda interviewed 200; and Deshpande slided down much below Issacs, and interviewed only 29 Harijan elites.

Two points of methodological and substantive nature emerge from these studies of scheduled castes and their elites: (i) The reliance is on the information which the researchers could gather from their respondents (elites in this case); and (ii) it is by and large realized that 'unevenness' among the scheduled castes inherently prevalent as well as created by the implementation of policies and programmes for their welfare is mainly responsible for their backwardness. Awareness about this unevenness could have a levelling effect on the weaker sections. However, it would not be correct that nature of elites could be understood by inter-viewing them. The number of respondents studied is not signi-ficant. The nature of investigation is important. Secondly, that diffusion of ideas about the welfare programmes and awareness about their status in the post-independence period could minimize the gap between the caste Hindus and the scheduled castes is also based on erroneous premises. It is quite likely that we get neither proper understanding of the structure of the scheduled castes *vis-a-vis* caste Hindus nor of the substantial reduction of the hiatus between the scheduled castes and caste Hindus as the problems of the scheduled castes are dealt at the surface level only.

Patwardhan observes: "The overall perspective is that there is an increasing possibility for upward mobility for all the Harijans." She further states that there are two processes of mobility:—(i) through corporate efforts; and (ii) by competing between castes and within a caste. Patwardhan also notices inter-caste variability in regard to social mobility, and "sacred and secular models in different contexts." Migration, education and white-collar jobs, particularly outside the village, have been the main source of social mobility among the scheduled castes. The gist of Partwardhan's analysis is that social mobility among the scheduled castes has been immense and a multiplicity of factors have contributed to this particularly since independence. However, Patwardhan's view that 'ascription' does not play such a role in social mobility looks only superficial. Ascription- achievement dichotomy is not viable for understanding mobility at the empirical level. Ascription promotes achievement, and in turn such an achievement adds to ascription, and in this way, in real life, it is found as a complicating process, and if it continues for decades and centuries no significant change may be brought by Constitution or Untouchability Offences Act of 1955 or other measures. In a recent study, Malik observes that as a consequence of social mobility among scheduled castes, their social status, pattern of interaction, levels of aspirations, family pattern, employment of wives and awareness of government policies have also changed. However, these aspects have been studied without knowing the basic structural questions and the complexity of ascription and achievement. Duskin and Lynch refer to unity among the scheduled castes beyond the village particularly for political action in towns and cities. Menchar and Mahar also find the similar political mobilization among the scheduled castes. Mobilization of such a sort may be counterproductive, and conse-quently the non-scheduled castes also mobilize themselves perhaps with greater resources and vigour than the scheduled castes.

All Dalits are not equally victims of atrocities committed by the landlords, the rich peasants and the upper castes. Why is it so? Is it perhaps due to the fact that the Harijans who are not victims belong to a higher 'class' than other Harijans who fall a prey to the rich landlords? The following questions are quite revelant:

Why some of the families of Harijans are tortured and exploited?

Why the Harijans of a particular village who have generally a low and poor status among the Harijans are victimized?

Why only certain sections of Harijans have extracted most of the benefits extended to them by the central and state governments and voluntary agencies?

Why some castes and groups have advanced in the field of education, and others have migrated to towns from their native places just for bare survival?

Why atrocities are committed only on Harijans and not on their non-untouchable counterparts (in the sense of class) from among the caste Hindus?

Massacre, loot and rape of the scheduled castes in Belchi, Agra, Pant Nagar, Mārathwada, Bajitpur and other places are known to all of us. In an attempt to understand the role of caste system *vis-a-vis* class struggle and class organization, the Atyachar Virodhi Samiti in Maharashtra was constituted. It observes: "The caste system functions both as a relation of production and as an ideology." The Samiti further observes: "The caste system functions as an extremely effective method of economic exploitation. The class which has economic power also acquires political power and social prestige which helps it to perpetuate, consolidate and justify its position in the hierarchy. Caste hierarchies also effect ownership of land. Economic hierarchy is closely linked with social hierarchy. The caste system is not merely division of labour. It is also a division of labourers. Capitalist relations make agricultural and industrial labourers into a distinct *class in itself,* but the caste system prevents them from being a *class for itself.*" Caste and religion are used to perpetuate a particular class structure. Caste persists as a part of feudal ideology. The Samiti observes that caste system has preven-ted formation of consciousness and struggle on class lines with any commonalty of interest or unity of function. This function is one of the main resources for its persistence. The Samiti agrees with Mencher's observation that "conflicts between social classes stem ultimately from the social relations of production." The new functions of the caste resemble with the old class-like functions of the caste system, hence discouragement to the emergence of class consciousness. Such a situation is not peculiar to Maharashtra only. Singh has reported about a similar situation in Punjab. One could find 'class character' in the 'spectre of caste war' in Gujarat in regard to reservation of seats for scheduled castes in state's medical colleges.

The above point is very well brought out by Bose in a study of the riots in Gujarat. He observes that literacy, education and employment are the most important indicators of social mobility among the scheduled castes, and geographical spread of the violence is closely related to social mobility of the scheduled castes affected by violence. Those sections of the scheduled castes who are relatively better educated, more mobile and have some access to jobs have been most seriously affected by the present caste riots. The areas, thus affected, have also a relative concentration of the scheduled castes. Bose also admits that there may be deep-rooted caste prejudices among the upper castes against the Harijans, but at the same time it is also a fact that the rivalry is now between the well-off scheduled castes and the caste Hindus who are entrenched into lucrative jobs, positions of power and high status. In effect, it is a 'class war' between the apparent caste riots, between the scheduled castes and *savamas*. I.P. Desai, who has earlier written a book on *Untouchability in Rural Gujarat,* also looks at the relations between the scheduled castes and the caste Hindus from a class point of view. Ingle finds that Untouchability Offences Act, 1955 has been flouted by caste Hindus in Maharashtra quite frequently, and without much corresponding corrective steps. Desai observes: 'The system of reservations, even though introduced by the state, has now become a weapon in the hands of the various deprived groups in their struggle against socially entrenched upper caste and upper class interests." The upper castes and classes want to maintain the social and economic status quo under the cover of seemingly progressive ideology and demand that 'merit' and not 'caste'should be the determining factor in higher education, jobs, promotions, etc. The scheduled castes and the scheduled tribes and other socially disadvantaged groups through their agitation have tried to attack on this status quo by insisting upon reservations which apparently might appear as a particularistic ideology.

Some empirical studies at the village level reveal a high concentration of socially backward castes among the tenant cultivators. Reddy and Murthy find that as many as 73 per cent of the pure tenant cultivators belong to the backward castes, and of the owner-cum-tenant cultivators 70 per cent belong to these backward castes. The backward caste tenant cultivators are predominant in the small and medium size groups. The socially backward castes in Andhra consists of Settibaliji and Harijan, and the socially advanced castes consist of Brahmin, Kapu, Devanga and others. Thus, most of the tenants of small and medium size belong to economically and socially depressed castes and pure rent receivers except 12 percent who belong to the dominant castes. The latter are getting more benefits from technological changes than the small size cultivators.

While discussing realities of agrarian relations in India, Mukher-jee discusses caste/class dichotomy and observes that at the root of different forms of social organization, namely, caste and class are the common causal factors which have brought caste, religion and class on the same political and economic dimensions. He cites the example of caste riots and observes: "Caste riots are frequent in those areas where the castewise 'social' deprivations are manifestly correlated with the classwise economic deprivations, such as in Bihar, Maharashtra, Tamil nadu, etc." According to Mukherjee, these caste contradictions are due to inherent class contradictions in the caste system.

Vagiswari compares the income and occupation of Harijans and non-Harijans. He finds that the position of the Harijans has worsened over the past ten to twenty years. He estimated that the per capita annual income of the Harijans in 1970 was Rs. 227 as against Rs. 406 for the non-Harijans. He finds that in terms of all economic indicators—size of landholding, employment, occupation, savings—the position of Harijans had progressively worsened between 1950 and 1970; also it had deteriorated compared to the non-Harijans during the same period.

Consequently, the *dalits* or Harijans are attacked, murdered, their womenfolk raped, and other cruel and inhuman treatment is meted out to them. The accounts of such atrocities are innumerable. In case the scheduled castes react even mildly against the atrocities, they are forced to pay a very high price including social boycott, denial of public facilities and employment on farms by the landlords. Such incidents have taken place quite frequently in Bihar, Uttar Pradesh, Gujarat, Maharashtra, Tamil Nadu, Rajasthan, etc. In the Belchi killings on May 27, 1977, nine Harijans and two others—all agricultural labourers were tortured and then burnt alive by dominant caste Hindus. Singh provides a vivid account of atrocities and oppression of the scheduled castes in Madhya Pradesh.

In a forthright despatch, Sinha comments on Bihar situation and observes that it is class war against Harijans, and not atrocities. In 1977, Bihar, among all states, accounted for the largest number of cases of atrocities against Harijans. The outrages occurred in Kargdhar, Belchi, Pathadda, Chhaundano, Gopalpur and Dharampur. People were killed or persecuted not because they were Harijans, but also because they were agricultural labourers and sharecroppers working with the rich and dominant landlords, hence cruelties against them were of the nature of a class war as the interests of the two did not coincide and class contradictions had become more than manifest. The issues behind these happenings were struggles for minimum wages, the occupancy rights of the sharecroppers, and a challenge to the absolute feudal power of the landlords. Therefore, such atrocities (class war) could be against the non-Harijan proletariat, the backward castes, and even against the poor intermediate and upper castes proletariat. Logically this view could be accepted on the basis of class war thesis. But it is only partially true. There is an element of Harijanness in the atrocities committed by the caste Hindus on the Harijans. There is a difference between a situation of atrocity and that of oppression and exploitation. There is a difference between a Brahmin prole-tariat and a Harijan proletariat, hence the differential treatment meted to the two by a Brahmin or Rajput landlord for the same reason. What is known as "the rise of the Kulak power at the centre and in the states", can be held responsible for the oppression of the scheduled castes. The attitude of patronhood or patronage has slowly been disappearing away particularly since independence.

Mukherjee, while writing about the peasant revolt in Bhojpur district of Bihar, observes that *izzat* (dignity) and *unche-neeche jaat ka sangharsh* (upper-lower caste conflict) are the two main causes of bitterness between the upper and lower castes and class people. He writes: "The dehumanization of the lower castes is violent and physical: rampant sexual tyranny perpetuated by the upper castes on lower caste women; the pride of Bhumihars, whose unwritten law prohibits lower classes to remain seated in their presence even at their doorstep; its viewing even the wearing of a clean *dhoti* or receiving education as intolerable ignorance; the 'hakim' suffix after every sentence; at places, the taking of *dole,* i.e., the Bhumihar or Rajput landlord's privilege to sleep with the new bride of a lower caste labourer on the wedding night." Movement for creation of Jharkhand State for the *adivasis* and slogans like "Harijanisthan lar ke leinge" (we will fight for a state for Harijans) are expressions of the oppression and sufferings of the Harijans and tribals at the hands of the dominant castes/ classes in Bihar.

In Marathwada, the riots began due to renaming of Marathwada University as Dr. Babasaheb Ambedkar University in July 1978. The Students Action Committee, which naturally consisted of *non-dalit* student activists, launched an agitation against the *dalits* which continued for 67 days. The Protection of Civil Rights Act did not help the victims in getting out of the inhuman situation prevailing in the region. The movement provoked violence including killing of people, molestation and rape of Harijan women, burning of Harijan houses and huts, pillaging their *basties,* evicting them from their houses and villages, killing of their cattle, denying them drinking water and refusing them work, etc. This act of the caste Hindu capitalists, landlords with the help of the state power was planned to give a serious setback to the *dalit* movement and its vocal leadership. Thus, an explanation for understanding the pitiable position of Harijans should be searched in the character of social structure of Indian society. The causes of their exploitation, oppression and intimidation are not casual, shortlived, and contingent in nature. Dignity and upper-lower caste/class have been the two focal points of discord and contradictions throughout the history of the Hindu society.

A study was conducted by the Harijan Sevak Sangh in 1976 in 179 villages of nine districts of Madhya Pradesh. It is reported that important programmes like land distribution, irrigation, distribution of homestead plots, debt redemption, freeing of bonded labour and financial help schemes were only marginally implemented. Most of the 54 lakh Harijans in the state are agricultural labourers or landless peasants and their future is in the hands of a few big farmers. They were paid as low as Rs. 1.50 for a day's labour. They were put to all sorts of inhuman treatment and indignity. Uttar Pradesh tops the list of atrocities, and Madhya Pradesh comes next to Uttar Pradesh. In the first half of 1973-74, 254 cases were reported, and 18 of these were murder, 37 rape, 38 arson, 81 grievously hurt cases, and 80 offences under Untouchability Offences Act. During 1974-75, 11812 cases were registered.

In 1977, there were 8,905 cases of alleged atrocities on the scheduled castes, and that highest number of atrocities were reported from Uttar Pradesh (4, 974), but according to another source the number was 5,739, and in 1976 it was 3,428 and in 1975 it was 6,760—higher than those of both 1976 and 1977. As many as 2,133 incidents of atrocities were reported from Madhya Pradesh. Other states had: Andhra Pradesh (70), Bihar (421), Gujarat (331), Kerala (136), Maharashtra (367), Rajasthan (179), and Punjab (81). The report refers to land disputes, payment of wages at lower rates, indebtedness and forced labour, forcing the Harijans to perform manual jobs and creating obstruc-tion in the use of public places, particularly drinking water wells.

In 1975-76 and 1976-77, the Scheduled Castes and Sche-duled Tribes Commission received, 2, 295 and 1, 761 complaints, respectively, regarding harassment and untouchability, land and agriculture, housing and education from the scheduled castes and the scheduled tribes. The Commission reports that all the cases are not reported, and out of the reported cases, only some are found punishable because of legalities and other factors such as lack of evidence, etc.

There was a time when studies on caste by ethnographers, anthropologists, sociologists and lately by political scientists, economists and historians became quite popular. Every aspect of the society was viewed in the idiom of caste. To the students who studied caste, class remained almost invisible as a social reality. But others who studied class quite consciously thought that 'caste divisions' persisted along with 'real class divisions' in Indian society. Scholars of either hue and orientation did not see the existence of the social formation of Indian society which absorbed caste, class, race, ethnicity, minorities, religions and regions. The change in the emphasis on the studies from caste to class, or from hierarchy to stratification, or from closed to open stratification or change in the application of the methods of study from 'indological' to 'empirical' and now 'experimental' are no doubt indicators of the realization of the need for studying what is more relevant than what was in the past. However, even these shifts in the foci of studies and research are not properly perceived. To think of Indian society simply in terms of 'caste' as the social formation implying harmony, hegemony, reciprocity, hierarchy, division of labour and stability of the society and vice versa from a class point of view would create confusions and misconceptions.

A scholar of the eminence of Srinivas does not take cognizance, perhaps inadvertently, of the continuity of 'social formation' of Indian society, and prefers to adhere to "caste model" of Indian society. He refers to 'rural caste' and 'urban caste' like some American scholars such as Rosen and Marriott. Caste and class, theoretically speaking, are principles of status determination, hence not concerned with 'rural' or 'urban' people as such. Rural and urban are patterns of living and not principles of ranking. Srinivas observes that "even today agricultural production requires the co-operation of several castes, and even traditionally competition between different castes did occur though it was not very common." He further notes that "caste idiom is widespread", but does not realize that it could also be called as 'class idiom', or idiom of Indian society itself. Srinivas states that there are caste continuities, discontinuities, and fuzzy/areas without clear-cut boundaries with multiple and contrary forces at work. Thus, Srinivas refuses to admit existence of 'class relations'.

We have pointed out that mode of production and differentiation of peasantry are dynamic in nature. Transformation in these could be understood by a framework which includes dialectics, history, culture, and structure. Structural-historical perspective is found quite useful. The rules and regulations to bring about social mobility among the scheduled castes have become quite ineffective. The frame of pure and impure and sanskritisation has been unable to account for structural changes among the scheduled castes. Differentiation among the scheduled castes has accentuated unevenness of a new sort among them. Atrocities and violence against the scheduled castes are a clear indicator of a 'class war' between the well-off caste Hindus and the well-off scheduled castes. Oppression and exploitation are not new to the scheduled castes. The only difference is that now there is more possibility of making a hue and cry than before whenever violence takes place. A class view of the status of the scheduled castes in the caste system could reveal the dynamics of social mobility. Srinivas is perhaps not prepared to accept clearly that caste has also been a system of class relations as well. He says: 'there is fuzziness," this is just to avoid the issue and clinch to his well known position of 'caste sociologist'. Leach feels that the tradition of British empiricism has been used the way it suits for the purposes of analyses—it has become a matter of convenience rather than a matter of scientific investigation. Leach's fear is that such an attitude in use of empiricism brings in the subjectivity and cultural idiosyncracies of the researcher. We are very often accused of doing Brahmin or Rajput or Raiyot sociology. We have to guard ourselves from such accusations by bringing refinement in our methodology and understanding.

Roots in Traditions

The untouchability is an age-old phenomenon. It has been said that the untouchables of India occupied the lowest position in the *varna* or caste system, hence untouchables and stratification were correlated. But this statement does not stand valid today in India to a large extent, and it was not completely true in the past as well. The untouchables were a highly differentiated category of people, and they had a hierarchy of their own, and therefore their relations with caste Hindus were not of a similar nature. In other words, different castes and subcastes of untouchables had differential relations with different caste Hindus depending upon the ranks of both the untouchables and the *swarnas*. Some of the families of the untouchables found positions of respect in the courts of the feudals while others did 'forced labour' during their life-time. Some untouchables were close to the upper caste families, while others were not so. Some castes and sub-castes were less impure than others, and therefore, they had different relations with the caste Hindus.

Such a situation was not just due to the notions of pollution and purity of birth ascription. Distinctions among various castes and sub-castes of untouchables were of a wholesome nature as they were reflected in their styles of life, traditional callings, relations with 'clean' and the upper castes and opportunities for mobility and migration etc. The situation of untouchables today cannot be understood without viewing the stratificational relations which they had in the past. Today, all types of Harijans are not equally victims of atrocities of the landlords, rich peasants and the upper castes. Why some of the families of Harijans are tortured and exploited? Why the Harijans of a particular village, who have generally a low and poor status among the Harijans, are victimized? Why only certain sections of Harijans have extracted most of the benefits extended to them by the central and the state governments and voluntary agencies? Why some castes and groups have advanced in the field of education and others have migrated to towns from their native places just for bare survival? These are some of the very relevant questions for understanding of the problems of the Harijans of India today.

The institution of untouchability is functioning selectively, but quiet effectively, in certain arenas of our social relations. It has eroded in regard to its pollutional aspect to a large extent, but it does not show encouraging trend of decline in regard to its social and economic dimensions. This shows that the institution of untouchability has been a dynamic institution of Indian society. Changes in the institution of untouchability have occurred from time to time corresponding with the changes in other institutions such as caste, property, land tenure, hereditary occupations etc. Some of the ex-untouchables are not strictly 'untouchables' today, and some others continue to sail in the same boat. Such a situation demands an analysis of structural factors which have brought about mobility, migration and awareness among the Harijans of today. Secondly, untouchability is a contextual and relational phenomenon. The untouchables are treated as 'untouchables' in a given context, and they are treated like 'non-untouchables' in some other contexts. We could call these as 'sacred' and 'mundane' contexts, respectively. Thus, the view that an untouchable must not be 'touched' physically, has no meaning in a secular context. For example, when the upper caste Hindus work with the untouchables on their farms, or when they wish to extract work from them, or when they visit Harijan houses during elections, we could refer these as secular contexts. However, the untouchables are treated as 'polluting creatures', when they are invited to eat at the patron's houses on certain occasions. The discriminatory treatment meted to them is an ample testimony of the 'sacred' context. It could be said, therefore, that all untouchables are not equally 'untouchables' among themselves, and also in relation to the caste Hindus. Further, it could be said that untouchability is not the sole criterion of untouchable's status in our society. Since untouchability and caste stratification are closely inter-related and caste has been a dynamic and adaptive system, untouchability should be studied through a processual perspective.

Various Opinions

There are different views regarding untouchability. First, the functions performed by the untouchables are considered necessary, useful and important for the entire society. In other words, untouchability would continue so long as the untouchables performed these functions. Contrary to this is the view according to which untouchability refers to a situation of exploitation, suppression and powerlessness. The untouchables are pauperized and the wretched of the earth. They are the lowliest of the lowest. Their exploiters are the well-off caste Hindu landlords and big peasants. However, both the views do not explain singularly or together the position of Harijans in relation to other castes. The positions of Harijans as well as caste Hindus have changed to a large extent, hence no traditional web of relations between the two. For example, the upper castes do not continue to be landowners, and the Harijans do not work on the traditional basis. The inter-mediate castes have gained the status of landowners, and the Harijans work on their fields as agricultural labourers on a daily wage basis. When the poor Harijans refuse to work due to some genuine reasons including less wages, they become a target of the fury of the landlords. Bihar, Uttar Pradesh, Haryana and Rajasthan have this sort of conflict between the Harijans and the rich peasants, and the latter are generally from among the intermediate peasant castes.

According to a third view, violence and insecurity are an offshoot of the elite sponsored developmental system. In such a situation, which we have, violence by elites on Harijans, and 'violence of protest' by Harijans are found simultaneously. However, the elites always get an upper hand even after the violence is deciding the affairs of the society and fate of the downtrodden. It is quite foolish to expect justice from the vested interests.

The institution of untouchability has changed in recent years, not due to the Untouchability Offences Act of 1955, but due to the pragmatism of the upper and upper middle castes and classes. They have realized lately that observance of untouchability might be quite disadvantageous for them economically and politically in the changed circumstances after independence. It is felt that without working with the Harijans on farms, in factories or in elections, the upper castes cannot continue to dominate or reconsolidate their position. This has been acquired due to some of the structural changes initiated since independence to bring down the age-old ascriptively determined monolithic dominance of the upper castes. However, partly due to legal loopholes and other lacunae, and partly due to pragmatic stratagems, the upper and the upper middle castes and classes have remained in positions of power, both politically and economically. Today, therefore, one finds dissonance between the formal and the real status of the Harijans, and there is also a hiatus between the form and the content of their position and standing in Indian society. One cannot understand the position of Harijans in terms of the existing legislation, constitution and other governmental measures.

The untouchables suffer a number of disabilities ranging from their most personal relations to the utterly formal and latent actions. These disabilities have been noted in regard to recruitment to army and police, admission to schools and colleges, bondage to the land, denial of services by Brahmins and other upper castes, use of sacred places and temples, and entry into shops and tea-stalls etc. The disabilities are not the same for all the untouchables as differential treatment given to the Harijans by the caste Hindus is found on the basis of their economic condition, education, occupation etc. Mahar observes that the nature of untouchability is too variegated in social and cultural phenomena and diversity of groups subsumed under such labels. Thus, there is no single measure or uniform criteria for identifying an 'untouchable'. Apparently, untouchability is a stigma, but in reality, it is a contextual phenomenon and a behavioural norm. It is not, therefore, just a cultural entity. The untouchables have complained against the upper castes on account of discrimination meted out to them, and the upper castes have complained against the Harijans as they have interfered in their exclusiveness of practices etc. The law does not provide a satisfactory solution to this antithetical, but apparently legitimate situation of self-righteousness.

Why there are atrocities only on Harijans and not on their other non-untouchable counterparts from among the caste Hindus? An answer to this question could explain the role of 'untouchability' as a factor responsible for the exploitation of the 'untouchables' by the *svarnas.* A number of studies have shown that the policy of preferential treatment has not given its desired fruits. The Harijans have not changed their traditional callings, nor they have acquired formal education to the extent caste Hindus have acquired. Moreover, these developments have created cleavages also among various scheduled castes. The Mahars, the Malas, the Balais, etc., are ahead of other scheduled castes of their respective regions. Thus, certain new forms of inequalities have emerged among the scheduled castes themselves. The caste Hindus and the Harijan elites have combined, may be unwittingly, to prevent the flow of facilities and new opportunities to the rank and file of the Harijans just to safeguard their vested interests or to promote further their own interests by directly or indirectly diverting the resources for sabotaging the welfare plans meant for the scheduled castes. The crux of the problem is that an equalitarian structure cannot be built without removing the structural bottlenecks of the already existing unequal groups.

We know that the Harijans earn their livelihood by working on land, and they are deprived of control over the land on which they have been working. The incidence of landlessness is more among them compared to other groups. The size of their land-holdings is also smaller than that of caste Hindus. As many as 33 per cent of the total agricultural labourers are from among the scheduled castes. Most of them have uneconomic landholdings. The Harijans have barren and fallow lands. The fertile and strategically important lands have been allotted to the caste Hindus with the connivance of the local leaders and district administration. Therefore, it is necessary to ask: What is the meaning of development for the scheduled castes? There is a need for a basic change among the planners, leaders, scheduled caste elites and administrators to ensure the filtering down of the benefits to the rank and file of the Harijans.

Eminent economists such as K.N. Raj, V.K.R.V. Rao, B. S. Minhas, Dandekar and Rath have shown that the planning has hit the poor badly, and they have become, indeed, poorer. The way modern education, technology and legislation have been initiated, has led to the breeding of inequality. The rich can escape, and the poor can be trapped. Consequently, the Dalits, the Chamars and Harijans are beaten, their houses are burnt and their womenfolk are molested and raped by the landlords and other caste Hindus. These victims are not the well-off Harijans, Harijan leaders and the Harijan white-collar workers. In fact, they are the people who could not have proper education, could not migrate to urban centres for better prospects, and who could not escape the fury of the landed interests. We have ample evidence to show that the poorest of the Harijans are dehumanized and oppressed by the caste Hindus.

In 1975-76, Uttar Pradesh had highest number of atrocities as reported by the state government. About 50 per cent of the total number of such inhuman incidents occurred in the most populous state of India. In 1976-77 also, Uttar Pradesh topped the list of atrocities followed by Delhi, Bihar and Madhya Pradesh. About 80 per cent cases were of beating, and only 10 per cent were of untouchability.

An overwhelming number of these clashes with Harijans are over land and agriculture. Atrocities by police have also been on the increase. However, the cases reported to the government are only a small fragment of the total atrocities which have been committed on the Harijans.

On June 22, 1974 two scheduled caste persons were killed by Kanbi Patels in Surendranagar district of Gujarat because they wanted to fetch water from a village well. The scheduled castes had a well, exclusively for themselves, but it had dried up. The Patels had to come to a compromise due to police intervention and allow the scheduled castes to draw water from the well during fixed hours of the day. However, the Patels did not tolerate the decision and considered this as their direct insult, and hence planned murder of two scheduled caste men who had raised voice for fetching water from the village well.

In 1976, a study was conducted by the Harijan Sevak Sangh in 179 villages of nine districts of Madhya Pradesh. It is mentioned that "important programmes, like land distribution, irrigation, distribution of homestead plots, debt redemption, freeing of bonded labour and financial help schemes were only marginally implemented." Most of the 54 lakh Harijans in the state are agricultural labourers or landless peasants, and their future is in the hands of a few big farmers. They were paid as low as Rs. 1.50 for a day's labour. The Harijans were terrorized by anti-social elements belonging to the upper castes. Their crops were destroyed or looted, houses were burnt and womenfolk were raped. All the Harijans suffered from one or another disability. Uttar Pradesh tops the list of atrocities on the Harijans, and Madhya Pradesh comes next to Uttar Pradesh. During 1972-73, 200 cases of atrocities were reported in Madhya Pradesh. In the first half of 1973-74, 254 cases were reported, and 18 of these were murder, 37 rape, 38 arson, and 81 grievous hurt cases, and 80 offences under the Untouchability Act. During 1974-76, 11, 812 cases were registered.

Arun Sinha, while commenting on Bihar situation, observes that it is 'class war' against Harijans, and not atrocities. In 1977, Bihar, among all states, accounted for the largest number of cases of atrocities against Harijans. The outrages occurred in Kargdhar, Belchhi, Pathadda, Chhaundadano, Gopalpur and Dharampur. The people were killed or persecuted not because they were Harijans and the actions of the landlords were not just atrocities. The issues behind these happenings were struggles for minimum wages, the occupancy rights of the sharecroppers, and a challenge to the absolute feudal power of the landlords. Therefore, such atrocities could be against non-Harijan proletariat as well belonging to the non-scheduled castes, the backward castes, the intermediate castes and even the upper caste proletariat. However, this view is only partially true. There is an element of Harijanness in the atrocities committed by the caste Hindus on Harijans. We could explain this point by making a distinction between a situation of atrocity and that of exploitation. It is true that all proletariat, irrespective of their caste background, are subjected to inhuman treatment by the caste Hindus. But there is a difference between a Harijan proletariat and a caste Hindu or a Brahmin proletariat. The differences between the two are found in regard to their occupational background, prestige of occupation, numerical strength in their respective castes, patronage from caste dominants and cultural milieu. The fact is that a Harijan becomes a target of landlord's fury, but a proletariat belonging to his own class does not get the similar treatment even if he works on his farm as an agricultural daily wage labourer. This is, what we would like to call as 'Harijanness' in the phenomenon of atrocities on Harijans.

We find somewhat different explanation of the atrocities on the Dalits. On May 27, 1977, in Belchhi, a village in Bihar, one villager was shot and 13 others were burnt alive. This was assessed as 'systematic harassment' of the Harijans by the upper caste Hindus according to one political party. However, the Janta Party maintained that the murders were the culmination of a feud between two groups of criminals, each including Harijans and upper caste Hindus. We do not have to enter into the controversy regarding the veracity of the incident, but it was said that the Bharatiya Lok Dal-Jana Sangh combine in eight of the Janta ruled states in 1977 encouraged the upper caste Hindus to persecute the Harijans. In other words, it was rumoured that the Harijans would remain defenseless so long as the Janta Party remained in power. A section of the Harijans made a demand for arms to protect themselves against the toughs and anti-social elements of the upper and upper middle caste Hindus. Thus, the emergence of Janta Party with BLD and Jana Sangh as its two important constituents was characterized as "the rise of the Kulak power at the centre and in the states." Oppression of the Harijans was considered a logical consequence of this change of power in the country.

The Atyachar Virodh Samiti recently made an analysis of riots in the Marathwada region of Maharashtra. The massacre, loot and rape of Harijans in this region have been quite frequent like Uttar Pradesh, Bihar and Madhya Pradesh. The Samiti observes that caste represents a specific form of oppression at the level of relations of production. There are both class and caste issues, because caste divisions persist beyond purely economic classes. A link should be established between fights against caste oppression and class exploitation, that is, caste discrimination and caste oppression are, in effect, representative of class hegemony of the upper castes.

It is reported that during 1966-76, 40, 000 cases of atrocities were recorded. During the 19-month rule of Janta, the cases of atrocities were more than 17, 000. Regarding the cases of atrocities (only murder and rape), Uttar Pradesh (183) tops among the states, followed by Madhya Pradesh (100), Bihar (100) and Rajasthan (78).

In Marathwada, the riots began due to renaming of Marathwada University as Dr. Babasaheb Ambedkar University in July 1978. The Students Action Committee launched an agitation against the change of the name of the university. The violence against the *dalits* took many forms which continued for more than two months. The Protection of Civil Rights Act did not help the victims in getting out of the inhuman situation prevailing in the region. The violence was of a wholesome nature. It included killing of people, molestation and rape of Harijan women, burning of their houses and huts, pillaging their *basties,* evicting them from their houses and villages, killing of their cattle, denying them drinking water and refusing them work, etc. It is reported by the Atyachar Virodh Samiti that 1,200 out of 9,000 villages of Marathwada were affected by the attacks of the caste Hindus, 5,000 people became 'homeless and stateless, and 2,500 became totally demoralized and helpless. This was an offensive launched by caste Hindu capitalist landlords with the help of police, patels, sarpanches and anti-social elements. Breasts of one woman were cut off after raping her. Those who had left their homes were not ready to go back in spite of starvation.

The Samiti observes that renaming of the Marathwada University was only a pretext; the real issues were different. These included preferential treatment given to the *dalits,* namely reservations in educational institutions and jobs, the policies and character of *dalit* movement itself and its leaders, the increasing unity among the *dalits* themselves and between *dalit* and *swarna* agricultural labourers, and the linkages between the rural and the urban *dalits.* Thus, the issues such as language, separate statehood, caste exclusiveness, communal freedom, establishment of steel plants, and opening or renaming of a university, etc. are only apparent causes of the atrocities on Harijans. The real cause of all this is the desire of the upper castes and the landlords to maintain their monolithic control over the resources of the society, and to keep the Harijans and other proletariat as their servants and slaves. As such, caste becomes a mechanism of exploitation of the poor people, particularly the Harijans. It is, in effect, a system of relations of production; it promotes conservatism and helps the rich and the entrenched few in Indian society.

Charan Singh when he was Home Minister of India said that the caste system was the root cause of the problems of the Harijans. Atrocities on Harijans would continue so long as the caste system continued. He made the suggestion that the preferential treatment should be given to those marrying outside their own caste. Attitude of the persons towards caste should also be considered while giving them jobs. Jagjivan Ram, an acknowledged Harijan leader, observed regarding molestation and rape of Harijan girls: "Why did such things happen? Harijan girls were not known for their beauty and there were far more beautiful girls in other communities. The reason was economic weakness of the victims. They would not put up a fight against the 'ruffians', whether they belonged to the police force or other communities."

The backward class movement particularly in Bihar and Uttar Pradesh has further sharpened caste divides in the countryside. Brahmins, Rajputs, Kayasthas and Bhumihars who comprise about 7 per cent of total population, hold 75 per cent of government jobs. In Karnataka, the backward classes constitute 38 per cent of the population, but hold only 12 per cent of the jobs. Besides this discrimination, the backward class people like Harijans are kept at a distance in social and cultural arenas by the upper castes. Parvathama observes:

> The Indian social structure itself is based on graded hierarchy of status where religious, economic, educational, political and judicial powers increase in the ascending order thus directly limiting the status of lower castes. While the instances of disabilities and backwardness are in the descending order, they are thinly spread over a whole range of Sudra castes, but greatest concentration obtains with reference to the untouchables who fall traditionally outside the *chaturvarna* scheme and thus constitute a class of *avarnas* called as *panchvnas.*

Thus, we must search for an explanation of the position of today's Harijans in the social structure of Indian society. The causes of their exploitation, oppression and intimidation are not casual, shortlived and contingent in nature.

Our study of educational inequalities among Rajasthan's scheduled castes shows that their alarmingly backward condition is connected to the deprivation they suffer in relation to the higher status groups and to the differential treatment they receive from the power elites from among themselves. We have found that the distributive disparities affecting the scheduled castes are at three levels: between the scheduled castes and the general population; between the various scheduled castes; and among scheduled castes in a particular district or area. Emergence of inequalities among scheduled castes has become a new stratificational problem, and this has accentuated class distinctions within the scheduled castes. Such a phenomenon would give a setback to unity, mobili-zation and movement among the scheduled caste people.

Available data reveal that the lowest castes, namely, Harijans, become the targets of violence. Such violence has very frequently occurred in Uttar Pradesh, Bihar, Maharashtra, Gujarat, Tamil Nadu, and Andhra Pradesh. Atrocities on Harijans are inflicted both by upper and upper middle castes in these and other states. Our view is that caste divisions in Indian society are not outside the purview of class divisions. Since caste and class co-exist, class consciousness and class unity are hampered by norms of caste divisions. It is, therefore, necessary to give a proper attention to the factor of 'caste' in the analysis of class relations, and also to see caste divisions from the class point of view. In fact, caste is a double-edged weapon being used against the Harijans by the caste Hindus, and to oppress them in the name of their exclusiveness and freedom. Resilience of the caste system has promoted the interests of the upper castes and suppressed the Harijans and other lower castes to a great extent. In other words, the processes of social change initiated after independence have helped the upper castes in the fields of education, politics and jobs. Violence against the Harijans is an expression of the hostile attitudes of the upper castes towards the Harijans, as this results into suppression of class consciousness among them and promotion of the vested interests of the caste Hindus.

13

The Aboriginals

The tribal people have been seen as an undifferentiated lot. However, they have/had gradations based on age-sets, sex and kinship which did not form the basis of social stratification as found among the non-tribal people like property, wealth, power and authority. Several studies of social stratification, ranking systems and class formation among the tribes all over the world have reported absence of social differentiation in tribal societies. Social stratification, as an existential phenomenon among the tribes, is, however, different from that of the advanced agricultural and industrial societies. It is not unique as it is generally considered. The principles of social stratification such as ethnicity, class and power are the same everywhere. The difference lies in the operationalization and actual functioning of these principles due to structural differences in various tribal societies in regard to their history, level of economic development, nature of colonial impact and exposure to modern forces of social transformation. Thus to the extent the tribal people are different in terms of these criteria social stratification and class formation are also different among them in comparison to the non-tribal societies.

For a long time it has been debated by the academia and policy-makers whether tribals should be allowed to retain their cultural identity intact or they should be assimilated with the rest of Indian people. This culrurological perspective is not specifically articulated for the study of social stratification as such among the tribal people, but rich data have been generated regarding intra-tribal and inter-tribal status distinctions (Vidyarthi, 1974). More specifically, the ethnic and class perspectives have been in currency for the study of tribal social stratification (see, for example, Sachchidananda, 1990; Badgaiyan, 1986; Doshi, 1990; Singh, 1985). Emphasis in the ethnic perspective is laid on inter-tribal distinctions in terms of historicity, land relations, colonial impact, contact with non-tribal people, economic development and socio-political awakening, etc. However, the class perspective emphasizes upon formation of class relations among tribes keeping in view their economy, patterns of exploitation, alienation, and backward-ness. In a couple of studies convergence between the ethnic and the class perspectives has been greatly emphasized (see Badgaiyan, 1986; Doshi, 1990).

Finally, we may identify the major tribal ethnic structures in terms of their internal differentiations and interethnic differences and ties to ascertain ramifications of social stratification and class formation. Class formation, as a structural process, is based on increasing differentiation among the tribal people in terms of property, wealth, landownership, exploitation, pauperization, education, political power, social movements, migration and social mobility. We may relate these aspects of class formation with the ethnic structures to find out the nature of correspondence/non-congruence between ethnicity and class.

Scheduled Tribes

'Tribe' may be distinguished from 'caste', but it is not that 'tribe' is a homogeneous entity and 'caste' is characterized by complexity and heterogeneity. There are distinctions within a given tribe and between different tribes. Certainly, tribes are considerably distinct from the non-tribes. But then the question is: What is so distinctive about 'tribe' that makes it distinct from other entities such as caste, class, race, etc. Some tribes are quite large in size and are also spread over several states of India. Surely, tribes are not 'organically' related to each other as castes are under a common principle. But tribes are also not exclusive systems as they are not small in size and bear a great deal of heterogeneity. Historically, a 'tribal society' has not been static, and yet it has retained its exclusivity from a 'caste society'. There are 427 tribes in India, and these can be classified on the basis of language, religion, degree of their isolation, and pattern of livelihood (Beteille, 1974). Some of these attributes of tribes often resemble with the non-tribal people in a given region than the tribal people of another region.

The tribals are hunters, fishers, shifting cultivators, settled agriculturists, plantation workers and industrial wage earners, hence some of them resemble with the non-tribal people. The large tribes such the Bhils, Gonds, Santhals, Oraons and Mundas are not only settled agriculturists, some of them are found in modern occupations in like members of caste Hindus.

Tribal economy is also largely like the peasant economy. Division of labour based on gender, work specialization, tenurial differentiation and class distinctions are found among the tribal people like any non-tribal peasant community. Despite these similarities, tribes remain distinct from castes because of their geographical isolation, language or dialect and religion (Beteille, 1974). Even these criteria are not a rigid basis of distinguishing tribes from castes. For example, Meenas in Rajasthan are listed as a scheduled tribe, but they have always lived in multicaste villages as a part of the village system. Meenas were also one of the functionary castes under the *jajmani* system and, in fact, they are/were always referred as a caste. Certainly, tribes have been large and small both, but never without internal social differentiation. Beteille argues that a substantial number of tribal people are peasants today, hence tribes are in transition (Majumdar, 1937; Sinha, 1965; Oraon, 1969). There is class and social stratification (implying stratified peasantry) among tribes in India. In no way, tribes can today be treated as 'primitive'. Besides differentiation of peasantry, there is also a middle class among the tribal people. Migration, education, mobility, social and political awakening have contributed to the emergence of a small middle class. State-sponsored measures including the constitutional provisions and special programmes for their development have set in a new process of differentiation and stratification which would mean consideration of more or less same criteria of status determination which are normally applied to the non-tribal people.

There is more or less unanimity among the students of tribal social life in India regarding the presence of social stratification. However, Roy Burman (1984) cautions that social stratification by itself is not enough to mobilize the people to actively resist alienation of their land. More important is the nature of social stratification. Roy Burman cites a few examples in support of this observation. The Gonds were a highly stratified community, but no significant revolt took place amongst them till the forties of the present century. The presence of a state structure and the shifting nature of political contacts with the outside world led to both stratification and segmentation of Gond society. Like the non-tribal people, "the upper strata emerged as a multi-focal aristo-cracy." A new elite emerged among the Gonds, and the British rulers transformed them into new Zamindars. Thus, the Gonds synthesized the old and the new, the tribal and the peasant cultures. A tribal movement gets a start generally when it has support of a combination of factors including iniquitous relations, middle class interests, philanthropism and ethnic/community identity. But the point is that tribal people are like other people engaged in similar pursuits in the same area(s), and they are also different from them, and it is this difference/dissimilarity that makes social stratification in tribal society somewhat different from the non-tribal people.

Let us describe a 'functional' formulation of 'tribes' here. Tribes are not castes or caste-like entities though some of them have followed the path of sanskritisation and conversion to Christianity and Islam. Tribes are a highly differentiated lot ethnically and culturally. Some adhere to 'tribalism', others have converted to Christianity by rejecting tribal pantheon, and some have taken up Hinduism by adopting vegetarianism, teetotalism and other Brahminic ideals and practices. Tribes are also differentiated based on landholdings, rural-urban background, education, occupation, income and political power. Tribes have been granted special treatment under the Constitution of India. They have also many attributes, practices and styles of life that distinguish them from the non-tribal people. It may be seen how their 'distinct' and 'general' characteristics get reconciled in their social life. What keeps them partly different from others, and what impinges upon their life to bring them closer to the non- tribal people? The tribal situa-tion is complex in the sense that the tribals depend upon forest-based sources of livelihood, they are also engaged in settled agriculture, they are working in factories and industries, some of them are educated and are employed as professionals, civil servants and white-collar workers, and some are active politicians and social workers. Ethnic and cultural differentiation can be seen in terms of tribal identities and religious pursuits. Thus, the nature of social stratification is also quite complex corresponding with the hetero-geneity of their socio-cultural and economic structure. Therefore, it would be unwise to consider tribes as the people dependent mainly upon forest produces, simple agriculture, living far off from modern civilization.

They are a people who have a lot of attributes in common with the non-tribal population, and at the same time, have their own 'tribal identity'. Social stratification among the tribal people is, therefore, neither simply based on criteria like age and kinship nor it can be characterized by property, education, occupa-tion, income and power. A semblance of the two sets of criteria may distinguish the tribal people from the non-tribal population.

The Backdrop

Sachchidananda (1990) reports that social stratification in the states of West Bengal, Bihar, Madhya Pradesh and Orissa in the pre-colonial period could be observed through the ranks such as the *khuikattidars,* the village headmen and the masses. Later on some artisan castes such as blacksmiths, potters and weavers further differentiated the tribal society. From class point of view, the village society was divided into the *khutkattidars* and the *paria lioroko* (masses). The later depended on the goodwill of the *khut-kattidars* and were rated as second class citizens. The *khutkattidars* were the real owners of the village land. Sachchidananda writes: "The *khutkattidar* system was thus an arrangement for the management of land resources on a communal basis. The headman managed the affairs of the village with the help of some influential village leaders. He dispensed justice, fixed the dates of village deities and collected dues from landholders for payment as *chanda* (contribution) to the tribal chief. Under such a situation lineage or clan was the basis of socio-economic differentiation. The *khutkatti* system was mainly confined to the Munda tribe. Thapar and Siddiqui (1991) also find the *khutkatti* system as the basis of the Munda society. The *mundas, pahans* and *mahtos* were heads of their clans. Besides these heads of the clans/ lineages, the *khut-kattidars* were powerful as they collected a tribute from the villages. Thapar and Siddiqui after tracing the history of social structure and its differentiation in ancient period write: "Thus, the tendency towards social stratification which had already begun with the *khutkatti* system was not only intensified and accelerated under the state, but was also made more complex with the interpolation of various levels of intermediaries". The tribal mode of production broke down and gave a way to the emergence of a new correlation of social status with landholding and power. The lineage rights over land became weak, and a feudal state on tribal society was superimposed. Tribal identity was also weakened by commodity production.

Individual ownership of land was found among other tribes. The headmanship was not confined to a member of a clan or lineage as it was in the case of the Munda tribe having the *khutkatti* system. But all the tribes had the institution of *headman* who acted as a patriarch. The *khutkattidars* were not completely autonomous as the king was the supreme authority in his state. Sachchidananda observes that such a system did not persist for long as feudal superstructure was set in place not only in Chhota-nagpur but also among the Gonds in Madhya Pradesh. He writes: "Scions of the Raja's family carved out feudatory estates and principalities, the most famous of which was the kingdom of Chanda. The emergence of the feudal system marked the beginning of the breakdown of the tribal polity characterized by communal ownership of land" (Sachchidananda, 1990). At this stage, a clearly visible system of social stratification could be seen among the tribal people. A sort of economic explanation of this is provided by Sachchidananda though without using clearly relevant concepts and categories. He writes: "Social stratification based on differential command over economic resources began to emerge. The development of trade and commerce facilitated the growth of small urban centres. A variety of castes, ranging from *brahmans* and *rautias* to many artisan communities, flocked to these centres".

Sachchidananda mentions about the grant of *jagirs* by the Raja of Chhotanagpur in early seventeenth century. As a result of this a new class of merchants, money-lenders and Brahmin priests emerged. The emergence of this new class proved antithetical to the principle of communal and equalitarian character of the tribal society. Since the new grantees of lands in the tribal areas enjoyed more or less permanent and usufructuary rights, they soon began to exploit the tribal people uninhibitedly with the help of village officers such as the *munda* and the *pahan*. The *khutkatti* system also began to crumble down along with the *parha* system. Thus, a new basis of power and social status emerged and replaced the traditional arrangement. Land did not remain any more a communally owned and controlled phenomenon. However, the village officers like the *munda,* the *manki* and the *majhi* were given police powers by the British in their interests to establish their rule over the masses by granting a small minority such benefits which made them to fight for the *raj* and to suppress their own people.

It can safely be deduced from the available literature that isolation of the tribal people has been decreasing, and this has benefited some sections of the tribal society and, at the same time, new forms of social stratification among tribes in India has been variously characterized in terms of peasantization, detribalization, Hinduization, conversion to Christianity, etc. Some caste-Hindus because of pre-eminence of tribal society in a given region have adopted some tribal attributes, and such a process has been called as 'tribalization'. Despite these changes, tribal society can be distinguished from the Hindu, Muslim, Christian and other non-tribal communities. However, this does not imply that tribes in India have remained or continue to remain isolated, homogeneous, small in size and unique compared to the non-tribal people.

The British affected the tribal people in several ways. The intrusion of the British in the management of forests dipossessed the tribals from their age-old control and use of forests. Besides the British officers, a lot of other sections like suppliers, traders, clerks and workers started living in the tribal areas. In course of time, some tribals were also benefited by the British encroachment, and they became a distinct class of the privileged few. Education was one way by which a select group of tribals became superior to the masses. Conversion to Christianity also helped the converts in education, employment, and in fact, in acclaiming a higher status for them.

Singh (1978) highlights some dysfunctional consequences of the British colonialism. The agency system established by the British was used for ruthless suppression of the tribal uprisings. The colonial system also strengthened the feudal elements in tribal society as it encouraged the chiefs and landlords to extract surplus from the tribals as much as possible for the well-being of the *raj* in India. The moneylenders had their heyday as no one was there to check the usurious activities perpetrated by them.

From various accounts, it is evident that during the British period class-based distinctions were replacing the traditional status system among the tribes of India. It could be seen in the alienation of land, control of forest economy by the state, emergence of moneylenders and traders, close but exploitative contacts by the non-tribals with the tribal people, etc. All these sections of society, including the British officers, Zamindars, moneylenders and traders and non-tribal agriculturists were superior in skills and resources even before they landed on the tribal soil. This implanted a hiatus between them and the tribals, and the policy of the government created status cleavages among the tribals. This is why some non-tribals are regarded as *diku* (exploiters). The tribals, in general, faced acute pauperization and were forced to migrate in search of employment to far off places in Bengal, Assam, Maharashtra, etc. The tribals are found divided even today due to the processes of acculturation started by the Christian missions and Hindu organizations. Conversion to Christianity and Hinduization brought about at least three orders, namely, Christian convert tribals, Hinduized tribals, and non-converts. All these tribals were also stratified internally based on their economic standing and ethnic status.

Inter-ethnic relations between different groups with varying degrees of structural distance have been highlighted by Badgaiyan (1986). Ethnicity and class as the two main principles of social differentiation have provided multiple ways to the people for organizing their social relations. Within the same ethnic group there are wide-ranging class differences, and the hostile ethnic groups may be found in the same class. The searching questions posed by Badgaiyan are: (1) How people resolve the contradictory claims on their sentiments and impulses to act? (2) Do they allow their ethnic sentiments to ride over class interests or do they let class interests prevail over their ethnic obligations? (3) Is it the context that decides as to which affiliation will prevail over the other? (4) Do all ethnic groups behave the same way? (5) Are ethnic groups swayed more by primordial sentiments than by contextual logic? These questions are explicated in the context of the historical development of Munda society. The four phases noted by Badgaiyan are: (i) the traditional Munda society before the emergence of kingship among them; (ii) Munda society under kingship but before the imposition of British colonialism; (iii) Munda society under British colonialism; and (iv) Munda society in independent India. The account provided by Badgaiyan about the pre-British period resembles with those given by Sachchidananda and Thapar and Siddiqui. The rent collectors in Chhotanagpur were recognized as Jagirdars (owners of land) after the British had taken over the Diwani of Bengal in 1765.

The Jagirdars accelerated the process of expropriation of native owners of land. Ejection became an easy affair, and some proprietary cultivators were forced to become tenants and agricultural labourers. By the middle of the last century the number of Jagirdars had gone upto 600. In addition to rent, they imposed new taxes and levies. Badgaiyan writes: 'Praetorian obligations of service, gifts and presentation now became necessary for holding the land. Forced labour came to be extracted more and more. The Jagirdars introduced the *thekedars* to collect revenue. These *thekedars* used all their means and power to extract as much as they could from the tenants". Thus, three new classes, namely, Jagirdars, *thekedars* and tenants emerged replacing the rent collectors and cultivators. With the intervention of the British, the moneylenders and the merchants also entered into socio-economic fabric of tribal life. Another dimension to social stratification among the tribes of middle India was added by the coming of Christianity as it brought about differentiation initially on religious basis and later on the basis of education, occupation and income. By the end of nineteenth century, the divide between the non-tribal elite and the tribal masses had become so wide that the Birsa movement emerged as a strong wave against the Hindus, Christians, Jagirdars, *thekedars* and colonialism.

Badgaiyan observes that by the end of the nineteenth century the tribal situation had become quite complex. For example, the Mundas had to deal with a number of other tribal groups like the Oraons, Hos and Cheros; they had also to deal with the non-tribal groups like the Hindus, Muslims, Sikhs and Christians and Birsaite sections from among themselves. These ethnic distinctions reflected to some extent status distinctions. The tribals who conver-ted to Christianity were able to improve their socio-economic status by having modern education and white-collar employment, hence were generally considered superior than those who adhered to their traditional pattern of social life. All these developments accentuated the role of class in patterning of social relations. What Badgaiyan observes is that "the objective reality was thus characterized by a multiplicity of social groupings based on ethnicity and class, religion and language. But the Munda consciousness visualized this diversity falling into a trichotomy: tribals, *diku* and non-tribals but *non-dikus*".

Around this time, the word *'diku'* became quite expressive signifying non-tribal exploiters such as Jagirdars, merchants and moneylenders. The character of the *dikus* has changed considerably after independence as the north Biharis employed in government departments are treated as *dikus* because they deprived the tribal people aspiring for white-collar jobs. In any case the word *diku* is used for the non-tribal exploiter of the tribal people. Thus, from the point of view of class, there are the classes of the exploiters and the exploited. However, both the classes are internally differentiated, hence no uniform pattern of exploitation. These outsiders also became local administrators and this too helped them in the oppression of the tribal people. But Singh (1978) takes a different view as he observes that the most of the tribal population in India was integrated within the administration of the provinces of British India or within that of the Indian states. He calls it the mode of protective administration. The administration established *chatties* along highways to supply the army which brought in merchants, traders and peddlers and set up canton-ments and centres of administration and trade. The colonial system ended the relative isolation of the tribal society; brought it into the mainstream of the new administrative set-up, policies and progra-mmes; but put an end to the political dominance of the tribes in the region; and roped the tribal communities which had been spared from the strain of the surplus generation by their states into a new system of production relations. Singh's observations thus do not synchronize with that of Sachchidananda and Badgaiyan. However, Singh makes a reference, though a passing one, about the dual policy followed by the *raj* as it strengthened the feudal crust on the one hand and the forces of market cutting the very roots of tribal economy and polity on the other. All these changes were reflected in social stratification. Let us now discuss the situation in the post-independence period.

Changed Situation

K.S. Singh observes that the economic and political processes of tribal transformation get reflected in social stratification. Social stratification among tribes has always existed in various forms such as social and physical distance, notion of purity and pollution, prestige and status, habits and customs, and the like. The system of social stratification in the form of the feudatory chief Zamindars at the top, the well-to-do headmen in the middle and the general mass at the bottom has changed since independence. A class of insider *diku* and professional tribal moneylender as a result of the anti-land alienation laws has emerged in the post-independence period. A small section of the tribes has gone up in socio-economic hierarchy, and they are engaged in land transactions and moneylending. In another context, Singh provides a four-fold classification of social movements with special reference to middle India. These movements are: (1) movements for political autonomy; (2) agrarian and forest-based movements; (3) sanskritisation processes; and (4) cultural movements based on script and language. All these movements could be understood as efforts on the part of tribal society to find for itself a place of honour and status at least equal to other sections of Indian society. In other words, the tribal people expressed their anger against their political and economic suppression and also desired to move up in socio-cultural hierarchy as reflected in their efforts to convert and or adopt Christianity and Hindu way of life.

There are not many studies available on social stratification among the tribes in India. The Indian State has provisions in its constitution with regard to uplift of the tribal people living in diffe-rent parts of India by reducing age-old socio-economic inequality. In the field of education, socio-economic and political awakening and employment part-successes have been achieved as a result of the policy of reservation of jobs, seats in educational institutions and earmarking of scheduled tribes' and scheduled castes' constituencies. The anticipated consequence of these provisions could be seen in new forms of socio-economic and political inequality between different tribal communities.

Sachchidananda seems to be (apparently though unintentionally) inclined towards an economic analysis of social stratification among the tribals of middle India. He writes: "Since the advent of colonial rule and the unrestricted movement of plainsmen into the tribal areas, the tribal population has been subjected to unemi-ting economic exploitation. Massive alienation of tribal lands to moneylenders and superior cultivating castes left the majority of agriculturists steeped in poverty and debt" (1990). Such a situation, characterized by isolation, economic backwardness, lack of educa-tion, social fragmentation, and distinctive ethnic, religious and linguistic affiliations, forced upon the state to declare the tribal people as a 'scheduled' category, providing them protective discri-minatory treatment leading to their integration with the wider society in India. Sachchidananda's description of the tribal situation lacks requisite rigour as it neither makes use of the categories like class, class consciousness, class antagonism, change, relations of production and role of state, etc. nor it examines the role of ethnicity, isolation, assimilation, kinship, etc. as the main tools of his analysis. However, studies by Rose (1981), Pathy (1984) and Shah (1979, 1986) examine the tribal situation from the class perspective about which we would make a brief reference later on.

Sachchidananda (1990) reports that the weak impact of the measures taken by the Indian State for the welfare of the scheduled tribes has resulted into the continued dominance of the new outsiders as the colonial rulers have been replaced by the indigenous elites. The illegal transfer of land from tribals to non-tribals has become an established fact of life. Surplus land has not been distributed to the poor and deserving tribals. Even the land distributed is in fact so meagre and qualitatively so poor that it has not proved to be a viable source of livelihood. Industrialization has displaced the tribals as their lands have been taken over by the state. A large number of outsiders have again come to the tribal areas due to industrialization further widening the gap between the tribals and the non-tribals *(dikus).* Contractors, petty businessmen and government officials have taken strong roots in tribal society though still they look to be anachronisms and unwelcome elements. Even infrastructural facilities like roads, electricity and means of communication have been made available in the tribal areas keeping in view the needs of the outsiders rather than the tribal inhabitants. Education, employment and representation in legislative bodies from village panchayat to parliament through the policy of protective discrimination have created an elite section among the tribals rather than bringing about social mobility among the tribal masses.

Sachchidananda observes that "a significant impact of politico-economic change in independent India is the accentuation of social inequalities in tribal society." Sachchidananda's argument is that most tribal societies in middle India were egalitarian. Social stratification emerged among them in the pre-colonial and colonial periods in the form of semi-feudalism and exploitation by dividing the tribal society into the upper class and the commoners. The outside moneylenders were a third notable class which has been replaced by the inside *dikus* after independence. Social stratification is a relational and relative phenomenon, and therefore, it can be observed only in terms of relations between individuals, between individuals and groups and between groups over a period of time based on a certain value-frame. It has been reported earlier that social stratification has always existed among the tribes of India though its value-frame has changed from time to time. Social stratification existed not only between tribals and non-tribals, but it was also found among tribes, clans and lineages based on kinship—status, age, sex, hereditary—office, possessions, etc. After independence, education, employment and political power, though these are in a certain way inter-related phenomena, have become the main bases of social stratification among the tribal people. Since these did not exist earlier, their emergence after independence in a particular way cannot be taken as an accentuation of inequality. A small section of tribals has come directly close to the non-tribals through these new bases of social status, and some of the tribals have even gone higher than the non-tribal people based on these criteria. Other tribals have been beneficiaries at the secondary and tertiary levels. A large number of tribals still remain unbenefited from these scarce resources like education, white-collar jobs and positions and offices of power. Class distinctions have crystallized among the tribals like the non-tribal people in terms of upper, middle and lower classes because all the people have not been benefited in equal measure, and it is hard to believe that a majority of the tribals have been harmed by the development process in the post-independence period. The high level of socio-political awakening among the Mundas, Oraons, Santhals, Hos, Bhils, Raj Gonds, Chaudharis, etc. is self-explanatory of their betterment compared to their own past during the British period.

The most important bases of social stratification among the tribes of middle India are ethnicity and class. Despite being inter-related aspects these are not found in the same proportions of interconnections and efficacy in all tribal societies. Tribal people who have been exposed more to the influences like Christianity, modern education, developmental programmes and industrialization would have more of *class* and power as the bases of status determination rather than ethnicity in the form of stratified lineages or clans. Let us have a look at these criteria in the context of the present day tribal society.

Tribe as Community

Ethnicity becomes distinctly observable if a community is viewed in terms of its independent existence rather than as an interdependent entity. The creation of scheduled areas, provisions for special measures for the development of tribal blocks, reservation for representation in parliament, state legislatures and local bodies and for admissions in schools and colleges/universities and jobs have further strengthened the ethnic identities of the tribes of India.

Thus, in any given region, we may find ethnic differentiation within a given tribe in terms of the non-converts and the converts. The benefits accruing from adhering to one's own religion or from conversion to Hinduism, Christianity and Islam would determine to a large extent social status of the tribal people.

Fuchs (1977) is, however, right in his observation that most tribes are divided in two sections—a Hinduized upper section and a lower tribal section. He cites examples of the Gond (Raj Gond and Jungli Gond), Kokru (Muasi and Paharia), Bhilala (Bara Bhilala and Barela), Raj Banshi and others. Hinduized tribes have been relegated to the status of outcastes and untouchables. Only some tribes living in Chhotanagpur have developed some degree of consciousness and they also assert themselves almost equal to the non-tribal people. Fuchs shows his serious concern about adoption of the Hindu way of life by the tribes in central India, but his silence regarding conversion to Christianity speaks volumes of his approval. Fuchs also deplores the absence of a strong tribal solidarity among the aboriginals of central India. They do not have organizational support-base nor they are economically and socially well-placed.

Thapar and Siddiqui (1991) ask the question as to how tribal identity survived. Though they do not provide a complete answer but observe that the preservation of tribal identity was in part due to the nature of land relations. The expansion of tribal identity was to some extent watered down by the cultural legitimation of the tribal elite in terms of a wider Indian context (sanskritic courtly culture). With the emergence of a well established agricultural base and a network of trade connections not only further elaborated the system of social stratification but also weakened the exclusivity of tribal/ethnic identity. Thus, going by Thapar and Siddiqui's view, we may infer that the tribal identity was always coloured by economic differentiation and power hierarchy.

Class and ethnicity were inextricably intermixed in Chhotanagpur in the nineteenth century (Badgaiyan, 1986). In the context of the Mundas of Chhotanagpur, Badgaiyan mentions about *khutkatti* clan Mundas, *non-khutkatti* clan Mundas, non-Munda tribals and Hindu caste functionaries in the period before the emergence of kingship among them. The Munda and the Manki were not only heads of their clans and villages, respectively, but were also *khutkattidars.* Later on the *khutkatti* system was destroyed and replaced by Bhuinhari, Rajhas and Manjhihas tenures. There were non-tribal jagirdars in large number when the Munda society was under the system of kingship. Hinduism made inroads into the tribal heartland, and it was strengthened by the recruitment of Hindu militia and administrative staff. Brahmin priests and other functionaries found a convenient place for themselves with the patronage of the king as lower level feudatories, Hindu and Muslim merchants also found opportunities for trade and barter in the region.

In the first phase, new ethnic groups entered into the Munda society as a subordinate class, the producers of surplus; but in the second phase the class that entered was the subordinate class, the appropriators of surplus. Badgaiyan observes: "Entry of this new class radically changed the production relations. In order to justify and support the new production relations new concepts of ownership and authority as well as new ideology came to be imposed on the Munda society and polity". "The Munda themselves became greatly differentiated on class lines". Thus a new complexity arose between class and ethnicity. In fact, Badgaiyan also analyzes the patterns of dominance along with ethnicity and class. He refers to the subordination of all non-Munda ethnic groups in the early period followed by the subordination of the Mundas by a dominant section of the immigrant ethnic groups. The ethnic divide gets further blurred by sharing of class positions by the Mundas with the non-Mundas. There were Munda Zamindars and non-Munda Zamindars, and there were similarly Munda tenants and non-Munda tenants. Perhaps ethnicity has an edge over class because "relations between non-Munda Jagirdars and Munda tenants were reported to be far more strained and antagonistic than those obtaining between Munda jagirdars and Munda tenants". However,

Badgaiyan infers a somewhat different conclusion from such a situation. He writes: "This leads one to hypothesize that agrarian relations are more strained when class stratification is compounded with ethnic differentiation." We may make two observations here: (i) the Munda Jagirdars had a legitimacy of their rule much before the non-Mundas encroached upon the tribal areas as jagirdars, hence they were not acceptable to the Mundas as their masters; and (ii) the strained relations between the Munda tenants and the non-Munda Jagirdars symbolized the non-acceptance of the alien rulers on the Munda land.

The ethnic structure of the Mundas became further weak due to two factors: (i) the British takeover of Bengal in 1765 (Bihar was part of Bengal); and (ii) Christianity. Rack-renting and ejection from Rajhas and Manjhihas land became frequent reducing the Mundas to the status of tenants and agricultural labourers. Forced labour was almost a routine activity. *Thekedars* as collectors of revenue were a new institution in the system of exploitation. Thus, with Jagirdars, *thekedars,* British administrators, money-lenders and merchants, the authority of Mundas and Mankis deteriorated further. Earlier Hinduism and later on Christianity proved to be an attack on the ethnically monolithic character of the Mundas as a community. The Birsa movement was a direct reaction to the onslaught committed on the Mundas by the British administration and Christianity.

Ethnic situation had become quite complex as the tribal groups came closer to each other and they also dealt with the non-tribal groups like the Hindus, Muslims, Sikhs, and Christians. Besides this, the Mundas had Hindu, Christian and Birsaite sections among themselves. Badgaiyan observed that it was not that every-thing was seen in terms of ethnicity alone. Social relations were defined by both ethnicity and class. Mundas and Hindus both had Jagirdars and tenants. Ethnicity was thus not coterminous with class. Objectively, there were several groupings based on ethnicity and class, religion and language. The Mundas perceived, according to Badgaiyan, three main groups, namely, tribals, *dikus* and non-tribals but *non-dikus.* Ethnicity and class co-exist among the Mundas. Badgaiyan writes: 'In the light of the behaviour of the Munda tenants and agricultural proletariats with regard to Munda and Hindu Jagirdars, it can be said that the ethnic solidarity is diluted by class differentiation and class hostility is heightened by ethnic differentiation." Class solidarity is eroded by ethnic differentiation. Identity of both class and ethnicity has resulted in greater solidarity among the Mundas. Today the question is: Whether ethnicity represents a bundle of primordial sentiments and ties or is it an identity which is contextually manipulated? Many a times ethnicity is articulated and twisted according to the compulsions of given situations. Badgaiyan writes: "Ethnicity is not just having a set of external attributes. It is essentially a question of subjective perception. It is this subjective perception that gives people a sense of belonging to an ethnic group." Members of one ethnic group could belong to more than one class, and members of one class could belong to more than one identity at a given point of time, and they may not be in mutual harmony.

Ethnicity in the context of wider socio-political and economic development has acquired a great deal of instrumental significance. Measures like the constitutional provisions and reservations and special schemes for development have strengthened rather than weakened the ethnic and primordial solidarities among the scheduled tribes. It is felt by the articulate section of the tribal people that they could persist with the existing benefits and also demand more and better amenities for their development by asserting their ethnic unity and solidarity as expressly as possible. In this way 'ethnicity' among tribes and 'caste' among Hindus have become a convenient means of political mobilization. Sachchidananda (1990) does not find any real contradiction between elaboration of stratification and hardening of ethnicity. Though apparently the two seem to be antithetical to each other, but in real life they are found in specific contexts without being anta-gonistic. Diversification and development impinge upon the monolithic character of the tribal society, hence weakening of ethnic solidarity becomes a logical and natural consequence, but 'ethnici-zation' is brought in by making best possible efforts to ensure availability of maximum benefits from the processes of deve-lopment.

Expression of ethnic identity depends upon the contexts and the issues at a particular point of time. Lack of inter-tribal solidarity has always been one of the serious obstacles in achieving the most urgent common ends. Different tribes have not come together to share the same platform mainly because of the perception of exclusivity of one tribe and a sense of pride of being superior or at least not inferior compared to any other tribe. Mobilization even against the non-tribal people has suffered from such perceptions regarding inter-tribal and intra-tribal relations and notions of superiority and inferiority. However, ethnic identity has found its place in different spheres of life such as language, education, politics and culture. Students have formed from time to time associations and unions comprising *adivasis* alone.

A detailed treatment of the 'tribal question' in Chhotanagpur is provided by Weiner (1978) as a part of his study of *Sons of the Soil: Migration and Ethnic Conflict in India.* One gets the impression from Weiner's study that the main cause of the backwardness among the *adivasis* is economic as he emphasizes on the problems of land alienation, exploitation by *dikus* (earlier moneylenders and Zamindars and now white-collar workers, politicians and traders and businessmen), unemployment, etc. This explanation is based on the perceptions of the tribals themselves about their own problems. Their perceptions about the outsiders and their impact on politics in the region have been considered by Weiner as the basis of his argument in regard to what he calls 'tribal encounters' for analyzing relationship between tribals and migrants. The economic problem forced the tribals to emigrate in large numbers to work as plantation labourers in Assam and Bengal. Ethnicity is reflected in some of the statements made by the respondents. All *dikus* were Bihari Hindus and that they (tribals) were exploited by the Bihari landlords. The tribals lost their lands to non-tribals. Weiner observes that some well-to-do tribals who have acquired land, and some of them are themselves substantial money-lenders are not hated by the tribal folk. In fact, some tribals feel proud of their wealthy tribals, whereas they express antagonism against the wealthy non-tribals. Thus, Weiner clearly advocates an ethnicist perspective rather than a structural view for analyzing relations between tribals and non-tribals. He writes: "given a choice, people prefer to hate others because of their religion, race, caste, or tribe, rather than because of their wealth. The wealthy in one's own community is a source of vicarious pride. The status (and accomplishment) of members of one's own community pro-vides self-esteem to all members of the community. For this reason, it is not easy to create class cleavages and class parties in a multi-ethnic society except where class and ethnic cleavages coincide. Class antagonisms then become veiled expressions of ethnic hostility. This is probably why ideological parties of the left based upon class appeal have not done very well in India, and why peasant revolts against landlords are more likely to occur when the peasants and landlords belong to different religions or castes, or one is tribal and the other is not".

Migration of the tribals from their native places has certainly weakened ethnic bondage because class differentiation forces to treat themselves also as unskilled workers, mechanics, clerks, teachers, rural, semi-rural and urban inhabitants etc. Some tribals have become professionals like university teachers, doctors, engineers, lawyers, social workers and politicians. Professionals from among the tribals identify themselves more with the non-tribal middle class people rather than with the rest of the tribal people. Weiner over-emphasizes the ethnic perspective undermining the role of class and power in weakening the ethnic character of the tribals on one hand and socio-political differentiation among the tribes on the other. All the queries made by Weiner refer to the ethnic question. Some of the questions are as follows:

(1) Why have the tribals remained 'backward?'

(2) Why are they looked down upon by non-tribals?

(3) Why have they not moved into skilled positions in industry, or into managerial posts?

(4) Why have they not successfully competed against the migrants who have moved into Chhotanagpur?

(5) What can be done to change the situation?

Certainly, ethnicity holds its strong ground among the tribes of India, but it is also a fact that as a result of some reforms, administrative measures and implementation of given policies, ethnicity has become visibly weak and class differentiation has surfaced significantly. Therefore, a simple formulation referring to tribals versus non-tribals or local people versus outsiders in the context of jobs and opportunities forecloses the analysis of the role of class and power in the context of social changes since independence. Without any conscious effort, class differentiation itself brings about de-tribalization among the tribes of India. Conversions to Christianity and Islam and impact of Hinduism and other cultural forces have already shown a great deal of de-tribalization. The Christian tribals are superior to the non-converts in socio-structural terms. The Hinduized tribes consider themselves culturally superior to the non-converts as they have adopted vegetarianism and have discarded drinking of alcohol.

Despite conversion to Christianity, the ethnic dimension remains intact though in a somewhat new and changed form. Conversion to Christianity has brought about 'double allegiance' among the tribals as they are unable to forget their past and simultaneously they are made to be a part of a new world-view, namely, Christianity. This double identity, though broadens economic and socio-cultural base of the converts, but they are not able to get out of ethnic bondage in larger sense of the term. Most of the educated tribals converted to Christianity have/had their training in theology and have remained attached to one or other church. Missionary schools, colleges and other organizations have invited strong reactions in which some of these convert educated tribals are employed.

Social Status

Economic and political processes, accompanied by urbanization, industrialization and political awakening, have brought about visible differentiation among tribal people on class lines. Singh (1985) observes: "The major thrust of change has been from tribes into peasants. By the end of the eighteenth century communities of peasantized tribals had emerged in Assam, Rajasthan, middle India, fete." A hierarchy of land tenures in the form of tribal chiefs and occupancy tenants emerged with the coming of the British administration. Taking over of the forests from the control of the tribals made them to work as manual workers. With the emergence of industrialization in post-independence period tribal people have also become unskilled, semi-skilled and skilled workers in industries. A class of well-off non-tribal people co-existed with the tribals in the form of moneylenders, shopkeepers and white-collar workers. These non-tribals are now expressly considered as 'outside exploiters'. Class differentiation is a double-edged phenomenon because there has been a differential impact of the factors and forces of social change due to the uneven nature of intra-tribal and inter-tribal situations. As a result of this, we can find today hunting and food-gathering tribal people on the one end of the continuum and highly educated people engaged in government jobs and other lucrative persuits on the other. Thus, there is no uniform principle of hierarchization among the tribes of middle India. The differentiation between various tribes and between the families of a tribe in a given context indicate clearly that different segments of tribes and specific families have carved out particular 'social spaces' or placements for themselves. In many ways, they resemble with each other and also with the non-tribals though in varying degrees. Neither all tribal people have been equally involved in class and power struggles against their oppre-ssors nor have they been benefited uniformly from the positive consequences of those collective or semi-collective mobilizations. But all tribals were not oppressed or deprived of in the same manner, hence their involvement in the emancipatory efforts has also varied. Some of these points have remained unattended in most of the studies of class and power among the tribes of middle India.

Observations made by Thapar and Siddiqui (1991) seem to be quite convincing about connection between socio-cultural and politico-economic dimensions among the Mundas in ancient period. They write: "The more fundamental changes however related to rights over land. The axis shifted from clan to territory: tenurial rights based on kinship were encroached upon by those based on professional services. The Raja granted lands and villages on perpetual tenures of military, administrative and personal services— the services required by the infrastructure of a state. The grantees were appointed to appropriate the maximum rights". Certainly, a distinction existed between the lineage lands or *bhuinhari* and the *rajhus* lands. Thapar and Siddiqui report presence of *manjhas* (grantee), *rajhus* (crown) and Kanwars, Thakurs and Lallas (who were given maintenance grants), and retainers. Thus, along with ethnic (clan, lineage) stratification, a quite elaborate class stratification existed. They write: 'Thus, the tendency towards social stratification which had already begun with the *khutkatti* system was not only intensified and accelerated under the state, but was also made more complex with the interpolation of various levels of intermediaries". Now, from lineage, economic and political functions passed into the hands of professionals outside the lineage. A new nexus emerged between social status, landholding and power, though lineage still did not become defunct. It is evident from this account that feudalism had taken over the tribal society and the classes mentioned above also existed in the princely states till India achieved her independence.

The hypothesis put forward by Thapar and Siddiqui regarding decline of ethnicity and emergence of class relations also finds substantiation in Badgaiyan's systematic historical analysis of 'class and ethnicity' among the Mundas of Chhotanagpur. Badgaiyan provides a detailed account of the simultaneous emergence of feudalism and complex class structure among the Mundas, and observes that "social relations were defined not entirely by ethnic membership. They were influenced also by the class structure." However, the two were not coterminous nor were they reducible to each other. Another important point in Badgaiyan's analysis is regarding what he calls "objective reality and subjective dispositions" particularly in the context *of dikus* (exploiters) in Chhotanagpur. The Mundas consider all the non-tribal exploiters despite their ethnic and class differences as *dikus*. "The definition of an objective situation is subjective" (1986). The tribal exploiters today and carrier the tribal jagirdars have/had not been perceived as *dikus*. Thus, the objective reality and its subjective perception do not necessarily coincide, and therefore class and ethnicity co-exist in certain respects and cut across each other in some contexts. When class and ethnicity are perceived in consonance, there is greater solidarity among the tribal people. Leaders of various tribal movements generally strive to emphasize on such an accord between ethnicity and class.

A large number of researchers observe that in the pre-British period with the encroachment of feudalism on tribal life, the process of emergence of a new class structure set in replacing the tribal patriarchal clannish system rooted into the *khutkatti* system of land tenure. Thus, feudal classes such as Raja, Jagirdars, grantees, *bhuinhars,* retainers, tenants on the one hand, and priests, merchants, moneylenders and masses emerged on the other. Such a change affected significantly the tribal polity too. Sachchidananda (1990) observes that the political authority of the head of the *parha* (confederation of villages) disappeared, and many Mundas migrated to other parts of tribal Bihar where they could retain their traditional institutions. In Madhya Pradesh and Orissa too, individual ownership of land had become a fact of life. The British used some traditional/hereditary village officers for collecting revenue by granting them powers of a police force. In Bihar, *munda, manki* and *majhi* thus became once again powerful under the British patronage. But the market forces further more rapidly accentuated in the British period along with new administrative system. Land alienation, moneylenders' usurious practices, heterogeneity brought in by the influx of non-tribal communities and new categories of people like traders, contractors and petite administrative officials not only proved a serious blow to the pre-colonial tribal system, but also accentuated two-pronged class-based stratification between the tribals and the non-tribals and among the tribals. Now one could easily find among the tribals proprietary tenants, tenants-at-will, share-croppers and landless agricultural and manual workers. The classes other than these were formed by the non-tribals to a large extent. These included government employees and officers, professionals like doctors, lawyers and professors and merchants and traders. The post-independence period has witnessed strengthening of this class structure, and side by side some new communities and social categories too have acquired an access to some scarce and much desired positions and offices. The new political system has certainly created a class of tribal power elite. This new class is largely a transformation of the class of educated tribals of pre-independence period who were engaged in various reform and other movements and also employed as professionals and administrative workers.

Socially and culturally, the tribals have not assimilated to a considerable extent with the non-tribals. Conversions and adoptions of other religions and practices have created somewhat limited cleavages among the tribals rather than restructuring the tribal society. But this is not true in the same way about economic and political relations among the tribals and of the tribals with the non-tribals. Class structure and relations among the tribals resemble with the non-tribals, and so are power relations. The hiatus between the socio-cultural and politico-economic structures and relations could be attributed to the differential impact of macro-structural forces and factors which was perhaps intended by the colonial rulers and it is persisting even today because of the policies pursued by the Indian State since independence. Ethnicity has thus remained a force to reckon with for mobilizing the *adivasis* against the atrocious class structure which was superimposed upon them by the pre-colonial and the colonial rulers and continues to be there to a great extent even after independence.

Some recent studies of social stratification among tribal people highlight on class hierarchy and its socio-cultural consequences. A study of the Chaudhari tribe in Surat district of Gujarat by Shah (1979) shows the presence of four economic strata on the basis of occupation and ownership of land. These strata are: (i) agri-cultural labourers and poor cultivators; (ii) middle cultivators;

(iii) rich cultivators; and (iv) white-collar employees. The first three constitute more than 92 per cent of the total working population of the Chaudharis, while in the fourth category there are less than 3 per cent people. Shah (1991) writes: "Labourers and poor cultivators are at the bottom of the occupational hierarchy. It is the single largest stratum, constituting 61 per cent of cultivators, of which 24 per cent are almost landless and 37 per cent have land between one and five acres. Their main source of livelihood is manual labour." Shah provides other details about economic life of this largest segment of the Chaudharis of Gujarat. Of the middle cultivators 33 per cent own land between five and 15 acres. These are a better off section as 20 per cent of them have wells for irrigation and half of them have diesel or electric pumps. They use chemical fertilizers, and about 70 per cent of them have a pair of bullocks. Rich cultivators are about 5 per cent and own more than 16 acres of land. They are better off than the middle and poor cultivators. They have electric or diesel pumpsets, use chemical fertilizers, hire wage labourers, produce for market, and their women-folk and children are educated and do not do manual work even on their own farms. All these three classes are related to agriculture though unevenly and enjoy different social statuses. The white-collar workers who are about 3 per cent of the population are engaged in non-agricultural white-collar jobs, particularly in lower level school teaching. Besides teachers, there are also clerks, postmen, *talatis, gram sevaks,* extension officers, etc. Some are employed in co-operative societies in various capacities. "Middle and rich cultivators dominate the stratum of educated white-collar employees."

In another study of stratification among the scheduled tribes in the Bharuch and Panch Mahals districts of Gujarat, Shah (1986) observes that status distinction based on achievement in such respects as wealth, property, income, occupation, education and power is emerging, and it is similar considerably with the pattern in the wider Indian society. Status determination based on ethnicity is being slowly replaced by the new criteria such as wealth, income, occupation, education and power. Economic and educational aspects and style of life are today the bases of newly emerging stratification. Differences in these aspects between the tribals and the non-tribals and within the tribals would provide an objective assessment of social stratification. The categories and groups in these two districts are more or less the same as Shah has found in Surat district. Different tribes are divided on the basis of interests. Besides land as the principal basis, there are differences of status based on education and life-style. Stratification is reflected in almost all aspects of social life of the tribal people. Contradictory changes have also been noted. Some have become quite rich and better-off, and others have slided down in class hierarchy. However, change in social stratification has not been uniform in Bharuch and Panch Mahals districts. Shah observes as follows: "There is sharper stratification in Bharuch than in Panch Mahals. The number of landless labourers is larger in the former area than in the latter district. The rich and the middle peasants of Bharuch purchased more land than their counterparts in Panch Mahals. So is the case with government benefits. The differences in life-style between the rich and the middle peasants on the one hand, and the poor peasants and the labourers on the other, are more widespread and sharper in Bharuch. These differences are perhaps because of uneven development in the two districts. Because the one which is more developed grows faster and develops sharper stratification, inequality increases and becomes sharp with development."

From both these studies of three districts of Gujarat, namely, Surat, Bharuch and Panch Mahals, Shah concludes that there is nothing like an all-India tribal culture and world-view. Tribals are also not isolated from the non-tribal people. It is a fact that they have become highly differentiated, socially and economically, and in certain respects the persisting socio-economic distinctions between them and the non-tribals have also accentuated mainly due to uneven consequences of lopsided development policies and their faulty execution. Despite this the tribal people are being 'integrated' with the wider society though not in a uniform manner. The better off tribals, namely, the middle class Chaudharis of Surat, have developed a certain commonness, cutting across tribal boundaries, with their counterparts of other tribes, in social and cultural matters and in life-styles. In fact, middle and rich cultivators as well as the middle class (white-collar workers) do not have a clash of interests, hence commonalty of attitudes and aspirations for further betterment of their status.

Bose (1981) also identifies four main classes among tribes in Gujarat, though mainly based on landholdings. These are: rich peasants, middle peasants, poor peasants, and agricultural labourers, and these have also been found by several researchers among the non-tribals as well. A given tribe is generally distributed among all the four classes. However, all the tribes are not the same as some are better off than others, and accordingly the proportions of different classes would also be different. Bose reports that the tribes in Gujarat today are equally affected by the processes of planned and unplanned change and by the continuous structural and institutional shifts in rural India. He writes: "They are stratified in terms of control over resources," hence the above mentioned four classes. This class hierarchy is reflected in all aspects of tribal life including education and political power. But Bose does not highlight the emerging patterns of social mobility among tribals brought about by developmental programmes and education as we find it in the two studies of three districts of Gujarat by Shah. Pathy's study (1984) of five tribal villages in Gujarat is similar in terms of its framework and methodology. The five economic categories in Pathy's study are: landlords, rich peasants, middle peasants, small peasants and farm workers. The distribution and characteristic features of these classes are the same as we find in the study conducted by Shah and Bose. It seems that in a broad sense, the studies of class stratification among the tribes of Gujarat reinforce each other. While referring to an earlier study by Pathy, *Political Economy of Kandhaland in Orissa,* Shah (1986) observes that "there is a case for closer examination in the tribal communities." Further, Shah finds that the rich have become richer, and the poor poorer, because of 'free competition' among the unequal competitors.

Roy Burman (1989) emphasizes on both class and ethnicity perspectives, but he does not spell out the nexus between class and ethnicity and status and class. The notion of status is inherently present in the ethnic identity and kinship system of the tribal society. In a recently published (edited) volume, Bhadra and Mondal (1991) also emphasize the role of class and ethnicity as the main bases of social stratification in North-east India. There are tribes like Meenas of Rajasthan which have hardly any tribal features in terms of ethnicity and class, and yet they are scheduled as tribes. The Tharus of Bihar have all the prerequisites for being scheduled as a tribe, but they are not scheduled as such.

Singh though admits the emergence of social stratification as a historical reality created by the colonial administration and the processes of sanskritisation and conversion to Christianity, but observes that "there are also contrary pulls in the opposition direction. The bonds of ethnicity and the appreciation of the political advantages of the tribe as an ethnic minority are still strong" (1985). This view is also shared by Sachchidananda. He writes while commenting on the class approach of Pathy: "These economic categories may be considered classes only in a limited sense; ethnic consciousness dominates over class consciousness. Similarly, production relations cannot be clearly characterized as feudal or capitalist. Primordial forms of slavery, revolving indebtedness of small peasants and agricultural labourers for consumption loans, the lack of a free labour market, forced labour, labour exchange, institutional credit and some commodity production confuse the total picture" (1990). But the question is: Do these four or five classes not exist among the tribes of Gujarat, Bihar or Rajasthan? Are they simply 'constructions' and not identifiable groups of people? Kulkarni (1979) observes that the question of class in the tribal society is more pervasive than the caste- tribal approach. Class interests do not obey caste or tribal boundaries (Sengupta, 1980). Land alienation is a class question. The demand for the formation of Jharkhand State is a class question. The 'tribal question', the 'forest-question' are all questions of 'class interests'. The forest policy in India in its present form serves the capitalists rather than the poor (Guha, 1983). 'Tribal unrest' is a class question. Both positive and negative consequences of the role performed by law and the state refer to the question of class in terms of gainers and loosers, more gainers and less gainers, more loosers and less loosers and so on. Thus, there are three viewpoints regarding ethnicity and class as the bases of social stratification: (i) mainly ethnicity, (ii) mainly class, and (iii) both class and ethnicity.

Social stratification among the tribes of India is different com-pared to the non-tribes to the extent the tribal people are dissimilar in terms of their history, level of economic development and impact of modern forces of social change. Several studies of social stratifi-cation bring out the convergence of ethnicity and class as the main basis of status distinctions within and between different tribes. However, emphasis on ethnicity and class as exclusive bases of social stratification remains central to some scholars who look at the tribal social stratification either in terms of ethnic reality or as an economic phenomenon—a part of global class formation.

The *raj* created new structures and institutions and thereby provided a new system of social stratification. Landlords, contractors and money-lenders were alien to the tribal society before the advent of the British. Differentiation of the peasantry in terms of tenure-holders, tenants-at-will and jagirdars was also created by the British. A class of outside exploiters in terms of Zamindars and moneylenders was not known to the tribals till the British took over the forests.

Since Independence ethnicity is being viewed in a changed form as a means of mobilizing the tribal people with a view to have access to economic and political opportunities. Inter-tribal and tribal-non-tribal distinctions on the one hand and processes of conversion and initiation on the other are being highlighted by the tribals as the basis for demanding special treatment by the government. However, the tribals are not an exclusive component in India's fast changing social situation. A new middle class is emerging among them like the one we find among the non-tribals.

Ethnicity is on decline on the one hand, and it is being revived in myraid ways on the other. De-tribalization and ethnicization co-exist today both as a reality and as a strategy for change. Unifor-mity is not found in regard to convergence between ethnicity and class. Processes of socio-cultural and structural transformation are also not uniform in different parts of India. At the same time, now the 'forest question' and the 'tribal question' are being considered more as class questions. The phenomenon of power and domi-nance is increasingly dependent upon the questions of ethnicity and class.

14

Impact of Education

From time immemorial Indian scholars have been famous for their learning. In the ancient times scholars from Persia and Greece, if not from Egypt also, and the scholars from China and Tibet came over to India to study either in the *gurukulas* established by the Hindu teachers or in the universities established in the Buddhist monasteries. However, the methods of learning in the *gurukulas* as well as in the universities of Takshashila, Nalanda, Kanjeevaram, etc., were traditional; they were only interested in theology, philosophy, etc. It is true that the great medical scholars like Charaka and Sushruta and mathematicians and astronomers like Bhaskara were empirically oriented and developed these positive sciences. But they were not able to proceed further along to what is now described as modern science.

Even when modern education was established in the nineteenth century, largely due to the efforts of the Christian missionaries Indian education was largely humanistic and philosophical rather than scientific and positive. It is only after the First World War that a scientific tradition on modern lines was set up by great Indian scientists like J.C. Bose, P.C. Ray, and C.V. Raman.

Even when the Muslim kingdoms were set up in India, there was really no change in the outlook of people towards education because the Muslims, like the Hindus, were traditional in their outlook and laid great emphasis on religion and philosophical education rather than on secular education. Of course, one should not forget that secular education received an emphasis even in

Western Europe only after the seventeenth century, and more recently since the nineteenth century.

When the Portuguese and other Western traders established their centres in the different parts of the country, the missionaries who came along with them established schools not only to give secular education to the Indian children but also to convert them to Christianity. The first printing press was set up in 1577 near Cochin in the South by the Jesuits. When the Protestant Danes established their centre in Tranquebar in 1706 they translated the New Testament to Tamil. They also produced a Tamil dictionary. Thus, through their desire to propagate Christianity, they also laid foundations for the modern methods of learning languages. The Protestant mission which came to Madras in 1727 started schools at Madras, Tanjore, and other centres.

The first school to be set up by the East India Company was in 1784 at Tanjore where courses were given in English and Tamil and Hindi and also in arithmetic and Christianity. The Company soon found they could acquire influence on the Indian citizens and the Indian society through education, and so established more schools with the Company's finances. Warren Hastings, the first Governor-General of India, started a *Madarsa* in Calcutta in 1784 at the Company's expense for the education of Muslim boys, through the medium of Arabic. He also started a Sanskrit college at Benaras in 1791. The chief aim of Hastings was to get well trained people in Hindu law and Muslim law to help the courts of justice set up by the British.

The next great step in Indian education was taken by Lord Wellesley when he started a college at Calcutta in 1800 to train civil servants of the Company in Indian languages, in Hindu and Muslim Law and in the history of India.

Thus, the main aim in the starting of the schools for children as well as the institutions for higher learning in the eighteenth century was to propagate Christianity, to have competent scholars in the Muslim and Hindu Law, and to train the British civilians in Indian languages, Indian law, and Indian history.

By the beginning of the nineteenth century there were thus three kinds of schools. There were the schools established by private efforts of the citizens or Indian rulers to teach the students traditional learning either through Sanskrit or through Persian and Arabic or through modem Indian languages. Secondly, there were the missionary schools which were established to teach English to the Indian children and also Christianity. Finally, there were the Government schools which were established to give Indian children secular education either through English or through Indian languages.

When the Charter was revised in 1813, the Company was directed to spend not less than a hundred thousand rupees each year on education. The Directors of the Company thought that this amount earmarked for education should be spent in encouraging oriental studies rather than in introducing Western education. In 1823, a committee on public instruction was appointed to dispose off annual grants for the benefit of the various educational institutions maintained by the Government both for elementary and for higher education.

When English was introduced, the enrolment in the Benaras College as well as in the Calcutta Hindu College went up; while there were only 70 pupils in the Calcutta Hindu College in 1819, the enrolment went up to 421 in 1829.

On account of the popularity of these steps in the field of education, Parliament raised the provision for education by ten times. While some of the members of the Committee on Public Instruction set up in 1823 were in favour of Western learning, others were opposed to it and were in favour of Oriental learning.

In 1834, Macaulay became the President of this Committee and it was in this capacity that he wrote his famous Minute in February 1835. The Committee was faced with the problem of mass education versus higher education. It was decided that it would be better to educate a few hundreds well than millions superficially. This is the famous theory of "Infiltration". The second choice before the Committee was between Oriental learning and Western learning. Oriental learning at that time was limited to a few families among the Hindus as well as among the Muslims. However, the records show that in the Hindu College as well as in Scottish Church College in Calcutta, large numbers of students had been enrolled where English was the medium of instruction, while there was comparative desertion in the Sanskrit college. As a result of this, Macaulay came to the conclusion that "English was a much easier language to master than Sanskrit or Arabic". He also affirmed that even the patriotic intelligent Indians like Rammohan Rai and others were greatly in favour of Western education. The decisive step was taken in March 1835 when William Bentinck, the Governor-General, proclaimed that the funds should be appropriated on "Ènglish education alone". Thus, this proclamation marked a turning point in the history of education in India. In the next few years there was a rapid increase in the enrolment in the Government schools where English was the medium of instruction, though the students had to pay fees, while the enrolment in Sanskrit and Arabic schools decreased though the Government paid stipends to them. Another important social change that came about with the introduction of the English medium in the Government schools was that children from all classes and castes entered the Government schools, while the enrolment in the Sanskrit schools was practically limited to the children from the Brahmin homes.

Because of the missionary effort to prepare dictionaries in the modern Indian languages, the schools with modern Indian languages as media of instruction also increased, but like institutions devoted to classical learning these schools with modern Indian languages also failed to attract large numbers of children; for example, Lord Hardinge started a hundred schools in Bengali in 1844, but half of them had to be closed down for want of enrolment. It must be recalled that the same Lord Hardinge issued a proclamation in the same year in 1844 directing that preference should be given to English educated persons in recruitment for Government jobs.

Thus, while 1835 established English as the medium of instruction in the Government schools, the year 1844 saw the promulgation that preference should be given to those educated in English in recruitment for government services. Thus, the aim of education became employment under government service. As Siqueira wrote, Hardinge probably never anticipated than in a caste-ridden society, with contempt for manual labour, there would be a great eagerness on the part of the higher castes to seek clerical employment in government service through a literary education. This, after a hundred years, created the problem of the "educated unemployed" in the country.

Education for All

As seen earlier, the nationalist movement in India became intensified by the partition of Bengal in 1905. The nationalist sentiments were further rein- forced by the defeat of the Russians by the Japanese at this time. So this period saw the first organized movement for national education in India. The National Council of Education was established in Calcutta. A national college was established which later became the Jadavpur University. The Indian National Congress, in its Calcutta Session in 1906, passed a resolution that the time had arrived for organizing a system of national education—literary, scientific and technical—to suit the requirements of the country,

In the following years the concept of national education was clarified by Gokhale, Annie Besant, Lala Lajpat Rai, Tagore, and later by Gandhi. It was held that a national system of education should promote the national consciousness in the youth and inculcate a deep love for the motherland and pride in the cultural heritage. To achieve this purpose it was felt that education should be imparted through the language of the people. It also emphasized scientific education and scientific research. Finally, it was asserted that emphasis should be laid on vocational education and technical education and research in order to help economic growth to eliminate poverty, and to provide decent living for all the citizens of the country.

The movement, however, was short-lived. When the First World War started the attention of the people was diverted. After the end of the First World War, due to the Jallianwalabagh incident and the Khilafat movement, the ideals of National Education were once again revived in 1920. Finally in 1937, when the Congress Party formed the Provincial Governments, it was again revived and led to the formulation of the Wardha Education Scheme; but it is not necessary to deal with this development at this stage.

Schooling a Must

When the fervour for national education was at its height the Maharaja of Baroda took a very significant step in the history of Indian education by making primary education compulsory in 1909 in the Baroda State. The great Indian leader, Gopalakrishna Gokhale (1866-1915), was greatly impressed by this practical step and the ideal behind it, and moved his famous resolution in the imperial Legislative Council in March 1910, "that a beginning should be made in the direction of making elementary education free and compulsory throughout the country." While introducing this policy he drew the attention of the Council that three great movements in the world combined to make mass education a duty of the State. He said "the humanitarian movement which reformed the prisons and liberated the slaves, the democratic movement which admitted large masses of people to participate in the Government and finally, the industrial movement which showed that the educated worker can produce goods in the factory more efficiently—all these led to the movement in Western Europe to introduce compulsory elementary education." He pointed out that the only way that the world had discovered to secure univer-sal education was by making it compulsory. So he rccommended that steps should be taken by the Government of India to intro-duce compulsion as far as education of children from ages 6 to 10 was concerned. He also laid down the condition as to when compulsion could be introduced. He said that when one-third of the boys between the ages of 6 and 10 years are already enrolled, then elementary education could be made compulsory. Finally, he asserted that compulsion could operate only when education was provided free of cost. Here again he pointed out that free education should be provided only for the children of those earning below Rs. 25 per month.

Thus, we find that in the famous speech in 1910, Gokhale defined not only the situation which compelled the State to introduce universal elementary education, but also defined stages by which compulsion could be introduced. The Bill was rejected on the ground that it was premature and unworkable. Though Gokhale failed in his attempt to change the educational policy of the State, his efforts bore fruit in that there was an unprecedented expansion of primary education by voluntary agencies between 1910 and 1917.

The year 1918 saw two significant developments with respect to the intensification of efforts to expand primary education and to make it compulsory. The national movement received a new impetus in 1918 under the leadership of Gandhi which became a mass movement instead of being confined to the educated classes.

The leaders realized the need for literacy among the masses. Gandhi himself started adult education classes in the indigo plantations at Champaran and among the industrial workers at Ahmedabad, as he realized that the national movement could never succeed without the cooperation and the involvement of the masses. The second change came about when the Govern-ment in 1919 entrusted the education portfolio in the provincial State to the Indian ministers in the Diarchy Government. Bombay was the first Slate to introduce compulsory education in 1918 at the instance of Vithalbhai Patel, though he restricted the scope to the municipal areas. After this, the State Legislatures in other parts also began enacting laws to introduce compulsory primary education and within the next ten years almost all the States had followed the lead of the Bombay State. However, legislation did not lead to the fulfilment of the aim. The State Governments did not have adequate financial resources for this purpose. Further, there was an adequate appreciation of the need for education among the lower castes and classes in the urban areas and practically the entire group in the rural areas. The little progress that was achieved in this decade was brought to an end by the worldwide economic depression in the thirties.

Elementary Education

With the introduction of provincial autonomy, the Congress Party came into power in some states in 1937 and intensified the expansion of primary education programmes. It was at this time that Gandhi gave considerable thought to the problem of education. He realized that the country cannot afford to raise the necessary financial resources to make elementary education wide-spread throughout the country. He had given thought to these problems even when he was in South Africa. He had developed the ideal of a new society where there would be no difference between classes and masses, and a society in which everyone would work with his hands. According to him, "manual work should be the basis of the social structure of a good society."

In July 1937, Gandhi wrote in *Harijan,* "As a nation we are so backward in education that we cannot hope to fulfil our obligations to the nation in this respect in a given time during this generation if this programme is to depend on money." He came with the startling suggestion that "education should be self-supporting." In order to realize this goal he asserted that the child's education should begin not with literacy but "by teaching it a useful handicraft to enable it to produce from the moment it begins its training." He further laid down the principle that the teaching of the craft should not be mechanical but should be educative.

In order to develop these ideas, he convened at Wardha, in October 1937, a conference consisting of national workers in the field of education and the education ministers of different provinces. The conference recommended that there should be free, compulsory education of seven years duration on a nationwide scale with the mother tongue as the medium of instruction. It further recommended that the educational process should centre round some productive form of manual labour and should be integrally related to the courses. Finally, it recommended that such an education should lead to production of goods by the students which could cover the remuneration of teachers.

The conference appointed a committee, with Zakir Hussain as the Chairman to draft a detailed syllabus. The report of this Committee was published curly in 1938 and was adopted by the Indian National Congress in March 1938 at Haripura. The Hindustani Talimi Sangh was formed to organize basic schools to train the teachers to conduct these schools.

The Central Advisory Board of Education of the Government quickly realized the merit of this new scheme and appointed a committee under the Chairmanship of Kher to examine it. The Kher Committee recommended that basic education should first be introduced in the rural areas to educate the children from 6 to 14 years, with the mother tongue as the medium of instruction and that all children should learn Hindustani, the national language, in the Urdu and Devnagari scripts. It also recommended that there should be no external examination. A second committee was constituted, again with Kher as the Chairman, to examine the details and the financial implications. The Committee recommended that the eight-year period should be divided into two stages—a junior stage of five years and a senior stage of three years. It further recommended that the children should go to the ordinary schools after completion of the junior basic stage. It also recommended that post-primary schools should have a course for five years at the junior basic stage, designed to prepare pupils for entering industry, commerce and the university. Finally, it recommended that the Central Government should bear half the cost, the other half being borne by the State Governments. However, the Central Advisory Board did not accept the financial clauses. Still, the Congress Ministers in the various states tried to put the basic scheme into practice. They established a large number of basic training institutions in each state. With the resignation of the Congress Ministries in 1939, when the Second World War started, the whole scheme came to a standstill and the political struggle from 1942-45 practically proved fatal to these institutions.

In 1944, the Sargent Scheme accepted many recommendations of the two Kher Committees but nothing came out of this due to the political struggle. After independence, an All-India Education Conference was convened by Maulana Azad, the Central Education Minister, in 1948 and accepted the recommendation of the Sargent Plan but proposed to achieve compulsory elemen-tary education throughout the country in a time shorter than the forty years proposed by the Sargent Plan. The conference appoin-ted a Finance Committee, again with Kher as the Chairman, which recommended that compulsory basic education should be introduced in the country within a period of 16 years during the Second Five-Year Plan and the Third Five-Year Plan by 1964. The Committee also recommended that the Centre should bear 30 per cent of the expenditure while the states would bear the rest. However, the scheme could not be implemented because of the paucity of finances.

The First Plan said, that all the new primary schools to be started should be of the basic type while the existing primary schools should be gradually converted to basic schools by introducing, in the meantime, crafts and practical work. An Assessment Committee was appointed by the Central Government to visit the various states and recommend further steps that should be taken. The 1956 Conference of Educalion Ministers discussed the report of the Assessment Committee and recommended that in order to facilitate the transformation of the non-basic schools, the important features of basic education like craft education, etc., should be introduced in all the existing and the new primary schools. The Conference also resolved that all the existing teacher training institutions should be convened to the basic type before the completion of the Second Plan. As a result of these recommendations, the Ministry of Education established the National Institute of Basic Education to conduct research studies in the fields and to prepare manuals and teaching aids.

Before proceeding further, we may briefly note the merits and demerits of Basic Education. One of the merits is that it is a child-centred scheme making the child an active learner by introducing the principle "learning by doing". Thus, Basic Educa-tion promotes purposeful and productive activity. By making the education craft-centred it seeks to emphasize dignity of labour in the minds of the children.

Among the demerits of the scheme are the lack of proper textbooks to guide the teachers as well as the students, the intrinsic difficulty of correlation, and the neglect of English, which is absolutely necessary for those who desire to go either to higher liberal arts colleges or to professional colleges. Finally, though the scheme was introduced with the best of intentions in the rural areas, the rural people never took to it because they suspected that an inferior system of education was being foisted on them by the urban people in order to keep them away from the fruits of industrialization. While the Gandhian ideals emphasized a rural type society, Nehru emphasized and took the necessary steps to develop an industrial society in India.

The Education Commission 1966 has asserted that it has incorporated the essential elements of Basic Education in primary schools of the conventional type.

We can now proceed to describe briefly the progress of primary education in India including the Basic type. It must be recalled that Article 45 of the Indian Constitution had directed in 1950 that the Stale shall endeavour to provide free and compulsory education from the age 6 to the age of 14 by 1960. However, only 60 per cent of the children of the age group 6 to 11 had been enrolled at the end of the Second Five-Year Plan (1959-60). Consequently the Third Plan reduced the target and expected that all the children in the age group 6 to 11 would have elementary education by 1966. However, during the Third Plan the enrolment of the 6 to 11 age group went up from 62 per cent to only 77 per cent in 1965-66.

It was 80.3 percent in 1971 and this went up to 83.6 per cent in 1979-80 and to 91.69 per cent in 1986.85.91 million children were enrolled in classes I to V in 1986, out of which 35.06 million were girls; the enrolment went up to 94.96 million in 1987-88, out of which 39.40 million were girls. The projected enrolment in 1989-90 in the Seventh Five Year Plan period was 95.96 million children in classes I to V, out of which girls were expected to be 40.96 million. The two formidable difficulties in enrolling all the children of this age group are resistance of the parents to send their girls to the schools (in 1986 out of a total enrolment in classes I to V of 85.91 million, girls constituted 40.81 per cent), and the enormous number of habitations in the rural areas with less than 500 people.

Among the causes for failure to implement the only directive principle of state policy in education may be included the large birth-rate and consequent population explosion, the inability of the Governments to raise the required financial resources, the apathy of the illiterate masses, the traditional resistance to the education of girls, the poverty of the parents which compels them to use the labour of children, small and scattered habitations, etc.

As regards the availability of the schools, the first All India Educational Survey, 1958-59, found that there were more than 750,000 small habitations with a population below 500 where 35 per cent of the rural people lived. The problem is to provide schools in these small habitations. It was found that more than 445,000 habitations had populations less than 200 each and more than 250,000 habitations had less than a population of 100.

The first survey suggested that there should be a rational plan to meet the requirements of these 750,000 small rural habitations and suggested that the aim should be to provide independent schools for every habitation with a population of 300 persons or more, and set up "Group schools" for a group of habitations with populations below 300 so that there is a school within one mile distance from the home of the child. It also suggested that peripatetic teachers could be appointed in the habitations which are too small to justify a school, and which are situated more than a mile from the group schools.

However, the second All-India Educational Survey, 1967 found that only 87.23 per cent had primary schools in the habitations or within walking distance. In other words, even in 1967, 12.8 per cent of the people living in 125,000 habitations were not served by primary sections.

This analysis shows that it is the children who are living in the small habitations of 300 persons and less, particularly those habitations in which the total population is below 100 persons, that do not have the facilities to go to schools near their homes.

The fourth All-India Educational Survey, 1980 found that out of 9,64,664 rural habitations (covering an estimated popula-tion of 50,91,63,428) 46.80 per cent (4,51,457) habitations have primary sections and another 33.44 per cent (3,22,541) habita-tions have primary sections within a walking distance of 1 km. In other words, 7,73,998 habitations are having primary schools/ either in the habitation itself or within a walking distance of 1 km. Amongst the rest 65,987 or 6.84 per cent habitations do not have primary sections even up to a distance of 2 km. In terms of population, 78.53 per cent rural population is served by primary sections in the habitation of residence and another 14.29 per cent by primary section up to a distance of 1 km, that is, 92.82 per cent rural population have either primary sections in the habi-tation of residence or within a walking distance of 1 km. But 2.15 per cent population is not served even up to 2 km.

The fifth All-India Educational Survey 1986, found that out of 9,81,864 rural habitations (covering an estimated population of 59 crores) 51.16 per cent (5,02,322) habitations have primary sections within the habitation of residence, and another 32.68 per cent (3,20,873) habitations have primary sections within a walking distance of one kilometre, in other words, 8,23,195 habitauons are having primary schools/sections either in the habi-tation itself or within a walking distance of one kilometre. Amongst the rest 1,06,139 or 10.81 per cent habitations have primary sections up to a distance of 2 kilometres. In terms of population, 80.38 per cent of the rural population in the country is served by primary sections within habitation of residence and another 14.07 per cent by primary sections up to a distance of one kilometre, that is 94.45 per cent of the rural population have either primary sections in the habitation of residence or within a walking distance of one kilometre but 5.55 per cent population is not served even up to two kilometres.

One gratifying feature is that planned action on the basis of surveys have enabled the State Governments to bring a school as near as possible to the habitations of 95 per cent of the population. This again highlights the basic problem in the country, namely, the existence of small habitations for which it is not possible to provide social services and other amenities. Unless revolutionary action is taken by the local authorities and the people move out of these small habitations and set up habitations in which at least one thousand five hundred persons live, it is very difficult for any Government to provide satisfactory education, health and other services. As already noted this is one of the important factors which stands in the way of economic as well as social development in the country.

Among the chief defects in primary education in India, three problems stand out as significant one of this is the heterogeneity of the age composition. Of the 16 million children enrolled in class I in 1961-62, only 32 per cent were between 6 and 7 years, the standard age assumed for this level. Nearly 20 per cent of the children were below 6 years and as high as 50 per cent, above seven. This again is a social problem; while the parents, mostly in the urban areas, are anxious to put the children below 6 years in the primary first year, many, probably mostly in the rural areas,, are unwilling for various reasons to put them in schools even when they are 7 years old.

Even more important are the two other problems of stagnation and wastage in the primary schools. As early as 1929, the Hartog Committee had drawn attention to these two problems. The Hartog Committee defined the term "stagnation" as the retention in the lower class for more than one year. Such a retention not only demoralises the children but it also demoralises the parents as well as the teachers themselves besides giving rise to enormous wastage in time and money. One of the reasons for the withdrawal of the children from the schools by the parents is repeated detention. The Committee defined the term "wastage" as the premature withdrawal of children before they complete the full course of four years. Studies have shown that permanent literacy needs at least the completion of five years in the school.

But when a child is withdrawn before this term, it leads to wastage not only of the efforts but also of money. The figures reveal that more than 60 per cent of the children do not complete the four-year period of education.

We find that there was stagnation as well as wastage at class I itself. Out of every 100 children admitted to class 1 nearly 45 children either leave the school or are detained in that class itself.

Analyzing the causes for the wastage of education, Naik points out 65 per cent may be due to economic reasons; the child is withdrawn because he is an economic asset at home, in the farm, etc., and the existence of incomplete schools, the dullness of the school atmosphere, absence of ancillary services like midday meals, and so on are contributory causes.

The Kothari Commission recommends that steps should be taken to reduce wastage and stagnation by seeing that not less than 50 per cent of children who enter class I reach class VII. Besides improving the general education of the teacher so that nobody is recruited who has not completed his matriculation, and improving the professional training of the teacher which should be at least two years in duration, the commission also recommends ancillary services like midday meals, free supply for textbooks, school uniforms, etc.

Thus, though there has been very significant expansion in providing schools for more than 95 per cent of the habitations in the country, the quality of education has in no way improved if we judge it from the point of view of the two criteria of stagnation and wastage, the problems pointed out in 1929 by the Hartog Committee. It is not enough if schools are established and children are enrolled in class I. It is necessary to take steps to see that they remain in the school for a period of at least five years, if not seven years, so that there is permanent literacy. This is one of the reasons, we shall see in a subsequent section, for the paradoxical situation, that while the enrolment in class I is continually increasing, the total number of illiterate adults in the country is also increasing.

Junior High School Level

While Article 45 of the Constitution contains the directive that universally free and compulsory education has to be provided for children up to 14 years, the Third Plan abandoned this aim on the basis of a "realistic" assessment of the situation and revised its target as provision of universal education at least up to 11 years of age by the end of 1966. We have observed that even this limited aim has not been achieved, since 5 per cent of the population live in very small habitations below 300 persons and thus it is difficult to provide schools for these children on an economic basis. Further, we have seen that the enrolment of girls has not kept pace with the enrolment of the boys.

We can now study the achievements with respect to the children who are between 11 and 14 years of age. At the commencement of the Plan year in 1951 only 12.5 per cent of the children of this age group had been enrolled, the sex breakdown being 21 per cent boys and 5 per cent girls. By 1960-61, at the end of the first two plans the enrolment went up to nearly 23 per cent. According to the 1957 survey, the target fixed was the provision of one middle school for a habitation with a population of 1,500 or more, and for those living in smaller habitations, one school which is at least within a walking distance of three miles. According to the 1967 survey, only 2.3 per cent of the habitations are in the population slabs of 2,000 and above, with a population which is 18 per cent of the total. On the other hand, 76 per cent of the habitations have a population below 500 in which 35 per cent of total population live. Thus the formidable problem of the middle school education is to provide schools in the small habitations which have a population less than 500.

In 1951, nearly 400,000 habitations constituting 47 per cent of the total habitations had middle schools in them or within a walking distance of three miles. The 1967 survey showed that 713,000 habitations, constituting 73 per cent of the total habitation, were provided with middle schools within easy reach. The survey also revealed that 95 per cent of the people living in habitations with more than 2,000 people and 88 per cent of the population living in habitations with more than 1,000 population are now being served with middle schools.

Thus, while nearly 80 per cent of the age group below 11 were in the primary schools, only 34 per cent of the age group 11 to 14 were in the middle schools in the year 1971, though the target according to the Constitution was that all the children below 14 should have been enrolled by 1960.

The third All-India Educational Survey, 1979 found that out of the 930,665 habitations, 80,837, or 8.69 per cent habitations have the middle sections in them 542,226 or 58.26 per cent and 729,930 or 78.43 habitations have the middle sections up to a walking distance of 3 km and 5 km, respectively including those having middle sections in them. In terms of population, 28.86 per cent of the rural population has got the facility in the habitation of residence. 71.97 per cent of the population in the rural areas is served up to a distance of 3 km (including the population served in the habitations of residence) and 86.91 per cent of the population is served up to a distance of 5 km including the population served in the habitation of residence.

According to the fourth All-India Educational Survey, 1980 out of the 964,664 habitations in respect of which information is available 103,604 or 10.74 per cent have middle sections in them and 644,971 or 66.86 per cent and 825,022 or 85.52 per cent habitations have middle sections up to a walking distance of 3 km and 5 km, respectively.

The percentage of population that is served with a middle section up to a distance of 5 km is 92.09 per cent. It includes about one-third (33.47 per cent) of the rural population that is served by a middle section within the habita- tion.

The fifth All-India Educational Survey found that out of 9,81,864 rural habitations in the country, 1,28,624 habitations or 13.1 per cent have an upper primary school/section within the habitation of residence. However, 74 per cent of the habita-tions have an upper primary school/section either within them-selves or within a distance of 3 km.

18,069 habitations (18.4 per cent) with a population of "1000 or more" are not served with an upper primary school/section within a distance of three km. 76 per cent of the unserved habitations have a population of less than 500.

Kerala, which leads in education, serves 94 per cent of its habitations and 96.2 per cent of its population with an upper primary school/section within a distance of three km. The corresponding percentages for Gujarat are 88.7 per cent and 94.4 per cent, for Punjab, 88.3 per cent and 92.5 per cent, and for Goa, 86.8 per cent and 91.8 per cent.

On the other end of the spectrum, the lowest percentages of habitations and population served are the States belonging to the north eastern region, viz. Arunachal Pradesh (19.6 per cent and 42.2 per cent), Nagaland (48.9 per cent and 66.4 per cent), Meghalaya (50.6 per cent and 65 per cent), Manipur (57.7 per cent and 80.2 per cent) and Mizoram (57.1 per cent and 82.8 per cent).

Out of all the unserved habitations in the country, 48.7 per cent are in five States, viz. Madhya Pradesh (17.4 per cent), Andhra Pradesh (8.3 per cent), Orissa (8.1 per cent), Bihar (7.7 per cent) and Rajasthan (7.2 per cent). Similarly, 49.2 per cent of the unserved population is accounted for by the five states, viz. Madhya Pradesh (14.8 per cent), Andhra Pradesh (10.1 per cent), Bihar (8.5 per cent), West Bengal (8.2 per cent) and Rajasthan (7.6 per cent).

Thus there is considerable leeway to be made up even after nearly 56 years of independence.

High School Level

The Hunter Commission of 1882 pointed out deficiencies in the academic type of secondary education and recommended diversified courses at this level. The Sadler Commission of 1919 reinforced this recommendation, and also asserted that university education cannot improve without the improve- ment of secondary education. Thus, the two main defects of secondary education in India are that it is academic, without taking into account either the variations in the interest of the pupils or needs of the society, and that even the academic education that is given by the secondary schools is not satisfactory, as it does not enable the students to pursue higher education at the university level. Right through, the various commissions and committees appointed by the Government have emphasized these two defects, for example, the Abbot Wood Report of 1937 and the Zakir Husain Committee report of 1937. The Radhakrishnan Commission of 1949 asserted "our secondary education remains the weakest link."

Secondary schools are of great national importance because (a) they provide teachers for the primary schools; *(b)* they provided the pupils for the universities; (c) they provide terminal education for those who enter life. The students of the age group 15 to 18 take up after their completion of studies and training, the occupations of the intermediate level in agriculture, industry, commerce, transportation, communication, etc.

While the main aim of secondary education is to prepare students for the university, the universities are absolutely dissatisfied with the secondary school students. They are ill-equipped to pursue a course of university education. It must also be realized that most of the students who complete secondary school educa-tion are not interested in higher education. They are interested in taking up some occupation, but the secondary education enables them to take up only clerical jobs or jobs as teachers in elementary schools, x»th of which they dislike according to the studies made. Educational administrators on their part are also not satisfied with them. They question the competence of secondary school graduates to serve as teachers in the elementary schools or in adult education work. The public also feel that matriculates are hardly qualified to do work entrusted to them. All these defects may be traced to the fact that secondary education, in spite of all the recommendations of the various commissions, continues to ignore the needs and the interests of the students on the one hand and the manpower needs of the society on the other.

In spite of these defects, one outstanding, though alarming, feature of Indian education in the recent years is the phenomenal increase in the number of schools as well as in enrolment. The schools increased from about 7,300 in 1951 to about 17,300 in 1961 and nearly 37,000 in 1971 Enrolment increased from 1.5 million in 1950-51 to 6.1 million in 1965-66 and the enrolment percentage of population in the age group increased from 5.3 to 20.4. The enrolment of boys increased in this period from 11 per cent to 29 per cent and the enrolment of girls from 1.8 per cent to 9.1 per cent. The increase has been phenomenal in the rural as well as in the urban areas. Of the 6.3 million children enrolled in secondary schools in 1966-67,2.8 million are in the rural areas and the 3.5 million in the urban areas. As regards habitation, the first Education Survey decided that habitations with a population of 5,000 or above should have a secondary section located in them and the habitations below 5,000 should have a secondary school within a walking distance of five miles, It has been estimated that the average annual increase in enrolment has been around 10 per cent per year from 1951-1966. It is expected that in 1973-74 about 22 per cent of the age group (14-18) will be enrolled and the target of the Fifth Plan is to enrol 26 per cent of the age group by 1978-79.

According to the All-India Educational Survey, 1979 24,049 habitations or 2.85 per cent have secondary sections. It covers a population of 5,83,99,577 or 13.67 per cent of the rural population. Further the survey observed that 4,56,165 habitations or 54.15 per cent with a population of 28,34,04,365 or 66.34 per cent are served by secondary sections within a walking distance of 5 km. It is also found that out of 3,745 habitations having population of 5,000 or more 3,437 (91.78 per cent), including 2,482 (66.2 per cent) habitations with secondary sections located in them, cover 92.32 per cent in this population slab up to a distance of 5 km. In the population slab '2000-4999' there are 28,484 habitations. Of these, 8,539 (29.98 per cent) habitations have secondary sections in them while 22,507 (79.02 per cent) habitations have secondary education facilities within a walking distance of 5 km covering a population of 80.83 per cent in this population slab. There are 76,518 habitations in population slab '1000-1999'. Out of them 6,356 (8.31 per cent) habitations have secondary sections in them while overall 51,508 (67.31 per cent) habitations have facilities within a walking distance of 5 km covering 67.40 per cent population in the slab. In the population slab '500-999' there are 1,49,780 habitations of which 3,601 (2.40 per cent) have secondary sections in them and altogether 91,925 (61.37 per cent) have secondary education facilities up to a walking distance of 5 km covering 62.33 per cent population in this slab. The remaining 5,83,868 habitations are scattered in the population slab 'below 500'. In this category 3,071 (0.53 per cent) habitations have a secondary section in them while 2,86,788 (49.12 per cent), including the preceding ones, covering a popu-lation of 52.61 per cent in the slab have schooling facilities within a walking distance of 5 km. The fourth All-India Educational Survey found that facilities for secondary education are available in 29,565 habitations which constitute only 3.06 per cent of the total of the 9,64,664 habitations in the rural areas of the country. Only 14.58 per cent of the rural population are, served within the habitations by secondary sections schools. The number of habitations served by secondary schools within 8 km is 6,99,804 (72.54 per cent), serving 41,84,55,278, that is, 82.18 per cent of the rural population. The survey also found that in the population slab of '5000 and above' 3,178 (72.11 per cent) out of 4,407 habitations are served by secondary sections within them and 4,318 (97.98 per cent) habitations are served within 8 km. In the population slab of 2,000 to 4,999 out of 35,069 habitations 11,030 (31.45 per cent) are served by the secondary section within them while 31,941 (91.08 per cent) habitations are served within 8 km covering 35.15 and 91.85 percentage of the population, respectively. In the population slab 1000-1999 out of 91,799 habitations only 7,493 (8.16 per cent) are served by secondary sections covering the population of 9.03 per cent in this slab. The number of habitations served within 8 km in this population slab is 77,197 (84.09 per cent) which covers 83.96 per cent of the population. There are 1,73,727 habitations in the slab 500-999 and out of them only 4,264 (2.45 per cent) are served by secondary sections within them and 1,38,082 (79.48 per cent) are served within a distance of 8 km. The population covered are 2.76 per cent and 79.66 per cent, respectively in this slab. Out of the total 9,64,664 rural habitations in the country 6,59,662 habitations are very small with less than 500 population. Among these only 3,600 (0.55 per cent) are served by secondary sections within them with a population coverage of only 0.86 per cent in this slab. But the habitations served within 8 km are 4,48,266 (67.95 per cent) with a population coverage of 71.66 per cent.

The Fifth All-India Survey found that out of 9,81,864 rural habitations more than three-fourths (78.92 per cent) have the facility for secondary education within 8 kilometers including 4.43 per cent enjoying it within habitations themselves.

The percentage of rural population having access to secondary sections within eight km is 86.54 including 17.73 per cent enjoying the facility within the habitation of residence.

In Assam, Bihar, Goa, Haryana, Jammu & Kashmir, Kerala, Punjab, Tamil Nadu, Tripura, West Bengal, Chandigarh, Daman & Diu, Delhi, Lakshadweep and Pondicherry more than 90 per cent of the rural population is served by secondary sections within eight km.

There are 3,591 habitations with a population of "2000 or more" which do not have access to secondary education even within eight km. These include 137 habitations with a population of "5000 or more".

The total number of secondary schools in the country is 52,560 of which 38,862 (73.94 per cent) are located in rural areas. The largest proportion of these schools (42.67 per cent) is run by private aided agencies. The corresponding figures in the case of Government, local body and private unaided schools are 36.88 per cent, 9.36 per cent and 11.09 per cent respectively.

The total number of children enrolled in classes IX and X is 1,15,19,996 of which 64,68,750 (56.15 per cent) are in rural schools.

More than half (50.19 per cent) of the total enrolment in these classes is in private aided schools. The corresponding percentage in the case of Government, local body and private unaided schools is 36.45, 6.85 and 6.51 respectively.

45.80 per cent of habitations are served by higher secondary sections within a distance of eight km including 0.91 per cent habitations having the facility within them.

50.97 per cent of the rural population is served within eight km by higher secondary education facility including 4.18 per cent population served within the habitations themselves.

Eight States and five Union Territories are above the All-India level in respect of the higher secondary education facility. More than 51 per cent of their rural population is served within an eight km distance. These are Assam (61.00 per cent), Goa (59.55 per cent), Gujarat (55.04 per cent), Jammu & Kashmir (54.30 per cent), Tamil Nadu (69.58 per cent), Tripura (72.39 per cent), Uttar Pradesh (72.35 per cent), West Bengal (72.40 per cent), A & N Islands (65.22 per cent), Chandigarh (100 per cent), Daman & Diu (81.24 per cent), Delhi (99.26 per cent) and Pondicherry (86.54 per cent). Of the 5,79,148 villages in the country only 7,765 (1.34 per cent) have the higher secondary education facility within them.

There are 15,465 higher secondary schools in the country of which 46.14 per cent (7,136) are in rural areas.

Majority of the higher secondary schools are co-educational (55.20 per cent), and run by private management (52.00 per cent).

Among the 15,465 higher secondary schools, 65.42 per cent have upper primary, secondary and higher secondary classes followed by 20.90 per cent schools with secondary and higher secondary classes, 8.61 per cent schools have all the 12 classes belonging to the four stages of school education and the remaining 5.07 per cent schools have only higher secondary classes, i.e. Classes XI and XII.

The total enrolment in Classes XI and XII in higher secondary schools is 35,09,571 of which 37.86 per cent study in rural schools and 30.77 per cent are girls.

Among the causes for this rapid expansion of secondary schools since independence may be mentioned the expansion in elementary education in rural areas, the general awakening among the backward sections of the population, particularly among the scheduled castes, the liberal concessions in the states, and finally, free education up to school final level in some of the states in India. In order to prevent this rapid expansion of secondary schools, which has resulted in reducing of the standards on the one hand, and heightened the level of frustration because of the lack of employment opportunities on the other, the Education Commission of 1966 has laid down that the objective of enrolment policy in secondary schools should not be universal but should be broadly governed by the need for trained man-power, and so the Commission laid down that at least 50 per cent of the enrolment should be in vocational institutions. Further, the Commission expressed itself against the proliferation of secondary schools and laid down that a secondary school should serve a radius of 5 to 7 miles with a total population coverage of 10,000 to 15,000.

Professional Training

One of the persistent problems of secondary education in the age group of 14 to 18, is to provide diversified courses to enable students with different abilities, aptitudes and interests to pursue courses which suit them instead of the traditional pattern of providing an unilinear academic course which leads to two insurmountable problems of educated unemployment and admission of students to the college courses which are not suitable to all the students of that age group.

As early as 1945, the Talimi Sangh prepared a scheme of post-Basic Education based on the principle of education through craft. The aim of this course is an all round development of the student both as an individual and as an useful member of the society, and the provision of diversified courses suitable to the pupils of different aptitudes. They recommended courses involving agriculture, medicine, engineering, mechanical, arts, commerce, artisanship, electricity, metallurgy, draftsmanship, printing, teaching, fine arts, home economics, etc.

The Mudaliar Commission on Secondary Education, 1953, recommended the starting of multipurpose schools as well as separate technical schools. According to the Commission, a Multipurpose school seeks to provide varied types of courses for students with diversified abilities and interests. It condemned the single track system followed by the traditional secondary schools in which all the pupils had to follow a heavy academic course.

The Commission recommended that the secondary school course should consist of two parts, one common to all students with five compulsory subjects, namely, English, general science, mathematics, social studies and crafts, and a specialized part which may be academic giving instructions in humanities and sciences, or practical, giving instruction in agriculture, technology, commerce, home science and fine arts. By such a design the Committee hoped that the multipurpose schools would remove the distinction between students preparing for the academic and the practical course and thus break down the sense of inferiority associated with vocational courses and enable secondary education to be truly democratic. The Commission also felt that this would ease the problem of educated unemployment so that all the young persons pursuing the secondary courses would not run after white collar jobs. It also hoped that there would be less wastage in education when pupils are given courses to suit their ability, aptitude and interest on the basis of vocational and educational guidance. Thus, the multipurpose schools required adequate space, adequate class rooms, laboratories, workshops, library, counselling rooms, etc. The commission recommended that each multipurpose school should provide at least two broad types of courses, one leading to the college and the other to a vocation. The work group set up by the Kothari Commission in 1965 found that both post-basic schools as well as the multi-purpose schools were not able to achieve the chief purposes set forth, nor were they popular because the enrolment in the academic type of secondary schools continued to increase with great vigour in the decade 1954-64.

Two reasons appear to have operated against the success of the post-basic scheme as well as the multi-purpose scheme. One of the reasons is the difficulty of finding the necessary finances to equip and staff these schools. In particular the multi-purpose schools need considerable capital outlay on land, buildings and equipment. Probably, the social reason may have been even more significant: than the financial and organizational reasons; the children of the rural people as well as the people of the lower castes who were coming in formidable numbers to enrol them-selves in these secondary schools, were eager to go for higher learning and prepare themselves for white collar jobs and professions. They have seen the success of the higher castes in getting the white collar jobs through education and so neither the parents nor the students were willing to encourage the non-academic secondary schools. The 1967 survey has shown that more than 70 per cent of the rural as well as the urban secondary schools are privately managed. It is much easier and cheaper for private organizations to set up academic type of secondary schools than the vocational schools.

The Education Commission of 1966 has emphasized the need to relate education to productivity. The primary resources necessary for the programme of mass education could be generated only if education is related to productivity so that expansion of education leads to an increase in national income which enables the state as well as the society to make further investments in education. In order to achieve this the Commission has emphasized the need for "work experience" among the students at all levels of education. Work experience is defined as participation in production work in the school workshop or on the farm or at home. Thus, the Commission is endorsing the view of Gandhi as well as the Secondary Education Commission about a craft. The complex techniques of production in modern agriculture as well as industry require a general education as well as technical training. Consequently, the Commission emphasized the need to give a strong vocational bias to secondary education.

Commenting on the agricultural section of the basic schools and the multipurpose schools, the Commission observed that these courses have not been able to impart the needed vocational competence to enable the students to become practising farmers since farming implies both hard work and mature judgement. The Commission is emphatic that agricultural training is not suitable either at the primary level or at the lower secondary level, at a time when the students are growing and are immature. The Commission points out that scientific knowledge and technical skills are basic requirements in modern agriculture.

As regards the industries, the Commission emphasized that technical education has really developed only after independence, by the establishment of the industrial training institutes, junior technical schools to train skilled workers, and polytechnics to train technicians. Here again, there is an urgent iced to bring about a social change so that the people change their attitude towards the status and the value of skilled craftsmen and technicians in the society.

Vocationalisation of education at the higher secondary stage was one of he important reforms included in the Sixth Plan. The programme has made limited progress with an enrolment of about 55,000 students in vocational education, confined to nine States and three Union Territories where it has been introduced. Measures have been initiated to establish the necessary links combining vocationalisation, skill training, in-plant apprenticeship and placement in gainful employment as composite parts of an integrated effort of raise the level of utility of the programme and its wider acceptance and success. The organisational requirements for the planning, implementation, supervision and evaluation of the integrated programme, along with the mechanism for effective co-ordination among the concerned agencies, are being assessed and defined.

During the Sixth Plan period, the major emphasis in technical education was on diversification and optimum utilisation of existing courses and instiutional resources. Efforts were made to provide facilities in areas such as ;computer sciences, instrumentation, product development, maintenance, engineering, bio-sciences and material sciences. Forty-six selected polytechnics were assisted and supported to develop them into a network of "community poly-technics" which would help transfer and apply available techno-logy with the object of modernizing rural structures. New man-power training programmes were undertaken for emerging areas in technology such as micro-processor application, remote sensing, laser technology, atmospheric sciences, and energy sciences. Pro-grammes of management education, particularly in the Institutes of Management, were reviewed by an Expert Committee and on its recommendation, the establishment of a new Institute of Lucknow was taken in hand.

Various Committees and Commissions that have considered the question if educational reform have underlined the need for diversifying secondary education by introducing knowledge and skills that may prepare the students or remunerative work without necessarily having to go for higher education, thhe VII plan document has also identified vocational and skill training programmes at different levels of education as one of the major thrust areas. PE, 1986 has accorded very high priority to the vocational education programme. The Policy has laid down the target of 10 per cent diversion to the vocational stream at the higher secondary stage by 1990 and 25 per cent by 1995.

The Centrally Sponsored Scheme of Vocationalisation of Secondary Education was started with effect from February 1988. Under this scheme, financial assistance has been provided to the State Governments/Union Territory Administrations for introduction of vocational courses in schools at the plus 2 stage. The Scheme has many components which include conduct of areas vocational surveys so that the vocational courses to be introduced in selected institutions are need-based, preparing curricula and course material, organising training of teachers, providing apprenticeship training to the extent possible and modification of recruitment rules so that some of the students passing out from the vocational stream can find employment in the organised sector. During 1989-1990, emphasis has been laid on the area vocational surveys and the establishment of a Joint Council for Vocational Education at the National level and counterpart bodies at the State and the District levels. The importance of creating a manage-ment structure at various levels for effective implementation and monitoring of the programme was also underlined.

State Councils for Vocational Education have been set up in Bihar, Delhi, Haryana, Himachal Pradesh, Mizoram, Punjab, Tamil Nadu, Uttar Pradesh and West Bengal. District Vocational Education Committees have been set up in Haryana, Punjab and Tamil Nadu. In other States/Union Territories they are in the process of being set up.

The States have been somewhat slow in creation and filling up of the posts sanctioned for management of the programme at the Directorate, SCERT and District levels. A few posts have been created/filled up in Bihar, Goa, Haryana, Himachal Pradesh,

Kerala, Madhya Pradesh, Orissa and Uttar Pradesh. In the States of Andhra Pradesh, Bihar, Goa, Gujarat, Haryana, Himachal Pradesh, Kerala, Maharashtra, Madhya Pradesh, Orissa, Tamil Nadu and Uttar Pradesh a large number of teaching posts have been filled up whether on full time or part time basis. Several vocational areas have been covered through the vocational courses and curricula for most of them have been prepared. A few States/ Union Territories have already developed instructional material for different vocational courses and in the remaining States/Union Territories work is still going on.

The Scheme also seeks to promote experimentation and innovation in vocational education through non-governmental organizations. The Society for Rural Industrialisation, Ranchi is engaged in developing technology for rural application and training tribals in use of such technology. The Society has trained 448 tribals in 6 trades including Land and Water Management, Building Block Production, Maintenance of Diesel Engine Pump-sets, Repair of Cycles and Mopeds etc. The Vigyan Ashram, Pune, seeks to develop an integrated course in Rural Technology to provide technical services to the community through students for jobs like water prospecting, bore well repair, electrical repairs and pest control etc. The project activities have been started in 3 schools and equipment and trained instructors have been provided to a large extent. Links with Rural Development Agencies (DRDA) have been established, and Community services in the various targeted areas are being provided.

Efforts are also being made to start vocational courses specific to the needs of the users which will ensure ready employ-ment to the vocational students provided they fulfil the minimum standards laid down. The Central Board of Secondary Education (CBSE) has started a vocational course in General Insurance in 19 schools during 1988-89 in collaboration with General Insurance Company. A course in Life Insurance has been started in 1989-90 in about 25 schools in collaboration with LIC. The course content of the vocational courses has been decided by GIC/LIC and approved by CBSE. The two organizations have committed to absorb continuously, year after year, the students coming out of the vocational course provided they have attained the minimum prescribed level. A similar sponsored course is also proposed to be started in collaboration with the Ministry of Railways for the Railway Commercial Staff. While the details have been worked out to start the course from 1990-91, the formal approval of the Railway Board is awaited. Discussions have also been initiated with the Ministries/Departments of Health and Family Welfare, Information and Broadcasting, Tele- communica-tions, Tourism, Handlooms and Handicrafts for starting vocational courses geared to their needs.

Any proposal to industrialize the country and modernize the industry is idle when the secondary education is not geared to meet the needs of industrialization. This points to the great need for a social change among the parents as well as among the industrialists. Today the parents are unwilling to send their children to the technical high schools and Industrial Training Institutes because they consider such education to be inferior and because they want their children to go in for white collar jobs even when there is a lack in ability and aptitude among the children for academic education. Further, the employers are not willing to recruit the trained young men and women in factories and workshops. They find it less bothersome to recruit illiterate unskilled workers and allow them to pick up in the course of working. Thus the old tradition of hiring the illiterate workers and training them on the job persists.

Students' Guidance

Diversified curriculum at the secondary level inevitably implies development of a strong and effective guidance programme. Guidance involves the difficult art of helping the boys and girls lo plan by themselves their own future in the light of the personal factors of ability, aptitude, and interest on the one hand and the social factors of job opportunities on the other. The Secondary Education Commission 1953 recommended that Educa-tional Guidance Bureaus should be established in every State and attempts should be made to broaden the pupil's under-standing of the scope, nature and consequences of various occu-pations and industries. The Kothari Commission also recommends that guidance and counselling should be regarded as an integral part of education assisting individuals to make decisions and adjustments.

Training the Teachers

Traditional Indian education never envisaged the training of teachers. It was assumed that a man who is well educated is in a position to educate others. This assumption continues to be widespread even now. Generally, teacher training is looked upon as an unnecessary aspect of modern education. Even now the private as well as Government schools continue to employ untrain-ed teachers. It was estimated that in 1947 only about half of the teachers were trained. Serious attempts are being made since independence to train teachers on a massive scale to meet the requirements of the massive primary and secondary education programmes.

According to the Fifth All-India Educational Survey, there are 8,86,935 schools in the country as on 30th September, 1986. Out of the above 6,31,308 are primary, 1,87,602 upper primary, 52,560 secondary and 15,465 higher secondary schools. These schools have 36,44,681 teachers working at all stages of education. Of these 69.45 per cent are working in rural schools. There are 14,92,721 teachers working in primary schools, 10,02,136 teachers working in upper primary schools, 7,23,625 teachers working in secondary schools and 4,26,199 teachers working in higher secondary schools in the country. Out of these teachers, 13.55 per cent, 12.58 per cent, 9.27 per cent and 10.57 per cent are untrained at the primary stage, upper primary stage, secondary stage and higher secondary stage, respectively.

According to the Fourth All-India Educational Survey there were 6,34,144 recognised schools in the country as on 30 September, 1978 out of which 4,74,636 are primary, 1,12,404 middle, 36,675 secondary and 10,429 higher secondary. These schools had 30,01,726 sanctioned teaching posts out of which 29,40,337 were filled. Of these teachers 20,60,527 (70.08 per cent were working in rural schools). Out of the 29,40,337 teachers working 25,47,033 (86.63 per cent) were trained and remaining 13.37 per cent were untrained. The Third All-India Educational Survey found about 14.65 per cent teachers untrained. The survey also observed that in rural and urban areas there is not much difference in proportion between trained teachers as 86.50 per cent teachers in rural schools and 86.93 per cent in urban schools were trained. The survey also found that in terms of professional competence there is not much difference between male and female teachers as 86.32 per cent male and 87.47 per cent female teachers were trained.

The New Education Policy attaches high importance to both pre-service and in-service components of teacher education for improvement in quality and coverage of education.

A programme of mass orientation of school teachers is already in operation since 1986, Under it, 10-day camps are organised, mostly during vacations, with a view to orienting teachers in improving their professional competence. About 13.5 lakh teachers were covered under this programme during first three years of its implementation. Another five lakhs were to be covered during 1989-90.

Under the new policy, a Centrally-sponsored programme of setting up District Institutes of Education and Training (DIET) and of strengthening Secondary Teacher Education Institutions (STEI) is also being implemented since 1987-88. These institutions impart pre-service and in-service training to elementary school teachers and personnel of adult and non-formal education. Besides, they provide extension and other academic support to elementary schools and adult and non-formal education systems at district level engage in locally-relevant experimentation and innovation. Likewise, selected STEI's are also being developed to impart pre-service and in-service training to secondary school teachers, and provide necessary academic guidance and support to the secondary schools of a group of two or three districts.

Central assistance is being given to states and union territories for setting up DIETs and strengthening STEIs, for construction of buildings, books and equipment, appointment of suitably qualified staff, conducting in-service training programmes, etc. During 1987-88, Central assistance was given, on project basis, for setting up 216 DIETs and strengthening 32 STEIs. States are now in the process of implementing these projects.

Higher Education

Though higher education has been valued and pursued even from the Vedic days in India, it was narrow in its conception in two ways. It was confined mainly to religion, grammar, logic and philosophy; only a few scholars specialized in secular subject like medicine, mathematics, and astronomy. Further, higher learning was confined to a microscopic minority of the population belonging to the twice-born castes particularly to those born in the Brahmin caste. It was in the Buddhist era that higher education was widened in its scope and thrown open to all castes. Fahien (A.D. 399-414) speaks of big Buddhist monasteries with about 300-400 monks in each monastery in Pataliputra where teachers and students had gathered from all parts of the land. Hieuen-Tsang (A.D. 629-645) and I-tsine CA.D. 673-6871 sneak of the great universities in Nalanda, Tamralipti and other centres of learning with thousands of students. These seats of learning encouraged both religious and secular learning, but all of them were destroyed by some short-sighted and narrow-minded Muslims early in the thirteen century A.D.

Though higher learning was pursued in the Muslim era, there were no organizations on the scale of Nalanda. It was also narrow in outlook in the Muslim as in the Hindu centres of learning both with respect to scope and regarding recruitment.

It was Woods Despatch of 1354 which sanctioned the establishment of three universities, but the greatest blunder was committed when the London University of those days, which was purely an examining body, was made the model. In 1857, there were 23 liberal arts colleges, 3 colleges of medicine and one college of engineering. Of these colleges, 18 were conducted by Government including four professional colleges and the remaining liberal arts colleges were conducted by the missionaries.

The three Universities of Calcutta, Bombay and Madras were established in 1857 with the sole purpose of examining students of the secondary schools and colleges. Thus the universities neither promoted higher learning and research, the essential tasks of a university, nor did they allow secondary education to develop on its own as terminal education with emphasis on vocational training to prepare the youth for a career and thus contribute to the economic development of the country. The youth who completed the secondary education course sought to go to the colleges though they had neither the preparation nor the desire to pursue higher learning. Because of the immense increase in the students who took the matriculation examination, a fourth university was started in the Punjab in 1882 and a fifth in 1887 in Allahabad.

In 1882, there were 7,400 candidates for matriculation examination but by 1906 the number went up to 25,000. This enormous increase in enrolment led to a phenomenal increase in the affiliated colleges. As against 68 colleges in 1882, there were 179 affiliated colleges in 1902. Side by side there was an enormous increase in unemployment from 1882 to 1916.

The Radhakrishnan Commission of 1949 asserted that the Indian universities should have a wider conception of their duties and responsibilities. They have to provide leadership in politics and administration, the profession, industry, agriculture, and commerce. They have to promote research and higher learning. They must enable the country to attain freedom from want, disease and ignorance by exploiting natural resources and human resources, thus ensuring a better standard of living. They emphasized that education is a universal right and not a class privilege. They further emphasized that it is the duty of the university to promote the general purposes of the State as outlined by the Constitution.

Since independence there has been a very rapid expansion in the field of higher education in the country. The number of universities increased from 19 to 176 including "deemed to be universities" according to Section 3 of the University Grants Commission Act.

Out of the total Science & Technology Graduates and Post Graduates enrolment in 1987-88, about 67 per cent were enrolled in the general faculty of science and only the remaining 33 per cent were enrolled in other faculties with a pronounced applied bias. There is an urgent need to execute a big shift for the general faculty of science to other applied faculties to ensure that these Graduates and Post Graduates become easily employable.

A complicating factor is that due to the irrationality of our educational system, many of the educated unemployed are really unemployable.

There has been an increase in enrolment from 2,66,000 at the lime of Independence to 38,14,000 in 1987-88. There is a 15-fold increase in medicine, 150-fold increase in engineering and 12-fold increase in agriculture during 1987-88 as compared to the enrolment in 1946-47.

At the beginning of the year 1989-90, the total student enrolment in Universities and Colleges was 39.48 lakhs. This was 1.34 lakhs more than the enrolment in the previous year. The enrolment in the University Departments was 6.55 lakhs and that in the affiliated Colleges was 32.93 lakhs.

Enrolment in the Faculty of Arts constituted 40.3 per cent of the total enrolment. In the Faculties of Science and Commerce the percentage was 19.7 and 21.5 respectively. Enrolment at the first degree level was 34.74 lakhs (88 per cent); at the postgraduate level 3.75 lakhs (9.5 per cent); at the research level 0.43 lakhs (1.1 per cent); and at the diploma and certificate level 0.55 lakhs (1.4 per cent).

The number of teachers increased to 2.49 lakhs during the year. Of these, 0.55 lakhs were in the University Colleges and the rest in the affiliated colleges. Of the 54,973 teachers in the Universities, 6,432 were Professors, 13,468 were Readers, 32,764 were Lecturers and 2,309 were Tutors/Demonstrators. In the affiliated Colleges, the number of senior teachers was 25,815, the number of Lecturers was 1,59,546 and that of Tutors/ Demonstrators was 8,734.

Technical education is one of the most significant components of human resource spectrum with great potential for adding value to products and services, for contributing to the national economy, and for improving the quality of the life of the people. In recognition of the importance of this sector, the successive Five Year Plans laid great emphasis on the development of technical education.

During the past four decades, there has been a phenomenal expansion of technical facilities in the country. But, a lot more remains to be accomplished in the field of technical education in respect of increasing its coverage and enhancing its accessibility to various categories of people, and in improving its productivity. Moreover, the changing scenario by the turn of the century in socio-economic, industrial and technological areas needs to be considered to enable the system to play its role with greater relevance and objectivity. Based on these considerations, several initiatives were taken to further re- vamp the technical education system. They include: modernisation and removal of obsole-scence, promoting institution-industry interaction, restructuring of courses/programmes, linking technical education with development sectors and application of science and technology for rural development.

However, there is a constant criticism that this rapid expansion of higher education has resulted in the fall in the standard of education. Every year the society is faced with violence and indis-cipline in some campus or the other. The Education Commission of 1966 has given a number of suggestions to improve the quality of higher education in India. They have recommended a greater freedom of choice to students regarding study in the colleges and universities. They reiterate the recommendations of the University Education Commission and urge that there should be an increase in tutorial work, discussion groups, seminars and independent study, and corresponding decrease in the lecture classes. They also recommend that there should be more frequent contact between the students, professors and research workers.

Education out of School

There are three functions of education: *(a)* the conservative function, i.e., the responsibility of transmitting the social heritage, *(b)* the progressive function, i.e., transmitting knowledge without engendering contempt for past tradition, and *(c)* to make education respond to the needs of today and the aspirations of tomorrow. This becomes pertinent in the context of societal change. For too long education had the task of "preparing for the stereo-typed function and stable situation"—for fitting the individual in a hierarchical world. This makes education lose its relevance to the living present and suffers from the gaps between its objectives and the living experience of its pupils, between the system of values it preaches and the goals set up by the society and the ancient curricula and the modernity of society.

The Education Commission of 1966 expressed that education should help in *(a)* increasing productivity, *(b)* achieving social and national integration, and (c) accelerating the process of modernization and then the cultivation of social, moral and spiritual values.

Education can no longer confine itself within the cloistered framework and within the portals of schools or colleges. In the modern times, one grows up by living inside and outside the institution. Educationists have therefore increasingly recognised that education should jump over its boundaries and move to the door-steps of the learners. As a result the Education Commission 1966 considered the problem of correspondence course and continuing education. It took another decade to change the whole concept of adult education and evolve a highly comprehensive idea of non-formal education which includes teaching-learning situations in which, irrespective of educational background, age and social background in life the individual at any stage of his life can learn as much as he wants in a situation completely non-formal, sitting in a farm, workshop, etc. The Central Advisory Board of Education at its session in November 1974 lent strong support to the introduction of adult adult and non-formal education in the country. The programme of adult education is of great significance for the success of universalization of adult education and the removal of illiteracy. It is also necessary for the intellectual participation of people in all programmes of national development. The Board therefore recommended that adult education should form an inbuilt part of every developmental activity, whether in rural or urban, private or public sector. The progress should be flexible, diversified and functionally selected to the needs and interests of youths and equip them to participate in developmental activities.

Shortcomings of Regular Education

It is now clear that the present formal system of education which is time bound and costly with a heavy load of academic discipline is hierarchical and elitist in character. This has caused social stratification and educational deprivation. While sizeable proportion of population lives under conditions of abysmal poverty or below the poverty line the parents belonging to economically backward and socially depressed groups show little enthusiasm to send the children to formal institutions. As a result universalization of primary education still remains a dream.

The child is attracted more by work than by knowledge. 'Doing' rather than 'knowing' is more attractive. Skill formation rather than mere verbal knowledge is necessary to attract them, The 'out-of-school' programme or 'learner-centres' are so designed and their tools and techniques so shaped that they can meet the needs and activities of the learners. This is in contrast to the "mass teaching-centres" system of formal education. In other words, learning should be self-motivated. This will help to overcome the problem of drop-outs who cause a drain on the meagre resources. However, it must be realised that non-formal education is not designed to replace the formal system of education. They supplement each other. What is non-formal education? It is not regulated by a formal course of induction lasting over a fixed number of years. Nor is it informal or incidental because it has a definite programme. It is an educational enterprise outside the traditional schools in which the content, media, time, admission criteria, staff facilities, etc., are adopted to the needs of the group and the situation. Its focus is on the improvement of social and personal living and occupational capabilities. It has immediate and practical utility to the learners. It is oriented to solve the problems facing the individual than to enable him to absorb a particular curriculum content. It involves the various communication media posters, flash cards, charts, comic books, puppets, audio and video tapes, films and filmsuips, etc. Non-formal education takes place at home, in the farm, factory, office, etc. It is learning by doing-performing specific tasks through association with peers. It has immense possibility as an alternate strategy for educating the masses.

One of the most important social objectives of education is to equalise opportunity enabling backward or under-privileged classes and individuals to use education as a lever for the improvement of their conditions. The Fifth Five Year Plan accepted the principle that formal and non-formal education should be correlated and integrated to meet the educational needs in view of the fact that full-time institutionalised formal education has not been able to meet the needs. To achieve social transformation and national development it emphasises non-formal programmes for non-school going children in the age group 6-14 and the youth in the age group 15-25. The greatest task is to improve the skills and outlook of the skilled and unskilled workers in agriculture, industry, commerce and other sectors. Just to think in terms of literacy and numeracy to them would mean nothing but chasing a wild goose, inasmuch as they would be unmindful and ignorant about the social change taking place around them. They have to be initiated to the ways and means of leading a good life to a proper and meaningful system of education. Awareness should be brought to them in personal and social hygiene, family planning, nutrition, child care, family budgeting, evils of dowry system, etc. In the above context non-format education assumes importance.

Article 45 of the Constitution of India provides for free, universal and compulsory elementary education in the country. Keeping in view this provision, the Ministry or Education set up a Working Group on Universalization of Education. The Working Group realising the difficulty of enrolling the large number of non-school going children in formal system, recommended the alternative strategy of non-formal education. The Union Education Minister announced on 5 April 1977 in Parliament the educational policy of the new government in which he stated that universal literacy would be attained in the country within a definite time frame of not more than 10 years. The strategy was to universalise elementary education for all children in the age group of 6 to 14 and remove illiteracy of the adults in the age group 15 to 35. It was estimated that there are 45.2 million non-enrolled children who would require to be brought into the school system by 1982-83 in order to reach the goal of universal elementary education. However, the feasible target by the end of 1982-83 would be to enrol 31 million of additional children. The hard core of non-enrolled children consists of children from the weaker sections of the community and majority of them are not attracted towards the formal schools due to socio-economic reasons. The children are required to help in augmenting the parental income and to help in household chores. However, even after enrolment in the formal school system, out of every 100 children that enter class I, only about 40 complete class V and only about 25 complete class VIII. To overcome this difficulty and bring the enrolled children to the completion of class VIII, it is essential to provide non-formal education on a large scale for the drop-out children. An additional enrolment of 12.40 million children is proposed during the period

1978-83. During the same period 9.38 million children are expected to be covered under the non-formal education scheme. During 1982-83 with the central assistance another 2.96 million are expected to be covered under NFE scheme thus bringing about a total additional enrolment of 24.75 million during 1978-83.

The fourth All-India Educational Survey, 1980 found that among 5,73,842 villages in the country only 25,194 (4.39 per cent) have provisions for non-formal education for one or more of the age groups: 6-14,14-35 and above 35. The survey observed that hardly 6,631 (1.16 per cent) villages in the country have facility for non-formal education for these age groups. Of an estimated child population of 1313.49 million in this age group, only 736.22 million children are studying in schools at different stages under formal system. This leaves a gap of 577,27 million children under compulsory education age group who are outside the formal system either having not attended the school at all or having withdrawn from the school prematurely before completing the formal system of education. 17,942 villages arc having facilities for non-formal education for adults in the age group of 14-35. Still this hardly covers 3.13 per cent of the total number of villages in the country. In 2673 villages, a 4.07 per cent of the total villages in the country have got facility for non-formal education for the age group of 35 years and above.

The Fifth All-India survey 1986 found that the number of villages having Non-Formal Education (NFE) centres has increased to 93,763 as compared to 25,194 during the Fourth Survey. Out of 93,763 villages having NFE Centres, the percentages of villages in population slabs '2000 and above', '1000-1999', '500-999' and 'below 500' are 22.11, 27.31, 2-4.55 and 26.03 respectively. 81.92 per cent of the 1,10,943 NFE Centres working at primary level are managed by Government/local bodies, compared to 94.57 per cent of the 6,297 NFE Centres working at the upper primary level, 71.64 per cent of the NFE Centres working at the primary level are in Andhra Pradesh, Bihar, Madhya Pradesh, Uttar Pradesh and West Bengal. 82.85 per cent of the NFE Centres working at the upper primary level are concentrated in Bihar, Madhya Pradesh and Uttar Pradesh.

Out of 3,878 urban areas in the country, 1,284 (33.11 per cent) have 8,386 NFE Centres working at the primary level compared to 328 (8.46 per cent) urban areas with 717 NFE Centres working at the upper primary level. 72.69 per cent of the 8,386 NFE Centres working at the primary level are managed by Government/local bodies, compared to 98.19 per cent of 717 NFE Centres working at the upper primary level. 2,284 NFE Centres at the primary level and 84 NFE Centres at the upper primary level cater to girls only. 80.23 per cent of the NFE Centres working at the primary level are in Andhra Pradesh, Bihar, Madhya Pradesh, Uttar Pradesh and West Bengal. 88.01 per cent of the NFE Centres working at the upper primary level are concentrated in Bihar, Madhya Pradesh and Uttar Pradesh.

Out of 31,88,582 children enrolled in NFE Centres at the primary level in rural areas, 13,52,264 (42.41 per cent) girls as compared to 55.450 (36.06 per cent) girls out of 1,53,777 children enrolled at the upper primary level. Out of 2,78,313 children enrolled in NFE Centres at the primary level in urban areas, 1,33,185 (47.85 per cent) are girls, as compared to 10,430 (41.41 per cent) girls out of 25,188 children enrolled at the upper primary level. Non-formal system provides education to only 2.19 per cent children in the age group 6-14. Only 1.94 per cent girls in this age group are covered by the system.

From the above it can be seen that the non-formal approach at all stages, particularly in the age group 6-14 has still a long way to go to make any reasonable impact on the masses.

Social Education

It has been noted earlier that both economic and social development require universal adult education in the industrial age. However, in spite of all the efforts of the State and voluntary agencies, literacy rate has risen only from 16.6 per cent in 1951 to 24 per cent in 1961 to 30 per cent in 1971 and to 52.11 per cent in 1991. Further, there is the paradoxical situation that because of the enormous increase in population there is actually an increase in the number of illiterates from 301 million in 1951 to 386 million in 1971 to 302 million in 1981 and to 324 million in 1991, (for 1981 and 1991 the data is for population aged 7 years and above and excludes Assam and Jammu & Kashmir), though there is an increase in the literacy rate.

Adult education in Indian culture is based on oral transmission of the cultural tradition. In ancient India literacy was confined to the small group of priests, kings, nobles and prosperous merchants. Further, education was confined to classical Sanskrit. It was in the Buddhist era that the scope of adult education was enlarged by the use of the popular languages Pali and Prakrit. But later Buddhism placed high value on Sanskritic tradition and so there was a decline in interest in adult education. There was a revival in the eleventh and twelfth centuries in South India when great religious leaders like Basaveswara spoke and wrote using the folk idiom. Right through centuries literacy has been associated in India with scholarship and so it was confined to a small section.

One of the essential features of an agricultural society, in contra distinction to the industrial society, is that the whole life is organized to function smoothly without involving any literacy. Even today the Indian farmers and the craftsmen, those engaged in personal services like the barbers or washer-men, men engaged in the construction of buildings and roads, the bus driver, the automobile repair man, all these people are functioning though they are illiterate. Many competent and skilled workers who use complicated tools which run with electricity are carrying on their work without any need for literacy. The villager can discourse on abstract subjects using the most sophisticated concepts like *Karma and Dharma* without being literate. Thus the rural as well as the urban worker and the businessman do.

There is not find any necessity to become literate and to educate themselves. They are quite satisfied to function at the level at which they are functioning. This is one of the important reasons why there is hardly any motivation to join an adult education class.

It was in the period 1918 to 1927 that new enthusiasm for adult education was generated by the intensification of the nationalist movement which at that time became a mass movement under the leadership of Mahatma Gandhi. It is in this period also that many Indian soldiers returned from the war fronts in Europe and the Middle East. This period also saw the growth of the cooperative movement. The Punjab Government took the lead by providing finances for starting literacy classes. In 1927, there were nearly 100,000 adults enrolled in night schools in the Punjab State. But in the years of economic depression which followed there was a slow down in the movement. It later acquired a new interest when the Congress Party formed the Government in 1937 in several States. Adult education was at that time accepted as a State responsibility. Again when these Governments resigned in 1939, the problem of adult education receded to the background. We are now witnessing another rise in interest in adult education with independence and the formulation of the Plans.

However, one of the most hopeful features of the Indian education scene since independence is the eagerness with which the illiterate adults are sending their children to primary schools. This may be taken as a manifestation of a social change in the illiterate adult. Though he did not himself respond to the call of education through the thirties and forties, he has changed his outlook with respect to his children. He has realized the need for the education of his children.

Another important thing is the change in the whole concept of adult education in the recent years, by the use of such terms like "social education", "fundamental education", "functional literacy", and so on, which not only include literacy, but also health education, citizenship training, recreation training, economic betterment, etc.

With the accelerated pace of social education, the Ministry of Education set up a new department of social education in 1948. Further, the Community Development programmes emplo-yed social education organisers in each development block. The Ministry also set up literacy workshops during the period 1953-55 to train writers to write books in a simple manner for the neo-literates. Still, the progress made by all these efforts has fiardly been impressive. Inadequate motivation and apathy on the part of the adult, inadequate training of the teachers, inadequate reaching material, lack of follow-up reading materials, all these have combined to make progress in adult literacy and social education very slow.

The population of adult illiterates in the age group 14-45 is estimated to be 150 million. This huge population is getting to be a hindrance to the progress of the plans for agricultural development, improvement of health and sanitation, etc. Though decentralization was effected by the introduction of Panchayati Raj with elected bodies in the villages to conduct the local self-governments, these bodies have not been able to function effectively. The Panchayat is an old institution conducted by the scheduled tribes in the interior jungles and also by the village people from time immemorial. So the illiterate village folk do not see any necessity to improve their education to fulfil the tasks of rural reconstruction assigned to them by the new Panchayat Raj constitution. Like the illiterate car driver who can manage the machine, like the illiterate mechanic who could repair it, the illiterate member of the Panchayat wants to look after the affairs of local self-government without bothering about improving his level of education and understanding the implication of the new Act.

In the meantime, however, considerable progress has been made in clarifying the concept and in developing the criteria. The Central Advisory Board of Education has laid down criteria for literacy, namely, the sight recognition of 250 words, 90 per cent comprehension of a piece of writing with this vocabulary, ability to read simple charts and posters displayed in the area, acquaintance with the money order forms, etc., and the ability to write simple sentences and the most often used names. Functional literacy has been defined by the UNESCO experts in 1962 as equivalent to five years ordinary schooling so that the adult is able to read with understanding newspapers, bulletins, advertisements, tax notices and letters.

Under directives of National Education Policy and implementation strategies of the Programme of Action, Government has formulated a comprehensive programme known as National Literacy Mission (NLM) in the field of adult education. It is one of the Seven National Technology Missions and aims at imparting functional literacy to eight crore illiterates in the 15-35 age group (three crore by 1990 and an additional five crore by 1995).

There are 513 projects under Central Scheme of Rural

Functional Literacy Projects (RFLP), besides 852 projects under state adult education pro- grammes (SAEPs). Whereas 454 projects under RFLP have 300 adult education centres each, the remaining 49 have 100 to 200 centres. Similarly under SAEPs also, projects have 100 to 300 adult education centres. Voluntary agencies are playing important role in creating environment conducive to literacy and actually imparting literacy. At present, about 628 voluntary agencies are implementing this programme by running over 45,433 adult education centres and 2,355 *jana shiksha nilayams* (JSNs). The overall number of JSNs has increased to over 30,000. Under Mass Programme of Functional Literacy, about 6.5 lakh students in universities, colleges and schools are participating in the Mission. Each student is expected to make at least one adult literate.

Kerala has taken the lead in the promotion of adult education programme. Two of its districts Kottayam and Ernakulam have achieved cent per cent literacy.

NLM is attracting support from people of all walks of life. Programmes for complete eradication of illiteracy have been taken up in Kerala, Gujarat, Karnataka, Goa, West Bengal and Pondicherry, in selected districts, blocks and villages by voluntary involvement of students, teachers and voluntary agencies. Emphasis is now on making persons actually literate rather than on enrolment. Thirty six *shramik Vidyapeeths* are also functioning in different states to cater to workers education. With a view to enlarging coverage of adult learners with reduced cost, a new technique, Improved Pace and Content of Learning (IPCL), is being introduced providing integrated learning material with in-built mechanism for evaluation at various levels. IPCL technique also aims at retaining the interest of adult learners. Eighteen state resource centres are providing academic and technical resource support to the programme by way of arranging training of functionaries, bringing out teaching-learning material, catering to varying needs of learners both in basic literacy and post-literacy stages and undertaking research and experimentation work relating to adult education programme. Seventeen voluntary agencies/ institutes of social science and research have been identified for evaluating the programme.

Forty two technology demonstration districts have been identified. Technopedagogic and research and development input like solar power packs, improved blackboards, slates, pencils, etc., are being provided to improve quality of the programme. A computerised management information system is also being developed in these districts to ensure reliable and steady flow of information needs for better management.

Over 23,000 *jana shiksha nilayams* (JSNs) have been sanctioned for providing facilities of post-literacy and continuing education so that neo-literates do not relapse into illiteracy.

Language Factor

India has always been a land of multiplicity of languages. In ancient times Sanskrit was the language of higher education. It was so even in the Buddhist and Jaina times though the Buddhists recognized the value of using popular languages like of Pali and Prakrit. The other Indian languages have also had a long history though they were not used in higher learning except probably Tamil. With the coming of the Muslim rulers, Persian became not only the court language but also the language for higher learning, along with Sanskrit. In the 19th century English became the State Language. As a result all the Indian languages languished. When the mass movement for national independence was started in 1920, emphasis was laid on Indian languages.

This was reinforced by the reorganization of the Congress organization which formed its Provincial Congress Committees according to the language zones. The Congress leaders practically gave up the use of English and used the regional languages in their contacts with the masses. Gandhiji also asserted that Indian languages should be the media of instruction in the schools. He was convinced that if the child is studying in the mother tongue he could master the social studies, nature studies, etc., with a greater ease and facility.

It was in 1937 that a big change came about and the regional languages were introduced as the media of instruction up to the secondary level, though English continued to be used side by side as the medium of instruction.

Another important change came up at about this time. With the expansion of secondary education in the rural areas the enrolment of the rural students in the colleges increased considerably. Though the rate of failure in the examination was more or less the same, it was asserted that the cause for a large percentage of failure was the use of the English medium at the college level since the universities continued to use English medium.

Since independence there has been a strong movement to replace English by the regional language as the medium for higher education. There was also another movement to replace English by Hindi so that higher education throughout the country is in one language, namely, Hindi. But side by side there was a third strong force in favour of English. In the urban areas, the parents belonging to the middle class could not imagine the possibility of higher education in any language other than English. Thus, since independence we could see two contrary trends, a strong opinion against English and an actual increase in schools with English as the medium of instruction.

The Indian Constitution recognized all- the 14 languages as the national languages [8th Schedule Article 344(1) and 351] though Article 343 lays down that Hindi shall be the official language of the Union. It also laid down that English should continue to be used for all official purposes for 15 years, i.e., till 1967. Article 350 lays down that the State shall provide adequate facilities for the instruction of children at the primary stage through the mother tongue, and Article 351 lays down that it shall be the duty of the Union to promote the spread of Hindi language so that it could serve as the medium of expression for all the elements of the composite culture of India.

Thus all these various articles created an atmosphere of controversy throughout the country. While the people in the Hindi states who form the largest single language group (about 38 per cent) were eager that Hindi should not only become the official language but also the language of higher education throughout the country taking the place of English, the people in the non-Hindi areas are keen that the regional languages should become the media of higher education besides becoming the official language of the respective States. In other words, they are eager that English should be displaced by the regional languages. There is also a third, equally vehement opinion in all the States, whether Hindi or non-Hindi, that the language of higher education should continue to be English because neither Hindi nor any other Indian language is now in a position to displace it.

There was another controversy as regards the stage at which the various languages should be introduced and the duration of the courses in these languages. The Secondary Education Commission of 1953 had recommended that the mother tongue or the regional language should be the medium of instruction throughout the secondary level. It recommended that a second language could be taught at the middle school level (5th to 7th standard). This may either be English or Hindi and at the high school level there should be at least two languages one of which being the mother tongue or regional languages and the other being either Hindi or English or a classical language or a modern Indian language. This meant that the student of the Hindi areas would learn Hindi and English and those in non-Hindi areas had to learn the regional language, Hindi and English.

The Central Advisory Board of Education did not agree with these recommendations. In 1956 the Board evolved the three language formula, and this was adopted with slight modification by the Conference of Chief Ministers held in 1961. According to this formula, all children should start their primary education with the mother tongue or the regional language. At the upper primary level (grades 5 to 7) they could learn English or some other modern European language and Hindi in non-Hindi areas or a modern Indian language in the Hindi areas. Thus, this formula provided for the learning of three languages by the children in all the areas of the country. It sought to equalize the burden of language learning by asking the Hindi students to learn a modern Indian language as the third language since in their case the regional language happened also to be the national language.

Though theoretically the formula is very sound and balanced, in implementation it ran into a number of difficulties. There was a general opposition that this formula imposed a heavy language load during the upper primary level. There was opposition to the "imposition" of Hindi in the non-Hindi areas. In the Hindi areas there was hardly any motivation to learn the additional modem Indian language. Thus, the third language, whether it was Hindi or an additional modern Indian language, was looked upon as an additional burden and an imposition. The provision of a third language involved tremendous expenditure. Further, the people of the non-Hindi areas looked upon this as a great threat. According to the Constitution, Hindi would become the sole official language from 1965 and English would be abandoned. This meant in concrete terms that only students from the Hindi areas could hope to compete successfully for the administrative jobs. In other words, the non-Hindi people felt that they would become second class citizens in their own country.

In order to overcome this fear, the Official Language Act was passed in 1963 which provided that from 1965, English may continue to be used for official purposes in addition to Hindi. This led to a violent anti-Hindi agitation in 1965 in the southern States, particularly in Madras State. More than 50 people were killed and much damage was done to public property. This created a national crisis and forced the Central Government to postpone the implementation of its language policies.

As a result of this, the Official Language Amendment Act 1967 was passed, which specifically provided that the English language would continue to be used for all official purposes in addition to Hindi, It also asserted that the officials in the Union services "will not be placed at a disadvantage on the ground that they do not have proficiency in both the languages." Finally, it provided that the use of English would continue till "all the States which have not adopted Hindi as their official language," passed resolutions for the discontinuance of the use of the English language.

One big change which has come about as a result of the recommendations of the Education Commission, 1966, the Official Language Amendments Act, 1967, and the violent anti-Hindi agitation in some of the southern States, is that the State Governments have now committed themselves to the introduction of the regional language as the medium of higher education, and the Central Government has made available huge sums of money to the universities through the University Grants Commission to prepare and publish books in the regional languages for higher education.

However, the students do not seem to be as eager as the Government. Very few of them have taken the regional languages as the media, they are eager to study with English as the medium since it offers the means for advancement to one's career as well as to one's knowledge.

There is always a fear that if all the universities adopted regional languages as the media of instruction, barriers will be created for the migration of students and teachers from one region to another. Even more disastrous would be the fragmentation of the intellectual community. While industrialization and the democratic form of Government promote mobility, the adoption of the regional language would hinder it.

15

The Renaissance

Great Reformers

In nineteenth century, the socio-religious awakening, was a remarkable feature of modern Indian history. It was a slow process in the beginning. Later it developed into a powerful force and deeply stirred thc masses, helping them to become politically conscious. The socio-religious awakening have indeed left beihind a rich legacy. They bequeathed us with the spirit of rational inquiry and taught us to change with the time. Contact with the West acted as an important stimulus to the awakening movement. According to Sri Aurobindo:

> "The renaissance in India is as inevitable as the rising of tomorrow's Sun and the renaissance of a great nation of three hundred millions with so peculiar a temperament, such unique traditions and ideas of life, so powerful an intelligence and so great a mass of potential energies cannot but be one of the most formidable phenomena of the modern world."

The socio-religious awakening movement which took place in India during the British rule were the expression of the rising national consciousness and spread of the liberal ideas of the West among the Indian people. The socio-religious awakening or reform movements were the expression of the national awakening in India and aimed at a revision of the medieval social structure and religious outlook on a more or less democratic basis, i.e. on the principle of individual liberty and human equality. The dominant feature of socio-political thought in colonial India were liberalism and nationalism. The liberal phase was characterized by attempts to rationalize and democratize the social and religious institution. In the social sphere, there were movements of caste reform, a campaign against child marriage and a ban on widow remarriage, equal rights for women, a crusade against social and legal inequalities. In the religious sphere, there sprang up a movements which combated religious superstitions, and attacked idolatry, polytheism and hereditary priesthood. The European missionaries and intelligentsia began to ridicule the idol worship and polytheism practised by the Hindus, for they believed these to be obstacles in the path of attaining enlightenment. The new wave of Western rationalism brought about the destruction of old customs that were prevalent in the society and religion. In the sudden invasion of the "Modern", India was supposed to have surrendered at discretion, and prostrating herself before the innumerable challenges of the present. While the age of illumination was inaugurated in Europe with a. temporary negation of religion, in case of India such an epoch was inaugurated by Raja Ram Mohan Roy, in the last quarter of the 18th century, following our traditional method of revitalizing decaying society through a new religion, by founding Brahmo dharma, based on the age old principle of unity underlying the vedantic monism.

The foundation of the British empire in India was laid just about the time when Europe was on the verge of a revolution, probably the most important, politically, socially and intellectually, which the world has even seen. The wave of liberalism which passed through England affected even her distant administration of India. They submitted to the despotism of the British as quietly as they had submitted to the despotism of any Hindu or Mohammedan power. The Govt. of the company had nearly until the close of the 18th century been a despotism, with scarcely any mitigating features to compensate for the loss of the manifold advantages of a native rule. All that the company had till than cared for was money. But since 1832, the year in which the bill crowned the cause of democracy in England, the benefit of India has generally been urged, at least by English statesmen, as the main object of retention of India. Though, in practise that object has not often been kept in view, its theoretical recognition bespeaks the liberal spirit of modern Europe. The charter of 1833 provided that no native of India be disabled from holding any place, office, or employment under the said government. It was Lord William Bentinck one of the few liberal minded statesmen that India has seen, to carry out the principles of the charter, and for the first time in the history of British rule, Indians were appointed to posts of any responsibility. The noble sentiments of the British have been reiterated over and over in official documents of which the most authoritative is the proclamation issued by her majesty queen Victoria in 1858 "we hold ourselves bound to the native of our Indian territories by the same obligations of duty which bind us to all our other subjects, and those obligations',... we shall faithfully fulfil. And it is our further will that,... our subjects of whatever race or creed, be freely admitted to offices in our service, the duties of which they may be qualified by their education, ability, and integrity, duly discharge".

The socio-religious reawakening movement in India was a byproduct of modern Western culture. India came into contact with Western ideas at a most oppertune moment. It was the age of the French illumination when the spirit of rationalism and individualism dominated European thought. It proclaimed supremacy of reason over faith and brought in its train new conceptions of social justice and political rights. A new ideology suddenly burst forth upon the static life, moulded for centuries by a fixed set of religious ideas and social conventions. The most important result of the impact of Western culture on India was the replacement of blind faith in traditions, beliefs, conventions characteristic of the Medieval age-by a spirit of rationalism which seeks to inquire and argue before accepting anything. The revolt of the mind against the tyranny of dogma and traditional authorities, beliefs and customs, is the first requisite for freedom of thought and conscience which lies at the root of progress in social, religious and political sphere of life.

Western conquest exposed the weakness and decay of Indian society. Thoughtful Indians began to look for the defects of their society. Western thought provided the key to the regeneration of their society. They were impressed in particular by modern science and the doctrines of reason and humanism. The influence of the West acted on the life and ideas of the people in multiple ways, forcing them to adjust their pattern of life to the new circumstances and thus effecting a continuum of social change. Standing out as landmarks in this gradual adaptation to new conditions are the reformers. These are the Indians who consciously reacted to the new situation and advocated deliberate changes in social and religious attitudes and customs, involving a break with tradition itself. They saw change not as a slow adaptive process, but as a positive value in itself. The British raj influenced Indian life through administration, legislation, trade, the creation of a network of communication, industrialization, urbanization, all had great influence not only on the many Indians who became directly involved in them, but also on society as a whole. According to Sri Aurobindo: "The renaissance in India had three aspects, it aimed at a recovery of the old spiritual gospel contained in the sacred books of 'the country... philosophers and thinkers like Emerson, Schopenhouer, Thoreau highly praised Indian wisdom in the past, Indian saints, and mystic leaders in India also helped the same process. This reinvigorated spirituality inspired fresh activity in the fields of philosophy, literature, art. And an attempt was made to deal in an original way with modern problems in the light of the new inspiration". In those early days-of the foundation of British power in India, the Indian people, had very little to boast of in the domain of politics and economics, both being dominated by the aggressive occidental nations who came to dictate the pace of our modern history. But even in that age of object degradation, the Indian people as a whole, not only the unlettered millions of villages, but also the elite, clung tenaciously to their ancestral faith and traditions; and faced successfully the deadly onslaughts of outlandish modernism. The Hindus and the Muslims, chastened by common suffering, the great equalizer, came to forget them as rulers or the ruled. Only the consolation of spirit, that never failed the nation, percolated the soul of the Hindus as well as of the Muslims through innumerably tols and Muktabs (village seminaries), so wonderfully efficient and pervasive in character as to put to shame the record of our bureaucratic primary education a century later. Sanskrit and the various verna-culars derived from it were cultivated side by side with Persian and Arabic.

The early religious reformers strove to extend the principle of individual liberty to the sphere of religion. Various socio-religious reformation movement tried to meet the needs of the new society. It is true that some of the reformers had the misconcep-tion that they were reviving the old pristine social structure of the vedic

Aryans, that they were returning to the golden age. In reality they were engaged, in varying degrees, in adapting the Hindu religious to the social, economic and cultural needs of the contemporary Indian nation. In fact, the reformers were forging a new society unknown to all past history. This illusion is the product of the contradiction between the old thinking and the new conditions of social being. "Man himself is composed like society, of current active being and inherited conscious formulation...Thus he feels, right in the heart of him this tension between being and thinking, between new being and old thought. ..The incomplete future is dragging at him but because instinctive components of the psyche are the oldest, he often feels this to be the past dragging at him. That is why we come upon the paradox that the hero appeals to the past, and urges man to bring it into being again, in doing so produces the future. The return to the classic dominated the bourgeoisie renaissance. Rome influenced Napoleon and the revolution. The return to the natural uncorrup-ted man was the ideal of 18th century revolutionists. Yet, it is the new whose tension men feel in their minds and hearts at such times... He may think it is the past he is born to save or reestablish on earth and only when it is done is it seen that the future has come into being. The reformer returning to primitive Christianity bring bourgeoisie Protestantism into being..." Similarly, Gandhi imagined that he was engaged in an effort to reproduce Ram Raj of the golden age of the Hindus while, in reality, he was attempting to evolve a modern democratic capitalist national state existence for India.

The reformers of the 19th century, while attempting to regenerate Indian society heavily drew from the experience of the West, more particularly the experience of Britain. The subtle combination of reinterpretation of religion and a passion for social regeneration, is a debt that we owe to the evangelical, the high Church, the oxford and the Christian socialist movements of Britain in the 19th century. All these 19th century movement in Britain were greatly responsible for the massive social legislation on India that was passes in order to ameliorate human life without neglecting people living at the lowest level of society. The failure of the mutiny of 1857 created a strong reaction among those who wanted to revive the Mughal empire and along with it all what the feudal ages stood for. The construction part of reaction manifested in the form of socio-religious reformation movement. In essence, the achievement of these constructive agencies is both of material and non-material nature. The material side of it impinged on Indian society-irrespective of religious or other considerations and it is basically an import from the West. On the other considerations and it is basically an import from the West. On the non-material level, it is rationalism, humanitarianism, scientific attitude and behavioural pattern and outlook of modern industrial society.

There is no denying the fact that the English education brought about a great change in social and religious outlook. The extent to which it was healthy and good for national life, or was instrumental in demoralizing the people is a subject of dispute. The first and foremost positive effect of English education is that it instilled in to the minds of the Indians, a spirit of rational inquiry into the basis of their religion and society. According to Naoroji: "The introduction of English education with its great, noble, elevating and civilizing literature and advanced science, will for ever remain a monument of good work done in India". A.R. Desai points out that the thought crystallized in precious scientific work. It not only enabled the Indians to absorb European ideas but also provided them with new and powerful means of interregional solidarity. R.N. Tagore writes:

> "We had come to know England through her glorious literature which had brought new inspiration in to our young lives ... It was chivalrous West which trained the enthusiasm of knight-errants ready to take upon themselves the cause of the oppressed, of those who suffered from the miserliness of their fate and we felt certain that the special mission of the Western civilization was to bring emancipation of all kinds to all races of the world. Though the West came to our shores as cunning tradesmen, it brought with it also the voice and a literature which claimed justice for all humanity."

Further, the modern means of transport were a formidable force in unifying the Indian people socially. K.M. Panikkar writes: "The establishment of the great principle of equality of all before law, in a country where under the Hindu doctrines a Brahman could not be punished on the evidence of Sudras and even punishments varied according to Muslim law an unbelievers testimony could not be accepted against a Muslim, was itself a legal revolution of the first importance". As a result, there developed among the people a critical outlook on the past and new aspirations for the future. Rationalism as the basis for ethical thinking, the idea of human progress and evolution, the possibility of scientifically engineering social change, the concept of natural rights connected with Individualism, were all alien to traditional Indian society. The British administration, English education, and European literature brought to India a constellation of fresh ideas. An equally strong influence was exerted by the works of the Christian missionaries.

The spread of the doctrine of equality in India is confined as yet to the educated community who form an insignificant fraction of the total population. It has not yet led to any serious disturbance of social order, not even a strike worth the name. The evils which are exercising the minds of philanthropists and philosophers in the West have not yet shown themselves among the Hindus. In politics, the democratic spirit of modern Europe has not yet gone further than strictly constitutional agitation by educated men for a moderate share in the administration of their country. In religion, it has led to movements like Brahmo Samaj. In literature, it has wrested the monopoly of authorship from the hands of the Brahmans. In this respect, however the spread of Western ideas of democracy has only intensified the change set on foot by the vaishnava revolution a few centuries ago, to a great extent, the order maintained under British rule throughout the length and breadth of India is undoubtedly favourable to progress.

The reformers did not altogether discard the past and did not mind involving some of the traditions from the past. But they were not revivalists in the sense that they glorified everything that existed in an imaginary golden age. They were critical of the Hindu doctrine of Karma. The reformers believed that man could determine his own progress. To the reformers, progress and change were a sign of life. Ranade summed up this aspect of the social reform ideology when he observed:

> "The change which we should all seek is thus a change from constraint of freedom, from credulity to faith, from authority to reason, from bigotry to toleration, from blind fatalism to a sense of human dignity..."

The sense of human dignity must reassert itself. The aim of social reform was to rediscover individuals and to make him free and creative. The reformers only protesting against blind acceptance of whatever was said by man who spoke in the name of religion. Above all the reformers put faith in human conscience. The Indian society in the 18th century was under the influence of several caste practices. The orthodox considered the caste rigidities as divinely ordained. Polygamy was widespread among the high caste Hindus, purdah was a way of life with both Hindu and Muslim, child marriage was widely prevalent, widow remarriage was not allowed. Indian society was groaning under the tyranny of customs and traditions. Due to the impact of Western education, a new spirit of inquiry developed among the Hindus. Similarly, nowhere in the world did religion dominate and determine the life of individual as in India. His economic activity, social life, marriage, birth, and death, all were strictly controlled by religion. The reformers fought the caste system, caste privilege enjoyed by the Brahman. The socio-religious re-awakening broadened in subsequent period. "The multiform world of Hinduism was stirred and awakened to a spiritual revolution in the 19th century much as Europe had been in the sixteenth. Like the reformation, they reverted to the earliest traditions and attacked the degeneration and superstition of later days. The reformers attacked polytheism, religious rites, dogmas, which undermined the critical intellectual power of the people. The socio-religious condition in the last quarter of 18th century was at its lowest ebb. "The country was overflowed with the rituals of idolatry. People here did not appreciate either the duties inculcated in the vedas or higher philosophy (Brahman) of the upanishad, but the festivities in which they used to find pleasure were the sacrifice of animals on the occasion of the worship of Durga... and similar things. People strongly believed that they could escape from the punishment of sin, purify themselves and earn religious merit by bathing in the Ganges... going on pilgrimage to the sacred places and by keeping fast.... the Brahmins who accepted services under the English used to make particular efforts to maintain their superiority and caste privileges.... The Brahmins, in those days were the newspapers... The influence of the Brahmins over the rich sudras was immense... The people were not willing to give up idolatry, but were willing to introduce some changes in their manners and customs." The

Hindus generally followed the traditional way of worshipping God. Mostly they were idolaters and pollytheists. The two ancient cult of Shiva and Vishnu, with many of their subcults which sprang up in course of time, had their followers spread over the country. Along with idol worship many other absurd and irrational practices had crept into the Hindu religion in the form of ceremonies and sacrifices. By religion they meant the observance of various rituals and dogmas and the strict adherence to caste system. Belief in the efficacy of magic spell, witchcraft etc. also formed an important element of popular religion. The 18th century saw the appearance on the fringe of the Hindu society of some heterodox religious groups and sects which denounced polytheism, idol worship and even the formal observance of caste rules. The founders of these groups mostly belonged to the non Brahminical classes.

The caste system thrived and persisted for many centuries in India. The precapitalist economy on which it rested was primarily based on the village autarchy. The caste system has stifled initiative, self-confidence and the spirit of enterprise. Since the caste system was hierarchically graded, it was based on social inequalities. It has created the untouchable problem. Caste has made birth the basis of social grouping. "It implies not only the negation of equality but the organization of inequality exclusively on the basis of inheritance. Differences there will be in any imaginable society, differences of function at all events. It is not in recognizing their inevitability that caste is peculiar, it is in the method it adopts to systematize and control them". Further, the caste system was sanctified by the sanction of religion. Its very genesis was attributed to God Brahman. On the other hand the reformers used rational arguments to show that caste was doing more harm than good. The division into numerous castes had destroyed all feelings of oneness and patriotism. The role of modern education in weakening the regard for caste should not be underestimated. The British government secularized education. It made it accessible to any one, irrespective of caste. The educated Indians who studied the liberal philosophy of Western countries, became the standard bearer of anti caste revolt. The spread of democratic ideas such as individual liberty kindled urges to revolt against caste distinctions and inequalities. Ram Mohan Roy considered the priests as the main culprits responsible for perpetuating the myth of the sacred origins of caste. National progress demanded the emancipation of the individual from the shackles of caste. The social reformers attacked inequality and separatism and stood for equality and cooperation. They attacked heredity as the basis of distinctions, and the law of karma which supplied the religiophilosophic defence of the undemocratic authoritarian caste institution. Raja Ram Mohan Roy, the founder of the Brahmo Samaj, invoked the authority of Mahanirvana tantra, an old religiosociological work of Hinduism to support his view that caste should no longer continue. The Brahmo Samaj opposed the rigid social divisions, which caste implied thus:

> "When will those pernicious distinctions which are sapping the very life blood of our nation be at an end, and India rise as a strong, united nation fit to fulfil the high destiny which providence has ordained for her?... That high destiny cannot be fulfilled without the utter destruction of the supreme root of all our social evils, the caste system."

In addition to the Barhmo Samaj, the prarthana samaj, the Arya Samaj, there were other movements which also carried on a campaign against caste. Further, the growth of the national movement weakened caste. According to R.P. Dutt:

> "The advancing forces of the Indian people are leading the fight against caste, against illiteracy, against the degradation of the untouchables, against all that holds the people backward. While learned lectures are being delivered on the antique Hindu civilization and its unchanging characteristics the Indian national movement, enjoying the unquestioned support of the overwhelming majority of the people, has inscribed on its banner a complete democratic programme of universal equal citizenship, without distinction of caste, creed or sex, abolition of all special privileges... state neutrality in relation to religion, and freedom of press, conscience, assembly and organization, for in advance of the semidemocracy of Britain."

Socio-religious reawakening movement served as a powerful ferment creating urges among the Indians against the caste system. "... The champion of caste privilege are already in retreat, and the retreat looks like becoming a route... if untouchability is deemed, can caste distinction survive?... No doubt the strength of Hinduism is neither in the temples nor in the legislature, but in the home. Yet, it is just in the home that the modernizing spirit is at work through the education of women. The Hindu joint family, the chief bulwark of caste, is being undermine by the education of women, and the facilities for travel and contact with the outer world."

The first important step towards the tejnoval of the restrictions against widow-marriage was the publication in 1855 by Iswar Chandra Vidyasagar of his work on widow-marriage in Bengali. Vidyasagar's efforts at reformation did not stop with exegetic disquisitions. Under his lead a memorial signed by two thousand Hindus was presented to Govt. for the recognition of widow-marriage, and an act legalizing such marriages, was passed on 13th July 1856. The widow-marriage movement had the sympathy of a large number of the educated Hindus. Under the influence of the Western environment, child-marriage is gradually becoming less common, at least among the educated community. The members of the Arya Samaj, denounce child-marriage. Further, it is becoming customary with parents to educate their daughters as long as they possibly can, because educational qualifications make them more eligible as brides. The educated Hindus are well impressed with the evils of child marriage and they are endeavouring to remove them. Besides, ordinarily there was no polygamy. All the Hindus acknowledge that it is a great mistake for a man to have two wives. Polygamy is tolerated amongst persons of high ranks. Plurality of wives is looked upon as an infraction of law and custom, in fact as an abuse. Raja Ram Mohan Roy, the first fearless champion of woman's rights in modern India, made a strong protest against polygamy. With the spread of education, the public opinion against polygamy is becoming stronger.

One shocking practise rampant in certain parts of India was sati, that is women burning themselves on the funeral pyres of their husbands. The efforts of some of the Mughal rulers to abolish it proved to be fruitless. During the 18th century it was more widely prevalent. After the establishment of the British rule, the first important step for the repression of sati was taken by Lord Wellesley. Compulsion may have been used in some cases by priests and relations to force women to offer themselves as satis.

But it often was the result of conjugal fidelity. During the 19th century amongst the Hindus themselves, Western ideas had already begun to spread. Ram Mohan Roy opposed sati with all his vigour and ability. In 1823 Lord Amherest made illegal the burning of a widow with the body of her deceased husband. Finally, Lord William Bentinck formed the determination of passing an act for the suppression of sati throughout the British territories. With the concurrence of his council, Bentinck promulgated regulation XVII of 1829 by which the practice of burning alive Hindu widows was declared penal. In their fight against sati, the reformers did not hesitate to use the scriptures against their opponents. The reformers dismissed the arguments of their opponent as metaphysical.

The fight against untouchability has been led, not by the British Govt., but by the progressive reformers. The untouchables were the outcastes of the Hindu society. Untouchability persisted in the Hindu society for centuries. Hardly any society condemned its sanction to physical segregation as the Hindu society did in the case of its untouchables. The Brahmo Samaj, the Arya Samaj, Harijan Sabha founded by Gandhi, strove by propaganda, education, to restore equal social, religious and cultural rights to the untouchables. Indeed, the incident will be recalled when certain famous temples in southern India, which had been traditionally closed to the untouchables were, under inspiration of Gandhi's crusade, thrown upon to them. The social oppression of the untouchables had religious sanction. Various organizations were striving for the removal of the disabilities of the depressed classes. The reformers strove in the direction of the democratization of the Hindu social system. The social reform movement aiming at eliminating social injustices such as un-touchability, in turn, contributed towards the building of the national unity of the Indian people on a democratic basis. The interests of the depressed classes and their liberation are inevitably linked up with the common national movement of liberation.

Society in general had feeling of reverence for its womenfolk. A Hindu woman can go anywhere alone and women are so sacred in India that even the soldiery leave them unmolested in the midst of devastation. This noble feature has been referred to by some other contemporary European writers like Forster, Buchanan. But, in fact the Indian women were leading a life which was not free from subordination. The spread of Western education, found expression in the movement for the liberation of the Indian women from the medieval forms of social subordination from which they suffered for countless centuries. The inferior status of women in society was made sacrocent by religious ordinances. The removal of the disabilities of the Indian, women and their freedom from various forms of oppression was a long process. With the spread of education and liberal and rational ideas among the people, the practise of purdah began to diminish. The institution of temple prostitution which new India had inherited from the past was analogous to similar institution in the ancient Greece. Devadasi formed an hereditary caste of women, who consecrated themselves in early childhood to temple service. The Devadasi were known to be prostitutes, actually degraded the arts they practised and made them distasteful to respectable women. The British rule were years of effort on the part of the progressive section of the Indian people to realize that democratic principle in politics, religion, and social sphere. Equal right of women to education and culture was recognized almost universally. The pioneering work of women's education was done by the reformers to a great extent.

Slavery was another common social evil. Slavery was prevalent in Indian during the 18th century. There were two types of slavery in India. Domestic slavery and feudal sèrvitude. In the latter the serfs attached to land were considered to be property. Buchanan holds that in Northern India, the Rajputs, Kayasthas openly kept women slaves of any pure tribe... But under the influence of humanitarian forces during the first half of the 19th century, slavery was abolished and the Indian act of 1843 removed legal recognition of slavery.

Raja Ram Mohan Roy : Raja Ram Mohan Roy is hailed as the "father of modern India." He attempted to combine the Western and Eastern philosophy. His writings and ideas are an example of a synthesis of ancient ideas with modern Western political principle. His contributions to Indian culture are so substantial that many of his contemporaries, whose contributions are significant but much more limited, have been largely neglected in the study of 19th century India. He set precedents in many of his activities. He was one of the first Indians to establish his own press and publish books as well as regular newspaper. He was the most prominent Indian, to become involved in the campaign for the abolition of Sati. Raja Ram Mohan Roy was a reformer, not a revolutionary. He wanted to combine tradition with modernity. He was a leader in the translation and distribution of traditional religious texts, and a spokesman for the defense of Indian religious thought against the criticism of Christian missionaries. He may be called as the father of Hindu reformation. Religion overshadows every thing in India, and he rightly attacked the Indian problems at their root when he started with religious reform. He emerged at a time when the light of the great encyclopaedists had not died down and when the influence of the utilitarians, was just beginning to be felt. Though he was proud of Indian culture and heritage, he yet, brought Indian into direct contact with the liberal humanism of modern Europe. In his religiophilosophical and social outlook, he was deeply influenced by the monotheism and anti-idolatry of Islam, Deism of sufism, the ethical teachings of Christianity and the liberal and rationalist doctrines of the West. He tried to interpret and assimilate into himself the highest elements of Islam, Christianity, and modern rationalism, and transformed them into a single creed which he found in the Upanishadic philosophy of his own community.

Raja Ram Mohan Roy was probably born in 1772 in an orthodox and wealthy Brahman family, at the village of Radha-nagar, Burdwan district, in West Bengal. He studied Persian and Arabic at Patna and this had enormous influence on his subsequent life. He soon became familiar with the work of Sufi poets and thus became critical of idolatry and polytheism. At the age of 14 he went to Benaras to learn Sanskrit. Knowledge of Sanskrit enabled him to study the Vedanta and the Upanishads. In 1796 he began learning English. He also learnt Greek and Hebrew and thus could study the Old and New Testaments in the original Hebrew and Greek. He published a book called the Precepts of Jesus. He rejected the divinity of Jesus but was much impressed by his ethical teachings. He had many Christian missionary friends but spurned the attempts of some of them to convert him to Christianity. On the death of his father in 1803, he moved to Murshidabad and wrote a Persian treaties entitled Tuhfat-ul-Muwa-hhidin or a gift to monotheists, a work protesting against idolatries and superstitions of all creeds and trying to lay a foundation of universal religion in the doctrine of the Godhead. According to him the socio-political progress of India, depend mainly on the successful revolution in the religious thought and behaviour. He attempted a spiritual synthesis, stressing the unity of all religious experience. He admired the Bible as much as he did the Vedanta and the Quran. He pleaded for an Advaita philosophy which rejected caste, idolatry and superstitious rites and rituals. Two fundamental principles have been discovered by Raja Ram Mohan Roy, the basic unity of mankind as the goal of human research on the intellectual plants and the welfare of society as the dominant consideration of our moral endeavour. Perfect free lance and free thinker that he was, Raja Ram Mohan Roy was not free from a legitimate pride in his Brahmana heredity which, amidst a thousand persecutions, held aloof the torch of Brahmavidya, the divine knowledge, which alone leads to immortality. His legitimate pride in the spiritual heritage of his ancestors was clearly expressed through the following memorable lines:

> "By a reference to history, it may be proved that the world was indebted to our ancestors for the first dawn of knowledge, which sprang up in the East, and thanks to the Goddess of wisdom, we have still a philosophical language of our own, which distinguishes us from other nations who cannot express scientific or abstract ideas without borrowing the language of foreigners."

Raja Ram Mohan Roy opposed polytheism and image worship, arguing for an iconoclastic, ethical monotheism. He defended the Hindu tradition against criticism of Christian and challenged the theological adequacy of trinitarian Christianity. Raja Ram Mohan Roy cannot be called a religious reformer in the sense Nanak, Chaitanya and Kabir were in the medieval period. He approached public as a religious reformer not because he was essentially religious minded, but because he was conscious of the evils of the society. The multitude of religious rites and ceremonies and the unnatural distinctions of caste and law of purification, had deprived the Hindus of any kind of common political feeling. He sought to combine the deep experiences of spiritual life with the basic principle of social democracy. Ram Mohan dealt with the rationalist, utilitarian, and liberal challenge of the West by rediscovering afresh in Hinduism the real source of its universal humanism, which had been concealed by the inertia and thoughtlessness of overgrown priestcraft and lethargic populace. He relied on the vedas to show that idolatry was not sanctioned by the highest religion. In the introduction to his translation of the abridgement of the Vedanta, Ram Mohan said:

> "My constant reflections on the inconvenient or rather injurious rites introduced by the particular practise of Hindu idolatry, which more than any other pagan worship destroys the texture of society together with compassion for my countrymen, have compelled me to use every possible effort to awaken them from their dream of error."

In Tuhfatual Muwahhidin, he criticized religious traditions and castigated religious leaders. He concluded his introduction to that work by asserting falsehood is common to all religion without distinction. His contribution to the modern articulation of the Hindu tradition is great. He defined the essence of the tradition in terms of the philosophical religious texts rather than the sectarian literature. He had accused religious leaders of self interest. "Most of the leaders of different religions for the sake of perpetuating their names and gaining honour,, having invented several dogmas of faith, have declared them in the form of truth by pretending some supernatural acts or some other measures suitable to the circumstances of their contemporaries, and thereby have made a multitude of people adhere to them so that those poor people, having lost sight of conscience, bind themselves to submit to their leaders". Further, he said that religious leaders emphasized the importance of rituals and image worship because these forms of worship required their services and were a source of their worldly advantage. He founded the Atmiya Sabha and began translating the upanishads into English and Bengali in order to expose the evils and abuses which had crept into the original Hindu faith. He began his reforming activity by preaching the unity of God. In 1820 Raja Ram Mohan Roy published the Brahmo Pauttalika Sambad. This book was written against the Hindu system of idolatry. By 1828, Raja Ram Mohan Roy felt that a reform within Hinduism was a necessity and established the Brahmo Sabha. He sought to unite the various communities on the basis of the fundamental unity and harmony of all religions. In 1829 the new religious society was known as Brahmo Samaj, a common place of meeting and worship of the different communities of the country. It was mentioned in the deed that the Samaj building was to be used as a place of public meeting for all persons, without any distinction of caste or creed, for the worship of the eternal being, who is the author and preserver of this universe, and that no image, statute, painting... or the likeness shall be admitted, nor any sacrifices or rituals even permitted there in. Only that form of worship would be allowed which would tend to promote the contemplation of God and the practise of morality...". The new society was to based on the twin pillars of reason and the vedas and upanishads.. Raja Ram Mohan Roy's religion was the crowning glory of his career as a scholar, a statesmen, and a patriot. His religious liberalism was meant to pave the way for social and political movement in India.

As a social reformer, Raja Ram Mohan Roy's interest was mainly in the appalling condition of women in Hindu society. He wanted to improve the condition of the Indian women. He took keen interest in and supported each and every movement aimed at human liberation. He revolted against the subjection of their rights. He vehemently opposed polygamy and he was in favour of the remarriage of women. He raised his voice against the practise of sati. He asserted that most of the sati cases were not voluntary, but forced. Raja Ram Mohan Roy started a press campaign against sati through his journal, Sambad Kaumudi. His constant advocacy urged the company Govt. to declare the practise of sati as illegal and punishable by law. Ram Mohan was a champion of the right of Hindu females to inheritance. He wanted not only social but also economic justice. As equality of sexes was an article of faith for Raja Ram Mohan Roy, he could not accept that women were inferior to men in any respect. He laid the foundations of the women's liberation movement in India. He had a clear idea of the evils of the caste system. He thought it to be illogical to assess the worth of an individual on the basis of birth and not on his merit. He asserted that the distinction of castes, introducing innumerable divisions has entirely deprived them (Hindu) of patriotic feeling and the multitude of religious rites and the laws of purifications have totally disqualified them from undertaking any difficult enterprise.

Ram Mohan Roy wanted that his country must keep pace with Europe, which had been making rapid progress due to its intellectual advancement. He welcomed the introduction of Western education and asked the Govt. to promote a more liberal and enlightened system of instruction, embracing mat..e-matics, natural philosophy, chemistry, anatomy and other useful sciences. He admired the British rule for inaugurating progressive measures of social reforms.

> "This was the period of courageous reforms, of such measures as the abolition of sati carried out with the cooperation of the progressive elements of Indian society, the abolition of slavery, the war of infanticide, the introduction of Western education and the freeing of the press, ...the deepest enemies of the British were the old reactionary rulers who saw in them their supplanters. The most progressive elements in Indian society, at that time represented by Raja Ram Mohan Roy and the reform movement of the Brahmo Samaj, looked with unconcealed admiration to the British as the champion of progress, gave unhesitating support to their reforms, and saw in them the vanguard of a new civilization."

His ambition was to change the educational system completely. In modernizing Indian antiquated System of education, he shines as one of the founders of Hindu college. His letter on English education to Lord Amherst is a veritable landmark in the educational history of modern India. He was a pioneer in the birth of vernacular press. He brought journals in Bengali, Persian, Hindi and English to spread, scientific, literary, and political knowledge among the people.

Ram Mohan Roy was the first Indian to speak of Indian liberty in the context of international development. Liberalism had emerged as the most valuable product of renaissance and reformation in Europe. Liberalism stands for the value and dignity of individual personality, it insist on human equality and inviolability of certain rights of the individual. His intense love of liberty was said to be the source of all his political opinions. He has a passionate attachment to the concept of liberty. He urged the necessity of personal freedom. In politics he insisted that every country should have a representative form of Govt. But he did not believe in the policy of laissez fairs. He wanted the state to protect the tenants against the landlords. He was in favour of rural basis of Indian civilization. He was also the initiator of public agitation. He demanded the abolition of the company's trading rights and the removal of heavy export duties on Indian goods. For him, liberty was a priceless possession of mankind. Separation for powers, codification of law were all expression of his intense love for liberty. He made a distinction between law and morality. He also suggested the revival of the age old panchayat system of adjudication. He was perhaps the first thinker of the 18th century who had a clear vision of internationalism. He knew that the ideal of human civilization does not lie in the idolation of independence, but in the brotherhood of interdependence of individuals as well as nations in all sphere of thought and action. Everywhere he championed the cause of nationalism, democracy and liberty. He held that, there must be frequent exchange of views in all matters among at the enlightened nations of the world. He has been rightly called the herald of new age. According to R.N. Tagore, he inaugurated the modern age in India, and he has been described as the father of Indian renaissance and the prophet of Indian nationalism. Raja Ram Mohan Roy's utilitarian approach to religious thought and social practice challenged the established priority of salvation (Moksha) over social order. He wrote very little about salvation but a great deal about social order. According to Collet, he stands in history as the living bridge over which India marcher, from her unmeasured past to her incalculable future. He was the arch which spanned the gulf between ancient caste and modern humanity, between superstition and science...". He was indeed the "morning star" of the great renaissance of India, the raja presents a most instructive and inspiring study for the new India of which he is the type and pioneer... He embodies the new spirit... its freedom of enquiry, its thirst for science, its large human sympathy, its pure and shifted ethics, along with its reverent, but not uncritical regard for the past and prudent, disinclination towards revolt.

M.G. Ranade : The middle of the 19th century witnessed a tendency amongst the younger members of the Bramho Samaj not only to broadern the basis of Brahmanism by advocating new social ideals but also apply the dry light of reason even to the fundamental articles of religious belief. They advocated female education, supported widow re-marriage, denounced polygamy, tried to rationalze Brahman doctrine. To this class belonged Keshab Chandra Sen, who joined the Bramho Samaj in 1857. Keshab Chandra Sen was responsible for the foundation of the Prarthana

Samaj (Prayer Society) in Bombay in 1867. In 1869 M.G. Ranade joined the Prathana Samaj in 1869. Ranade was born at Nasik in an orthodox Brahmin family. He was instrumental in giving a progressive shape to public life in Maharashtra by participating in the working of the Pune Sarvajanik Seva, Prathana Samaj, the Indian social conference and the Indian National Congress, He carried forward the message of Raja Ram Mohan Ray. He wanted to establish a free democratic society in India which would be based on justice, equality and liberty. Ranade wanted the reformation of Hindu religion. He was against polytheism, idolatry. The two main planks of the Prarthana Samaj were theistic worship and social reform. It did not produce any new philosophy". He expolnded the theistic interpretation of the universe and wrote against materialism. With the progress of science, he hoped that man would be able to understand some aspects of the spirit. According to Ranade, the spirit was immanent in everything and every being. For Ranade, truth was not to be found in sacred books, but it was to be searched. The central idea of his philosophy was morality. According to Ranade, the Prarthana Samaj seemed to have been "Perfectly satisfied with a creed which consists of only one positive belief in the unity of God, accompanied with a special protest against the existing corruption of Hindu religion..." He did not believe in the non-dualistic monism of Adishanka-racharya because he held that God and man were not one and the samething. According to him, the essence of salvation was living a saintly life guided by truth and morality. According to Ranade, the Prarthana Samaj was a continuation of the Bhakti movement. The sources of its inspiration were indigenous and its practices had local roots. He did not regard the veda as divine or infallible, nor believe in the doctrine of incarnation of God. Above all, the Prarthana Samaj draws its nourishment very largely from the Hindu scriptures.

The greatest service of the Samaj, was the organization of social reform movement. The Samaj laid stress on the abandonment of caste, and the abolition of Purdah, encourage-ment of female education. He was critical of the lack of freedom in the Hindu society. According to Ranade "we do not want to break with the past and cease all connection with our society. There was an ideal Hindu society in the past but evils crept in during a period of depression, when in panic and weakness, a compromise was made with the brute force of ignorance and superstition". He was a critic of the caste system." He believed that the caste system did not permit free choice of vocation. He pleaded for the abolition of caste system and argued in favour of intercaste marriage. He also favoured the introduction of secular education in India. Education for him had a liberating influence, Education of women and backward communities were subjects dear to his heart. He was a champion of Indian languages and sought their development so as to enrich the cultural life of the Indian people. He came round to the view that the only basis of social reform was the real need of the country as rationally conceived. When the Indian National Congress was formed there was a proposal to make it a forum for discussing not only political but also social reform. Because political advancement was not possible without social reform. In 1887 Ranade founded the Indian National Social Conference.

Ranade realised that foreign rule had adversely affected the intellectual, moral and cultural health of the society. But he believed the Indians could benefit from the British experience. Further, he believed that interaction with the Islamic tradition enriched the indigenous Indian society and culture. He was profoundly impressed by the personality of Shivaji and undertook a deep study of the historical processes involved in the Maratha uprising. He likened the Bhakti movement in Maharashtra to the protestant reformation movement in Europe. He held that the Bhakti movement was heterodox in its spirit of protest against all forms of ceremonies and class distinction based on birth and in its preference of a pure heart. He held political elevation, social emancipation and spiritual enlightenment as three important goal that should be pursued. Essentially he was a moderate and his political method was essentially constitutional. According to him, the state must perform regulative, productive and regulative functions. He held that Indian Govt. should be developed around the following six principles Supremacy of law, representative Govt., common constitution for states, parliamentary Govt., decentralization of judiciary and representation of India in the imperial parliamenl. He was the first Indian thinker to insist that national development must be based on the principles of democracy, secularism and liberalism. He wrote "the inner spring, the hidden purpose not consciously realized in many cases, is the sense of human dignity and freedom which is slowly asserting its supremacy over national mind. It is not confined to one sphere of family life. It invades the whole man and makes him feel that individual purity and social justice have paramount claim over us all which we can ignore long without being dragged to a lower level of existence". In the economic field, he supported state initiative to bring about the industrialization of the country. He did not approve of the extreme individualism nor the social indifference of classical economists. He favoured curtailing the rights of landlords in favour of tenants. For the improvement of agriculture Ranade suggested capitalist farming, establishment of cooperative credit societies, stabilization of land settlement and formation of state farms. He was in favour of an integrated scheme of national economic development. Above all, he was a liberal thinker in the humanistic tradition and stood for progress and welfare of all human beings.

Dayanand Saraswati : Just as the impact of Islam gave a fillip to Bhakti movement in India in the middle ages, so has the inroad of Western civilization given rise to a number of reform movements in Hinduism in modern times, of these, the Arya Samaj takes its stand on the bedrock of the Vedas, which it is believed, hold the key to all our socioreligious problems. It challenges the good sense of humanity to subject to a crucial test, the time-old wisdom revealed to the saint and see if their life giving message can be replaced to advantage by the varied materialistic 'ism' of modern days. Northern India produced a new Hindu Luther, whose reform work was to have the deepest and most lasting effect. Dayanand Saraswati was unique as a man in the sense that while all other thinkers of the period had a effective knowledge of English language, Dayanand was innocent of it. And his message was unique in the sense that while the other thinkers of his time were moving away, in one way or another, from the dogma of infallible revelation, Dayanand declared that the vedas were not only true, but they contained all truth, including the ideas of modern science.

Dayanand, known in early life as MulaShankara, was born in 1824, in an orthodox Brahmin family living in the small town of Tankara in the old Morvi state in Gujarat. He revolted against idol worship at fourteen and became a sanyasi (religious mendicant) of the Sarasvati order. He spent the next 15 years as a wandering ascetic. In 1860 he found a real guru in Swami

Virajananda, who was blind from infancy, but was a man of great learning and piety. He told Dayanand "people do not know the right from the wrong, they wrangle about caste and creeds and neglect the study of the vedas". Having imbibed the teachings of Virjananda, Dayanand went out into the world taking his stand on the vedas, India's rock of ages. He attacked the excrescences of Hinduism. After his contact with the Brahmo and Prarthana Samaj leaders, a new approach emerges, that of the organizing reformer. He successfully adopt the modern reform technique, the vernacular, publication, organization, education. It was the powerful combination of all these elements that made Dayanand into a unique figure among the 19th century reformers. Dayanand's inter pretation of the vedas, the primeval scripture of humanity, has given a new orientation to the Hindu faith. "I hold that the four Vedas as infallible and as authority by their very nature". His theological vision was one that emerged neither from a personal mysticism nor from Western ideas, but from the intimate observation of the corrupt Hinduism of the day.

According to R.C. Majumdar:

> "The absolutely authoritative character of the vedas, and vedas alone, formed the fundamental creed of Dayanand. At first he included within the vedas both Brahmans and upanishads themselves repudiated the authority of the vedas as the highest or the early revelation. He modified his views, ultimately the Samhita portion of the vedas, and particularly the Rigveda Samhita, was alone held to be the real vedic revelation, at least for all practical purposes".

Dayanand's thoughts are contained in the Satyarth Prakash, the bible of the Arya Samaj. In this he extolled the virtues of Hinduism, and criticized Islam, Christianity, Buddhism, Jainism. He declared there are three things beginningless, namely God, souls and Prakriti or the material cause of the universe. He had declared Moksa (Salvation) to be an eternal state. Dayanand's religion, whilst denouncing much of contemporary Hinduism, kept close to orthodoxy in several basic ways, belief in the vedas, and in Karma and transmigration, allegiance to the six darshanas and to the various Hindu names for the one God.

Dayanand founded the first Arya Samaj at Bombay in 1875

and another at Lahore in 1877. When the Arya Samaj was founded to propagate ideas, one of these was represented by the motto "Go back to the Vedas". The veda is precisely the sign, perhaps the only one, of Hindu orthodoxy, as distinguished from Hinduism. He preached in favour of returning to an unqualified adherence to the Veda, and claimed that explicit principles of pure monotheism and of social and moral reform could be found in the hymns. The intensity of belief in the vedas Dayanand seems to share with the mimamsa and vedanta Schools of Hindu philosophy, although the form of his belief seems to be more in the tradition of the Nyaya school, for he bases the authoritativeness of the Vedas not on the doctrine of their eternal self-existence, but on the Nyaya belief that the vedas were uttered by Ishwar (God) himself. Dayanand gave his own interpretation to vedas, defined as consisting of the Samhita portion only.

According to Sri Aurobindo:

> "There is nothing fantastical in Dayanand's idea that the Veda contains truths of science as well as truths of religion. I will even add my own conviction that the veda contains other truths of a science which the modern world does not at all possess...The character of the veda is fixed in the sense Dayanand gave to it, the merely ritual mythological, polytheistic interpretation of Sankaracharya collapses, and the merely meteoro-logical and materialistic European interpretation collap-ses, we have instead a real scripture, one of the world's sacred books and the divine word of a lofty and noble religion."

Swami Dayanand argued that the vedas were the fountain-head of science and religion for all mankind. He kept the basic rites of Hindu, the five daily sacrifices and the sixteen sacraments. To these he added the new reformist type of communal worship, including the singing of hymns, sermons, besides the new home sacrifice. Though, Dayanand considered the vedas as the only repository of true religion, he was at once conservative and aggressive, traditional and dynamic, for he wanted not only to revive Hinduism but also to reform it. He looked forward to the day when the religion of vedas would become the religion of the whole human race. He wanted to make Hinduism a proselytizing religion. He asserted that atleast in matter of religion and in the domain of philosophy the best modern European thought did not come up to the level of the best ancient Hindu thought. Dayanand claimed that the people of Egypt, Greece, and the continent of Europe were without a trace of learning before the spread of knowledge from India, and he believe, that the most recent invention of science were known, at least in their germ, to the poets of vedas. He did not want to found a new religion and he said that his ideas were based on vedas. He summarized his beliefs thus, "He, who is called Brahma or the most high, who is Paramatma or the supreme spirit who permeates the whole universe, who is true personification of existence, who is omniscient, formless, infinite, almighty, who is the author of the universe, who awards all souls the fruits of their deeds... even him I believe to be the great God... I hold that the four vedas... are absolutely free from error.... He aspired after Mukti, but which one got-rid of all suffering, was freed from rebirth, and realized God. The means to attain such mukti was, to practise truth, to acquire the knowledge of the vedas, to associate with men of truth and to practise yoga for eliminating all kinds of untruth from the mind and soul.

The constitution which was drawn for the Arya Samaj laid down some of the fundamental doctrines. The Arya Samaj shall regard the vedas as absolutely authoritative. The primary object of this society is to do good to the whole world. One's dealing with all should be regulated by love and justice, in accordance with dharma. Dayanand's conception of his church was that of a democratic body. He did not recognize the intervention of any intermediary between God and his worshipers. The most important characteristic of the Samaj is the emphasis it laid upon the work of Suddhi. This means the conversions of these Hindus, who had once been willingly or forcibly converted into other religions, but were now willing to come back to the fold of Hinduism. The leaders of the Arya Samaj realized, from the very beginning, the vital importance of education in opening the eyes of the people to their true cultural heritage. In order to propagate knowledge among the people, the Samaj has spread widely a network of Gurukulas, Colleges, and Schools, both for boys and girls throughout the country. The Dyanand Anglovedic College at Lahore became the foremost agency for planting a study and independent nationalism in the Punjab. The D.A.V. has resuscitated the vedic and Sanskrit studies and assimilated to them modern art and science. By the; revival of the ancient institution of Brahmacharya and by giving morality the first place in its scheme, the Samaj has made it possible to make character the basis of Juvenile education. The uncompromising attitude of the Arya Samaj against what it regard as false Gods and the gauntlet it has thrown in the name of the ancient sages have earned it the epithets "Church militant and aggressive Hinduism."

The Arya Samaj had a programme of social reform. Though opposed to the hereditary caste system, it stood, however, for the four caste division of society to be determined by merit not by birth. It stood for equal rights of man and woman. This was a distinct democratic conception. The Arya Samaj was generally inspired with the spirit of nationalism and democracy. It attempted to integrate the Hindus by destroying the subcaste. The contemporary caste system was nothing but the utter degeneration of the original Veidc Varna system. The Arya Samaj represented a form of national awakening of the Indian people. He was a cultural nationalist. He was the first Indian to speak of Swaraj. He also believed in Swadeshi. He believed in everything indigenous. He emphasized the value of education, specifically with a veidc orientation for all, irrespective of caste and sex. He favoured cow protection and is believed to have been the first who pleaded for the protection of the cow on a utilitarian principle. Initially Dayanand advocated education for all, sudras were to be excluded from Vedic education and he consequently modified his views to include sudras which is more in line with the vedic hymn. Thus, the germ for the movement for the amelioration of the depressed classes had been laid. He did not approve of foreign rule, a sentiment which Gandhi was to echo later on. He advocated indigenous rule and harked back to the universal and presumably golden rule of the vedic age. He believed in some form of representative government. The Arya Samaj attacked religious superstition, dictatorship of the Brahmins, denounced polytheism, and opposed caste system, child marriage. But the Arya Samaj could not be a cosmopolitan religion since it demanded of its followers the recognition of the principle of the infallibility of the vedas. On the other hand, the Arya Samaj was considered as the leading instance of revivalism rather than of reformation, despite the fact that Dayanand shares the dynamism of the other leading lights of modern Hinduism. Swami Dayanand represents a transitional stage and inaugurate future developments with his vision of a complete overhaul of Hindu society and his creative amalgamation of reform and nationalism. It cannot be denied that the movement of Swami Dayanand Saraswati, as organized in the Arya Samaj has contributed more than the rational movement of Brahma Samaj to the development of a new national consciousness in India.

Annie Besant : Annie Besant once said that an India, whose citizens have conquered their baser passions, could become the centre of the British empire. The centre could then shift from the West to East. Nehru, who first saw her in 1901, was overwhelmed by her personality and he wrote "I became a devoted admirer... undoubtedly she was a dominating figure of the age". She had a magnetic personality. She was known in the English speaking world as one of the most remarkable women of her time. She was a freethinker and a radical political agitator. Annie Besant exhorted educated Indians to renounce the hybrid and sterile ideas of Anglicized Indianism, and so to work India could take her position in the world as evolver of the innerman, as teacher of the possibilities of the human soul. The theosophical society was founded by Westerners who draw inspiration from Indian thought and culture;. Madame H.P. Blavasky of Russo-German birth laid the foundation of the movement in the U.S.A. in 1875: Later, Colonel Olcott of the U.S. joined her. In 1882 they shifted their headquarter to Adyar, an outskirts of Madras. The society accepts the Hindu beliefs in reincarnation, Karma, and draws inspiration from the philosophy of the upanishads and vedanta school of thought. It preached universal brotherhood of caste, creed, race or sex. It stood for the development of a national spirit among the Indians. It considered ancient Hinduism as the most profoundly spiritual religion in the world. The movement became popular in Indian with the election of Mrs. Annie Besant as its president.

Annie Besant had a remarkable education. In 1867 she married an Anglican clergyman. Later on, she became an atheist and joined the free thought society. The reading of the secret doctrine by Blavasky virtually converted her to theosophy. Gandhi once said "though we had political differences, my veneration for her did not suffer abatement." Besant defended Hinduism not only against the attacks cf Christian missionaries, but also against the criticism of English educated social reformers who, after studying spencer, Mill had turned sceptics. The needs of India, Mr. Besant wrote in

1905, are among others, the development of a national spirit, an education founded on Indian ideals and enriched, not dominated by the thought and culture of the West, Besant, a foreigner, was teaching the Hindus their Shastras, irked some orthodox Hindus. Theosophy reconciled the idea of universal brotherhood with the caste system and the fundamental unity of the supreme being with the worship of numerous Gods and Goddesses of Hinduism. Besant translated the Bhagwad Gita into English and became a pillar of Hindu revivalism. She was also associated with the founding of the central Hindu College at Benaras. She once declared that caste system had outlived its utility and must go. She also started the home rule league movement. She was elected as the president of the Indian National Congress in 1917. As president she told the delegates "while I was humiliated, you crowned me with honour... while I was crushed under the heel of bureaucratic power, you acclaimed me as your leader..." India, she said, was deeply grateful for the inspiration she had breathed in from English literature, from Milton, Burke, Shelley, Mill. Indian does not suffer with the blood of her sons and the proud tears of her daughters in exchange for so much liberty. India claims the right as a nation... S.P. Sinha described India as a patient, but Besant objected to this analogy saying India is no sickman. She is a giant who was asleep and who is now awake. As a nation India was entitled to freedom. She defined a nation as a spark of the divine fire, a fragment of the divine life, out breathed into the world and gathering, round itself a mass of individuals whom of bound together into one. Thus, India had the duty of spreading the idea of dharma. Indian feeling of nationality grew out of British rule was silly and absurd. Liberty, she maintained, could not come through non-cooperation, it could come only through a change in the hearts of men. Liberty could never descend upon a nation by the shouting of crowds, nor by arguments of unbridled passion. She had faith in India's future and destiny. She spoke of democratic socialism. For her democracy does not mean majority rule. She maintained that only those who were intellectually trained and morally disciplined should be allowed to govern. She said, a democratic socialism, controlled by votes, guided by numbers, can never succeed, a truly aristocratic socialism controlled by duty, guided by wisdom, is the next step upward in civilization.

Rama Krishna Paramhansa : From the close of the 18th century right upto the middle of the 19th century, Indian had been wading through a bewildering welter of cultural ideals. Gradually the hypnotic spell of foreign civilization began to recede, before a rising wave of self-consciousness of the Hindus. Mighty movement of socio-religious reform sprang up, to resuscitate the ancient culture of India. It was also accompanied by sweeping changes in social customs. The orthodox masses, under the traditional lead of Hindu saints, pleaded on in their old socio-religious ruts. In the eyes of the reformers, this attitude of the orthodox masses appeared to be fanatic. But the orthodox society had not to wait long, when a phenomenon of paramount importance took place to infuse enormous strength in to the entire range of Hindu convictions. The life and message of Sri Ramakrishna constituted precisely such a phenomenon. According to Gandhi, "The story of Ramakrishna Pramahansa's life is a History of religion in practise. His life enable.us to see God face to face... In this age of scepti-cism, Ramakrishana presents an example of bright and living faith which gives solace to thousands of. men and women who would otherwise have remained without spiritual light" The radicals, found in the realization of Sri Ramakrishana a wonderful solution of their intellectual doubts. This is why an advocate of modern thought like Narendranath (Vivekananda) who had drunk deep from the dangerous fountains of rational atheism and also from the refined springs of Brahmo theism, could surrender himself completely to this extraordinary man of phenomenal spiritual insight. Ramakrishana had no Western education and he was no scholar. But it is to this simple village saint, the illiterate, shrunken, unpolished, diseased, half-idolatrous devotee that many highly educated, sceptical, and Westernized Indians came and in him they found the faith, serenity, and strength which they lacked. Ramakrishana combined simplicity of preaching, mystical and philosophical depth, spiritual intensity, and direct earnestness, with a pure Hinduness to such a degree that even sophisticated could hardly withstand his fascination. In course of his spiritual experiments he had tried to understand and practise not only the religious tenets of Hinduism but also those of Islam and Christianity. He had gone to Muslim and Christian mystics and came to the conclusion that Krishna, Buddha, Allah, Jesus were but different names of God, and that the pursuit of all religious would lead to the same goal.

His life lacks the aristocratic dignity of Maharshi Devendranath Tagore, the reputed oratory and majestic personality of Keshav Chandra Sen, and the vast erudition of Swami Dayanand Saraswati. Neither aristocracy of birth, nor wealth, nor academic distinction, nor power and prestige in the temporal sense had anything to do with his career. Yet, this humble life had something of immense value and significance. Gadadhar Chattopadhyaya, who was known in later life as Ramakrishna Paramahansa, was born in 1836 in a poor Brahmin family in a small village called Kamarpukur in the district of Hooghly in West Bengal. His formal education did not proceed much further beyond the elementary stage as he had no liking for school and enjoyed for more the society of the Sadhus. Fur he was of a religious and contemplative mood. At the age of 17 he came to Calcutta, and later, adopted the coveting of a priest in the temple of Goddesses Kali, founded a short while ago by an aristocratic lady named Rasmani, at Dakhineswar on the bank of the Ganga. This was the turning point in the life of Ramakrishna. He was seized with the idea that the Goddess Kali, whose idol he worshipped, was not an image of clay, but the Goddess herself personified. With a devout heart and scrupulous care, he would go through the daily round of scheduled rituals and chant, in his melodious voice, sacred hymns in the prescribed order. Ramakrishana's thought were glued to the service of the divine mother, and soon he became intoxicated with a great yearning for seeing the Goddesses in her glory. He led a God-centered life characterized by constant search for, and continuous approach to God, through various modes prescribed by tradition. One day, seized by a grim determination, he rushed frantically to put an end his life, when all on a sudden, the mother's descended upon him. The veil was off, and he became immersed in an ocean of ecstasy. Ramakrishna experimented with different religious practices. He followed the tantric discipline into which he was initiated by Bhairavi Brahmani. Then he passed through the Vaishnava phase going through all the traditional practices of the bhakti school of approaching God as parent, master, child, friend. Next he was initiated into the concept of impersonal absolute and the advaita by Totapuri. He never gave religious lectures and founded no sect or ashram. After having gone through all the austerities, he came to the conclusion that it was not necessary to give up the world to find God, but that it was only necessary to transform one's mind and heart. Everything was in the mind. Ramakrishana spoke simply and homely language. He said "Live like an ant". It knows sugar from sand, The world contain truth and untruth, discriminate between them.." The most characteristic trait of his teachings is that he expressed the highest wisdom or greatest truth in simple sentences and parables. The theme of all his discourses was the realization of God as the highest human ideal, attainable only by development of high spiritual life. This was possible by discarding desire for material prosperity. His tireless journey on the various roads of religion had practically come to an end with his Advaita realization. The universe lay unmasked before his illuminated eyes. Ramakrishana without beat of drums or flash of stump oratory, breathed life into Hinduism with all its Kaleidoscopic phases and ushered in an era of Hindu renaissance. His realization of divine immanence had convinced him of the existence of two distinct phases of maya, which are termed Avidya Maya and Vidyamaya. The former is the grosser aspect of appearance that fixes human souls on the world of the senses and whirls them 'through the round of births and deaths, and it is this aspect of the illusion that the Advaita Sadhakas are rightly taught to fight. He realized that after one had perceived one's identity with the supreme Brahman, and come back to the world of appearance, Maya would appear altogether in a new role. The transcendental appeared to be immanent in the realm of relative existence. It was this aspect of the appearance that Ramakrishana designated as Vidya-Maya.

Ramakrishna, who regarded Sarda Devi (wife) as the divine mother and actually worshipped her as such looked upon her as his wife as well. He received from his wife her unbounded and pure love, genuine devotion, and earnest service. His uncommon attitude towards his wife left no room for sex suggestions. To him the absolute and the relatives were equally divine. It was this position of his on the threshold of relative consciousness that enabled him to fuse the apparently contradictory schemes of monastic and householders life into an undivided synthetic attitude. Besides, his heart would break with the sight of misery. He made it clear that the Jiva was no other than Siva, that every creature was God himself in a particular garb of name and form. The service of suffering humanity with the subjective outlook and the attitude of worshipping divinity is by itself an entire programme of a new form of spiritual practice that can independently lead an aspirant up to goal of God-realization. This is an innovation as a precious acquisition in the world's store house of religious sadhana, Further, he regarded the development of character as superior to knowledge. No spiritual progress can be made without discrimi-nation and dispassion. Though preaching against carnal passion he did not hate women nor tried to avoid them as source of evils. Spiritual life and the means to attain it were described in ancient Hindu scriptures, but they were either forgotten or disbelieved, and nothing but an actual vision of it in Ramakrishna could have impressed upon the modern Hindu minds the real meaning, nature, and value of this great treasure of ancestral knowledge. He was a visible embodiment of the spiritual attainments of India during three thousand years.

Ramakrishana's emphasis on spiritual experience and his praise of renunciation did not appeal to many educated Indians who had come in contact with the liberal, activists, and humanitarian ideals of the modern West and who were seeking a religion that promised not merely personal salvation but emphasizes primarily the obligation of individual to society. Ramakrishna said that God alone will the blissful mother ask him to work for the world. According to P.C. Mazumdar "Rama-krishana's religion itself was a puzzle. He worships Siva, Kali, Rama, Krishna, and is a confirmed advocate of vedantic doctrines... He is an idolater, yet is a faithful and most devoted mediator on the perfection of the one formless, absolute, infinite,... His religion is ecstasy, his worship means transcendental insight his whole nature burns day and night with a permanent fire and fever of a strange faith and feeling. By his strong conceptions of an everready motherhood he helped to unfold God as our mother in the minds of men. He made his own life a laboratory for the synthesis of different systems of religion, a wonderful synthesis of higher forms of spiritual discipline with rituals and ceremonies, of Sakara with Nirakara, of vedanta with devotion, of rationalism with emotion. He was a store house of spiritual powers.

His unprecedented record of purity and love, his amazing synthesis of opposing phases of life, thoughts, and emotions, his edifying contacts with the old school, scholars and devotees, and also with the modern intellectual, broadening their religious outlook by his message of harmony of religions, disseminating of all the spiritual ideas uphold by some of the most important faiths of the world had a deep impact on his disciples. He found that it was not the physical conditions that determined the mystic visions, as in the case of hallucination, rather, he observed, with empiric accuracy how events occurred in physical world according to the will of the divine mother. Before his spiritual vision was unfolded a majestic and magnificent oneness of the universe, towards which all sciences and philosophies are steadily converging. It is this realization of a living oneness that alone can furnish the world with the rationale behind the Concept of equality and fraternity, and provide it with the basis on which it may build up the much needed edifice of universal brotherhood. Religion was the breath of his life and morality his backbone. In his perspective realization of God was the worthiest object of life, and devotion, purity, sincerity, love and humility constituted the real wealth of man. By his deep and extensive spiritual experience of the entire range of the upanishadic truth, and he certainly heralded an epoch making Hindu renaissance. He discovered the spirit of Catholicism within the sealed bosom of Hinduism. His feeble violence, has been raised in the modern world by a distinguished band of thinkers, poets, philosophers and scientists, a voice that is tending to rationalize the wisdom of the prophets, and thus to lift up the eyes of mankind towards spirituality

Swami Vivekananda : Indeed, like Bhagiratha of Hindu mythology, Narendranath, betterly known as Swami Vivekananda brought down the clear and vitalizing stream of spirituality from the celestial heights of seclusion of Ramakrishan's life. In 1893 Vivekananda electrified the world by his address at Chicago. He was a orator by divine Right. His brilliant presentation of Hindu spirituality was hailed as a triumph of the East. The image of the warrior monk marching into the citadels of Western materialism and successfully demonstrated the powers of Indian spirituality is so strongly believed by his disciples that one may not be easily able to find the historical Swami Vivekananda. He was certainly a gifted youth, sociable, free and unconventional in manner, the soul of social circles, a brilliant conversationalist, altogether an inspired Bohemian, but possessing what Bohemians lack, an inspired will. Vivekananda, the great disciple of Ramakrishna, was strongly influence by very different streams of thought. The influence of Ramakrishana on him was very great, it gave him an overriding pride in the theoretical and practical achievements of Hindu. When he went to Dakhineswar and met Ramakrishna, he said, "Ah, you have came so late... you are Nara, the ancient sage, the incarnation of Narayan. You have come back to earth to take away the suffering and sorrow of humanity." He summed his estimation of the master, even if insane, this man is the holiest of the holy, a true saint, and for that alone he deserves the reverent homage of mankind.

Vivekananda was the monastic name of Narendranath Dutta, who was born on the 12th January, 1863, in an aristocratic kshatriya family of Calcutta. His mother was a spirited and accom-plished lady, and his father an enlightened freethinker with liberal views. The childhood legend seem to indicate that his mother and relatives believed that this child was a gift from Siva, that he had a special destiny, that he would become a sanyasi. He was a naughty boy. demonstrated kingly attributes, had no caste consciousness, and confounded his teachers. In 1878-79 when he was 16, he passed the entrance examination and began studies at Presidency College. During his college career he was a member of the most social reform minded faction of the Brahmo Samaj movement. But, later on, he changed to the Scottish Church College, and switched his affiliation to the Adi-Brahmo Samaj which was more conciliatory to the Hindu community. About Vivekananda, Hastie, the principal of the college where he studied said that he was a genius. I have travelled far and wide, but I have never yet come across a lad of his talents, even in German universities among philosophical students. As a member of the Adi-Brahmo Samaj band of hope he abandoned theism and became an agnostic. In adolescence, he grew up to be a rationalist to the core of his being. He was at heart a seeker of truth. His nature rebelled against the idea of accepting anything on faith. When he reached almost the verge of scepticism, he met the great saint of Dakhineswar temple, Calcutta, accidentally in the house of a Brahmo devotee. This chance meeting of the two souls really proved to be pregnant with all the possibilities of Narendranath's subsequent career. The meeting of the two, which ended eventually in their spiritual union, appears to symbolize the meeting of the ancient Culture with the modern, scriptural faith with imperious reason, mysticism with positivism.

Narendranath was very much impressed by Ramakrishna's overwhelming power, and felt a great attraction towards the sage

Sri Ramakrishna had used his powers (Siddhis) and influence to modify the religious path of Narendranath. Ramakrishna had led Narendra to an experience of Kali as the supreme mother of the universe. Ramakrishna also had Narendra study the vedanta to see that his Brahma Prejudices were wrong about it as well. Ramakrishna taught that the absolute of vedanta, Brahman, and the Goddesses of form of Saktism, Kali were the same. He said that the goal of life was God-realization through renunciation of women and money. Narendranath's intellectual predilection for positivism did not, however, ruffle Ramakrishna's equanimity. After Ramakrishna passed away in 1886, he took charge of his disciples at the Baranagore monastery. With a nontraditional self-initiation they began wearing Ochre robes. Narendranath, with all the ardour of his impetuous soul, started an enthusiastic career of spiritual practice, in order to verify the worth of Ramakrishna's instruction by his own realization. Vivekananda convinced that a reinterpretation of the vedas would provide a scriptural base for a socially concerned vedanta. This reformed vedanta would be free from caste-distinction. Meanwhile, he undertook a pilgrimage over North, West and South India. This was a landmark in his career, for it brought him into intimate contact with the peoples of India. "As a common feature, of India as a whole, he found poverty, loss of mental vigour and hope for the future disintegration of age old institution, conservatism trying to hold its own under the guise of spirituality, the waves of Western science and culture as well as Christianity beating against her shores... The only hope she still held on to the one source of her life her religion." In May 1893 Swami Vivekananda (He received his name from a suggestion of the Maharaja of Khetri) went to the United States to attend the parliament of religions. He told the organizers he was a member of the oldest order of Sanyasis in India founded by Sankara. His majestic appearance, expressive of a virile manhood, made him conspicuous among the oriental delegates. He opened his lips to accost the audience endearingly as sisters and brothers of America and he was overwhelmed by deafening cheers from all corners of the hall. The surging stream of spirituality, of endless love for God and defied humanity, of universal faith in all religions - the stream that had its birth on the snow-capped heights of the heavenly life of Ramakrishna and had descended to the immaculate heart of his chosen disciple suddenly broke through all barriers and gushed out in a torrential rush of apostolic love and wisdom. The house was flooded by waves of spirituality. Within two months of his first speech the statesman (Calcutta) carried the first news of the Brahmin Sanyasi. The reputation won by Vivekananda through the parliament of religions made him a world figure and raised the prestige of India and Hinduism very high. He spent more than three years of the best part of his life in America and Europe. He acquainted his Western audience with the faith of the Hindus rooted in the oldest of scriptures, the vedas, he told them its message of unbounded Catholicism, its presentation of various readings of divinity, monistic, and also about various kinds of religious practice grouped under four fundamental types, namely, Jnanayoga, Rajayoga, Bhaktiyoga, and Karmayoga, covering the entire range of human taste. According to Vivekananda, the goal of the West was individual independence, her language was money making education, and her means, politics, while the goal of India was mukti, and her language was that of the vedas, and her means, renunciation. He said that whereas the West needed the spirituality of India, India needed her science, and he wanted a synthesis of the two.

Swami Vivekananda, with his devoted followers returned to India in 1897. Soon he founded the Ramakrishna mission in 1897. For seeking God, Vivekananda did not discard image worship. It was he who acted as the messenger, the ideas of Ramakrishna just as St. Paul for Jesus and Ananda for the Buddha. Vivekananda said that, if you want to find God, serve man. That is why the befitting tribute of Nehru, "Rooted in the past and full of India's heritage, Vivekananda was yet modern in his approach to life's problems and was a kind of bridge between the East and the West." On the other hand, he lectured throughout the length and breadth of the country thundering against indiscriminate Westernization. He asked his countrymen not to forget that the ideal of their womanhood was Sita, Savitri, that the God they worshipped was the great ascetic of ascetics, the all renouncing Shankara... that the lower classes, the ignorant, the poor, the illiterate, were their flesh and blood. He asked every Indian to proclaim that the ignorant Indian, the poor and destitute Indian was his brother. He regretted that the social reformers had confined their activities to the upper castes and had not touched the masses. He condemned the outrage of untouchability. He believed in the uplift of the masses, rather he stood for a spiritual and cultural fraternity in which there would be not only social, economic and political freedom, but also moral and intellectual kinship. He laid before his countrymen practical formulas of social service deduced from the fundamental teaching of the vedanta. He enjoined on the privileged classes to feel intensely for the misery of the teeming millions and to serve them with all the devotion. The sunken vitality of the helpless victims of social tyranny was to be restored by providing them with life giving food, physical, intellectual, as well as spiritual. In the words of S.C. Dasgupta "Swami Vivekananda did not believe in a religion which could not give a morsel of food to the mouth of the hungry. He diagnosed all the evils of life as. due to weakness and ignorance. Strength was life, weakness death. He advocated muscles of iron and nerves of steel, and if necessary throw away the Bhagawat Gita and acquire strength in the field of games". He want man who possess minds wrought from thunder. Stand up, do not be afraid, stamp upon fear and it dies. If you are fit to worship God without form, discarding any external help, do so, but why do you condemn others who cannot do so. He condemned the meaningless rituals and touch-me-not religion of the conservatives. He asked the Indians to elevate their country. His real hope for India's revival rested on the spread of education among the masses. He had little faith in politics, but his contribution to the resurgence of India is undisputable. He said the powerful men in every country are moving society whatever "way they like and the rest are only like a flock of sheep. About the upper classes in India he wrote:

> "That they were but mummies ten thousand years old, they are real walking corpses... Fleshless and bloodless skeletons of the dead body of past India that you are... You merge yourself in the void and disappear and let new India arise... out of the peasants cottage grasping the plough, out of the huts of fishermen, the cobbler and the sweeper. Let her spring from the grocer's shop... let her emanate from the factory, from the marts and the markets".

He said I am a socialist, not because I think it is a perfect system, but half a loaf is better than no bread. He was a Karma Yogi. He said who cares for your bhakti and mukti... I will go into a thousand hells cheerfully if I can rouse my countrymen immersed in inertia, to stand on their own feet and be man inspired with the spirit of Karma Yoga. He warned his people that it would be futile for them to attempt to make politics, and not religions, the centre of their national life.148 He came as a tonic to the depressed and demoralized Hindu mind and gave it self-reliance. His contribution to nationalism is certainly praise worthy. To use Hegalian terminology, the reforms inaugurated by the Brahmo Samaj may be taken as representing the thesis, the Hindu revivalism antithesis and the Ramakrishna-Vivekananda doctrine, the synthesis. He said after me hundreds of Vivekanandas will be born, if this man is not a Godman who else? In fact Swami Vivekananda is one of the greatest reformer that mother India has produced.

Bibliography

Aggarwal, Pratap C., *Caste, Religion and Power: An Indian Case Study,* Shri Ram Centre for Industrial Relations, New Delhi, 1971.

Agrawal, S.N., *Indian Population,* APH, Bombay, 1960.

Ambedkar, B.R., *The Untouchables,* Amrit Book Comp. New Delhi, 1948.

Ambhirajan, S., *Political, Economic and British Policy in India,* Cambridge, 1978.

Anstey, V., *The Economic Development of Modern India,* London, 1949.

Aurora, G.S., *Tribe, Caste, Class Encounters,* Administrative Staff College of India, Hyderabad, 1972.

Bagchi, A.K., *Europe and Indian Entrepreneurship in India,* OUP, London, 1970.

Bailey, F.G., *Caste and Economic Frontier,* Oxford, 1884.

Bali, D.R., *Modern Indian Thought,* Sterling, London, 1989.

Balkrishna, R., *Commercial Relations between India and England,* Madras, 1958.

Bansil, P.C., *Agricultural Problems of India,* Vikas Publishing House, New Delhi, 1969.

Bell, D., *The Coming of Post-industrial Society,* Heinneman Educational Books Ltd., London, 1974.

Berger, PL. and Luckmann, *The Social Construction of Reality,* Doubleday and Co., New York, 1966.

Berna, J.J., 1960, *Industrial Entrepreneurship,* New York, 1960.

Beteille, A., *Caste, Class and Power,* Barkeley, 1964.

Bettelheim, C., *India Independent,* MacGibbon and Kee, London, 1968.

Bhatt, Anil, Caste, *Class and Politics: An Empirical Profile of Social Stratification* in *Modern India,* Manohar Book Service, New Delhi, 1975.

Bipin Chandra, *The Rise and Growth of Economic Nationalism in India,* Delhi, 1977.

Bose, N.K., *Culture and Society in India,* Bombay, 1967.

Broomfield, J.H., *Elite Conflict in a Plural Society,* Oxford University Press, New Delhi, 1968.

Buch, M.A., *Rise and Growth of Indian Liberalism,* 1938.

Buchanan, D.H., *The Development of Capitalist Enterprise in India,* New York, 1934.

Burns, Tom, *Industrial Man,* Cox and Wyman Ltd., London, 1969.

Chaudhury, K.N., *Economy and Society,* OUP, London, 1979.

Chopra, Puri, Das, *A Social, Cultural and Economic History of India,* Macmillan, Delhi, 1974.

Choudhury, R., *The Evolution of Indian Industries,* Calcutta, 1939.

Cicourel, A., *Cognitive Sociology,* Cox and Wyman Ltd., London, 1973.

Cohn, B.S., *Structural Change in Indian Rural Society,* London, 1969.

Das, M.N., *Studies in the Economic and Social Development of Modern India,* Calcutta, 1959.

Das, Nabagopal, *Industrial Enterprise in India,* Calcutta, 1956.

Das, R.K., *The Labour Movement in India,* Berlin, 1923.

Datta, R.C., *The Economic History of India,* Delhi, 1990.

Durkheim, E., *The Division of Labour in Society,* Macmillan Company, New York, 1933.

Dutta, R.P., *India Today,* Calcutta, 1989.

Gadgil, D.R., *The Industrial Evolution of India,* OUP, New Delhi, 1942.

Ghosal, H.R., *Economic Transition in the Bengal Presidency,* Patna, 1950.

Giddens, Anthony, *Consequences of Modernity,* Polity, Cambridge, 1990.

Giri, V.V., *Labour Problems in Indian Industries,* APH, Bombay, 1958.

Gough, Kathleen, *Class Developments in India,* McGill University Press, Montreal, 1975.

Habib, Irfan, *The Agrarian System of Mughal India,* Bombay, 1963.

Ishwaran, K., *Tradition and Economy in Village India,* Allied Publishers, New Delhi, 1966.

Johnston, H., *Pioneers in India,* Delhi, 1977.

Kapadia, K.M., Marriage and Family in India, Bombay, 1958.

Karnik, V.B., *Indian Trade Union,* Manaktalas, 1966.

Lokanathan, P.S., *Industrialisation,* Oxford, 1946.

Malhautra, M.; *New Century: Whose Century?* UBSPD, New Delhi, 2001.

Mandelbaum, D.G., *Society in India,* Chicago, 1968.

Mannheim, Karl, *Man and Society,* Routledge and Kegan Paul Ltd., London, 1940.

Mehortra, S.N., *Labour Problem in India,* Delhi, 1981.

Mehta, S.C., *Caste in India,* New Delhi, 1965.

Merton, R.K., *Social Theory and Social Structure,* The Free Press of Glencoe, 1968.

Mill, J.S., *Principles of Political Economy,* London, 1920.

Nehru, J.L., *The Discovery of India,* Calcutta, 1946.

O'Neill, John, *Sociology as a Skin Trade,* Harper and Row Publishers, New York, 1972.

Prasad, R., *Social Reforms: An Analysis of Indian Society,* Y.K. Publishers, Agra, 1990.

Pusalkar, A.D., *History and Culture of the Indian People,* London, 1951.

Rao, M.S.A., *Urbanisation and Social Change,* Orient Longman, Delhi, 1970.

Revri, C., *Indian Trade Union Movement*, Orient Longman, New Delhi, 1972.

Shelvankar, K.S., *The Problem of India*, London, 1940.

Singer, Milton, *Traditional India: Structure and Change*, Aldine Publishing Company, Chicago, 1968.

Spencer, H., *Principle of Sociology*, D. Appleton and Company, New York, 1898.

Srinivas, M.N., *Social Change in Modern India*, Orient Longman, Delhi, 1972.

Thapar, Romila, *Past and Prejudice*, National Book Trust of India, Delhi, 1975.

Tiryakian, Edward A., *Sociologism and Existentialism*, Prentice-Hall Inc., New York, 1962.

Tumin, M.M., *Social Stratification—the Forms and Function of Inequality*, Delhi, 1987.

Vidyarthi, L.P, *Conflict, Tension and Cultural Trends in India*, Punthi Pustak, Calcutta, 1969.

Weber, Max, *Essays in Sociology*, Routledge and Kegan Paul Ltd., London, 1952.

Index

❑❑❑